On the Warpath

On the Warpath

The Psychology of Public Support for Armed Action

JIM ORFORD

OXFORD
UNIVERSITY PRESS

Oxford University Press is a department of the University of Oxford. It furthers the University's objective of excellence in research, scholarship, and education by publishing worldwide. Oxford is a registered trade mark of Oxford University Press in the UK and certain other countries.

Published in the United States of America by Oxford University Press
198 Madison Avenue, New York, NY 10016, United States of America.

© Oxford University Press 2024

All rights reserved. No part of this publication may be reproduced, stored in a retrieval system, or transmitted, in any form or by any means, without the prior permission in writing of Oxford University Press, or as expressly permitted by law, by license, or under terms agreed with the appropriate reproduction rights organization. Inquiries concerning reproduction outside the scope of the above should be sent to the Rights Department, Oxford University Press, at the address above.

You must not circulate this work in any other form
and you must impose this same condition on any acquirer.

CIP data is on file at the Library of Congress
ISBN 978-0-19-767675-2

DOI: 10.1093/oso/9780197676752.001.0001

Printed by Integrated Books International, United States of America

*For my grandson Lewis Orford
in the hope that he will experience
a lifetime without war*

By the Same Author

Excessive Appetites: A Psychological View of Addictions
Community Psychology: Challenges, Controversies and Emerging Consensus
Addiction Dilemmas: Family Experiences in Literature and Research
Power, Powerlessness and Addiction
The Gambling Establishment: Challenging the Power of the Modern Gambling Industry and Its Allies

Contents

List of Illustrations   xi
Acknowledgments   xiii

   Introduction: Posing the Question, Why Is War Supported?   1
1. Wars, Old and New, Costs and Controversies   14
2. The Personal Attraction of War   46
3. War in Defense of National and Other Identities and Values   74
4. Thinking of Us and Them, Enemies and Heroes   98
5. Embedded Militarism and Readiness for War   125
6. Engineering Consent: Propaganda and Persuasion   155
7. Just War? War as a Moral Dilemma   180
8. An Answer: Toward a Unified Understanding of War Support   207

Notes   243
Bibliography   277
Index   291

List of Illustrations

Figures

2.1	The personal attraction of war: a summary of the main themes	73
3.1	War in defense of national and other identities and values: a summary of principal conclusions	97
4.1	Thinking of us and them, enemies and heroes: a summary of the main ideas	123
5.1	A summary of some of the ways in which militarism is embedded within culture and civic society	153
8.1	The war support model: a summary of three factors driving support for war	224
8.2	The war support model: the three factors form a system of interacting and mutually reinforcing parts	225
8.3	The war support model: the three war support factors grow in strength as we tread the path to war	226

Tables

1.1	Ten Points about War, and the Debates around Them, to Bear in Mind when Constructing a Psychological Understanding of Support for War	44
2.1	Seven Recurring Aspects of Masculinity Crucial for Understanding Support for Wars of the Conventional "Old" Kind, Many Equally Important for "New Wars"	65
6.1	The Contrast between Respectful Dialogue and Propaganda	172
7.1	Our Moral Rough Guide to Making War: The Jus ad Bellum Just War Criteria and Some of the Reasons Why Their Application Is Problematic	188
7.2	Six Mechanisms of Moral Disengagement	199

Acknowledgments

Writing this book has been a very personal task. It owes no straightforward debt to the world of work as a community and clinical psychologist with a main interest in addiction which I have inhabited for so many years. Nor can I acknowledge any experience in or alongside the military, for I have none. It has drawn, rather, on a lifetime of influences, both in and outside work, and on the encouragement and support I have been so fortunate to have received from so many people. Among them have been teachers and mentors, colleagues and students, whom I first met when I was at the Institute of Psychiatry, Psychology and Neuroscience in London or later at the University of Exeter or later on at the University of Birmingham. I hope they will understand how much I owe them collectively and will forgive me for not mentioning them by name.

I shall have to confine myself to mentioning a very few people, principally my family, first and foremost my wife and life partner Judith. As a young woman, a participant in one of the earliest Aldermaston marches in protest against the siting of atomic weapons in England, she was appalled by war and its accoutrements well before I was. We share our views on this as on so much else.

I would like to thank Nadina Persaud at Oxford University Press for taking a risk with an author who was coming afresh to the field of war studies and for supporting me throughout the process of shaping the manuscript into its final form. I must also acknowledge the role played by a number of anonymous reviewers who made comments on earlier drafts. From my experience as an academic writer, I am all too familiar with the sinking feeling one can get when reading criticisms and requests for redrafting. Equally familiar, however, is one's somewhat reluctant appreciation, after further work, that the result has indeed been an improvement. I believe that was the case for *On the Warpath*.

Jim Orford
Brighton, England
February 2023

Introduction

Posing the Question, Why Is War Supported?

> Even if there is a group of individuals who hope to profit from waging a war, why are they so enthusiastically followed by the rest of the citizens of their nation? . . . It is crucial to understand why war is so popular among humankind.
>
> Lawrence LeShan, *The Psychology of War*[1]

> *Suppose They Gave a War and Nobody Came?*
>
> Title of film, 1970

My Background and Motivation for Writing This Book

I have worked in psychology for over 50 years but not in war studies nor even in the branches of the discipline most likely to have an interest in war—political and peace psychology. My areas have been firstly clinical psychology and later, with perhaps somewhat greater relevance, community psychology. My day job, so to speak, has been addiction: how to understand it psychologically; how it affects those who experience it directly, either being addicted or being closely affected by someone else's addiction; and how to treat and prevent it. I have sometimes been tempted to pursue the addiction analogy when it comes to studying war: are we addicted to war? But I believe that would just be an analogy. There are much better ways to explain why we go on making war. So, I come to the field of war studies afresh, without any established background in the subject (other than writing a couple of minor articles). I am what is sometimes unkindly referred to as an interloper. That rather damning charge chimes with the uncertainties I had personally when embarking on the project some years ago. What claim did I have, as someone whose work has been in other areas of psychology, to make a contribution to such a well-worked-over topic as war?

War was, however, something that I had been thinking about, reading about, and promising myself I would write about, for many years. To be more precise, what I had been contemplating was exploring, as a psychologist, how it is that we seem to embrace war, to so often support it. Several early experiences come to mind. One, very early on, the first four years of my life in fact, may be relevant to my later interest in the subject, although I cannot be certain of that. I was born in London during the Second World War. My father was in the forces, and my mother was in effect a single parent. My father hardly spoke of his experiences during the war, and I never asked him. He ended his war service in India, and the Indian carpet he had sent home, the smattering of Hindi phrases he used and I sometimes trot out to this day, plus the introduction of curry as a regular item on the menu at home, long before it became a national British dish, were among the main legacies of the war in our home of which I was aware.

But I did grow up to develop a horror of war, an instinct for pacifism, a failure to understand how people could deliberately kill and maim others of their own kind. As a rather studious teenager for whom libraries and bookshops were some of my favorite places, I was surprised, appalled, but intrigued at the rows of books about wars and weapons of war. It was then that I began to form the idea that many people might actually rather like war, have an appetite for knowing about it, be attracted to the means of making war, give their support to the leaders who executed it on their behalf. Later, when our sons were teenagers in the 1970s, my wife and I put up a poster, from the film of that time, posing the conundrum, *Suppose They Gave a War and Nobody Came?* But it was only much later, having retired, at least to the extent of no longer having duties to an employer that I had to perform, that I was able to set to and draft the book I had wanted to write for so long. As it happened, the COVID crisis enabled me to make faster progress than would otherwise have been possible.

What the Book Is About

I believe I now have a better understanding of why we allow wars to happen. So powerful, I have concluded, are the psychological drivers of war support that it is much to our credit that we remain at peace so much of the time. But the dangers of modern warfare are sufficiently great that we cannot afford to congratulate ourselves. We must try to comprehend why we continue making war and thereby to diminish the risks faced by future generations. In the final chapter I bring together, in the form of a war support model (WSM), what I believe I have learned. My conclusion, summarized in the model, is that three factors propel support for war.

First and foremost, we accept an ever-readiness for the possibility of war. That acceptance rests on a militarism deeply embedded in our country's or group's history and culture, its memorials and heroes, our support for the military and admiration for weapons of war, along with the belief that war can be necessary and just, even virtuous. A chauvinistic national or group identity and a war-supporting form of masculinity that values power and dominance also play their parts. The second factor is the way in which we deal with threats, real and supposed, to our nation's or group's security. Threat perception flourishes more strongly when we believe the world is a dangerous, threatening one, when threat is perceived to be coming from an identified rival or enemy out-group, the less contact with and understanding of that group we have, and the more we subscribe to a threat-laden narrative encouraged by our leaders and the media. War support requires a large dose of mental simplification. That is the third factor. Support for war rests on cognitive simplicity regarding the circumstances threatening war, the enemy, and ourselves. It draws on our repertoire of simplifying mental mechanisms that enable us to distance ourselves from the costs of war and to disengage from normal moral constraints about harming others.

The strength of those three factors—acceptance of readiness for war, threat perception, and over-simplification—varies with time. One might think of there being three phases to war support: preparedness for war, contemplation of war, and engagement in war. All the factors that drive war support, especially acceptance of readiness for war, are present all the time, more or less quiescent until circumstances provoke them. They may then operate as a mutually reinforcing system with a tendency, unless checked, to grow exponentially, spiraling out of control. The outbreak of armed hostility is a tipping point beyond which the system escalates rapidly and is more difficult to reverse.

That understanding of the mystery of war support that has bugged me all my adult life is what this book offers. None of the individual insights contained herein are novel. Each of the elements of my model have been studied, written about, and reflected on by many others. What I aim to offer in this book, which I believe is original, is a bringing together of the various psychological facets involved. As I outline below, my sources include a wide variety of expert, detailed, and thoughtful contributions on the subject. Each has been illuminating. None, however, has as far as I know provided the integrated, psychological overview of war support which I am attempting here.

What the Book Does Not Do

To be clear, the purpose of the book is to explore what leading psychological ideas there are for explaining why we so often and so willingly support war. By *we* in that sentence I mean the ordinary people, the general public, not only in Britain, or in the West generally, but anywhere the drumbeats of war are sounded. The research I have done for the book has confirmed my initial suspicions that, compared to the voluminous amount of attention given to the war roles of political and military leaders, states, or organizations, the territory this book explores has been relatively uncharted.

I need to insert an important caveat here. One early reviewer of the book proposal took me to task for appearing to be making the assumption that we possess a natural tendency to favor war. I hope I make it clear, especially in Chapter 2, that I do not argue for there being any such *natural* tendency. I start from the premise that we as humans with agency have often, but certainly not always, given support to war, that we continue to do so, and furthermore that war continues to threaten. Nor do I assume that people necessarily have, or have had, full say in the matter; people may be coerced into supporting war, and the degree of popularity for wars varies from time to time, place to place, and person to person—examples of that variability of support for war come into the book in almost every chapter in one way or another. But in modern democracies, at least, we do believe some degree of support for war on our part is required. I am not trying to prove that we as a species either do or do not support war. It seems to me evident that we sometimes do and sometimes don't. In fact, the whole purpose of the book is to explore what leading psychological ideas there are for explaining the circumstances under which warfare is likely to have support—which I believe is surprisingly often. The aim is thus to contribute to the prevention of war on the grounds that it is highly destructive in so many ways and is best avoided.

Obvious though it may sound, I also need to make clear that the book's perspective is a psychological one. The question I set out to explore—Why, when we are called on to support war, do we so often agree?—is a question, not about politicians or military leaders or nation-states but about the rest of us, the ordinary citizens of the world. It is a question about which psychology should have a lot to offer. Only a relatively small number of psychologists have written works on the subject of war, but in common with books by non-psychologists, it is the perceptions, attitudes, intentions and actions of political and military leaders, or of anthropomorphized states or organizations, which get the most attention, rather than those of ordinary people who are called on to support war. As is almost always the case with important questions of a psychological kind, many non-psychologist authors do have a lot to say on the matter. In fact, in this case they outnumber professional psychologists by a large margin. I have tried to integrate psychology's specific contributions on the subject with psychological theories which *could* have useful application to answering the book's key question, along with many insights of a psychological kind offered by international relations experts, historians, war correspondents, military veterans, and other writers.

The Book Is an Exploration of Ideas

The spirit in which I approached the project I like to describe as one of exploration. I wanted to try and get some answers to the question that had been forming in my mind ever since my teenage years. Support for war was a mystery to me. I felt like a naïve, perhaps foolish, explorer. Surely the discipline of psychology that I had been party to for half a century would have some answers. My aim was to discover what were likely to be the leading psychological ideas of relevance for understanding war support, a territory which, surprisingly, appeared still to be poorly charted. The book is about ideas. However, that does not mean it is uncritical about those ideas. For one thing, I have chosen to include those ideas which have stood the test of time and empirical research—although that has often been in general rather than in their application to war support specifically since there has been relatively little of the latter type of research—or which have been emerging recently as leading candidates for studying war support. The interpersonal contact theory, dealt with in detail in Chapter 4, is a good example. There is a large body of research in support of it; it has had some application to war support and has been refined in the course of research over the last few years. The model of moral disengagement (Chapter 7) is another where there has been much less war support–related work but which I and some others believe is a strong candidate. Also, I have aimed to interrogate these candidate ideas by critically reflecting on them and their relevance. Nationalism (Chapter 3) is a good example: I have tried to unpack the idea, present variations on it, and question its relevance in any simplified form.

It was not my aim to carry out a systematic review of the research literature on each of these topics. For one thing that would be an impossibly large task, probably the work of multiple PhDs. What is more, many of these ideas are difficult to test in the context of war support, particularly given the variations in the circumstances surrounding different wars. War in general is a topic with very few theories whose validity is widely accepted: that democracies relatively rarely make war against one another is one of the few accepted in the international relations field, for example. To explore, reflect on, and integrate psychological notions that may account for war support is, I would argue, a worthwhile scholarly task in itself. I hope it will contribute to an understanding of one of the great issues facing us all and at the same time help to open up a relatively new area of psychology. The prevention of war continues to be of the utmost importance for the future health and prosperity, even survival, of humankind. Armed conflicts and threats to security continue. War between Ukraine and Russia erupted during the writing of the book, and great power rivalry between China and the United States and its allies, and associated military posturing, have continued to be in the news. There are warnings of conflicts to come if climate change is not mitigated. In order to prevent war, we need to understand how it happens, including why it has our support.

My Sources

Because relevant publications on the subject of war are so diverse, my main sources have included books written by psychologists; by others with varied social science, history, and policy backgrounds; as well as by some who bring experience as war correspondents or military veterans. Works by psychologists that have been particularly useful include Mark Pilisuk and Jennifer Rowntree's *The Hidden Structure of Violence: Who Benefits from Global Violence and War* and Steven Pinker's *The Better Angels of Our Nature: A History of Violence and Humanity* (both relevant at several points in the book); David Winter's *Roots of War: Wanting Power, Seeing Threat,*

Justifying Force and Anthony Stevens' *The Roots of War and Terror* (both especially relevant for Chapter 2); and Lawrence LeShan's *The Psychology of War: Comprehending Its Mystique and Its Madness* (Chapter 4). Books written by international relations scholars that have proved very helpful include Mary Kaldor's *New and Old Wars: Organized Violence in a Global Era* (especially for Chapters 1 and 3); Martin Shaw's *The New Western Way of War: Risk-Transfer War and Its Crisis in Iraq* (Chapter 5); and Philip Seib's *Information at War: Journalism, Disinformation, and Modern Warfare* and Barbara Walter's *How Civil Wars Start: And How to Stop Them* (both Chapter 6). Those by historians include Azar Gat's and *The Causes of War and the Spread of Peace: But Will War Rebound?* (relevant at several points); Keith Lowe's *The Fear and the Freedom: How the Second World War Changed Us* (Chapter 1); Joanna Bourke's *Wounding the World: How Military Violence and War-Play Invade Our Lives* and George Mosse's *Fallen Soldiers: Reshaping the Memory of the World Wars* (both useful for Chapter 5); Niall Ferguson's *The Pity of War* (Chapter 6); Oona Hathaway and Scott Shapiro's *The Internationalists: And Their Plan to Outlaw War* (Chapter 7) and Graham Allison's *Destined for War: Can America and China Escape Thucydides's Trap?* (Chapter 8). Those by other social and political scientists include Miguel Centano and Elaine Enriquez' *War and Society* and Jack Levy and William Thompson's *Causes of War* (both of value throughout); William Wiist and Shelley White's *Preventing War and Promoting Peace: A Guide for Health Professionals* (Chapter 1); David Duriesmith's *Masculinity and New War: The Gendered Dynamics of Contemporary Armed Conflict* (Chapter 2); John Hall and Siniša Malešević's *Nationalism and War* and Arie Kruglanski, Jocelyn Bélanger, and Rohan Gunaratna's *The Three Pillars of Radicalization: Needs, Narratives, and Networks* (both Chapter 3); Philip Taylor's *Munitions of the Mind: A History of Propaganda from the Ancient World to the Present Day* (Chapter 6); and Helen Frowe's *The Ethics of War and Peace: An Introduction* (Chapter 7). War correspondent Fergal Keane's *Wounds: A Memoir of War and Love* has been useful in several places. Among works by military veterans cum academics that have been drawn upon are David Wood's *What Have We Done: The Moral Injury of Our Longest Wars* (Chapter 1) and Andrew Bacevich's *The New American Militarism: How Americans Are Seduced by War* (Chapter 5). *The Shadow World: Inside the Global Arms Trade*, by campaigner and South African Member of Parliament Andrew Feinstein, and philosopher Grégoire Chamayou's *Drone Theory* were both useful for Chapter 5. Classicist Ian Morris' *War: What Is It Good For? The Role of Conflict in Civilisation, from Primates to Robots* was relevant at several points. Among helpful works by general writers were Barbara Ehrenreich's *Blood Rites: Origins and History of the Passions of War* and A. C. Grayling's *War: An Enquiry*.

Scholarly journals constitute the other main source of material for the book. A wide range of journals were found to at least occasionally contain material relevant to the question the book poses. Those that have been most useful can roughly be divided into three groups. The first, valuable sources throughout, comprises journals of peace and conflict: *Peace and Conflict: Journal of Peace Psychology, Political Psychology, International Journal of Peace Studies, Conflict Management and Peace Science, Journal of Conflict Resolution*, and *Global Change, Peace and Security*. The second group consists of other psychology journals, especially social psychology journals: *Journal of Personality and Social Psychology, European Journal of Social Psychology, European Review of Social Psychology, Social Psychology, Journal of Language and Social Psychology, Group Processes and Inter-group Relations*, and *British Journal of Social Psychology*. They were drawn on particularly for Chapters 2, 3, 4, 6, and 7. The third group of journals which from time to time contained highly relevant articles, especially when drafting Chapter 5, consists of those devoted to international relations and military affairs: *Armed Forces and Society, Analyses of Social Issues and Public Policy, Cambridge Review of International Affairs*, and *International Studies Quarterly*.

The Book's Structure

There are eight chapters to the book. The first provides what I believe is important material about war, necessary as background before embarking on the book's main business. The final chapter presents my overall conclusion in the form of a War Support Model. The six chapters in between, Chapters 2 to 7, are where the reader can find the detail. The order in which those chapters are presented, although not totally arbitrary, could have been different. Hence, a reader could dip in to any of those chapters and need not read them in the order presented. Though, having said that, I recommend reading them in order, the better to follow how they build toward the development of the model offered in the final chapter.

Chapter 1 sets the scene by covering some basic topics which need to be kept in mind when thinking about the psychology of war support. The chapter begins by discussing what is included in a reasonable definition of war and what excluded. It continues by covering some topics familiar to scholars and students of international relations but which will be less well known outside that discipline. They include the role of the state in war, variations in types of war, and in particular how recent "new," civil or *intra*state wars may or may not differ from "old" *inter*state wars. A brief summary is then given of the varied "costs" of war, including mortality for combatants and civilians, dislocation, injury, ill health, and environmental damage. The chapter proceeds to discuss two areas of active controversy: whether there are positive outcomes from war and the evidence that war has been in decline. The chapter concludes by listing 10 points about war, and the debates around it, to bear in mind as background when constructing a psychological understanding of support for war.

Chapters 2 to 7 are the book's core chapters, exploring six domains, each offering a partial answer to my question, Why do people support war? Chapter 2 begins the search for a psychological understanding of war support at the level of the individual. It starts by making the point, with quotations from historians, ordinary citizens, and veterans, that the experience of war has often been described as a positive one, even sometimes a healthy or spiritually uplifting one. The notion that war can provide meaning and purpose to life is a common theme and one that has been taken up by war theorists and researchers including those who have recently been studying terrorism and the "new wars." A main line of work has looked for individual differences in support for war, focusing on such factors as beliefs in a competitive or dangerous world, authoritarianism, and social dominance orientation. The gendered nature of war, and to an extent of war support, has suggested to some that war is inherent not in human nature generally but rather in maleness and masculinity. The conclusion of the chapter is that masculinity, along with a number of individual beliefs and circumstances, makes some people more prone to support war than others but that war and thoughts of war carry positive associations for many and that they strengthen as the drumbeats of war sound more loudly.

The focus of Chapter 3 is the part in support for wars played by personal, strongly held values and beliefs which are based on state, ethnic, religious, or regional identity. The presumed central role of nationalism as the basis of people's support for war is questioned. Any nationalism is complex, multi-factorial, contested, and ever changing, masking crucial distinctions which are of relevance to war: for example, between nationalism and patriotism; between national attachment and national chauvinism; between civic, cultural, and ethnic nationalism. Nationalism, in its traditional sense of psychological attachment to the state, may, in any case, be less relevant to many recent wars, which are more likely to draw on identities of ethnicity, religion, or region. One claim is that such identities, as well as nationalism, do not themselves provide a strong basis for war but, rather, that they are exploited as a means of enlisting support for war, even that war causes nationalism and other values based on exclusive identities rather than the other way round. The apparent contrast between such values and cosmopolitanism—a feeling of citizenship of the world—is discussed. The chapter concludes that the more a set of identity values departs from cosmopolitanism and the more it carries the elements of superiority over others, dominance or chauvinism, the more available it is to be exploited in support of armed hostility. That potential for war may lie dormant for years, even for generations; but given the right circumstances, it may harden and escalate rapidly.

Chapter 4 examines the mental processes that it is thought are necessary in order to construct the idea of an enemy and which might justify the use of armed conflict against it. It covers a number of relevant areas of psychological theory and research. They include enemy images, processes of dehumanizing and demonizing members of potential enemy groups, and mental mechanisms that over-simplify, bias, or distort reality in ways that support the justification of war. Two leading theories are examined in some detail: social identity theory and interpersonal contact theory. The importance of perceived threat is discussed. The chapter concludes by considering the spiral conflict model and its implications for how cognitions and feelings about the enemy escalate as conflict develops.

Chapter 5 moves the search for answers to the question about war support into the realm of how society encourages war support, the social structures of militarism, and how they are justified. It begins by defining militarism as the normalization of a set of shared beliefs and practices which support developing and maintaining the means for making war as a valued way of defending the nation's or group's common interests. Ways in which militarism is embedded in culture and civic society are explored, including the role that games, films, and other entertainments have played in the "military–industrial–entertainment complex." The militarization of education is discussed, as is the controversial question of whether war graves and war memorials serve the cause of peace or of war. The chapter then goes on to consider the complicated issue of how important weapons themselves are as part of militarism and support for war. The long-term trend toward the development of more lethal weapons, enabling fighting at a greater distance; the West's modern preference for "risk-transfer war"; and the sometimes corrupt nature of the arms trade are noted. Drones are discussed as a controversial modern weapon. A distinction is often drawn between militarism and "militarization," the latter focused more closely on valuing and supporting the nation's or group's military organization and personnel. The chapter concludes with a discussion of the possibility of a growing "cultural gap" in some countries between the public and the military and whether militarism in general is in decline.

Chapter 6 looks at how we are persuaded to support war by means of propaganda. It begins with a brief excursion into the modern history of propaganda, during, between, and since the two world wars, including its use in the "new wars." The key role played by the media, including social media, and by control and censorship of the media as a vital part of the need to silence opposing voices and present a biased view of the enemy's intentions and the reality of war is considered. The chapter goes on to discuss the use of war discourses and other propaganda techniques and how "perception management" is achieved. Psychological strategies for successful propaganda are discussed. There is agreement about the importance of encouraging fear and the perception of threat. There are widespread misgivings about propaganda as a form of persuasive communication which departs from mutually participative dialogue between equals. What makes for persuasive war leadership is also discussed. An older psychology of leadership encouraged the personality cult of a heroic, great leader, while the newer psychology of leadership is more about how an effective leader acts as the group's champion, supporting in-group identity. Although its role in promoting war can be exaggerated, the chapter concludes that propaganda has played an important part in encouraging support for war and continues to do so.

Support for war may rest on our confusion about its morality or immorality. Chapter 7 examines the moral dilemma which war poses, the justifications we offer for war, and the relevance of just war theory. The contested nature of war in all the world's major religions is discussed first.

The two parts to modern just war theory are then described. The first, jus ad bellum, talks of the criteria for deciding to wage a just war, all of which are to a degree subjective, leaving room for them to be challenged in relation to specific wars. The second, jus in bello, about the ways in which wars may be justly prosecuted, includes the criterion of non-combatant immunity which has always been problematic. Citizens of countries objecting to war as a matter of moral conscience and combatants rebelling in various ways and suffering "moral injury" illustrate the moral dilemma war poses. There is now concern that widespread flouting of the principle that non-combatants should be protected and an enlarged conception of what constitutes self-defense are amounting to abandonment of the concept of just war. The chapter then broadens out, drawing on psychological models of morality and ethics, such as the mechanisms of moral disengagement model, to discuss how we try to distance ourselves from responsibility for supporting the killing and cruelty of war. Finally, the chapter poses a question rarely articulated: If war is a moral dilemma, is it one to be faced by us as potential supporters of war or one principally for combatants or one for our political and military leaders?

Building on the conclusions presented at the end of each of the foregoing chapters, Chapter 8 brings them together in the form of the integrated WSM. Central to the WSM is a triumvirate of ideas which recurred over the course of the earlier chapters—acceptance of readiness for war, threat perception, and mental over-simplification. It is my contention that each of these three factors is relevant at each of three phases in the spiraling buildup to a war—preparing, contemplating, engaging—although readiness for war is of special importance in the early phase. The model presented is obviously preliminary, but if taken up by others, it should lead to refinement, to a consideration of how it might apply to different types of war, and to the generation of specific, testable hypotheses and hence to a growing body of productive research. Wars and threats of wars continue. Chapter 8 closes by using the war in Ukraine, which flared up during the writing of this book, and the growing tension between China and the United States and its allies to illustrate the application of the WSM and its implications for attempts to reduce support for war.

One of the book's aims is to help establish a new area within my own discipline of psychology. The latter either has been relatively silent on the question of war support, has taken an ambiguous position on the subject, or has positively contributed to war support rather than clearly opposing it. Understanding the roots of support for war and the roles that ordinary citizens can and must play in resisting rather than supporting war and its horrors needs to be a much greater focus in public affairs and in academia and the professions generally, including in psychology specifically.

1
Wars, Old and New, Costs and Controversies

> War is nothing more than the continuation of politics by other means
> Carl von Clausewitz, *On War*[1]

> Good rarely comes of war. The human misery and the wreckage are hard to overstate.... Beyond this criminal waste, the inevitable strategic miscalculation and wildly unpredictable consequences of war far overbalance the glorious benefits of armed conflict touted by politicians
> Conscientious objector and US war reporter David Wood, *What Have We Done: The Moral Injury of Our Longest Wars*[2]

This chapter sets the scene for what follows. From Chapter 2 onward, my focus will be on identifying psychological ideas and theories to try to get some purchase on the mystery of support for war. This opening, scene-setting chapter is necessary in order to introduce the reader to some of the lines of thinking and debates about war and its causes more generally. What is war? Are there different types of war that need to be distinguished? Why is it so difficult for nations to share the planet amicably? What are the human and other costs of wars? And should we acknowledge that there are some benefits? Should we be grateful that there is so much less war than there was? We need some guidance on those questions before tackling the book's main task.

We shall settle for a definition of war that sees it as *collectively* organized violence between *organizations* which have *political* purposes. The collective nature of war is something we shall need to constantly bear in mind as we proceed. We may have our own individual thoughts and emotions concerning war, but it is how we collectively support war which counts in the end. In the last several centuries at least, nation states have been the preeminent political organizations making war, although rarely between two democratic nations. We shall see that in recent decades the nature of war has been changing, with fewer state-to-state conflicts and more intrastate civil wars of various kinds. These are the "new wars," concentrated in the poorer parts of the world, involving the breakdown of unified state-controlled order, and a confusing mix of military and paramilitary forces. Any psychological explanation of war support that claims to be at all comprehensive must be applicable to all types of war, "old" and "new." In this chapter we shall also meet a feature of war and support for war that will recur throughout our exploration of the subject and which must be a part of our thinking—namely, the escalation of conflict, often remarkably rapid and hard to control. We shall briefly catalogue war's costs. The list is a long one. It includes combatant and civilian casualties, malnutrition and disease, war traumas affecting adults and children, displacement and forced migration, and widespread economic, social, and infrastructural damage. Those costs need to be continually borne in mind since any support for war has to contend with them. War, to be supported, must be justified despite them.

This scene-setting chapter will conclude by tackling two major areas of controversy. One is the claim that, in spite of the costs of war, it has, over the long term, made humanity safer, richer, and fairer and, even in the quite short term, brought benefits to both winners and losers in the form of such things as innovations in healthcare, science, communications, and transport; welfare provision; increasing female suffrage; and decreasing inequality. The other controversial claim we shall discuss is that war has, over a long historical period, been on the wane and that we are now actually less supportive of war than ever. We must deal with both claims since each, in their different ways, might contribute to war support and lessen the urgency in trying to understand why war-making continues to be supported.

Defining War

Embarking on the question of why we so often support war, other questions immediately presented themselves. The first was, simply, What is war? What should be included as *war* and what excluded? When I started on this project, like many of my compatriots I had in mind the Second World War, the war in which my father served. When, in Britain, we talk of *the war* or use expressions like *post-war*, it is that war we understand is being referred to. That was the image of war I grew up with. But it doesn't take much study of war to realize that World War II was, in many ways, exceptional historically and quite unlike most of the wars that have taken place since. So, how should we define war?

A good place to start is with a definition offered in their book *Causes of War* by Jack Levy and William Thompson, both professors of political science at universities in the United States. They define war as *sustained, coordinated violence between political organizations*.[3] What they say is useful to us because they devote several pages to a defense of their definition, word by word. To qualify as war, they say, reasonably enough, it must involve violence. So, for them the Cold War, per se, was a rivalry, not a war, even though wars followed from it. Similarly, for the Arab–Israeli rivalry,[4] though again wars have broken out as part of it. Not all agree with even this first point; some definitions of war do include the idea of "armed hostility" as in the Cold War.[5]

The word *between* in their definition is important because in their view, like dancing the tango, it takes two parties to make a war. They illustrate what they mean by referring to two events that were important in my adolescence and young adulthood because they did so much to disillusion the left in the West about Soviet communism. By their definition the Soviet invasion of Hungary in 1956 *was* a war because Hungary resisted, whereas the Soviet invasion of Czechoslovakia in 1968 was *not* because there was no armed resistance.[6] That may sound reasonable, but it could rule out very significant military actions that we might be uncomfortable leaving out. For example, government suppression of a civilian uprising might be one and genocide another: an estimated 37 cases of geno-/politicides are said to have occurred between 1955 and 1997.[7]

The qualifier *sustained* they defend because they want to keep the term *war* for those incidents that escalate and exceed a certain violence threshold. Some border clashes between China and India, for example, would not qualify because they ended quickly with limited casualties, whereas others, such as that in 1962, which escalated and involved sustained fighting, could be referred to as the "Sino–Indian War." Unlike some other authorities on war, such as the Correlates of War Project, a data set to which international relations experts frequently refer, which for research purposes requires 1,000 battle-related deaths, Levy and Thompson decline to offer an exact threshold that needs to be crossed in order to meet their definition.[8] That does, of course, underline the obvious fact that precise definitions, necessary for scientific study, may be problematic in this as in so many other fields of social and political science.

Note the word "escalated" there. At many points in later chapters, we shall witness the importance of how support for a war can change over time, sometimes rapidly, as the drumbeats sound and matters accelerate, sometimes appearing to move out of anyone's control. The element of change with time, and the concept of escalation, will play a part in the understanding of war support that I develop as the book progresses.

Central to the theme of the present book, and to much theorizing and debate about war, is their not wholly successful attempt to define the expression "political organization." About the actors who engage in war, they say, categorically, these are "not individuals. Individuals do the actual fighting, but they fight on behalf of a larger collective political unit, under the direction and coordination of political and/or military leaders, to advance the goals of the collectivity, or at least of its leadership."[9] The phrase "or at least of its leadership," with its hint that wars may not always be in the interests of the ordinary citizen, raises the question of whose interests are being served by wars. We shall return to that question. But for the moment we might note that Levy and Thompson never define quite what they mean by a political organization. They do acknowledge that, although at least in Europe since the seventeenth century wars have mostly been between states, other collectives, such as "terrorist" organizations, also make war. As A. C. Grayling concludes in his book *War: An Enquiry*, wars are fought between a variety of nation states, tribes, and other organized groups of people "between whom conflicts of interest can arise over resources, territory, ideology, religion—in short, the political structures, taken in the broadest sense of 'political.'"[10] Others[11] have made the point that an organization's war objectives may indeed be political, but they might equally be economic, ideological, philosophical, or religious. This will become clearer when we consider later on the many so-called new wars.

It seems that even coming to an agreement about what constitutes war, and which are its essential elements, turns out to be considerably more complicated than I, in my naïveté, had assumed. Finally, adding further confusion, the designation *war* is often used metaphorically, as in "the war against the coronavirus." But when does such a war become a real war? What about the "war on drugs," which we might reject as a real war but which sometimes tests any definition of war. In Mexico, for example, it has involved tens of thousands of deaths and collective action on the part of the state, which is certainly a political organization, and on the part of well-organized and armed criminal groups, which might not qualify as "political" by most people's definition.[12]

While recognizing that any definition of war is bound to be fuzzy around the edges, from hereon when I use the word I shall for the most part be using it in the Levy–Thompson sense of organized and sustained armed conflict between political actors, with the word "political" broadly defined. Later in this chapter we shall move toward a consideration of the human costs of war and in the following chapter start to discuss the psychology of support for war. Before we leave the realm of international politics, however, it will serve us well in later sections of the book if we first delve a little more into ideas about the nature of the political organizations that make war.

The Role of the State in War

If it is political organizations that make war and, in the world as it is, states are the main repositories of political authority, then it follows that the state is going to be the principal war-making body. That has not always been the case and might not always be so in the future. But for now at least, states remain the chief holders of military power. We accept that military capability, usually nowadays officially called "defense" or "defense and security," is a central function of state government and that defense ministries are among the most important arms of the state.[13] In federal or united states, defense is one of the functions most likely to be retained by the central government and least likely to be devolved: while Scotland remains part of the United Kingdom, it is the UK government which is responsible for Scotland's defense, for example, not the Scottish government. But the ties that bind the state and war are stronger than a simple matter of where in government responsibility for war preparation and war-making lies. Reading around what international relations experts have been writing on the subject of war, one soon comes across a statement, much quoted since it was made in the mid-1970s by the sociologist Charles Tilly: "war made the state, and the state made war."[14]

What did he mean by that? Mary Kaldor (of whom more later) explains it as well as anyone. From the fall of the Roman Empire to the late Middle Ages wars had been fought by such collectives as barons and their dependents, barbarian tribes, city states, or the Church; and if monarchs were able to raise armies, they could only do so by drawing on coalitions of feudal chiefs. What we usually think of as war, she says, in fact took shape in Europe between the fifteenth and eighteenth centuries and was closely "bound up with the evolution of the . . . centralized . . . hierarchically ordered, territorialized modern state."[15] Mercenary armies were replaced by standing armies, and the whole military edifice of garrisons, uniforms, and drill was erected on behalf of the state. The idea that the state has a violence "monopoly" is an important one: "To distinguish war from mere crime, it was defined as something waged by sovereign states and by them alone. Soldiers were defined as personnel licensed to engage in armed violence on behalf of the state."[16] As others have put it, strong states have the necessary means, and effective institutions, "to control the means of violence in their sovereign territory."[17] So central was the military to the European states that by the eighteenth century, military spending, Kaldor tells us, was accounting for about three-quarters of their budgets.[18]

Princeton University international relations sociologists Miguel Centano and Elaine Enriquez, in their book *War and Society*, tell much the same story but emphasize the "war makes the state" causal effect running *from* war *to* state formation. As they describe it, it was the military revolution of the sixteenth and seventeenth centuries, with the need to acquire the means of war, including the administrative efficiency to run a large armed forces and the great costs involved, that was the driver. A larger, more bureaucratic state could be seen as a by-product.[19] The increased size of states and the decreased number of them are impressive. In the fifteenth century, the number of states in Europe, according to some accounts, stood at about 1,500. Other historians suggest that the total number of independent political units may have been nearer 5,000. By the end of the nineteenth century the number of European states had decreased to less than 30. In the process, state populations had increased from the tens of thousands to the millions.[20]

But the world wars of the twentieth century, particularly the second, were not just state wars; they were what have sometimes been called "total wars." They weren't only actions decided upon by political leaders and executed by the military; they involved the total population. The leaders had to take the people with them. This is still quite evident in the United Kingdom today. As I was drafting this chapter, we witnessed the 75th anniversary of the air Battle of Britain, the D-Day Normandy landings, and, just as poignant in our collective national consciousness, if not more so, the death of the Second World War "forces sweetheart," the singer Vera Lynn.

The origins of total war are often traced back to the American and French Revolutions.[21] As Ian Morris says about the founding of the United States in his *War: What Is It Good For?* (of which more later), "it was the people in arms, not paid professionals or mercenaries, who rose against the British. Lacking their enemies' wealth and organization, the American revolutionaries had raised armies by enthusing them with patriotism instead of paying them."[22] The same is said of the American Civil War: "a critical moment in the path to total war . . . both sides depended on their civilian populations. . . . This was not a war between soldiers, but between peoples." And the French Revolutionary wars: "the most significant transformation was that armies stopped being seen as the playthings of rulers and became emblems and tools of the nation."[23] Napoleon's army, based on conscription, the *levée en masse*, was the largest Europe had seen, over a million men under arms, not repeated until the First World War.[24] Not that the breakdown of the distinction between state and citizens may have been invented by American and French revolutionaries. As Mary Kaldor points out, accounts at the time of the wars between Greek city states centuries earlier tended to refer to wars between "the Athenians" and "the Spartans," not between "Athens" and "Sparta."[25]

Anarchy Rules in the International System

"The word state is identical with the word war." That was said by Kropotkin, the famous nineteenth-century anarchist, yet another who recognized the close association of state and war.[26] It is often pointed out that one of the great weaknesses of a global system based on separate states is that, while the states themselves may have a monopolistic control of legitimate violence within their sovereign territories, they exist within a world system that has no effective control over them. The global system can be described as "anarchic," lacking a higher authority with anything like the same degree of control that states possess within their borders.[27] Mary Kaldor makes the same point when she compares the position of the UN secretary-general today, who in order to raise a peacekeeping force has to rely on voluntary contributions from individual states, with that of medieval European monarchs, who were similarly reliant on raising an army with the help of the feudal barons.[28] Anarchy ruled within nascent countries then, as it does now, so it is often said, in the international system.

What does that mean for the behavior of states? In short, existing in an anarchic system with "no legitimate, higher authority to regulate disputes and enforce agreements,"[29] no "policeman" to keep order, makes it difficult for states to behave well. The school of international relations thinking that has been dominant for many years is the "realist" school. Adherents to one or another variety of that school of thought share the basic assumption that states (or other territorially based groups) are being rational and realistic when they act to promote their own power or security.[30] The Hobbesian world of organizations, typically states, in competition and potential conflict with one another, leads to what international relations theorists call the *security dilemma*. As Azar Gat, Israeli national security professor, historian, and ex-major in the Israeli Defense Forces, describes it,

> When the other must be regarded as a potential enemy, his very existence poses a threat, for he might suddenly attack one day. For this reason, one must take precautions and increase one's strength as much as possible ... [since] precautionary and defensive measures often possess some offensive potential ... measures that one takes to increase one's security in an insecure world often decrease the other's security and vice versa ... suspicion and insecurity are difficult to overcome because it is difficult to verify that the other side does not harbour offensive intentions.[31]

Rivalry between states can persist for decades, and empirical findings suggest that earlier disputes make later ones more probable and that the more disputes there have been, the more likely that any subsequent dispute will result in war. The issues pertaining to specific disputes can become less important than the rivalry underlying them: "The alchemy of rivalry works in such a way that objects of limited value can become important symbols of which side is moving ahead or falling behind. Rivalries also become weighted down with mutual suspicion and mistrust."[32]

Those are the arguments of the more "offensive" variety of realist international relations theory. Other forms of realist theory are more "defensive," leaning toward viewing some weapons systems and strategies as able to provide for one's own security without threatening that of others. The deterrence model argues that building a state's security apparatus need not lead to an escalating action–reaction conflict spiral and thereby constitute a step on the path toward war. On the contrary, war occurs when deterrence fails.[33] The deterrence model therefore argues in favor of military buildups and coercive strategies to preserve peace, supporting the old adage *Qui desiderat pacem, praeparet bellum*, "If you seek peace, prepare for war. "[34] Or, as former French president Nicolas Sarkozy put it, "We know what becomes of continents and countries whose sole ambition is to be left in peace: one day, they see the return of war."[35]

The balance of power between states has been the focus of much international relations theory. One of a state's goals, theory has it, is the avoidance of "hegemony," one state becoming so powerful, in the region or even globally, that it can dominate the rest and compromise other states' sovereignty. One model posits that balances of power have been the norm throughout most of international history, with hegemonies rarely forming. Hegemonic theories, on the other hand, argue that such concentrations of power have been common; they de-emphasize anarchy in favor of the hegemon's role in managing the system within a hierarchical order and thereby contributing to world stability. Hegemonic stability theory, developed in the 1970s by MIT professor Charles Kindleberger, proposed that a dominant power, having both the ability and interest to ensure world order, is the best antidote to costly and dangerous international chaos.[36] Ian Morris likes the word "globocop," to refer to what others have called an international hegemon; and he rather approves of there being one. Without strong government—a *Leviathan*, as Hobbes called it in his classic treatise of that name—we would be perpetually caught up in conflicts, and our lives would be, in his famous phrase, "solitary, poor, nasty, brutish, and short."[37] Britain played the role of globocop for some time, Morris says, because it uniquely had the financial resources and incentives to play that role up to the time of the First World War. Two new hemispherical cops emerged from the Second World War, with the United States becoming later the unrivaled globocop.[38] At least for a while. According to power transition theory, "The most dangerous and warprone situation is one in which a state that is rising and dissatisfied with the status quo begins to approach the strength of the leading state in the system and threatens to surpass it in power."[39] Globally, the present concern to many is the rise of Chinese power and the dangers of a Chinese–US conflict, something we will return to in the final chapter in the light of what we will have learned in the meantime about the psychology of war support.

The great complexity of the causes of war is a theme of much erudite writing on conflict. The immediate triggers for war may often be apparent, but unearthing the more fundamental causes has proved much more difficult.[40] Almost every theory has its critics who say it can at best make very general predictions but not more specific ones. One leading exception seems to be what is sometimes incorrectly referred to as the *democratic peace theory*. This should more correctly be called the *inter-democratic peace theory* since the findings are that two states, both of which can be categorized as democratic (itself not always a straightforward thing to do), scarcely ever go to war with each other. According to Levy and Thompson, it is "the closest thing we have to an empirical law in international relations"—which is not to say there is much agreement about why this appears to be a regular finding. As they say, "it remains a strong empirical regularity in search of a theory to explain it."[41] What the theory does not say is that democracy makes an individual state less likely to make war against others which are, or are considered to be, *un*democratic. Another theory, of particular relevance to civil wars, suggests that countries with unstable regimes, moving toward or away from democracy and lying in the middle ground between democracy and autocracy—they have been termed "anocracies"—are the most prone to interstate warfare.[42]

The Attempt to Outlaw War

The twentieth century, as well as witnessing two of human history's bloodiest wars, also saw serious attempts to outlaw war, or at least interstate war. Those efforts are described in detail in *The Internationalists: And Their Plan to Outlaw War*, by Oona Hathaway and Scott Shapiro. The key plan they focus on is the 1928 General Treaty for the Renunciation of War, sometimes referred to as the *Kellogg–Brand Pact* and later more generally known as the *Paris Peace Pact*. It declared that the parties,

> in the names of their respective peoples ... condemn recourse to war for the solution of international controversies, and renounce it, as an instrument of national policy in their relations with one another ... [and] agree that the settlement or solution of all disputes or conflicts of whatever nature or of whatever origin they may be, which may arise among them, shall never be sought except by pacific means.[43]

In January 1929 it was passed in the US Senate, and within a few years nearly every country in the world had ratified the agreement. US Secretary of State Frank Kellogg won the Nobel Peace Prize. Hathaway and Shapiro see the pact as being a turning point, marking the end of The Old World Order under which war was seen as a legitimate way of righting wrongs. Waging war had been viewed as legal, even as civilized. The First World War had been the old order's "terrible culmination."[44] From now on war would be regarded as an uncivilized way for states to engage with one another. Others similarly see the pact as having been a watershed in international relations.[45]

Of course, it didn't prevent the Second World War. Hathaway and Shapiro say, "The Great Powers had absolutely no intention of renouncing war; on the contrary, they were busily preparing for it."[46] Japan interpreted the pact as not preventing it from protecting its interests in the region and Britain and France as not interfering with them defending their empires. Indeed, it appealed to the West because it promised to secure and protect previous conquests and their dominant international position. For a time, disarmament of major military powers looked appealing as an important step toward honoring the pact's prohibition on resort to war, but the seizure of control by the Nazis in Germany changed that. There was also the question of neutrality. Under the old order, other countries were required to maintain neutrality, for example being able to manufacture and supply goods and munitions to both belligerents at war prices, and could not take sides between belligerents; but the new rules allowed the United States to take sides in Europe and against Japan's invasion of China.

The post–Second World War United Nations (UN) Charter of 1945 and the later International Criminal Court created in 1998 are now considered as "the foundational instruments of modern international law."[47] The UN Charter is more realist than was the between-the-wars Paris Peace Pact: for example, it preserves a state's right of self-defense and does not preclude use of force on another state's territory if that state expressly consents to it. The UN Security Council may authorize force as "necessary to maintain or restore international peace and security," but parties to any serious dispute are obliged to first "seek a solution by negotiation, enquiry, mediation, conciliation, arbitration, judicial settlement, resort to regional agencies or arrangements, or other peaceful means of their own choice."[48]

Opinions differ about whether international law can constrain impulses to take up arms. Some are impressed by an extraordinary proliferation of organizations, treaties, international laws, and conventions which more and more countries have signed up to—a growing institutional framework of global cooperation indicating a greater moral consensus about the proper behavior of nations,[49] nothing less than a colossal shift of power in the world. Others are more doubtful about the capacity of the law to outlaw war. Joanna Bourke (of whom more in later chapters) is one. Law, she says, provides the justification and rationale for armed conflict, and hence is a "blessing to militarists everywhere ... the laws of war are a creation of powerful elites and they reflect the limitations that these elites are willing to accept. They privilege the military necessity of the great powers."[50] For example, in the war crimes trials after the Second World War the Allies ensured that unrestrained submarine warfare and aerial bombardment were not prosecuted as war crimes—not even the atomic bombing of Hiroshima and Nagasaki. Nor may laws designed to restrain states from making war be applied so easily to what have come to be called *new wars*.

The New Wars

There is now general agreement that war has changed again since the mid-twentieth century. Not only were the nineteenth- and twentieth-century European and world wars untypical of war historically, but wars between states no longer account for most modern warfare. The organizations that fight modern wars are, for the most part, not states. Writing in 2011, John Arquilla believed the world had entered "an era of perpetual irregular warfare."[51] The state's monopoly on the legitimate use of violence had been broken. Wars were being fought, less often by state forces and more often by some combination of terrorists, insurgents, pirates, and criminals, plus a growing army of private companies carrying out military and security jobs once reserved for state military or police. Levy and Thompson characterized the changing nature of war as "away from the great powers, away from Europe, and, increasingly, away from state-to-state conflict and toward civil war, insurgency, and other forms of intrastate and trans-state warfare."[52] The shift, they say, was away from the Westphalian model of "symmetric" warfare, involving battles between two sides, toward increasingly "asymmetric" violent conflict, with rebel groups adopting guerrilla, insurgency, and terrorism tactics and an increasing targeting of civilians. It had been said to amount to a "barbarization of warfare," with criminal networks and illicit black markets now playing significant roles. Many central players were ethnic or religious groups, and some termed their wars as "ethnic wars" or "identity wars." Others had questioned whether that masked other, familiar, realist, and mundane motivations, such as achieving security goals, economic resources, or political power or furthering private interests.

No one has described these "new wars" better than Mary Kaldor, professor of global governance at the London School of Economics and Political Science. Two features emerge with shocking clarity from her description of them. One is the context of "failed states," the term Madeleine Albright, former US secretary of state, used to describe countries with "weak or non-existent central authority."[53] New wars, Kaldor wrote, "arise in the context of the erosion of the autonomy of the state.... In particular... the erosion of the monopoly of legitimate organized violence"[54] and a withering of the formal economy. That, in the wider context of "a global risk environment," to which poverty, inequality, climate change, insecurity, and war all contributed, provided fertile ground for nationalist and religious groups to step in.[55]

The other outstanding feature of the new wars was the disintegrated character not only of the states in which they take place but of the very nature of the wars themselves. Although most were "localized, they involve a myriad of transnational connections so that the distinction between internal and external, between aggression (attacks from abroad) and repression (attacks from inside the country), or even between local and global, are difficult to sustain."[56] Unlike in total wars between states, national participation tends to be low. Only 6.5% of the Bosnian population took part directly in the war there, for example. Because the warring parties lack state legitimacy and resources, "the war effort is heavily dependent on local predation and external support,"[57] and zones of war and apparent peace are not so marked. It is difficult to draw a clear distinction between combatants and non-combatants, and there is a blurring of the distinctions between war and crime.[58]

Kaldor cites the wars in Slovenia, Croatia, and Bosnia-Herzegovina as archetypal new wars.[59] This was a story, she says, of the breakup of the Yugoslavian military–industrial complex into "a combination of regular and irregular forces augmented by criminals, volunteers and foreign mercenaries ... a bewildering array of military and paramilitary forces ... cooperating with each other in differing combinations."[60] The UN Commission of Experts identified no fewer than 83 paramilitary groups on former-Yugoslavian territory. The privatization of military forces, paramilitaries, child soldiers, foreign mercenaries, private security firms, and the availability of light weapons through the black market or by looting military stores all played their parts, she says.[61] Globally, the size of the private military services market, virtually non-existent a generation previously, grew to be worth, according to one rough estimate, in the region of a hundred billion dollars annually from the early 2010s.[62]

The internal wars in the Great Lakes area of central Africa, the core of which consists of the former Belgian colonies of the Congo, Rwanda, and Burundi, provide another example. One authority on the area, René Lemarchand, like Kaldor, contrasts the nature of old European wars with the newer wars of the Great Lakes area: "where the context of warfare is that of a failed state, and where the stakes involve access to mineral wealth, the privatization of sovereignty is all too predictable, along with the proliferation of private armies."[63] He continues, "in no other area has ethnic cleansing been conducted with such savagery as in eastern Congo. So far from promoting a sense of 'We Congolese' in the face of armed invasion, the result has been the surge of factional conflict and fragmentation on an unprecedented scale."[64] Referring to the Congo wars of 1998 to 2004, dubbed *Africa's First World War*, he lists five militia groups and six foreign forces from other African countries as the main groups involved, although even that provided only a highly simplified picture since it was hard to keep track of ongoing splits and realignments among the different factions.[65]

The Correlates of War data certainly do show that there were fewer and fewer European interstate wars since the Second World War—60% of all conflicts from 1816 to the 1940s, 45% in the 1950s, 26% in the 1970s, and by the 1990s only 5%.[66] Azar Gat points to evidence that war zones are now concentrated in the poorer parts of the world. Since the end of the Cold War, up to the mid-2010s, he charts intra- or interstate wars having involved only two of the world's countries in the top two deciles by wealth—they were the 9/11 attacks on the United States (and that would not count as a war by some definitions) and the invasion of Kuwait by Iraq—versus 15 in the bottom two wealth deciles.[67] Almost all of the latter were concentrated in sub-Saharan Africa, the Middle East, South and Southeast Asia, Latin America, and the former Soviet Union and Soviet bloc. He concludes, like others, that "non-state armed forces thrive where state structure is weak and productive economic opportunity is lacking."[68]

Of course, he grossly understates the recent involvement of rich countries in warfare by conveniently leaving out their military actions that have taken place in other, poorer countries, as Mark Pilisuk and Jennifer Rowntree describe. If "terrorism" is the calculated use of force against civilians for political purposes, they argue, then we can identify "state terrorism," including kidnapping, assassination of political opponents, imprisonment without trial, and persecution. Their own country, the United States, they recount, has a long record of supporting state leaders responsible for such terrorism—using force to overthrow legitimate governments, engaging in preemptive military action in Iraq, and supporting violent military rule—and has continued to act militarily in those ways in other countries since the Cold War.[69] Azar Gat acknowledges that war might perhaps now be concentrated in the poorer parts of the world "because the rich countries... are powerful enough to take them there and avoid war on their own territory." But he dismisses the validity of that claim on the grounds that it is between or within poorer countries themselves that most wars are now occurring.[70]

Another question is whether the so-called new wars really are so new after all. Some experts see many elements of the new wars in the wars of earlier times.[71] Others have criticized the idea of new wars as being Eurocentric and inaccurate historically, even for Europe.[72] Kaldor recognizes that "old wars" changed in many respects from the seventeenth and eighteenth centuries up to the late twentieth. As she sees it, war waged by absolutist states evolved into war between nation states, then between coalitions of states, later by empires, then by the Cold War blocs. The conflicts that underlay wars moved from those between dynasties to border conflicts to those between rival nations to ideological conflict. Types of armies and military techniques evolved. So did the type of war economy, from regularization of taxation and borrowing, to expansion of administration and bureaucracy, to a mobilization economy, to the military–industrial complex.[73] Many conflicts, both those branded as *new* and those of earlier times, contain both interstate and civil war elements, sometimes simultaneously, in other instances sequentially. War in Iraq, from 2003 onward, is an obvious modern example, starting as an interstate invasion, then involving domestic insurgency, civil war, secessionist war by the Kurds, and international intervention by both state (e.g., Iran) and non-state (al-Qaeda) actors.[74] The Second World War, in all its complexities, contained new warlike aspects, including preceding and subsequent civil wars, for example in Spain, Italy, and Greece.[75]

Such complications aside, there can be no doubt that many modern wars do have the features that Mary Kaldor has described. Most of what is written in the current literature about war focuses either on war between states or on civil war but less often on both.[76] Any discussion of the psychology of why people support war must apply to any type of war, "old," "new," or otherwise, that meets the basic definition of war. That makes the task of understanding why "we"—by which I mean all of us as humans—so often support war even more difficult.

The Costs of War

The nature of war may have changed in the last few centuries and in recent decades, but for our purposes here the essence of war, as organized, collective violence against an enemy for political purposes, and my central question of how it is that we so often support it, remain the same. The costs of war, though they may vary greatly in extent from one war to another, are still with us. No one denies that war is hugely *costly* and in almost every sense of that word. States and other organizations that make war have to weigh up whether it is worth it. When wars are fought in our name, we do too. That is what the present book is about. For now, let us just consider briefly what some of the costs of war are. They are various: "War kills people, destroys resources, retards economic development, ruins environments, spreads disease, expands governments, militarizes societies, reshapes cultures, disrupts families, and traumatizes people."[77] The first and most obvious cost is death. World War II, usually portrayed as a necessary and justified war, was staggeringly costly in terms of lost lives: 50 million according to some estimates, up to 70 million according to others. Around one in six Poles died, for example, as did up to one in five Ukrainians, and at least 20 million Soviet citizens and 15–20 million Chinese.[78] One effect in several countries after the war was demographic: an excess of women to men, with a high proportion of all women who came of age in the decade before the war remaining unmarried for at least the next 20 years and millions of children across Europe growing up without a father.[79] Since then, during the long period of comparative peace that I have experienced in my part of the world, the carnage has continued. The Korean War, for example, is said to have resulted in three million deaths.[80] More than 2.5 million Vietnamese died in the Vietnam War and more than 650,000 Iraqis in the two Iraq wars. Altogether there have been more than 250 major wars, taking over 50 million lives, since the Second World War.[81]

Those who are actually doing the fighting, the combatants, are obviously at particular risk of dying. But one of the ways in which recent wars are "new" is the greater proportion now surviving with severe injuries due to advances in body armor and battlefield medicine: the ratio of wounded to killed was similar in the two world wars, about 1.7 to 1, rising to 2.6 to 1 in Vietnam and to 7 to 1 in Iraq between 2003 and 2011.[82] And the pattern of injuries has changed. Classic injuries to combatants in World War I were trench foot and exposure to poisonous gases. Exposure to ionizing radiation was a greater factor in World War II and frostbite injuries in the Korean War. In Iraq and Afghanistan, traumatic brain injury was the "signature injury" due to improvised explosive devices. Hearing impairment due to noise exposure has been one of the most common service-related disabilities of many wars—as it was for my father who, about 30 years after the end of World War II, was granted a small war disability allowance for that reason.[83]

Being a war combatant, although it can be very boring at times and at other times very exciting (see Chapter 2), can, needless to say, be frightening and traumatic, not just physically to the brain and other parts of the body. The mental health ill effects have been in focus since "shell shock" was recognized in the First World War by British and US doctors, and the French recognized *commotion* (concussion) or *obusite* (shellitis).[84] Post-traumatic stress disorder (PTSD) is now a recognized diagnosis and one for which combatants are known to be at special risk. Associated with PTSD are unemployment; violent behavior; marital, parental, and family problems; and psychological problems for spouses. Reports, especially from the United States where the impacts on the health of military service personnel have been exposed and written about more openly and extensively than almost anywhere, have catalogued the high rates of PTSD, depression, and suicides among veterans of recent wars.[85] In most of the places in the world where people are recruited for military service and where wars occur, these impacts, and worse, are a reality but are more difficult to expose.

Although PTSD, as an accepted diagnosis, has undoubtedly advanced our appreciation of the horrors of fighting in a war, there are now many who believe that PTSD does not fully capture the psychological costs of engaging in an activity where there is a possibility of being killed and of killing others. The "moral injury" which killing others inflicts on combatants who are called on to kill has started to receive greater attention.[86] I shall return to that idea in Chapter 7, where I consider more generally the moral issues surrounding war support.

Civilian Casualties of War

The focus on those who do the fighting, overwhelmingly men, of course gives only a partial picture of war's traumas. The casualties are as much civilian as military, women and children usually in the majority. In fact, as a proportion of all war casualties, civilian casualties rose dramatically during the twentieth century. Civilian deaths are notoriously difficult to count, but they are thought to have accounted for 19% of war-related deaths in World War I, 48% in World War II and in Vietnam, and yet more by the time Mary Kaldor was writing about the "new wars." It has been estimated that more than 90% of those killed in conflicts in Africa in the 1990s were civilians; 3.9 million people in total are thought to have died in the Democratic Republic of Congo civil war alone, the large majority civilians.[87] The point has been made, though, that what we have seen in the later twentieth century is really only a return to what war was like for civilians before the European military revolution's limited wars of the eighteenth and nineteenth centuries, which were a historical exception. The high civilian death toll in World War II and since might therefore simply be a return to the mass killing of civilians in the seventeenth century's Thirty Years War and throughout much of history, across the world, when the distinction between combatants and civilian populations was much less clearly drawn.[88]

Short of death, civilians are injured by war in a great variety of ways.[89] Their injuries may result from them being among the direct targets of landmines, improvised explosive devices, and chemical agents of various kinds—nerve agents, vesicants (which produce chemical burns on the skin and in the respiratory tract), harassing agents (e.g., sarin, mustard gas, and tear gas), and sexual violence employed as a weapon of war. Civilians caught up in conflict zones, including journalists, even though they may not always be intended targets, may suffer some of the same wounds as combatants, including burns and shrapnel fragment wounds. Airports, dams, crops, electrical grids, power stations, and roads are often war targets affecting civilians quite as much as, if not more than, combatants; and targeting of medical facilities, aid, and healthcare workers has increased in recent wars such as the Syrian conflict. Since living in an area where war is taking place and experiencing its horrors and threats at close quarters must be among the most traumatic of experiences, it is not surprising to find that the diagnosis of war-related PTSD has been applied to civilians too.

One of the most traumatizing effects of war for civilians is being forcibly displaced from one's own home, often into overcrowded and impoverished refugee camps. Huge displacements occurred during and after the Second World War. Keith Lowe spells out some of the facts of which I was unaware, brought up as I was in the glow of Britain's victory. At the end of the war, nine million were homeless in Japan, 20 million in Germany, and 25 million in the Soviet Union. All of Czechoslovakia's three million Sudeten Germans were expelled from the Czech borderlands between 1945 and 1948, he tells us, as were almost the whole populations of East Prussia, Silesia, and Pomerania, annexed by Poland and the Soviet Union in 1945, and 1.8 million ethnic Germans from Hungary, Romania, and Yugoslavia.[90] In 2022, the creation of refugees from Ukraine has been a particularly notable feature of the war there.

The biggest killer of lives due to war has been disease. Disease brought by conquerors to populations lacking immunity, and the political and social disruption which epidemics caused, played a huge role in European colonial conquest in the Americas and in other places such as India and Australia. The conquerors themselves often fell to disease in large numbers, especially in Africa.[91] It is estimated that infectious disease accounted for two-thirds of the over 600,000 soldier deaths in the US Civil War. Yellow fever was responsible for 13 out of every 14 deaths in the 1898 Spanish–American War. The 1918 so-called Spanish influenza epidemic, which killed my maternal grandfather, is thought to have killed in the order of 500 million people globally, partly attributable to troop movements and close quarters, sometimes aided by the deliberate policy of starving the enemy into submission. Malnutrition and starvation have also been frequent accompaniments to war. In Java in the Second World War over two million are thought to have died of starvation and perhaps another million on the other Indonesian islands.[92]

The costs of war for children can be devastating. They include the traumas of death of parents or other close family or friends, loss of home and of personal possessions, exposure to attack, and famine and disease. Well-documented examples include the experiences of refugee Croatian children following the war in Kosovo and of children in Angola displaced by the 20-year civil war there.[93] One further disturbing feature of war, perhaps a particular feature of modern "new wars," is the coercion and control of children as soldiers. The *War Child Annual Report 2009* gave 250,000 as the estimated number of child soldiers in the world, of whom 40% were girls.[94] The increased availability of arms such as assault rifles plus technological innovations have made it easier for children to carry and use them. For example, the Kalashnikov AK-47 weighs only 10.5 pounds, has only nine parts, and can be assembled and fired by a 10-year-old.[95]

War's Destructive Costs to Societies' Infrastructures and Economies and the Environment

Those are the most obvious human costs of war. But the true extent of the damage war causes is far greater still. As William Wiist and Shelley White say in the foreword to their volume *Preventing War and Promoting Peace*,

> War causes much morbidity and mortality, directly and also indirectly by damaging the health-supporting infrastructure of society. . . . War destroys communities and sociocultural institutions. War damages the environment. . . . War diverts huge amounts of human and financial resources. . . . War and its long-term consequences may be the most important public health problem worldwide.[96]

To the direct human costs must be added the less direct social and material effects for civilian populations such as exacerbation of poverty, strife within communities, destruction of social networks and support, sexual exploitation, and breakdown of infrastructure and of law and order, with resulting impunity for criminal activity. Women and children suffer disproportionately from these indirect costs of war.[97]

The sheer destruction of war is something we are more familiar with as a result of media images of ravaged towns where fighting has taken place. Bomb sites were a common sight in the London of my early childhood. An estimated 200,000 houses were destroyed and a further 250,000 rendered uninhabitable in Britain, and the destruction was far greater in France, in Germany where a fifth of all dwellings were lost, in the Soviet Union, and particularly in Poland. In the Soviet Union around 32,000 industrial enterprises had been destroyed and 65,000 kilometers of railway tracks torn up.[98]

There are economic costs of war, both for countries that go to war and for their citizens. Wiist and White comment on the US war in Iraq, that it "was pouring more than a billion dollars a week into the . . . war that could otherwise have been spent on healthcare, schools, and infrastructure at home."[99] That was a foreign war with comparatively few US casualties. The economic effects on war-affected countries in the Second World War were massive. The economies of many countries including France, the Netherlands, Greece, Philippines, South Korea, and Taiwan all halved in size during the war. Britain was dependent on billions of US dollars in lend-lease aid. Consequent rises in inflation and cost of living, during and immediately after the war, although comparatively moderate, at about 30%, in Britain, the United States, and Australia, were far greater in some countries such as Mexico and Japan (in the region of 150%) and greater still in France during and immediately after the war.[100] Referring to the most recent "new wars," Kaldor writes of the spread of war's economic and other costs to neighboring countries, affected for one thing in terms of the cost of lost trade. She gives the example of land-locked African countries with trade routes via Mozambique having been affected by the war there. The burden of refugees borne by countries close to war zones is another obvious neighbor war effect, experienced, for example, by the rings of countries around Bosnia-Herzegovina, close to Syria more recently,[101] and neighboring Ukraine most recently.

War also exerts costs in terms of environmental damage. Wiist and White list the following: destruction of fauna and flora, water supply contamination, effects of movement of heavy military equipment (in just one decade around 35,000 aircraft collisions with birds were reported by the US Air Force), noise pollution, radioactive contamination from nuclear weapons, the toxic remains of explosives, depleted uranium, landmines, long-lasting chemical contamination with implications for wildlife, oil and other spills at sea, chemical defoliants such as Agent Orange in Vietnam, and pollution associated with military bases (although they acknowledge the existence of some evidence that because of the exclusion of the general public, bases such as US bases in Europe can actually improve biodiversity). As they say, "Wars devastate the biological, chemical, ecological, human, and physical environment for years following the end of a conflict."[102]

The Other Side of the Argument: Does War Bring Benefits?

The litany of war's horrendous costs seems endless and incontestable. We must, however, deal with the argument that war, paradoxically, has its benefits, even that on balance its overall effects might be positive. Nowhere is the war-has-benefits thesis more eloquently put than in Ian Morris' book *War: What Is It Good For? The Role of Conflict in Civilisation, from Primates to Robots*. Professor of classics at Stanford University, he relentlessly pursues, over the course of almost 400 pages, his conclusion that war has made humanity safer, richer, and fairer. Whether it was the ancient empires—notably the Roman, Parthian, Mauryan, and Han—of the last millennium BC, the

500 years of European conquest spanning the fifteenth to the twentieth centuries, the two world wars, or even the Iraq War, they have been responsible, he argues, for falling rates of violence and rising prosperity. It is important to note, however, that unlike some others, whom we will consider shortly, Morris does not claim that war is good, or even a mixed blessing, at the time it takes place or even in the short term thereafter. His perspective is a long-term one. He knows that the experience, especially for the losers and the conquered, was one of "death, destruction, and wastelands." He also acknowledges that the claim that the horrors and misery of war are not in vain and will bring benefits to all eventually would seem like a cruel joke to those bearing the brunt at the time. But that can't stand in the way of the real truth, as he sees it, that "war has always been the prime mover in reducing violence, creating bigger societies ruled by Leviathans." In place of Tilly's maxim "War makes the state and the state makes war," he says "war made the state and the state made peace."[103]

None of that may seem controversial. The conclusions of a classicist taking such a long-term and intriguing view of war need not detain us long you might think. Except that his conclusions get a bit more concerning as his overview approaches the present day. When it comes to the European colonial conquests, a subject under renewed debate in the United Kingdom as I write, he opines that this Five Hundred Years' War, as he terms it, "was as ugly as any . . . but . . . was the most productive war in history. . . . On the whole, the conquerors did suppress local wars, banditry, and private use of deadly force, and began making their subjects' lives safer and richer." The process was "brutal and exploitative"—he acknowledges that historians who call the effects on the native populations of the New World the "American Holocaust" do have a point—but by creating yet bigger Leviathans, the overall effect was to create "the biggest, safest, and most prosperous society (or world system) yet," reducing violence and generating wealth on a massive scale. But on the question of who benefits from this increased wealth, Morris is again on dangerous ground. Like the Roman Empire before them, the European colonial empires "eventually drew their subjects into larger economic systems, which, in most cases, made them better-off . . . as the nineteenth century drew to a close, the rising tide of the Five Hundred Years' War was lifting all the boats." Closer still to our own times, he thinks the Second World War, although "the most destructive ever fought . . . also managed to be among the most productive . . . because the war began the process of clearing away the chaos left by the demise of the British globocop," leading eventually to the United States taking its place.[104]

Morris acknowledges his debt to Azar Gat's 2006 *War in Human Civilization*. Indeed, one reviewer of Morris' book refers to it as "essentially a popularisation of Gat's work."[105] In his later 2017 book, *The Causes of War and the Spread of Peace*, Gat puts it this way:

> Despite the general overall loss of resources in war, there were also spin-off and long-term productive gains ... the most significant spin-off effects appear to have come from the state itself ... securing increased internal peace and imposing coordinated collective efforts, some of which, at least, were in the common good ... [and] the seemingly paradoxical huge gains in terms of longevity, development, and well-being.[106]

Such arguments for the benefits of war are by no means confined to just a few prominent writers like Ian Morris and Azar Gat. Perhaps more difficult to deal with are the frequent claims that war, even in the quite short term, brings benefits beyond the fact of victory for some. War may be costly in many ways, the argument goes, but looking at the cost–benefit balance sheet presents a less clear picture. Listen, for example, to the authors of *War and Society*:

> War makes a significant contribution to national wealth. The economy of the US is partly shaped by the results of the Civil War, which provided the economy of the North with an immense boost. . . . For the losers, the very destruction of war may be beneficial as it eliminates outdated technologies ... and allows the creation of new industries. . . . War can also develop group cohesion within the state.[107]

Although war can be associated with suppression of civil rights, it can advance egalitarianism, for example, offering opportunities for the disadvantaged in society, as it has, they suggest, for African Americans in the military.[108] They point to wartime need as the driving force for improvements in health services after the Second World War in several countries including France and Russia,[109] as indeed it was for developing clinical psychology, my own training, in Britain, part of the inauguration of the National Health Service. Taking a longer perspective on the twentieth century's two world wars, French historical economist Thomas Piketty sees there to have been a benefit in terms of reducing inequality in the world's richer countries. He is clear that the economic shocks those wars brought about were responsible for a dramatic fall in private wealth relative to national income in most of those countries and, as a consequence, a reduction in wealth and income inequality.[110]

In the 2018 Reith Lectures, broadcast on BBC radio, Margaret MacMillan, professor of history at Oxford University, considered the subject of war and humanity. This annual lecture series is important, commemorating as it does the foundation of the BBC. Like the BBC itself, the Reith Lectures are a much admired and valued feature of British life. Of the five lectures that made up the 2018 series, the first two were held in London but the third and fourth, respectively, in Beirut and Belfast, both places that have experienced organized armed conflict in recent times. The fifth was held in Canada, Professor MacMillan's home country, at the Canadian War Museum in Ottawa. What she had to say was full of insights into the nature of war and our attitudes toward it, but overall the lectures troubled me.[111]

She began her first lecture by staking out her main thesis, that we are ambivalent about war, which we fear but also admire due to the positive qualities it enables such as sacrifice and organization. Among the "paradoxes of war," the title of her second lecture, were benefits such as penicillin, the jet engine, even the very welfare state, which she attributed to the Second World War. War can bring other benefits such as female suffrage and a decrease in inequality. A recurring theme for her was the role of women. Women had served as combatants in the past, although they had often been written out of accounts of war. Although she also recognized the role of women as war resistors, women now being acknowledged as playing the same roles as men in the military was clearly seen by her as an advance for women (something I take up in Chapter 2). Her final lecture focused on how the arts deal with war and how we commemorate war. Although art had been used to prepare for war, as propaganda, often distorting the reality of war in the process, MacMillan reminded us that great art can come out of war (she cited Benjamin Britten's requiem and the novel *War and Peace*), from some wars more than others—the First World War and the Vietnam War, for example.

MacMillan hesitatingly wondered if we could aim to end war, especially because technological change has made it so much more dangerous potentially, although she sounded doubtful. On the question of whether war is natural, she thought the truth was closer to the Hobbesian view that it *is* than to that of Rousseau who thought it was *not*. She was asked directly at the end of her last lecture, Isn't war the aberration? She replied that she found it hard to believe that, because there has been so much war. She says we must understand war because from it we learn something about being human. This comes dangerously close to the idea, now rejected by most of psychology, including the American Psychological Association, that war is natural to humankind because of some built-in aggressive drive or instinct.[112] We shall be examining that and similar ideas in the next chapter.

Nowhere in MacMillan's lectures was there any clear repudiation of militarization policy in the United States, Britain, Northern Ireland, Lebanon, Canada, or elsewhere. Indeed, she was critical of, or at least less than wholeheartedly supportive of, an explicitly anti-militarist stance because we should recognize war's benefits, its admirable qualities. She might object to being construed in that way if it were not that she was quite explicit in her criticism of those who take a one-sided condemnatory approach to war. We may think of war as an aberration, something barbaric indeed; but this is not helpful, she suggested. We need to be aware of the functions it has served. We need to take war more seriously, to try to understand it, so that we can reduce it, or even abolish it, however unlikely that might be.

Others, such as Jungian analyst Anthony Stevens in his book *The Roots of War and Terror*, seem obliged to at least nod in the direction of acknowledging war's benefits:

> War brings out both the best and the worst in us ... inspired human ingenuity and inventiveness and stimulated the development of consciousness ... the discovery of capacities for collaboration, leadership, and subordination indispensable to running a civilized state.[113]

Yet others, like David Wood, cited at the beginning of this chapter, and Lawrence LeShan in *The Psychology of War*, remain on Rousseau's side. LeShan's view is "no war will ... make the world safe for democracy ... nor organize a new world order ... nor establish the perfect society, nor end war, nor do anything else except solve a particular problem, at a high cost and with unpredictable changes following it."[114] Those, whole-heartedly negative, views of war are the ones that come closest to my own. But the very fact that an acknowledged expert on the subject, with as high a media profile as MacMillan has, can highlight our ambivalence about war, believe it to have some admirable qualities, and find it hard to explicitly acknowledge war as a human aberration helps make the central point of the present book. We are not, as the appalling costs of war might lead you to think we should be, always set against war. Indeed, we are sometimes inclined to think that war is not on balance always a bad thing.

The Optimists' Argument: We Should Be Celebrating the Decline of Support for War

A related idea that we need to discuss is the argument that humanity has become less and less warlike, to the point where we are now more civilized in that respect than at any time in history. It is important for us to consider that optimistic perspective for two reasons. One is the same reason we had for looking critically at the arguments of Morris, Gat, MacMillan, and others, that war is a mixed blessing. The danger is that these arguments may detract from trying to understand why war-making continues to be supported and using that understanding to prevent war. But the other, more personal and professional, reason for considering the views of the war optimists here is that one of the best known among them is perhaps the most widely quoted psychologist on the subject of war these days, Steven Pinker.

In the preface to his book *The Better Angels of Our Nature: A History of Violence and Humanity*, he says, "Instead of asking, 'Why is there war?' we might ask, 'Why is there peace?' We can obsess not just over what we have been doing wrong but also over what we have been doing right. Because we *have* been doing something right, and it would be good to know what, exactly, it is."[115]

Let us try and unpack his, and others', argument. One question is whether the decline thesis is about war or about violence more generally. Sometimes it appears to be about one, sometimes the other. What he says early on suggests it is war, or at least militarism, he has in mind. He believes there has been, in the West, "a decline of martial culture."[116] But elsewhere, especially when theorizing about the causes of declining violence, war itself becomes a less obvious focus. He draws on the theory of Norbert Elias that the decline in European violence can be attributed to a larger psychological change beginning in the eleventh and twelfth and maturing in the seventeenth and eighteenth centuries, during which "Europeans increasingly inhibited their impulses, anticipated the long-term consequences of their actions, and took other people's thoughts and feelings into consideration."[117] He views with favor two triggers of this civilizing process. One, already familiar to us through the ideas of Ian Morris and Azar Gat, is "the consolidation of a genuine Leviathan after centuries of anarchy in Europe's feudal patchwork of baronies and fiefs."[118] The second was economic, the positive sum games, the need to plan, control impulses, take other people's perspectives, exercise social skills, all involved in the rise of business and trade. This is sometimes referred to as the *economic interdependence, commercial pacifism,* or *capitalist peace hypothesis*. Levy and Thompson's conclusion, in *Causes of War*, is that, "The evidence so far suggests that, on average, trade tends to reduce the probability of war, but that the strength of the relationship is relatively modest."[119]

An important decision, announced early in Pinker's book, is to look at rates of violence corrected for population size, rather than at absolute numbers. He admits that, "In absolute numbers, of course, civilized societies are matchless in the destruction they have wreaked." Using rates per capita or per 1,000 or 100,000 of the population, he presents statistics showing that modern Western countries, even in their most war-torn centuries—the seventeenth with its wars of religion and the first half of the twentieth—experienced no more than around a quarter of the average rate of death by violence of non-state societies. He refers to western Europe at the turn of the twenty-first century as "the safest place in human history," with an annual homicide rate of about 1 per 100,000 of the population. Civilization therefore makes a huge difference, and in that he seems to include colonization: "Though imperial conquest and rule can themselves be brutal, they do reduce endemic violence among the conquered."[120]

As one of the leading optimists on the subject of violence and war, Pinker does not hide his disdain for pessimists. Those who take an anti-militarist stand are, if anything, portrayed as obsessive, pundits, innumerate, unwilling to see the truth. For example, he refers disparagingly to aggressive academics, the *Peace and Harmony Mafia* as they have been called, who favor Rousseau's romantic theory over Hobbes' realism. They fail to see the enormous progress that has been made. One of the great constraints of contemporary social criticism, in his view, is a loathing of modernity, a delusional nostalgia for a peaceable past: "the decline of violence is an accomplishment we can savor and an impetus to cherish the forces of civilization and enlightenment that made it possible."[121]

Azar Gat is another prominent declinist. He too defends, against some of his critics, mixing discussion of war and of violence more generally, on the grounds that their underlying causes are the same. Like Pinker, he also relies on war casualty figures expressed as percentages of populations rather than as absolute numbers. The combined effect of those two analytic preferences is to stack the figures in support of the declinist thesis. Yes, the archaeological and historical evidence reviewed by Gat and Pinker looks convincing that, despite wars continuing, our chances of dying in our beds rather than in organized wars or violent attacks and skirmishes have improved greatly. But that need not automatically translate into the positive view of the trends in war that the declinists offer. Their interpretation of history is a statement of preference. Others, and I am one of them, prefer to emphasize the continuing costs and dangers of war.

Gat is also in broad agreement with Pinker about changing attitudes toward war. He agrees that democracy and trading relations between states are part of the explanation for war between the old great powers declining, but he thinks there is a more fundamental cause. He calls this the "modernization peace." Economic modernization, rising prosperity, affluence, and comfort have been the main drivers, as he sees it, with urbanization, aging populations, and sexual liberation all playing a part. It is not the cost–benefit balance of war that has changed, he argues, but the appreciation of the greatly improved benefits of remaining at peace compared with the anticipated loss of those benefits if war were to be resumed. As he puts it, "rising prosperity has been associated with a decreased willingness to endure the hardship of war . . . with the individual's life and pursuit of happiness elevated above group values, sacrifice of life in war has increasingly lost legitimacy in liberal democratic societies."[122]

All the war declinists take a long-term historical perspective. Their main difficulty is dealing with recent history. Like Pinker and other declinists,[123] Gat has to explain the apparent anomaly of the twentieth century's two world wars which don't seem to fit the picture of a steady transformation of values and attitudes from earlier to modern times. He can only deal with this by describing what he sees as the special circumstances that existed prior to the First World War, notably the imperial and economic rivalries between the great powers. This is hardly good enough. There are always likely to be special circumstances that help account for the start and continuation of any war. The awfulness of World Wars I and II is surely sufficient to drive a massive hole through any theory of a steady historical decline in warfare. The second and longest long peace, according to Gat, is the three-quarters of a century, and counting, since the end of the Second World War.[124] But here again his inclusion criteria help support his optimistic picture. He confines his analysis to wars between the nineteenth-century great powers, thus excluding all the many other wars, including those where Britain, France, Russia, or the United States took military action against other states.

There is agreement, however, that there has been a striking reduction in the numbers of territorial changes between states taking place during militarized conflicts. Analysis confined to armed conflicts resulting in such changes between 1948 and the first decade of the twenty-first century, using the Correlates of War project data set, found one such conquest taking place on average every 10 months reducing to one every 4 years, the likelihood that any individual state would suffer a conquest plummeting from 1.33% a year to 0.17%, and the amount of territory conquered also falling dramatically. Furthermore, territorial conquests that did occur were viewed differently, now more likely to be contested as contrary to international law and more likely to be reversed.[125]

Oona Hathaway and Scott Shapiro, while not disagreeing with the conclusion that war, or at least interstate war, has declined, do see the causes for war's decline very differently from Pinker. They think it is correct to say that democracy, free trade, and nuclear deterrence also have contributed to the decline. But those explanations are incomplete. The missing element, which Pinker and other declinists fail to emphasize, is the outlawing of war from the Peace Pact onward (see above). It was not principally a civilizing of our natures, an evolution in empathy, reason, and self-control, but rather a gradual rejection of the assumption underpinning the interstate wars of the old order, a dawning of a new enlightenment that Might No Longer Makes Right.[126]

There are then those who disagree altogether with the decline-of-war thesis. Miguel Centeno and Elaine Enriquez, in *War and Society*, provide an example:

> What we observe over the past 10,000 years is not necessarily the decline of violence, as some have argued, but its aggregation. Violence is not necessarily declining, but rather becoming ever more organized and affecting ever-larger groups with ever-greater amounts of killing power. Stephen Pinker may be right in that we kill each other much less randomly than we used to, but the twentieth century would indicate that when we set out to do so, our capacity for violence is ever larger.[127]

Those hundred years, they argue, were unprecedented in their bloodiness, with roughly 80 million deaths from interstate wars and over 100 million in other kinds of war—colonial, civil, revolutionary, genocides. For the first time in history wars were occurring simultaneously across the world; each decade witnessed a major war in every region.[128]

Attempting to arrive at a balanced position on the is-war-declining? issue, A. C. Grayling may have got it about right. Pinker, he says, is correct that violent premature deaths as a percentage of population have declined throughout history, most sharply since the eighteenth-century Enlightenment, and that numbers of wars between major powers have declined since the sixteenth century. But deaths in major battles—admittedly not representative of all wars—more than doubled from the fifth to fourteenth centuries, more than doubled again from then until the early nineteenth century, and increased by as much as a factor of 10 from then until the twentieth. As Grayling puts it, "Absolute numbers of war-related deaths have risen; the world has been growing more peaceful; these two facts are not inconsistent. But the relevant fact is that war still happens. That is an aspect of history which has not yet come to an end."[129]

Conclusions

What have we learnt in this chapter after our brief dip into the world of war and the debates that surround it? I suggest that the 10 points summarized in Table 1.1 are ones which we should bear in mind as we go on. They form part of the necessary background to an exploration of the question of war support. I shall have reason to refer back to these points several times in the course of the remaining chapters.

There is then an additional, general point of great importance. Throughout my brief excursion into the world of international relations and conflict, I have been struck by the absence of a truly *personal* perspective. Discussion remains largely at the level of the state or other political organization. In the process the latter is anthropomorphized, as if it were an individual actor with feelings, aspirations, and motivations. I am certainly not alone in noticing what others have called *unitary actor framing*—referring to states as if they were individual people.[130] When real individuals are the focus, that is usually the personalities or decision-making of political or military leaders. When, less often, reference is made to public opinion, it is usually about how state leaders can mobilize it or is discussed as a reflection of the political system, for example whether or not that is democratic. The remaining chapters of the present book are an attempt to develop a psychological understanding of the factors promoting war among the generality of the population; how we, the public, individually or collectively, contribute to causing war. We shall need to be constantly alert to the danger of retreating from that purpose and regressing to the more familiar view of war as something perpetrated solely by organizations and their elites.

Table 1.1 Ten Points about War, and the Debates around Them, to Bear in Mind When Constructing a Psychological Understanding of Support for War

1 A definition of war.	There is a large measure of consensus that war involves collectively organized violence between organizations which are political, broadly defined. War is a *collective* action. It is always done with others, as part of a group, never alone. If our group is at war, we are involved, like it or not. And the action which we are asked to support, is a *political* one.
2 Conflicts escalate.	The escalation of conflict, often remarkably rapid and hard to control, is a feature of war and support for war. How support for a war changes over time, and the concept of escalation, must play an important part in any model of war support.
3 It is often nation states that make war.	In the last several centuries at least, nation states have been the preeminent political organizations making war. Indeed, that "war made the state, and the state made war" is a widely accepted idea. Our relationships with our nations, including our feelings of nationality or patriotism, are therefore likely to be of great importance when considering war support.
4 The world system is a mix of anarchy and attempts to construct international law.	Despite attempts to construct international law, the global system is often referred to as "anarchic," lacking a higher authority, a kind of insecure Hobbesian world of nation states in perpetual competition and potential conflict. This is used to support the realist argument that, despite the risks, being militarily prepared is necessary to guarantee security: "if you seek peace, prepare for war."
5 Historically, wars have changed. Some modern interstate wars have been "total wars."	The nature of wars has changed over the centuries. Perhaps starting with the American and French Revolutions, and characteristic of the twentieth century's world wars, modern state wars have been called by some "total wars," involving the total population. They required the people's wholehearted support. Relying on allegiance or coercion was not enough.
6 Intrastate wars, the so-called new wars, have been the more common recently.	In recent decades the nature of war has been changing again, with fewer state-to-state conflicts and more intrastate civil wars of various kinds, concentrated in the poorer parts of the world, involving the breakdown of unified state-controlled order and a confusing mix of military and paramilitary forces. Any discussion of the psychology of why people support war must apply to any type of war, interstate, "new," or otherwise.
7 There is support for the inter-democratic peace theory.	There is little agreement about the fundamental causes of war as opposed to its immediate triggers. One theory which comes close to being an established empirical law is the *inter-democratic peace theory*, that two states, both categorized as democratic, rarely engage one another in war, although there is less agreement about *why* that appears to be a regular finding.

Table 1.1 Continued

8 Wars are costly in so many ways.	The catalogue of war's costs is a long one. In addition to combatant deaths and injuries, physical and psychological, it includes civilian casualties, which, as a proportion of all casualties, rose dramatically during the twentieth century. Malnutrition, famine, starvation, and death due to disease are common accompaniments to war. War traumas, particularly serious for children, include death or injury of close family or friends, displacement from home, and forced migration. War's devastation includes widespread economic, social, and infrastructural damage.
9 But the idea that war also has its benefits is often heard.	A familiar thesis is that war, at least over the long term, has made humanity safer, richer, and fairer. An alternative, frequently voiced claim is that war, despite its many costs, brings benefits even in the quite short term, and not just to the victors: for example, contributing to national wealth; stimulating innovations in healthcare, science, communications, and transport; welfare provision; increasing female suffrage; and decreasing inequality.
10 The "optimists" claim that historically humankind has become less and less warlike.	There are good grounds for challenging the conclusion that we are now less supportive of war than ever. If war is on the wane, and if it is a mixed blessing in any case, perhaps there is less urgency in trying to understand why war-making continues to be supported and using that understanding to prevent war. It might even challenge this book's premise, that we continue, remarkably often, to support war.

2
The Personal Attraction of War

> The enduring attraction of war is this: Even with its destruction and carnage it can give us what we long for in life. It can give us purpose, meaning, a reason for living.
>
> Chris Hedges, *War Is a Force That Gives Us Meaning*[1]

> War has universally been a masculine problem. Women do not make war; men do.
>
> Anthony Stevens, *The Roots of War and Terror*[2]

One of the ten general lessons about war that we learned in the preceding chapter was that war is a collective activity. It may seem strange, therefore, to begin our exploration of the psychological roots of support for war with a chapter focusing on the possible attractiveness of war to us as individuals. My defense of starting here is twofold. First, and to state the obvious, collectivities like states and identity groups are just that, collections of individuals who bring their contributions to the group. More personally for me, this is where my interest in the subject began, with the observation that a lot of individuals seemed to be, in some way I didn't comprehend, attracted to war and things connected with war.

This chapter, then, will explore the thesis that for many people there are things about war that are personally attractive. The old idea that war is inherent in human nature can be dismissed as unhelpful and, in the end, unanswerable. It is undoubtedly the case, though, as the words of historians, ordinary citizens, and veterans make abundantly clear, that the experience of war has often been described as a positive one, even sometimes a healthy or spiritually uplifting one. That war can provide meaning and purpose to life, a sense of renewal, a feeling of exhilaration, an experience of togetherness, are common themes. Another line of investigation has looked for individual differences in support for war, finding evidence that those with a greater belief in the world as a competitive or dangerous one and those who measure higher for authoritarianism or for social dominance orientation are the more inclined to support war. It seems that some people are more inclined than others to interpret events and circumstances as threatening. Threat perception will have an important part to play in the model of war support I develop as we go along and which is presented formally in the final chapter. Another thesis we shall examine in the present chapter is the idea that war is not inherent in human nature generally but rather in a form of maleness that values gendered characteristics such as strength and competitiveness, aggression, emotional detachment, and loyalty to a male group. We shall have reason to return to this theme also when constructing the overview model of war support later: the gendered nature of support for war, I shall argue, is one of the elements that make up our preparedness for war, even long before the drumbeats for a particular war start to be heard.

The changing strength of war support, and its tendency to spiral out of control, was something else we learned about in Chapter 1. A theme in the present chapter is the personal meaning and significance experienced by those caught up in an actual war. But that experience is not exclusive to war combatants, although they may experience it most acutely. It is widely shared by non-combatants in a given war. And, of particular significance for my argument, it is an experience shared even more widely, perhaps one might say vicariously, by many of us at times when war is merely contemplated or feared and, furthermore, at an even earlier time when war is prepared for but not yet specifically contemplated. The outbreak of armed hostility—not, in any case, so clear-cut in many modern wars—may act as a tipping point beyond which war support escalates dramatically. But the factors promoting war support do not, I believe, change in kind as war moves from contemplation to engagement. They are with us all along the path to war.

Is War Inherent in Human Nature?

There is a lingering but still widespread belief that war is a natural, ever present, inevitable accompaniment to human affairs.[3] Freud's idea was that of a constant struggle between the life instinct, Eros, and the death instinct, Thanatos. The latter needed to be turned outward if it was not to be turned inward and become self-destructive.[4] Freud himself in the end felt that was an unsatisfactory explanation for war. Others have held more specific ideas about what this human propensity to war was exactly or how it had come about.[5] For example, Robert Ardrey, whose writings were very influential in the 1960s and 70s,[6] believed war was a legacy of our hunter background, our genetic heritage, and that the military was a remnant of the hunting party, accounting for "our fascination with the chase and kill" and with weapons. Writing at the beginning of the twenty-first century, Jungian psychoanalyst Anthony Stevens stressed that war should not be seen as simply a matter of coercion, as pathological or as some kind of perversion, or as a reaction to provoking circumstances:

> These circumstances do not act on an unstructured organism. On the contrary, they act in such a way as to release aggressive behaviour in a creature already equipped and primed to act aggressively when just such an eventuality should arise.[7]

There continues to be scholarly disagreement over whether we are, so to speak, "hardwired" for collective hostility. More specifically, the debate is about whether war predated the rise of settled agriculture and the civilizations of Mesopotamia, Egypt, the Indus valley, and China. Some readings of the evidence suggest war was absent up until the last 10,000 years.[8] The editors of *Nationalism and War*, John Hall and Siniša Malešević, are among those who accept that reading of the evidence. Before that, humans were gatherers and scavengers and, they say, "generally did not engage in warfare."[9] The existence of some present-day Indigenous cultures apparently without any history of war—admittedly few, the Fore of New Guinea is one that has been proposed[10]—was further evidence for some that "human nature" could not be a satisfactory explanation for war.[11]

Others, whom we already met in the previous chapter, read the evidence very differently. Azar Gat is one. He is convinced by the archaeological and anthropological evidence of war throughout human history and is particularly impressed by evidence of communal fighting throughout Aboriginal Australia. He makes a good point when he says that, of course, any definition of war that requires complex, organized militaries is bound to exclude such communal fighting. The argument that war only came with complex civilization then becomes tautological. But collective violence, he concludes, *is* one tool in our toolkit. It is in our repertoire. He applauds the 1986 Seville Statement on Violence, from a group of international scientists under UNESCO auspices who concluded that "biology does not condemn humanity to war," but thinks they were wrong to go one false step further and claim that warfare "is a product of culture." He is a fan of modern evolutionary theory, in which war is viewed as serving the goal of acquiring scarce resources of food, land, and sexual partners. Other supposed motives for war, such as power, status, honor, and revenge, he views as merely secondary derivatives of the basic struggle for the resources necessary for optimizing reproduction.[12]

Psychologist Steven Pinker is in broad agreement. It is only in very recent times, he says, that ethnographers and forensic archaeologists have been able to compile reviews of the frequency and damage of fighting in prehistoric, hunter–gatherer societies—including Europe's last tribal society, the Montenegrins. Intergroup violence, particularly the much more common deadly raiding, as opposed to larger battles, was endemic in such societies. He goes on to discuss what he concludes is the now clear evidence that lethal aggression is part of chimpanzees' normal behavior repertoire. Bonobos, to whom we are as closely related, are certainly less aggressive—they never raid one another, for example—but they are certainly not peaceful across the board. He says, "This reinforces the suspicion that violent competition among men has a long history in our evolutionary lineage."[13]

Although new evidence is emerging all the time, the debate concerning our basic human nature, and whether it supports war or peace, goes on. It is often cast as the Thomas Hobbes[14] versus Jean-Jacques Rousseau[15] debate. Supporters of the former incline toward believing that fighting each other is basic to our natures and that some imposed authority or discipline is required to keep the peace. Followers of the latter are more attracted to the view that we humans are basically peaceful: it is war that requires special inducement in order to overcome our natural pacifism. As we saw in Chapter 1, modern-day international relations experts of a "realist" persuasion lean in Hobbes' direction, and those who emphasize war as behavior which has to be promoted or learned are drawn to Rousseau—the former perhaps the more pessimistic about war, the latter the more optimistic.[16]

Whether one is more of a Hobbesian or a Rousseauian may be very important for one's support of war. But the fundamental question of which way human nature inclines is unanswerable and probably beside the point in any case. Others take the more helpful view that humans are, quite evidently, capable of both acting cruelly and violently, individually and collectively, against their own species *and* demonstrating toward one another the kinds of altruism, cooperation, support and trust which we celebrate. There are those two sides to human nature. The variable nature of war and peace has to be explained; war is not a constant.[17] Writers like Pinker and Gat, too, although they argue for the roots of collective intergroup violence being deeply anchored in our human nature, in the end are in favor of a strategic approach to war which focuses on the incentives and disincentives for violence.

The Personal Attraction of Taking Part in War

In the search to understand why we support going to war, the simple idea, attributed to Freud and other psychoanalysts like Carl Jung, that we do so because there exists a deep-seated, archetypal, or primal instinctual propensity for it may simply lead us into a dead end and is mostly rejected now.[18] In 1967 the American Anthropological Association, for instance, concluded that the evidence did not support instinct theories of war.[19] But that is not to deny that there may be profound, personal reasons for war support. Indeed, such assertions abound.

In his magisterial *The Pity of War*, about First World War, British historian Niall Ferguson writes of the deep-rooted fascination we have with war. He posed the question, given the conditions soldiers endured, why were there not more deserters, more mutinies? Coercion, the presence of military police, the threat of execution played a part. But the explanation he concentrates on and finds most convincing, "not very palatable" though it may be, is "men kept fighting because they wanted to." Before the war, Wyndham Lewis, an artist of the Vorticist school, wrote, "Killing somebody must be the greatest pleasure in existence." But it is not necessary to be a Freudian or a Vorticist to have such feelings. Upper-class cavalry-type Julian Grenfell said, "I *adore* war. It is like a big picnic without the objectlessness of a picnic. I've never been so well or so happy." Such sentiments, Ferguson claims, were widespread but also "shocking," especially given the subsequent, very different, legacy of that war left to us by the likes of Wilfred Owen and the other First World War poets.[20]

The focus of George Mosse's *Fallen Soldiers: Reshaping the Memory of the World Wars* was also the First World War. He drew on a thorough study of the diaries and letters of Australian soldiers which concluded that while some veterans wanted to forget their war as quickly as possible, others recalled the security and companionship of war and the feeling of purpose they experienced. Some even thought of those years as the happiest of their lives. Young men, Mosse says, "were taken out of the routine of daily life and placed in a new environment, which for many of them held the promise of fulfilling a mission in life," the attraction of "a sacred mission" which is found, he says, throughout the history of war volunteers. He points to the wish to escape "the tyranny of school or family, especially father" as a theme often to be found in novels and plays in the last decades of the nineteenth century onward. Young men going to Spain to join the International Brigades were said to have been motivated by something very similar two decades later. John Cornford, for example, wrote "It was partly because I felt myself for the first time independent that I came here."[21] US Second World War veteran Glenn Gray echoed those feelings when he wrote, in *The Warriors*, of the "powerful fascination" of battle, the desire "to escape the monotony of civilian life and the cramping restrictions of an unadventurous existence. . . . This sense of comradeship is an ecstasy."[22]

Nor were positive sentiments about the First World War confined to those doing the actual fighting and killing. May Sinclair recalled "exquisite moments of extreme danger" working in a Belgian ambulance unit, and Vera Brittain and Violeta Thurstan were others who relished the "thrill" and "fun" of working as nurses near the front.[23] Even French priest Pierre Teilhard de Chardin, Ferguson tells us, wrote of his experience as a stretcher-bearer: "You . . . see emerging from *within yourself* an underlying stream of clarity, energy and freedom that is to be found hardly anywhere else in ordinary life."[24]

Nor were such feelings foreign to those on the "home front." Barbara Ehrenreich, in *Blood Rites*, says, "Not only warriors . . . undergo the profound psychological transformation that separates peace from war. Whole societies may be swept up into a kind of 'altered state' marked by emotional intensity and a fixation on totems representative of the collectivity." "The war is so horribly exciting. . . . It is like being drunk all day," wrote one British suffragette. After the war, American psychologist G. E. Partridge referred to the war mood as one of "ecstasy," the "social intoxication, the feeling . . . of being a part of a body and the sense of being lost in a greater whole." British historian Arnold Toynbee was one of many who noted the similarity with religious feelings. The "passions of war," Ehrenreich writes, are "among the 'highest' and finest passions humans can know: courage, altruism, and the mystical sense of belonging to 'something larger than ourselves.'"[25] William James, writing a few years before the First World War, said of the sentiments tapped by war that they "represent the more virtuous dimensions of human existence: conceptions of order and discipline, the tradition of service and devotion, of physical fitness, of unstinted exertion, and of universal responsibility."[26]

Nor confined to the First World War—although sentiments about that war are the ones often quoted. Citing psychiatrist Anthony Storr, Stevens talks of people without a sense of purpose in their lives or who are dissatisfied with their ordinary mundane existence and who "find an almost religious satisfaction in devoting themselves to one main objective, and in orienting their lives in submission to the single wartime aim of victory."[27] Historian Eric Hobsbawm was a Marxist—at least he was a member of the Communist Party most of his life, although by no means an uncritical member—and he served in the British Army in the Second World War. In a letter to his cousin Ron, he wrote, "Frankly for a historian these times are absolutely unique. Since the fall of the Roman Empire or the French Revolution there has been nothing half as fascinating. It is unpleasant to have been born in this age, but by God, I wouldn't have missed it for anything."[28] In *The Psychology of War*, Lawrence LeShan quotes Julian Symons, writing of his experience during the London bombing in Second World War: "A wretched time people say. I recall it as one of the happiest periods of my life. Living became a matter of the next meal, the next drink. The way people behaved to each other relaxed strangely. Barriers of class and circumstance relaxed."[29]

LeShan draws attention to something else, even more shocking than the notion that we might actually like war. This is the complementary idea, articulated time and time again by philosophers, poets, and historians, that peace, the absence of war, might be degrading or unhealthy in some way. We are told that Roman poet Juvenal wrote, "Now we suffer the evils of long peace. Luxury hatches terrors worse than wars" and that philosopher Hegel opined that "War has the higher meaning that through it . . . the ethical health of nations is maintained."[30] There is also to be found the extraordinary idea that war might be something to look forward to, not only because it might serve to right wrongs but because it might be liberating, "cleansing," restorative of health even. Prior to the First World War, Mosse tells us, the Futurists spoke of *guerra fiesta*, "war as a festival": "The outbreak of war in August 1914 was like a festival to many youths, an extraordinary event, a liberation from normal life," a feeling of restless opposition to the "petrified society" of their elders. He quotes George Heym, a German expressionist, who wrote in a diary entry in 1907, "I can say for myself, if only there was war I would be healthy again. Now one day is as the next, no great joys and no great pain . . . everything is so boring."[31]

In his book *Wounds: A Memoir of War and Love*, Irishman and distinguished BBC war correspondent Fergal Keane cites the words of Patrick Pearse, a leader of the 1916 Dublin Easter Rising: "We must accustom ourselves to the thought of arms, to the use of arms. We may make mistakes in the beginning and shoot the wrong people," he wrote, "but bloodshed is a cleansing and a sanctifying thing, and a nation which regards it as the final horror has lost its manhood. There are many things more horrible than bloodshed; and slavery is one of them." Coming from very different national standpoints, writers Rupert Brooke and Patrick Pearse were among those who "employed a language of redemptive blood sacrifice."[32]

LeShan makes a further, interesting, and vital point, of central relevance to the present book, when he says that it is not just the case that "our species consistently acts in ways that indicate we are *attracted* to the idea of war" but, what is more, "Mostly this attraction is concealed and denied."[53] It is that denial, and the constantly voiced claim that it is only peace we crave and that we go to war only as a last resort, that makes addressing our support for war so difficult.

Supporting War May Enhance Life's Meaning

A wide range of different psychological theories and concepts have been proposed to try and explain support for war at an individual level. One of the ideas that crops up repeatedly in one form or another is this idea, noted by historians, journalists, and others, that war enhances life's meaning. In 2002 a book came out with precisely the title *War Is a Force That Gives Us Meaning*. Its author, Chris Hedges, says

> Most of us willingly accept war as long as we can fold it into a belief system that paints the ensuing suffering as necessary for a higher good, for human beings seek not only happiness but also meaning. And tragically war is sometimes the most powerful way in human society to achieve meaning.[34]

As I was writing, a war broke out between Armenia and Azerbaijan over the disputed region of Nagorno-Karabakh. Footage of excited citizens waving flags, shouting slogans, assuring journalists that history is on their side, that they will not give up the struggle, and, significantly, that they will win certainly conveys a strong impression of meaningfulness. Other footage, though, showing scenes of women crying and of the injured, silent, and dazed, being treated in hospital, suggests that, for some, the violent conflict is bringing a different kind of meaning to their lives. The same was witnessed later, on a larger scale, in Ukraine (see Chapter 8 for more on the war in Ukraine).

There have been several quite recent academic papers looking at meaning or its opposite, meaninglessness, and their relationships with conflict. One aimed to test the hypothesis that "the mere *presence* of conflict in one's life can *itself* fulfil an important human need... the psychological need for meaning."[35] That need, the authors state, lies at the very heart of the human condition. They go on to describe two general components of meaning in life which have been identified. One is a sense of *purpose*, which can be fulfilled through many activities, accomplishments, knowledge or relationships. Importantly, one way of fulfilling this component of meaningfulness is by "attaching oneself to a larger philosophical framework." The second component of meaning is *comprehension*, sometimes called *coherence*, which they define as "the ability to make sense of and understand one's life and the surrounding world in a coherent manner." More precisely, conflict can enhance purpose and coherence, they postulate, because it can do five things. It can give us a feeling of exhilaration and arousal, the perception that we are becoming personally stronger, a new perspective on our lives and our priorities, a sense of unity and connectedness, and a feeling that we are part of something of importance that transcends the self. They argue that once people experience the meaning that conflict often provides, even though that may not be responsible for the start of wars, it may be a powerful enough factor to at least help prolong conflict and provide an obstacle to ending it.

These ideas were tested in a series of studies of different kinds. One study involved participants who were themselves living through an actual conflict, the 2014 Israel–Gaza war. In other studies, about the American Revolutionary War, the US-led campaign against ISIS, and the November 2015 Paris attacks, participants were exposed to reminders of intergroup conflict. A measure of "perceived meaning in conflict" was based on the degree of agreement with ten statements, such as "The national unity my country displays during times of conflict is very uplifting," "It is exhilarating to see our nation restore justice after being attacked or threatened by our adversaries," and "Knowing that our servicemen and women fight for our country... gives me a greater appreciation for the value of life." Across the studies, being involved in a conflict, or being reminded of one, increased "meaning in conflict" as well as support for "conflict-perpetuating beliefs" (e.g., "We live in a world in which perpetual war is more likely than perpetual peace") and "general militaristic attitudes" (e.g., "Only the militarily strong can negotiate successfully in international conflicts").

One theory which has come to prominence and has now spawned research in multiple countries and a large literature is *terror management theory* (TMT). The theory is based on the idea that nothing is more terrifying than being reminded of our own mortality, that life is uncertain and full of dangers, even that events that impact us may be random and meaningless, beyond our control. Anything which reduces that existential uncertainty, imposing some order and meaning on our lives, providing a comforting balm for anxiety in the face of the possibility of tragedy and eventual mortality, is to be welcomed. According to one account of the theory, it is about "efforts to transcend one's biological finitude and buffer death anxiety by providing a sense of personal significance and by signifying the fusion of the self with something greater and more enduring than physical existence."[36]

A leading candidate to fulfill the role of that "greater something," and one which is central to TMT, is a particular "cultural worldview" with which one can strongly identify.[37] Some exponents of the theory stress that a person's cultural worldview is a very individual matter, influenced by personal life experiences. At the same time the word "cultural" indicates the importance, for the development of a worldview, of the collective culture shared with others, including its political and socioeconomic aspects. Remembering that war is a collective activity, it is that shared aspect of the cultural worldview which gives TMT its relevance for war support. The theory posits that defending our cultural worldviews, and personally living up to the standards they demand of us, is vital to managing the distinctively human experience of mortality awareness, and hence to the maintenance of our self-esteem. Hence, the potency of support for war in defense of a cause linked to a worldview, shared with others and at the same time so important for the mental health of each of those who share it.

It is not hard, then, to see the attraction of TMT as a way of explaining the otherwise mysterious phenomenon of widespread support for war. Although relatively little of the research relating to TMT has focused directly on war, much of it is on the subject of prejudice toward others who do not share one's own worldview. There is good evidence that exposure to others who do *not* share our view of the world can make us feel uncomfortable and may result in increased prejudice and defense of our own view, although there is other evidence that, depending on circumstances, such exposure can result in prosocial responses including generosity and forgiveness.[38] Other experimental research has provided evidence consistent with the hypothesis that self-sacrifice for a cause might function to buffer death anxiety. For example, one study[39] found that making mortality salient heightened Iranian college students' support for fellow students who committed martyrdom attacks against the United States and increased willingness to join their cause. Another found that young English adults, asked to think about their death, were then more likely to endorse statements such as "I would die for England."[40]

There is much subtlety to TMT, which there is not the space to elaborate on here. For example, the ways in which people may be reminded of their mortality are varied and need not necessarily involve arousal of strong emotions, such as terror, hate, or rage, at the time. Furthermore, responses to being reminded of one's mortality can include direct ways of defending against conscious thoughts of death as well as responses to less conscious such thoughts, including enhanced support for one's cultural worldview and for others who share that view. Some have proposed that it is not death itself which is terrifying but, rather, the terrifying uncertainty associated with it. Others have responded by suggesting that TMT provides the specific explanation for that uncertainty in terms of reminders of the inevitability of death.

But why should engagement in, or support for, collective armed conflict be necessary for one to achieve a feeling of meaning in one's life? Something is missing from a simple conflict-gives-meaning or mortality-defying theory. Fortunately, there are a number of related theories which contain the further idea that the boost to meaning in life which engagement in conflict can offer may be especially attractive to those of us who have particular reason to need such a boost on account of our circumstances. A number of such theories focus on perceived threats and humiliations. One such is the *3Ns model* of terrorism.[41] Some may question the inclusion of ideas arising from the study of terrorism, which is not the same thing as war. In justification I would argue that wars, especially the "new wars," with which we have become familiar, often include acts of terrorism. The distinction between terrorism and war is not at all clear-cut. Furthermore, the study of terrorism has produced ideas about support for armed conflict which can be helpful to us. The 3Ns model provides a good illustration of that. It contains the idea that the attraction of violent collective conflict can be motivated by deep-seated personal anxiety—the personal *need* part of the theory, one of the theory's three Ns. Behind all the various motivations to which terrorism has been attributed—honor, vengeance, religion, loyalty to a leader, heavenly reward, among them—is something more fundamental. In the model this is called the "quest for significance." Individuals, the model suggests, are motivated to engage in violent conflict not only for political ends but also for existential reasons. The latter can include feelings of shame, humiliation, and meaninglessness or the restoration of a lost or threatened sense of meaning, control, justice, honor, or dignity. Experiencing traumatic events plays a special role in such theorizing. In fact, any strongly felt *loss of significance*, actual or threatened, is especially likely to activate significance quest. Significance loss may arise through a personal failure or humiliation or loss—including loss due to enemy action—as well as a state of *anomie*, helplessness and personal insignificance due to one's deprived economic and social conditions, or disrespect for one's cultural and social identity, as may be felt by Muslim immigrants who encounter Islamophobia in Europe, to give just one example. The model's definition of loss of significance is therefore a broad one, and the circumstances that can motivate a quest to restore meaning are widely set.[42]

There are many studies which could be cited in at least partial support of models like the 3Ns. One I particularly noted because it came from a part of the world where warfare, of the "new wars" kind, has been endemic in recent times, as we noted in Chapter 1, but which has not otherwise been well represented in research. A team of researchers—from Sweden, Norway, and Italy as it happens[43]—used survey data from a representative sample of households in the North Kivu province in the east of the Democratic Republic of the Congo, an area which had seen very high levels of violence for 10 years from the start of the First Congolese War in 1993. It remained tense due to a combination of threats to livelihoods owing to climate changes, especially drought, and the continued threat of violence. The study looked at variation in support for the use of political violence. Respondents were asked to respond to two statements—"The use of violence is never justified in Congolese politics" and "In this country, it is sometimes necessary to use violence in support of a just cause."

The findings indicated that threat due to having been exposed to drought *plus* lower household resilience was a combination most likely to be associated with support for political violence. Both objective and subjective indicators of resilience were employed. A widely used objective *Resilience Index* estimated resilience capacity based on four "resilience pillars": access to basic services (e.g., improved sanitation, improved electricity supply, distance to school, distance to hospital), assets (e.g., wealth, agricultural wealth, land), social safety nets (e.g., access to credit, transfers, others you can rely on), and adaptive capacity (e.g., years of education, salary, training). An example of the subjective resiliency questions was "If an extreme rainfall irregularity occurred, what is the probability that your household could recover completely during the next six months?" The combination of drought threat and low resilience identified by those researchers certainly fits that part of the notion of a need to restore meaning to one's own or one's household's life due to deprived and threatening economic and social conditions.

The research team referred to such conditions giving rise to anomic feelings of lack of control. The concept of anomia, sometimes called simply *alienation*, is one that has also been used to understand support for various kinds of politically motivated violence, including state terrorism such as Iranian-backed Hezbollah attacks in Lebanon in the 1980s, armed struggle by large groups representing minorities such as by the Kurdistan Workers' Party in Turkey, as well as protest violence—not necessarily meeting our definition of war (Chapter 1) however—perpetrated by smaller factions such as far-right or anarchist violence in countries like the United States or France.[44] A typical definition of anomia sees it as a psychological state with five main components: feelings of meaninglessness (that one's life has no purpose), powerlessness (that one's actions have no political consequences), social isolation (that one's values do not fit with those of one's society), normlessness (that behavior is not efficiently socially regulated), and self-estrangement (that one's daily actions are motivated by external factors such as working for the wage only).[45]

Whether couched in terms of meaninglessness, loss of significance, alienation, or awareness of one's own mortality, these ideas and theories all support the widely held view that an important function of war support may be the bolstering of our very *personal* feelings of meaning and purpose. We need to be reminded, though, of one of the conclusions of Chapter 1: war is waged, not by individuals, but by organizations. It is a collective undertaking. We will pick up the idea of war support and meaning again in the following chapter, where the focus will be on *collective* values and beliefs based on state, ethnic, religious, or regional identity.

Individual Differences: Are Some of Us More Personally Inclined to Support War Than Others?

Meaning and mortality have significance for us all and may be especially salient under certain conditions. But is there something even more personal at play? Surely individual differences are relevant too. Aren't some of us more personally inclined to support military action than others? One of the most enduring individual difference concepts in political psychology is that of *authoritarianism*. The idea goes back to the post–Second World War era and the publication of *The Authoritarian Personality*,[46] which proposed the first measure of authoritarianism as a personal trait. It was sponsored by the American Jewish Committee's Department of Scientific Research and was motivated by the desire to understand the roots of antisemitism and the appeal of fascism. There have been significant revisions to the construct since then, notably Altemeyer's[47] understanding of authoritarianism as comprised of three components: aggression, submission, and conventionalism. The view now is that authoritarianism combines deference to authority with support for conformity, conventional values, and harsh punishment for violations of in-group norms and authority. Those high in authoritarianism are more inclined to perceive out-groups as threatening.[48]

Because scores on measures of authoritarianism correlate with conservative political values, at least in the United States and other Western countries where most of the research has been done, the revised concept of *right-wing authoritarianism* (RWA) has become prominent in the psychological literature. It is seen as consisting of three personal traits: submission to in-group authorities, support for social conventions and values, and aggression toward non-conformists and conventional targets as defined by social authorities.[49] Not that all forms of authoritarianism would necessarily be thought of as "right-wing," especially in the context of various "new wars" and anti-colonial and civil wars.

A particularly interesting study of direct relevance to support for war was one conducted in 2015 with several hundred Russian adults recruited through political discussion forums.[50] That was a time, the authors say, when attitudes toward war were particularly salient in Russia: both the 70th anniversary of the victory in Second World War, with its demonstration and celebration of the country's modern armed forces, and the then current conflict in eastern Ukraine were being regularly discussed in the media. The study drew on RWA but combined it with *social dominance orientation* (SDO). The latter refers to a general positive orientation toward social hierarchies in which some social groups occupy a dominant position and others a more submissive one.[51] The rationale for including both RWA and SDO was that each, in their different ways, encourages prejudice toward various out-groups, including gender and sexual prejudices but also prejudice toward migrants, ethnic minorities, and residents of other countries. The dual-process model of prejudice[52] suggests that it thrives on two things. One is the belief that the world is dangerous, unpredictable, and threatening as opposed to safe, stable, and secure (*dangerous world belief*, or DWB: a typical example of the questions used to measure it is, "Our world is a dangerous and unpredictable place in which the values and way of life of decent people are under threat"). The other is the belief that people are basically competitive and manipulative as opposed to being naturally kind and cooperative (*competitive world belief*, or CWB: a typical question is, "It's a dog-eat-dog world where you have to be ruthless at times"). RWA, it is supposed, is an expression of DWB, and SDO an expression of CWB.

The dual-process model of prejudice has generally been supported, but, as the authors of the Russian study say, most of the relevant studies have been conducted in New Zealand, the United States, Germany, and Belgium. In three-quarters of the studies, the questionnaires were completed by students—hence the importance of the Russian research. The main interest was to try and understand variations in Russian adults' attitudes toward war, assessed with a scale including 12 statements covering the moral justification for war and its economic, societal, and humanitarian consequences. Other studies have shown that RWA is associated with positive attitudes toward military action to resolve international conflicts, and some studies, but not all, have shown the same for SDO. In the Russian study, statistical modeling showed that both dangerous and competitive world beliefs were associated with more positive attitudes toward war, both directly and via their expressions in RWA and SDO. The influence of CWB was the stronger of the two orientations. It is also interesting to note that men scored higher for both CWB and SDO than women, and also held the more positive attitudes toward war. Both CWB and SDO diminished with age.

Another program of research using these popular concepts of RWA and SDO is summarized by political psychologist David Winter in *Roots of War: Wanting Power, Seeing Threat, Justifying Force*.[53] Over an 8-year period following the 2003 US invasion of Iraq, he and his group conducted a series of surveys with a total of over 1,750 college undergraduates at a large public university in the US Midwest. Students were on average negative about US engagement in Iraq, but attitudes varied; and both RWA and SDO were highly correlated with belief that the Iraq War was just and with support for it, RWA the more strongly so in this case. But Winter sees something yet more fundamental behind such psychological results. He has concluded that the motivation to exercise *power*, often implicit rather than explicit, is more basic for understanding war—Nietzsche's "will to power." He shows how, in both interstate and "new wars," "both insurgents and governments may be driven by the drive for power."

Unfortunately for our purposes, however, his greater focus, as it is in political psychology generally, is on the leaders who take us into and through warfare, not on those who support them. Winter is not alone in emphasizing the centrality of power motivation, but others who have done so have also generally failed to distinguish between the elite decision makers and the general public, assuming that to all intents and purposes they can be treated as being one and the same.[54] This failure to uncouple the citizens and their leaders, the inclination to speak of human motives that encourage war as if they applied in the same measure to the mass of the people and to the elites, is remarkably common.[55] This is the same issue that I identified, at the end of Chapter 1, as a shortcoming in war-related research and commentary generally. It will recur time and again as the following chapters proceed.

Theory and research in psychology and related disciplines, which has grown steadily since the Second World War, has been pointing to the conclusion that we, the people, bring a variety of sentiments, desires, attitudes, and beliefs supportive of war. Among those that have received attention are the quest for meaning, the need to be part of something greater than our individual selves, which can turn into support for collective violence when aided by belief in deference to authority and belief in a dangerous, competitive world and promoted by personally threatening circumstances. There remains one idea, prominent in writings about war and war support, which such generalizations miss altogether. That is the idea that war is a gender issue: war is a boy's game, underpinned from start to finish not principally by the personal factors common to the sexes which have been covered in this chapter so far but by masculinity.

Is War Inherent in the Nature of Men and Maleness?

There has been no shortage of observations that warfare has the appearance of being a male institution. Military strategy, coordination, and support, as well as the fighting itself, it is often pointed out, are dominated by men, as are the design and production of arms and the buying and selling of them.[56] Even at the turn of the twenty-first century, men constituting 97% of the world's soldiers and 99.9% of those who could see combat are figures often cited.[57] In 2016, Miguel Centano and Elaine Enriquez were able to say in *War and Society*, "War has been nearly the exclusive domain of men."[58]

Nor is it just the over-representation of men that has drawn attention. It is the dominance of masculine values that has been so impressive. For example, war is now "one of the most rigidly 'gendered' activities known to human kind.... It is an activity that has often served to *define* manhood itself," wrote Barbara Ehrenreich in her 1997 book *Blood Rites: Origins and History of the Passions of War*. Some writers, she says, "are so struck by the link between masculinity and war that they find in masculinity . . . a satisfyingly complete explanation of war."[59] A comment a few years later claimed that military establishments and state defense departments operated in "highly masculinist institutions that glorify and promote the traditional male values of strength, power, and competitive advantage."[60] So, is that the real truth? Support for war is not so much due to something inherent in human nature, or necessarily in certain personality types, but it is, rather, inherent in the nature of men and maleness.

What has been recorded and written about the twentieth century's two world wars provides endless material to support the thesis that maleness makes war. The evidence is particularly strong in relation to the experiences of those who served in the military in the First World War. Joanna Bourke, writing about the justifications for sacrifice in First World War in *Dismembering the Male*, argued that society "encourages the soldier's delusion of masculine virility and calls him a hero in order to lure him into becoming a sacrificial victim."[61] Based on about a thousand accounts of the lives of men born between the 1890s and the 1930s, Humphries and Gordon's, *A Man's World: From Boyhood to Manhood 1900–1960*,[62] a book which accompanied a BBC television series, is just one of many sources. Chapter 3, "The Soldier," is based on accounts of serving in one of the two world wars. Of the first, the authors say,

> That so many men could allow themselves to be used in this way as cannon fodder was in part due to the idea that the battlefield—however gruesome—provided a crucial test of manhood. Deep-rooted values of manliness also lay behind the regimental pride and camaraderie which were so important in helping to keep the men going. Traditions of honour, strength in

adversity, brotherly love and a fearless attitude to danger and death formed the bedrock of army life and shaped the aspirations of the ordinary soldier during the First World War.

Although the quotes from the men's accounts are even more replete with references to the fear, horror, sadness, and disillusionment they felt at the time or since, being a man is a theme well represented too. For Norman Edwards, who rose to be an officer and was wounded in the First World War, trench warfare "made a man of me, I think. . . . You had the satisfaction of knowing you'd not only done your duty, you'd been wounded doing it. You had a stripe on your arm which showed that you'd been wounded in action, you'd actually been in the front line." Ted Francis, who joined up in Birmingham at the start of the First World War, said,

> I suppose I only felt a man when I joined up, became a soldier. . . . But especially when I had a uniform and especially when I had a gun, then I felt a man. When we got to France you could see some of 'em swelling up absolutely fit to burst with pride and I too. Being cheered by the French and mostly girls too. We thought it was great to be a soldier . . . . It was just the thoughts of really young men who didn't know any better.

Frank Davies, too young to be sent abroad at the start of the Second World War but who finished the war in a Japanese prisoner of war camp, remembered looking up to older boys: "There were lads walking round with these fancy uniforms. To me they looked like heroes and that's what I wanted to be. I wanted a crack at being a soldier hero and so I went off to join up."

George Mosse's *Fallen Soldiers*, cited earlier,[63] is another source, though not so confined to Britain or so completely focused on those who served in the military. The concept of manliness, he tells us, summed up most of the ideals shared by articulate German youth at the time of the First World War. The German Youth Movement described the "ideal German male" as having a superbly formed body, being in control of himself, modest, restrained, decent and fair in daily life as well as in battle and sport, and chivalrous toward women. In England, upper-class education such as at Eton or Harrow consciously instilled an ideal of manhood, with fair play and chivalry emphasized as well as patriotism, physical prowess, courage, and energy. Although the heady August days were shared by men and women, "in the last resort war was an invitation to manliness." Decisiveness was at the core of this definition of maleness. For men, to the fear of being effeminate was added that of being thought decadent. "Decadence," the exact opposite of masculinity, was a word often used. After the war, "The feeling that war had created a new masculine type existed all over Europe." In England Christopher Isherwood held that young men after the war had to face the question, "Are you really a man?"; and in Germany Ernst Jünger wrote about a new race of men loaded with energy, men of steel.

A book that came out in 2016, entitled *Masculinity and New War: The Gendered Dynamics of Contemporary Armed Conflict*,[64] attempts to bring this debate up to date. The author, David Duriesmith, discusses seven recurring aspects of masculinity which he concludes were crucial for understanding support for wars of the conventional "old" kind. Summarized here in Table 2.1, they are what he refers to as "the basic building blocks of what it means to be a man in the Global North.... They are the tools that make males men, and make men willing to fight. Similarly, they serve to normalise war and patriarchal violence."

His own analysis focused on recent wars in sub-Saharan Africa such as those in South Sudan, Sierra Leone, Nigeria, Liberia, the Democratic Republic of the Congo, and Uganda. He takes issue with Mary Kaldor over her failure to recognize the important issue of gender in such "new wars." Many of the same seven factors he identified as important in old wars he concludes are likewise important for understanding these wars too.

Duriesmith goes further, seeing masculinity and war within a broader framework of gender and power, of patriarchy: "Conventional interstate war tends to serve the interests of a small constituency of dominant men and is made possible by the structures of gender that place them in a position of power ... old wars are justified through the masculine narrative of militant nationalism ... the state is a masculine institution."[65] He is not alone in viewing the association of war with masculinity as drawing on a still deeper patriarchy. Study of elite groups of military planners, almost all male, psychologists Pilisuk and Rowntree tell us, shows that their vocations "provide gratification for masculine identities ... often pursued without conscious awareness of an underlying preoccupation with the subjugation of the weak and the feminine ... reinforced by a clandestine organizational culture."[66] Although he was coming to the subject from a very different perspective—that of Jungian psychoanalytic theory—Anthony Stevens also saw the association of war with masculinity as part of a more general domination by things male. His book, although it purports to fathom *The*

Table 2.1 Seven Recurring Aspects of Masculinity Crucial for Understanding Support for Wars of the Conventional "Old" Kind, Many Equally Important for "New Wars"

Violence	Men socialized to respond to threats with violence, priming men for involvement in the military.
Militarism	Valorization of military heroes: men's claims to manhood by emulating military in various ways, including competitive sports, games, etc.
Emotional detachment	Emotions seen as signs of weakness, feminine; desensitization primes for violence, disconnects consciousness from experiences and the possibility of destruction and the pain violence may cause.
Aggressive bravado	Male culture encourages competitive expressions of bravery, skill, strength, sexual bragging.
Risk-taking	Including hard-contact sports, heavy drinking, sexual risk-taking
Aggressive heterosexuality	Opposing homosexuality in the military receding, but "the social enforcement of compulsory heterosexuality remains" through group sexual activities like joint visiting of strip clubs and brothels.
Loyalty to a male group	Full admission through training and first combat experience; subsumed by squad, eat, sleep, bathe, fight, die together; harsh tests; ritualized humiliation; must demonstrate manhood, superiority over lesser men, other squads, and civilians.

Source: D. Duriesmith, *Masculinity and New War: The Gendered Dynamics of Contemporary Armed Conflict* (London: Taylor and Francis, 2016), chap. 3, see 30.

Roots of War and Terror, refers throughout solely to men and maleness. As he sees it, war is rooted in "archetypal structures residing in the male psyche."[67]

Earlier we met political psychologist David Winter, author of *Roots of War*, which contains his arguments for putting power and power-seeking at the center of our understanding of war. One source of evidence he summarizes comes from a number of data sets showing that the number of wars countries engaged in and the number of years they were at war, between the end of the Second World War and the first decade of the twenty-first century, were significantly greater in countries where women had lower status—judged by indices of gender inequality, poorer physical security, and lower comparative female literacy rates, life expectancy, and number of seats in parliament. It was also the case, however, that lack of social progress more generally, with which lower status for women is highly correlated, as well as geography and military spending were even stronger correlates of war. He concludes, nevertheless, that across countries "the external violence of war is correlated with internal violence toward women" and, indeed, that "the patriarchal pattern of social relations between the sexes ... becomes the primary model for understanding power."[68]

Many writers remind us that sexual abuse of women in war has been well documented.[69] Throughout history, rape of women, and sometimes of men too, has been a frequent accompaniment, sometimes even seen as a perk, of war. Azar Gat lists as examples rape of women on a massive scale in eastern Germany in 1945; later, rape being a feature in wars in Bosnia, Rwanda, Darfur, and West Africa; and female prostitution for the military, often on a huge scale, state-organized for Japanese soldiers serving abroad, low-cost for American and Allied troops in ruined western Europe after Second World War, and among the desperately poor in Vietnam.[70] The civil war in Libya provides an even more recent example of war-related rape.[71]

In fact, the theory behind social dominance orientation (SDO), which has become such a popular concept for capturing support for hierarchy as a personal characteristic associated with war support (see the previous section), also makes a very clear link between gender inequality and social power more generally. *Social dominance theory* (SDT) has it that many of the sources of hierarchical stratification, such as those based on ethnicity, vary from one society to another; but two are so basic that they can be found everywhere to some degree. One of them is gender, some degree of disproportionate male power being universal according to SDT—the other is age, adults universally having social power over children and adolescents.[72]

Are Men More Supportive of War Than Women? Are Women More Peaceful?

Our interest is not only with those who do the fighting but also with support for war more generally. Is it in fact the case that men hold more positive attitudes toward war than women? Are women generally against war? Indeed, it *is* a common finding that there are significant differences between the sexes in terms of attitudes toward war and that it is nearly always women who are the more negative about it.[73] A review of almost 300 US public opinion polls between the 1930s and 1980s found men to be the more supportive of the violent or forceful option in answer to 87% of questions asked.[74] The difference is not always found, and when it is, it is not always a very strong sex difference. For example, in Winter's 8-year study of US students' attitudes toward the Iraq War, men were significantly more supportive of the war and more likely to consider it a "just war." However, although significant statistically, those results paled into insignificance beside the much stronger associations between support for the war and both right wing authoritarianism (RWA) and social dominance orientation (SDO).[75] Nevertheless, the sex difference in war attitudes, with men being the more supportive, is such a common finding that it has to be concluded that there is something in the idea that women are not, other things being equal, so supportive of war as men are.

The other side of the same coin is the possibility that women are simply more peaceful than men. Another study of university students' views, conducted in both Denmark and the United States using a more qualitative approach, showed that there was a sex difference not just in stated attitudes but also in the way men and women talked about war and peace. Women, talking about war—and the same was true for those women *or* men who held more negative attitudes toward war and for Danish students compared to those in the United States—were more likely to talk about violence, fear, inequality, and poverty, whereas men spoke more often of armed conflict and social order.[76]

Some, such as psychologist Steven Pinker, see all this as a reflection of basic biological sex differences that have evolved to strengthen the male incentive to compete for sexual access and the female incentive to stay away from risks that could harm their children. In every society, he says, males more than females fight, carry weapons, enjoy violent entertainment, fantasize about killing, start wars, and fight in them. A part of the brain, the hypothalamus, implicated in what has been termed *inter-male aggression*, is, he tells us, twice as large in men as in women; and the system of which it is a part is full of receptors for testosterone, which is several times more plentiful in men's bloodstreams than women's. This is a notoriously controversial area, certainly among psychologists and among biologists too; but Pinker believes that men, young unmarried men especially, are thereby primed to respond to dominance challenges, including those involving sexual or sporting competition.[77]

We do not need to resort to psychology and the brain—the now rampant fields of neuropsychology and neuroscience more generally—or sociobiology to find support for the idea that women and men, whether by nature or nurture, have such different outlooks on life that differences toward war and peace are unsurprising. While the "essentialist" view of sex differences may view them as anchored in women's and men's different reproductive roles, biologically based and socially transmitted, the "constructivist" believes such differences have less to do with the biological sexes and more to do with certain definitions of femininity and masculinity with which people identify. It is several decades ago that Harvard psychologist Carol Gilligan argued in her influential book *In a Different Voice* that women have a different ethical experience than men, one which is less individualistic and pays more attention to the essentially interpersonal or social nature of human passions. It is rooted both in women's own experience of social subordination and in their sensitivity to the needs of others. Women assume greater responsibility for taking care of others, which leads them, more than men, "to attend to voices other than their own and to include in their judgement other points of view."[78] Women might therefore be expected to subscribe more strongly than men to what some have called an *ethics of care* code. Women would, it follows, be more sensitive to the personal and family harm inflicted on *all* sides in a conflict, not just on "one's own side."[79]

Would war be less often supported, then, and the world be more peaceful, if women were in greater charge and less often marginalized in matters to do with war and avoidance of war? Women have been associated with peace movements throughout history, as feminism was with pacifism in the nineteenth century.[80] The courageous and persistent occupation by women of the Greenham Common air force base, where nuclear missiles were to be stored, is a long-remembered feature of anti-war campaigning in Britain in the 1980s.[81] Mary Kaldor draws attention to the role of women's groups in paving the way to peace in several regions and countries that have experienced "new wars"—Central America, the Balkans, West Africa, and Northern Ireland, for example—or, like the League of Iraqi Women, supporting victims of war. She also points out that, despite their greater potential as peacemakers, women's groups have often been marginalized in such conflicts.[82]

As a solution to the war problem, Anthony Stevens favored assigning to women a proportion of places in decision-making bodies dealing with defense and war. Even better, he thought, would be "the rebirth of feminine consciousness in both men and women."[83] Steven Pinker too was of the opinion that "A recognition of women's rights and an opposition to war go together... all else being equal, a world in which women have more influence will be a world with fewer wars." In fact, he believes that has to an extent already happened. Part of the civilizing process that has, in his view and that of the other "declinists," driven a reduction in war casualties (see Chapter 1) is feminization, along with women taking more control over their reproductive capacity. He refers to a more "female-tilted value system" having emerged during the mid- to late twentieth century, which "saw a deconstruction of the concept of dominance and related virtues like manliness, honor, prestige and glory." Female-friendly values should reduce violence.[84]

Others are not convinced. LeShan argues that giving women the vote made no difference to support for war: "It has become increasingly plain that the reason women have been less involved in war than men is only that they have not been offered the opportunity to participate more fully."[85] Not being able to serve directly in the fighting does not mean women have never been enthusiastic supporters of war. As Centano and Enriquez put it, "in some ways, women serve as the enforcers of the masculinity of war." Joanna Bourke speaks of women "buckling men's psychological armour."[86] Even women suffrage leaders shared in the growing chauvinistic nationalism in the early months of the First World War. The mental image of women humiliating men who didn't volunteer to serve by pinning white feathers on them is one that always comes to mind whenever it is suggested that women do not support war.[87]

Shakespeare captured the theme of women standing behind their menfolk going to war and bolstering their resolve to fight in one of his most warlike plays, *Coriolanus*. A central character is Coriolanus' mother, Volumnia. She eggs her son on, sharing with him his past glories, his honor, his expectations of further triumph, and even his heroic wounds: "My praises made thee first a soldier... let thy mother... feel thy pride... for I mock at death with as big a heart as thou.... Thy valiantness was mine, thou suck'dst it from me."[88] But the play also reflects woman's ambivalence toward war. Virgilia plays the part of any wife, left behind to fret and later to grieve Coriolanus' death. By the play's end, Volumnia too, now sharing Virgilia's grief, regrets the support she has given his violence.

The First World War may have been a good example of a type of state war in which women were confined to serving in support roles, notably as nurses— the "angels of mercy,"[89] standing apart from the actual fighting. But that has by no means always been the case for women in wartime. Roles have been more equal in certain conditions, for example, on both sides of the Arab–Israeli conflict.[90] Centano and Enriquez believe women are more likely to be found partaking in the fighting the more "transgressive" is the cause their group is fighting for—groups "on the side of a radical social change, when they belong to a marginal group, or when they find themselves geographically or politically distant from the center of social power." Frontierswomen or twentieth-century guerrilla armies would be examples.[91] "Revolutions and insurrections have again and again utilized women in combat roles," says Barbara Ehrenreich. A feature of new wars—although she prefers the term "transformed" war—is that they are less exclusively male. It represents a "de-gendering" of war, as she puts it. Even when those conditions did not obtain, historians can offer many examples of women passing as men in order to fight.[92]

Women have now obtained access to positions in the military that were closed to them previously, although compulsorily drafting women into a state's military remains a rarity.[93] The United States is a prime example of a country having moved to encourage women to volunteer. Women in the US military now serve in roles such as directing artillery, piloting helicopters, operating supply depots, some even as fighter pilots. These changes have gone hand in hand with developments in military technology such as improved armored vehicles and body armor, night vision wear, and drones. "Whether measured in terms of numbers, roles, or responsibilities, women in uniform achieved hitherto unimaginable prominence after the Cold War," including full combat positions in 2013.[94] India is another country that started to recruit women to non-combat roles in the 1990s, and in 2016 both India and the United Kingdom announced they would follow Israel and the United States, and others like New Zealand and Germany, in allowing women in combat roles.[95]

Opinions differ about whether this has yet much altered the fundamental masculinity of the military. According to one view from the United States, a result has been that "the identity of the American warrior shed much of its traditionally masculine character."[96] Another refers to women who do fight "obtaining an honorary male status, but not challenging the underlying sexual specialization" of the military.[97] Women have no "innate inhibition against fighting," says Barbara Ehrenreich: "We no longer hail 'our boys' . . . but 'our men and women.'" But for her that doesn't mean masculinity will cease to be desirable, just that it will be an attribute that women as well can possess. At every step, she says, women have met with misogynist resistance and sexual assaults and harassment (see Chapter 1): "But the inclusion of women has gone far enough to cast serious doubt on any theory of war that derives exclusively from considerations of gender."[98]

Nonetheless, a significant body of research finds women to be more concerned than men with a variety of issues that affect the overall well-being of society, placing greater emphasis than men on societal issues such as healthcare, childcare, education, and care for the elderly.[99] Furthermore, several researchers have found women to have stronger negotiation and conflict-resolution skills, being better at facilitating discussion among others, while men may be more inclined to express their own views—a study involving a series of interviews with Members of the Legislative Assembly in Northern Ireland is one example.[100] If one accepts those two sets of findings, it should follow that women being more prominent in decision-making roles should be more likely to encourage peace and less likely to lead to war.

In an article entitled "Gender Equality and Intrastate Armed Conflict," which appeared in *International Studies Quarterly*, Erik Melander addressed that hypothesis head on. He used international data sets to test whether there was a relationship, across 163 independent states and territories, between the proportion of women in government (WIG) and lower violence levels as captured by the Global Peace Index (GPI). The latter is a measure of the absence of violence or fear of violence as indicated by lower levels of ongoing domestic and international conflict, less discord within the country, and a lesser degree of militarization. Economic development was controlled for. WIG was indeed significantly associated with GPI, as predicted. But another variable of relevance was even more significant in the analysis. That was freedom from corruption, measured with the Corruption Perception Index (CPI) created by Transparency International. The relevance of the CPI rests on the general consensus that corruption negatively affects efforts to build and sustain peace, plus a body of research that links women to lower levels of corruption. Melander cites the Liberian Women's Initiative as perhaps one of the most evident examples of the success—after 14 previous peace negotiations in Liberia that had failed—of deliberately involving women in negotiation bringing popular support to bear on politicians and warlords to disarm before elections. In October 2000, the positive effect of women on building and maintaining peace was recognized in the unanimous passing of the United Nations Security Council's Resolution 1325 on Women, Peace and Security, which specifically calls for women's increased participation in conflict-prevention and -resolution efforts.[101]

Perhaps the truth of the matter is that, despite the existence of some notable measurable sex differences in attitudes toward war, such differences come and go with changing times and circumstances. Perhaps women in general, like men in general, are ambivalent about warfare, do not speak with one voice, and can change their minds quite quickly, as Russian women did toward the Chechnyan war and as the "security moms" in the United States did toward a military response by their country to the 9/11 attacks.[102] Gender, unlike biological sex, is, to a large extent at least, a social construction. Ideas about what constitutes masculinity and femininity, as well as how exclusive and changeable they might be, are constantly altering. Some have been of the opinion that war support might change with changing ideas of masculinity: "Until we redefine manhood, we shall not end war" has been a popular sentiment.[103] But there is also a constant reframing of femininity, of women's rights and women's roles, women's increased participation in the military being just one example.

Conclusions

What can we provisionally conclude from this brief and very partial dip into the colossal body of writing, research, and opinion about whether war is inherent in human nature? Do we have an instinct for it? Are we stuck with it, come what may? Informed opinion says *no*, although perhaps as much in hope as in certainty. Are we inclined toward it, given the right circumstances which have obtained so often in human history and continue to obtain to this day? Evidently *yes*. At the same time, it is true that most of us, most of the time, live in peace. Facing the task of preventing war, we must therefore try to understand in more detail when and why we are supportive of it.

The picture is a complicated one. In Figure 2.1 I have tried to summarize some of the themes touched on in this chapter. My present conclusion is that some combination of circumstance, personal belief, and the forefronting of the masculine side of our natures goes a long way to predicting who will support war and when. But that is only half the story of what it is about war that may be personally appealing. Thoughts of war can, for many, provide us with purpose, meaning, significance. They can bring a sense of renewal, a feeling of exhilaration, an experience of togetherness, comradeship. A large part of the material I have drawn on for this chapter, particularly in the earlier part of the chapter, has focused on personal feelings experienced during wartime. Although such feelings strengthen as we tread further along the path towards war, and the more so once war is engaged, they are part of our acceptance of

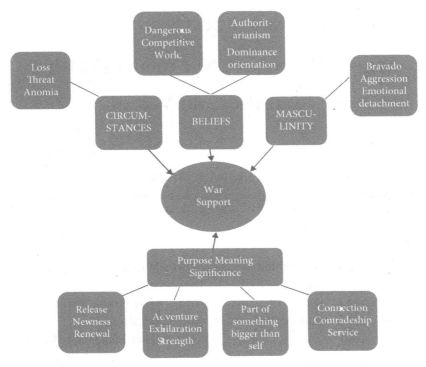

Figure 2.1 The personal attraction of war: a summary of the main themes

preparedness for war at all times. This will become clearer in the following chapters and will be brought together in the final chapter with a discussion of how support for war can grow and develop over time. Meanwhile there have already been regular hints in the present chapter that personal support for war is not confined to wartime. Authoritarianism, male bravado, belief in a dangerous world, reminders of threats and losses, and reminders of the sense of purpose and meaning which war has given one's predecessors are always present to some degree, waiting for their moments to stir up support for another war. An important element is a transcendent feeling that we are ready to contribute to something greater than our individual selves. It is that "greater something" that I want to explore in the following chapter.

3
War in Defense of National and Other Identities and Values

> I remain in the curious position of disliking, distrusting, disapproving and fearing nationalism *wherever* it exists... but recognising its enormous force, which must be harnessed for progress if possible.
>
> Historian, Eric Hobsbawm[1]

> A man who has nothing which he is willing to fight for, nothing which he cares more about than he does about his personal safety, is a miserable creature who has no chance of being free, unless made and kept so by the exertions of better men than himself.
>
> Philosopher, John Stuart Mill[2]

In the previous chapter it emerged that support for war is, in part, promoted by one's individual beliefs and values—belief that the world is dangerous and threatening and male values of strength and competitiveness, for example. The present chapter remains focused on beliefs and values but takes a turn toward those that are more obviously shared collectively. These are the belief systems and philosophical frameworks that help provide a coherent and meaningful understanding of one's place in the world. They are frequently based on state, ethnic, religious, or regional identity or adherence to an ideology and are often very strongly held. We will begin by looking closely at nationalism since it has often been claimed as central to people's support for war. We shall find the idea of nationalism to be less straightforward than might be supposed. Furthermore, its relevance to the "new" type of wars can be questioned. Some important distinctions need to be drawn; for example, that between nationalism and patriotism. Crucial, I shall conclude, is the distinction between, on the one hand, cosmopolitanism and, on the other, a nationalism or any other strongly held collective identity which is exclusive and chauvinistic, implying superiority over others. It is the latter that forms one component of preparedness for war and which can most easily be exploited in support of war. It may for long remain dormant, but given the right circumstances, it may harden and escalate rapidly.

If a state or other potential war-making group develops a collective narrative claiming that they are exposed to threat from another group out to harm them, responding with armed hostility may be increasingly viewed as justified, and support for war may grow. Indeed, such a threat-laden narrative may *demand* violence and sacrifice, as has so often been said. By John Stuart Mill (see above), for example, who would accuse any of us, unwilling to support fighting for a cause, as "miserable creatures," or by Irish independence fighter Patrick Pearse, who, like so many other fighters for independence, thought that putting up with the "slavery" of submission to English rule justified bloodshed (see Chapter 2).

What Is Nationalism?

Embarking on the quest to try and explain our support for war, one of my first assumptions had been that the idea of nationalism as a value would constitute a central part of the explanation. If, as international relations scholars maintain, war in the twentieth century, and perhaps ever since the American and French revolutions, was "total" or "absolute," involving the whole of a country's population in one way or another (see Chapter 1), then feelings toward one's nation have surely been crucial. In their book *War and Society*, Miguel Centano and Elaine Enriquez[3] conclude, with reference to World War II, "Without the political legitimacy of nationalism, no armed force could rely on the support of their society for such long periods and with such immense sacrifice."

I still believe feelings of nationalism to be very important, but I have come to understand that the link between nationalism and war support is far from straightforward. In any case we have to face the fact that many of the so-called new wars are fought for values other than state nationalism. Leaving that aside for now, the first complication is that when one looks closely at the idea of nationalism and tries to unpack it, it turns out to be less than simple. Take my own nation, England—my state, of course, is the United Kingdom, although we sometimes, confusingly for us and everyone else, speak of the United Kingdom being composed of four "nations." Nor do things stay the same forever. Since the issue of independence for Scotland has become more salient, and further complicated by Northern Ireland's position following the United Kingdom's decision to leave the European Union and by somewhat different policies toward controlling the coronavirus, it has become noticeable how more frequently the term *nations* is being used to refer to England, Scotland, Wales, and Northern Ireland.

In his book *English Nationalism: A Short History*, Black[4] explains how any sense of national solidarity is carried by such things as a collective name, shared history, distinctive shared culture, and association with specific territory. Like many nationalisms, the English variety has a "deep history," the result of a long, cumulative process. Among the contributions he picks out are the rise of standard English as the main language in the fourteenth and fifteenth centuries and the religious break with Rome. Military triumphs have been especially important, focusing aggressive feelings of identity and carrying forward ancestry myths and symbols of collective identity such as St. George. Differentiation from Scotland has been important—the English tend to be fairly evenly divided on the issue of whether their Englishness or their Britishness is more important—but in so many respects, Black reminds us, it is being different from France and Frenchness that has been historically so foundational. Antipathy toward, or at least definition in distinction to, another nation is, Black argues, a key element in nationalism. The Napoleonic wars in particular "underscored a patriotic discourse on British distinctiveness . . . a memorialisation of identity through victory," there for all to see in Nelson's Column, Waterloo Station, and street names up and down the country. That visual legacy is coupled, regrettably, with "a fleshing out of a sense of national greatness . . . attitudes of national uniqueness, national self-confidence, and a xenophobic contempt for foreigners."

England is not unique in such things. Those who have studied nationalism more generally have tried to characterize it. The following puts it well, referring to national identity as

> the group's definition of itself as a group—its conception of its enduring characteristics and basic values; its strengths and weaknesses; its hopes and fears; its reputation and continued existence; its institutions and traditions; and its past history, current purposes, and future prospects . . . [a basis for] distinctiveness, unity, and continuity . . . and a sense of belonging . . . claim to ownership of the land and control of its resources . . . bolstered by a national narrative.[5]

All nations have their symbols of national unity, national flags, heroes, anthems, songs and poems, recognition and respect for such symbols, various pledges, or other acts of allegiance. Indeed, according to some, "feelings of closeness to and pride in one's country and its symbols" is the very definition of identification with one's nation.[6] Flags, fireworks, and food are integral parts of Independence Day celebrations in the United States. The right to display the Irish flag, which had been banned, "became a central feature of political mobilization" during the Northern Irish "Troubles."[7] National anthems often use the language of victory over others, and their militarism is scarcely disguised. "La Marseillaise" and the UK and US anthems are examples. During the writing of this book a dispute broke out about whether the annual tradition of singing "Land of Hope and Glory" on the last night of the BBC Promenade Concerts—that series of events itself is a national symbol if ever there was one—should be suspended during the coronavirus lockdown and perhaps, with increasing recognition of how inglorious much of the British Empire had been, done away with altogether. In the event, the BBC backed down, and it was sung, by the choir and without the usual audience. On the other hand, nationalism need not be of the flag-waving variety. It can be quite "banal," as described by British social psychologist Billig, including such things as dress, food, sport, even a romantic view of the countryside. Non-political though these "everyday" aspects of national life may be made to appear, they can nonetheless be used by governments to support their ideologies, as was the case in Franco's Spain where bullfighting, flamenco, and traditional roles for women were deliberately promoted—even the popular dish *ensaladilla rusa* (Russian salad) was renamed *ensaladilla imperial*.[8]

Nationalism can evoke very varied images and sentiments. It can stand for prestige, dignity, pride in achievements. But on the other side of the same coin can be heightened sensitivity to perceived insults, frustrations, or aggressive behavior by others.[9] It is not surprising, then, that support for nationalism varies between people. Writing about attachment to the nation in the journal *Political Psychology*, Herrmann and colleagues[10] said, "Across the twentieth century, national identities have been seen as the foundation of peace and the cause of war. For liberal nationalists the emergence of nations and their independence from empires secures a sense of dignity that provides a foundation for international cooperation." For its critics, on the other hand, nationalism leads to "ego-enhancing social comparisons and discriminatory behavior toward other nations." Those on the left politically have tended to be hostile to nationalism, except when it underpinned independence movements in former colonized countries. The Marxist—but unconventionally so—historian Eric Hobsbawm, whose comment on nationalism was cited at the head of this chapter, was one such.[11] Contrary opinions I have heard expressed, often in the context of debate about UK separation from the European Union, include the view that nationalism may start in banal fashion, with folk dancing and fireworks, but always transmutes into barbed-wire fences and hostility toward others and, contrariwise, that there is nothing wrong with wanting sovereignty and self-government and that nationalism has now come to be unfairly "demonized."

Taking a Closer Look at Nationalism: Some Important Distinctions

Are we in danger of confounding different things? Let us have a closer look. One of the distinctions which is very often drawn is that between nationalism and patriotism. Whether they are different and, if so, how are questions that are frequently asked, especially in the United States where the latter term is often preferred and where much of the relevant research on public attitudes has been carried out. Worrying over this, and other distinctions regarding nationalism that I shall discuss, may seem of little account. That might be true if it were not for the fact that nationalism, in some of its guises, shows a war-supporting face, while in others, not. As I hope to show, attempting to pin down exactly what it is about nationalism that encourages war then becomes a critical task.

One relevant US study, from the late 1980s, used the statistical technique of factor analysis to test whether agreement with the kinds of attitude questions found in nationalism questionnaires were sufficiently consistent, that they could be said to form a single "factor." Although the results of such analyses are highly sensitive to the exact wording of the questions, the makeup of the survey sample, and the era in which the study is carried out, it does give us some purchase on the issue of whether nationalism is uni-factorial or multi-factorial. This particular piece of research found two separate factors. One, which the report's author called "patriotism," was tapped by agreement with such statements as "I am proud to be American." On the other hand, agreement with statements such as "In view of America's moral and material superiority, it is only right that we should have the biggest say in deciding UN policy" contributed to the second factor, which was duly labeled "nationalism."[12] Not only were these factors fairly independent of one another, but they also correlated in unexpected and apparently inconsistent ways with expressed support for certain policies and personal commitments. For example, nationalists—those scoring more highly on the nationalism factor—indicated stronger support for nuclear armament policies and for readiness to go to war but were less willing to risk their own lives than were patriots. That would come as little surprise, however, to those[13] who have pointed out the irony that modern US militarism is strongly supported by many US citizens who at the same time express little enthusiasm for risking their own or their children's lives in war (see Chapter 5 for more on this).

Another piece of research produced some results which, on the face of it, might appear puzzling. It bore the provocative title, "Sowing Patriotism, but Reaping Nationalism?"[14] It reported on two experiments conducted with US undergraduate students—the sample constitutes an obvious limitation—to test the effect of exposure to the US flag. A random half of the participants completed a questionnaire in a room where the country's flag was prominently displayed, either on the wall or on the questionnaire itself. The first experiment was conducted three years before the 9/11 attacks on the United States, the second three years after 9/11. The results were the same. Exposure to the flag, compared to the control condition without the flag either on the wall or on the questionnaire, did not affect patriotism, but it did increase nationalism (e.g., "The United States is the best country in the world"). At the same time, it also increased "group-based dominance," a general tendency to favor group hierarchy (e.g., "Some groups of people are simply not the equals of others," "It is probably a good thing that certain groups are at the top and other groups are at the bottom"). It seemed that exposure to the flag, rather than supporting a comparatively benign type of patriotism, might be reinforcing a more dangerous form of nationalism in which feelings of superiority play a part. The authors viewed the results as alarming but not surprising in view of the role that the nation's flag plays in US life. Thought of as a potent symbol of patriotism, it is also of great significance for the US military and appears in increased profusion whenever the United States is engaged in warfare.

There can be little doubt that nationalism can show an ugly face. One kind of nationalism is "the arrogant idea that this country is the centre of the universe, exceptionally virtuous, admirable, and superior," perhaps achieving its height with the Nazi notion of Aryan superiority.[15] *Patriotism good, nationalism bad* is a not uncommon attempt to clarify the issue. Many in the modern social sciences do distinguish patriotism—love for one's own people and homeland—from "nationalism," used pejoratively, or "blind patriotism" or feelings of superiority or arrogance toward other countries. One study of the US adult population used the term *chauvinism* for the latter. It concluded that patriotic feelings were "pervasive in the American public."[16] For example, asked "How close do you feel to America?," 81% said "close" or "very close," and 80% and 88%, respectively, said they felt proud of America's "political influence in the world" and "its history" (although only 57% were proud of America's "fair and equal treatment of all groups in society"). Chauvinism was less pervasive. For example, 44% and 32%, respectively, agreed that "America should follow its own interests, even if this leads to conflicts with other nations" and "people should support their country even when it's in the wrong." Although independent to a large degree, patriotic and chauvinistic sentiments were somewhat positively correlated, and both were associated with support for more spending on defense, chauvinism the more strongly.

A related distinction, sometimes made by historians, is that between nationalism—sometimes referred to as "civic" nationalism—based on citizenship, sovereignty, and civic equality, often traced back to the French Revolution, and "ethnic" nationalism based on a sense of shared blood, language, ethnicity, and history. Although in reality they are thought to overlap, nationalism may be ultimately based on territory, ethnicity on lineage. Nationalism can be taken to imply that a citizen's overriding group loyalty to the nation takes precedence over other possible loyalties based on identity, such as ethnicity.[17] In the United States of 2001, when the survey referred to in the previous paragraph was carried out, the national creed, the report's authors said, was one of democracy and individualism, assimilation of newcomers, trumping ethnicity. A later review of US surveys, on the other hand, concluded that ethnic group identities were salient for many and were inconsistent with the "melting pot" ideal, with European Americans having the stronger patriotic attachment to the nation than those from other ethnic groups.[18]

Moving beyond the United States brings further nuance to the debate. For example, one review of the evidence about nationalism in Latin America, including opinion polls conducted by the Latin American Public Opinion Project, concluded that more support was to be found for patriotism than for nationalism. As the reviewers described it, this seemed to combine elements of what some have called patriotism, others "cultural nationalism," "a 'love of place' . . . pride in folklores, natural beauty, and culture," in contrast to civic, state, or political nationalism. There was a consistently higher level of pride in being of a certain nationality but much lower levels of pride in the political systems in their countries.[19] Of course, such a combination of sentiments may be common everywhere to some degree. As Mark Twain is quoted as having said, "My kind of loyalty was loyalty to one's country, not its institutions or its office-holders."[20]

Back in the United States, the *Political Psychology* paper cited earlier[21] took the matter further in several ways. For one thing, it tested, and found support for, a three-dimensional conception of national identity. The three dimensions or factors were *national attachment*, *culturalism*, and *national chauvinism*. *National attachment* was defined as individuals' feelings that they belong to a nation and that this membership defines, both cognitively and emotionally, who they are. Drawing on the distinction that has often been made between nations that are first and foremost "cultural" and those that are more "civic," *culturalism* was the belief that cultural markers were what defined the boundaries of the nation. The third dimension, *national chauvinism*, was "When members feel their nation is vastly superior to others and feel the world would be better if others emulated them."

A strength of the study, carried out in 2004, was that the participants were random samples of the adult populations in two countries, Italy and the United States, quintessentially cultural and civic nations, respectively. That part of the analysis of most interest to us here focused on how the three nationalism factors appeared to combine in their association with the participants' degree of "militarist disposition." In the best-supported model, the total effect of national attachment on militarism was positive. But much the larger part of that effect was indirect via chauvinism. The two-country nature of the study also provided an example of a rather unsurprising principle: although the general picture may be the same in two separate countries, the details may be different in important ways in a country other than the United States where most of this kind of research has been carried out. In this study, it turned out that culturalism could also play a role as a mediator of the effect of national attachment on militaristic disposition, but that was only significant in Italy, not in the United States.

The results of the Italy/United States study, the researchers said in their conclusions—the conclusions authors draw at the end of academic papers, which is where their otherwise strict scientific objectivity can slip, are nearly always as interesting as the results themselves—were consistent with the "liberal nationalist" contention, to which they supposed that both Italy and the United States subscribed, that attachment to a nation is not per se the cause of a disposition toward militarism. The findings, they said, "suggest the beliefs most associated with justifying a resort to force are not necessarily rooted in feelings of national attachment but emanate from chauvinism and a sense of cultural exclusivity."[22]

They did acknowledge that critics of the liberal nationalist perspective may be concerned that, even if separating attachment from culturalism and chauvinism was analytically possible in the way the analysis had done, in the real world the three factors cannot easily be separated. They may fear that national attachment lies at the root of the other two (as the results of the US flag experiment mentioned above might suggest). Indeed, in their study the three dimensions were substantially intercorrelated; it was only by using a statistical method of examining the effect of each factor while controlling for the influence of the others that the likely effect of the factors separately could be examined. The understanding of national attachment itself, favored by these researchers, was as something that can "inject emotional fuel" into one's sentiments about another country, depending upon the circumstances surrounding the current relationship between one's own and the other nation.[23] That opinion chimes with another distinction, made by some, between a more ideological nationalism, expressed openly and strongly in opposition to other, incompatible, ideologies, and a relatively naïve, unreflective nationalism, often lying dormant but available to be promoted and aroused during times of state unification or war.[24] Others have noted that one form of cultural attachment to a nation implies something deeply "essential" and lasting. It may also have negative implications for attitudes toward outsiders. For example, one 2008 set of studies of German adults found that belief in that kind of nationalism (e.g., "True Germans are characterized by certain cultural attributes that will always remain as they are," "Different generations may do things differently, but there are certain cultural characteristics that true Germans will always share") was associated with prejudice toward immigrants.[25]

Cosmopolitanism: An Alternative to Nationalism and Other Exclusive Identities?

In his book *The Fear and the Freedom: How the Second World War Changed Us*, Keith Lowe reminds us of the strong movement for world governance and world citizenship, supported by, among others, prominent figures such as Albert Camus, Jean-Paul Sartre, Yehudi Menuhin, and Albert Einstein, which arose in the aftermath of World War II. In Britain, up to 200 members of the All-Party Parliamentary Group for World Governance identified nationalism as the major source of war and advocated global federalism and the reduction in importance of nation states' sovereignty. The United Nations (UN) gave this movement cause for much hope, which was quickly disappointed when it became clear that it would be dominated by the national interests of members, especially those of the war's most powerful victors who would have veto powers and would soon be locked in Cold War conflict.[26]

More recently this debate has resurfaced in the form of "cosmopolitanism." What some have been referring to as the cosmopolitanism–nationalism debate has attracted a lot of attention among those who research public attitudes toward state foreign policy.[27] In her book *New and Old Wars*, Mary Kaldor speaks of "an emerging political cleavage" between what she calls cosmopolitanism "based on inclusive, universalist, multicultural values" and identity politics, whether based on nationality, clan, religion, or language. This is sometimes portrayed as a contrast between "the local" and "the global" and its adherents as "somewhere" and "anywhere" people—those with identity linked to specific location and those not.[28] Kaldor refers to "a growing cultural dissonance between those who participate in transnational networks, which communicate through e-mail, faxes, telephone and air travel, and those who are excluded from global processes and are tied to localities." At the core of cosmopolitanism is the idea of being a citizen of the world, part of a global community of human beings. Cosmopolitans, more generally, have in common the view that all people have equal moral worth or value, that those people who happen not to belong to our particular group (ethnic, national, or political, say) are not less valuable than those who do.[29]

Like nationalism, cosmopolitanism, when looked at closely, is not so simple, consisting of several strands loosely woven together. Online survey data from over 8,000 participants from 19 very varied countries showed it to be consistently made up of three distinguishable factors: cultural openness (CO), global prosociality (GP), and respect for cultural diversity (RCD). CO was defined as being open to learning about other cultures and different peoples, recognizing equal personhood and humanity, "entering into the mind" of others, as the Stoics had it. GP is more practical, to do with providing support and help to others, regardless of their cultural background or how great the social distance is between one's own and the other's culture. RCD is more prevention-focused, about respecting cultural differences, helping to preserve cultural diversity, and preventing discrimination. Although that was not a study of war attitudes, it can be noted that all three factors predicted more positive attitudes toward immigrants, and GP was the best predictor of trust in the UN.[30]

Cosmopolitan proposals are frequently criticized as being unrealistic. Such accusations are often based on a belief that valuing the whole global community is contrary to something very basic to human nature. That belief can take a number of different forms. The most common, introduced into modern social science by William Sumner over a hundred years ago[31] and widely taken for granted to this day, is that in-group attachment and out-group hostility go hand in hand as part of our deep-rooted need to belong to groups (we shall be looking more closely at this in the next chapter). A simple reading of evolutionary theory—evolutionary psychology, for one, has been enjoying a resurgence—is sometimes forwarded in support: ability to discriminate between friend and foe might confer fitness benefits and have become consolidated in the human genotype. There are alternative, more popular sources of support for the claim that in-group favoritism, including nationalism, is anchored in basic existential human needs, such as those discussed in the previous chapter. These are based in notions of a need to find meaning to our lives, a need for identity, or even a basic individual need for self-esteem. That may not imply that nationalism is the only or the best available option to satisfy such personal needs. In fact, a review of such psychological supports for the importance of nationalism which appeared in the journal *Ethical Theory and Moral Practice* in 2008 concluded that the human needs that nationalism is said to satisfy are complex and can be well met in ways other than through "national identification and bias . . . nationalism is no more an innate or necessary part of the human psyche than is a sense of global community."[32] For example, studies suggest that nationalism is not particularly effective in boosting self-esteem.[33]

Others have argued that cosmopolitanism alone is not attractive to most people and that cosmopolitanism and nationalism are not incompatible. One such argument is that the "local" continues to provide most people with their moral compass and their political organization. Another is that cosmopolitanism, far from denying national or other local identity, celebrates the diversity of multiple overlapping identities. As Kaldor points out, the term *cosmopolitanism*—which combines being a citizen of the world (the cosmos) and of the city or locality (the polis)—originates in philosopher Immanuel

Kant's idea of cosmopolitan right combined with recognition of individual sovereignties, uniting universalism and diversity. Notions of the "cosmopolitan patriot" or "rooted cosmopolitan," and variations on the theme of nationalism such as "plural" or "multicultural" nationalism, reflect the same idea.[34]

Other relevant psychological theories offer support for the compatibility of cosmopolitanism and nationalism. Basic to them is the acceptance, obvious to most thoughtful people but which was not always properly recognized in earlier theories, that people can have multiple social identities (e.g., as British, a Muslim, a woman, a doctor, a daughter) and generally manage to integrate them into a coherent whole. There is much in the literature on social identity theory about the emotional and behavioral strategies we use to do that.[35]

Nor it seems, from the evidence of much research, does a sense of belonging to an in-group mean that we automatically feel hostility toward or hold negative views about others who are not in our group (although we may be more inclined to cooperate with co-members of our in-group). More specifically, national identification need not be associated with negative sentiment toward non-nationals. A more specific and highly relevant variety of social identity theory is the theory of *optimal distinctiveness*, which proposes that in-group identification can occur without out-group derogation. What it does posit is that, however multiple and complex our group identities, they must satisfy both the need for a sense of belonging to an in-group and the need to be distinct from others. A purely cosmopolitan identity may not be very good at doing the job of giving one a sense of both belonging and distinctiveness. Humanity is too big and amorphous a social category, it is argued, for it to offer us a meaningful sense of belonging. Cosmopolitan identity fails at the task of defining "who and what we are," critics say. It is only to be expected, therefore, that those of a cosmopolitan persuasion will, at the same time, maintain their national distinctiveness and identity. They will, in effect, have a dual identity, as citizens of both the world and their local country or community.[36]

This question is explored in an empirical paper that drew on data, collected between 2010 and 2014, from the World Values Survey involving 85,000 people from 60 countries. To capture cosmopolitan identity, participants were asked to indicate their agreement or disagreement with the statement "I see myself as a world citizen." Similarly, national identity was measured by asking respondents to indicate their agreement or disagreement with the statement, "I see myself as a part of the ... nation." Contrary to any prediction that cosmopolitan and national identities are opposites, they were in fact *positively* correlated. The coefficient of correlation was not large (indicating that only about 5% of the variation in how people responded to those two statements was common variation), but with such a large sample it was highly statistically significant; and, anyway, it was the positive direction of the relationship that was of importance.

The study went on to test the further prediction that cosmopolitan identity is also positively associated with willingness to go to war for the country ("Of course, we all hope that there will not be another war, but if it were to come to that, would you be willing to fight for your country?"). After controlling for a number of other variables, including confidence in the military, support for democracy, and sociodemographic variables, *both* cosmopolitan and national identities were significantly associated with willingness to go to war, although national identity, and particularly a variable termed *national pride* ("how proud you are to be [nationality]," with response choices spanning from "very proud" to "not at all proud"), had the stronger relationship. The author concluded,

> Attachment to national roots persists... world citizenship does not rule out patriotic sacrifice. Contemporary cosmopolitans are attached to the nation and are willing to sacrifice for it in ways the Greek Cynics or Kant did not imagine.... The number of people who identify as cosmopolitan world citizens in global public opinion surveys has increased considerably in the last two decades. Yet we also know that nationalism is on the rise... cosmopolitan world citizens do not shed their national identity and patriotic obligations.... Rather, they merge their cosmopolitan and national identities into an integrated dual identity.[37]

That may be true, but it is also the case that cosmopolitanism varies; some people are more signed up to it than others, and the same is true of nationalism. A more optimistic view of cosmopolitanism draws on the *common in-group identity model*, which maintains that intergroup bias and prejudice can be reduced by adopting an overarching superordinate identity. The theory was first presented long ago by Sherif and colleagues,[38] who proposed that a competitive "us versus them" stance can be changed to a cooperative "we" position through cooperation. There is now a large body of research supporting the idea that when groups share a strong common goal and cooperate together, that changes people's group identities and reduces intergroup negativity. The authors of the *Ethical Theory and Moral Practice* journal article, referred to earlier, speculated about the extent to which such basic social psychological findings could be applied to cooperation between nations and reducing international biases:

> *At the moment*, the chances of achieving this seem to be greatest where cooperation allows a superordinate identity to be established *without compromising national identity*. This is encouraging news for cosmopolitans ... we can maintain something of the familiar—retain people's comfort zone, so to speak—while working to extend that comfort zone at the same time. In addition to creating a superordinate identity, it may also be possible to dilute the importance of national identity through more complex identities.[39]

Cosmopolitanism, seemingly the very antithesis of the kind of chauvinistic, my-country-right-or-wrong nationalism, turns out not to be as straightforward a deliverer from war support as I had hoped it might be. Having discovered some of the complexities lurking behind the very concepts of nationalism, patriotism. and cosmopolitanism, it turns out that authorities on war are in any case skeptical about the role nationalist sentiments play in war support.

Nationalism and Willingness to Go to War: A Complex Relationship

Carl von Clausewitz, who served in both Prussian and Russian armies against Napoleon and often described as the greatest of all military thinkers, thought the emergence of nationalism had changed the character of fighting. It had become "the business of the people ... instead of governments and armies as heretofore." He particularly attributed the change to the patriotism underlying the American and French revolutions of the late eighteenth century (see also Chapter 1): the "We the People" of the US draft constitution and the "people's war" to defend the new French Republic.[40] It has been accepted ever since that states' ability to make war rests, at least in large part on a sense of national cohesion and citizens' willingness to defend and make sacrifices for their nation. Citizens are expected to be concerned for their country's prestige and dignity and prosperity, willing to take action to rectify perceived affronts, be responsive to their leaders' appeals for support in defending the nation's interests, and willing to serve in the military.[41]

Although in what has been written on the subject of war nationalism received plenty of attention as a leading cause in the last half of the twentieth century,[42] in fact much of what has been written more recently has been surprisingly lukewarm about the link between nationalism and war. The introduction to the 2013 book bearing the name *Nationalism and War* suggests that the link has often been overemphasized. Authors who contributed chapters to the book make several points. One is that warfare long predates the rise of the nationalism that von Clausewitz was referring to. In fact, wars may have been more frequent in the pre-nationalism period. Nor is there anything inherently aggressive about nationalism. And a further point is that nationalism may play little role in the motivations of modern military troops for whom professionalism and the use of highly technical weaponry are much more important.[43] In his *War: What Is It Good For?* Ian Morris[44] is dismissive of "the grand ideas for which men and women laid down their lives," which are as insignificant as "foam on the surface of waves, driven by much deeper forces." Others, such as the authors of *War and Society*, sometimes appear to be equally dismissive, at other times less so. They say, "there is little indication that men fight or die for patriotic reasons." But, as we noted earlier, they also acknowledge that the "political legitimacy of nationalism" may be necessary to sustain the use of armed force.[45] A position that is probably reflective of much modern thinking on the matter was taken by Daniel Druckman in his 2001 piece[46] on nationalism and war from a social psychological perspective. Although nationalism was often cited as providing much of the motivation for war fighting, it might not be "either necessary or sufficient to initiate or sustain combat," he thought. The manipulation and mobilization of nationalistic sentiments by leaders and elites was another matter, however, and one we shall be looking at more closely in Chapter 6.

Admittedly, nationalism can take a turn toward aggression when associated with hatred of other nationalities, but the causal relationship is not so clear. Although war is often "augmented with and legitimized through nationalist ideologies,"[47] if anything it is war that causes nationalism, not the reverse, some conclude. As an illustration, Michael Mann refers to the idea that nationalism caused World War I as a myth: "the downward slide to war involved tiny diplomatic and military elites with almost no popular participation in the process." Anti-war protests outnumbered pro-war demonstrations, and only later was there a heating up of a "banal nationalism" based on symbols of national unity, the "rally round the flag," and the over-optimistic prediction that the war would be a short one, "over by

Christmas." Nor, he adds, was public opinion in favor of the Second World War, outside Germany.[48]

There is an important variant of that theme, however, which recurs in writings about nationalism and war. It speaks of nationalisms having the potential to stoke violence, while for long periods of time remaining dormant. At certain times, for example, under threat, during social crises, or in response to out-group actions, and manipulated by political leaders, the content of group narratives can change and become more hostile. Historian of the First World War, Niall Ferguson, cites several writers who think much the same happened in Britain and in other countries including Germany and France at the outbreak of war.

> The patriotic "spirit of 1914", it is argued, was the product of years of indoctrination—in schools, universities, nationalist associations and (on the continent) in the armies themselves. . . . The masses—or at least the middle classes—had been "nationalized" by relentless exposure to nationalist music, nationalist poetry, nationalist art, nationalist monuments—and, of course, nationalist history.

English so-called public schools, it has been argued, fostered the very qualities necessary for supporting war, including loyalty, honor, leadership, and patriotism.[49] One of England's best-loved poets, Edward Thomas, brilliantly expressed his ambivalence about nationalism in the poem he wrote on Boxing Day 1915. Its first lines capture his deep dislike of what he saw as the jingoism and xenophobia, and the profiteering, among his fellow countrymen: "I hate not Germans, nor grow hot/With love for Englishmen, to please newspapers./Beside my hate for one fat patriot/My hatred of the Kaiser is love true." He argued bitterly with his father about it and fell out with friends on account of his opinion that Germans and British—he was as much Welsh as English—were basically the same.[50] But he volunteered for service in the war which took his life, and the last few lines of the poem express the nationalistic position to which the events of the First World War had propelled him: "But with the best and meanest Englishmen/I am one in crying, God save England . . . /She is all we know and live by, and we trust/ She is good and must endure, loving her so:/And as we love ourselves we hate her foe."[51] It is hard to imagine any clearer or more poignant expression of the two faces of nationalism and how nationalist sentiments can change with circumstances.

Historian of the Second World War, Keith Lowe, describes the same phenomenon happening in regions of Europe such as a part of the old Austro-Hungarian Empire, where those who identified as or spoke the language of Slovakia, Germany, or Hungary lived together "in a spirit of mutual cooperation" as they had done for generations but where the war changed the atmosphere and started to make nationalism a source of conflict. "The world . . . in which Slovakians, Germans and Hungarians had lived side by side without excessive regard for their differences . . . was fast disappearing."[52]

There are many who support the claim that war creates nationalism rather than the other way round. As one military historian, writing about Athens at the height of the ancient Peloponnesian War, put it, "For a brief moment they were all Athenians." Even when not at war, the centrality of the military and service in it can be critical in the development of a country's nationalism; Japan in the past and Israel more recently may be good examples.[53]

Some agree with Ian Morris, doubting altogether the power of national identities to motivate war. They argue that nationalism is simply a "romantic veneer," encouraged by governments, providing a cover for collective violence which is caused by other factors. Others, such as liberal nationalists a century ago and Huntington[54] in recent times, have argued that attachment to the nation can potentially lead not to chauvinism but to the "democratic peace" (see Chapter 1). The public, "comfortable with the idea that they are members of a distinct nation . . . protected at home by democracy and abroad by equal sovereignty," become more peace-loving, often more so than the elite in fact.[55] On the 75th anniversary of the D-Day Normandy landings, the BBC radio program *The Moral Maze*[56] debated the question whether we are now more individualistic, hedonistic, less civically minded than we were 75 years ago. Even if faced with an existential threat, would we now be less willing to defer to state calls for the kind of self-sacrifice that our parents and grandparents made then? Mary Kaldor certainly thought that was a pertinent question. She wrote, "What has become clear in the post-war period is that, at least in Western countries, there are few causes that constitute a legitimate goal for war for which people are prepared to die." The comfortable, materially well-off "laissez-faire cosmopolitans" living in modern democracies may be rejecting state militarism as much as "the restless young criminals, the new adventurers" who join the fighting in the "new wars," she suggests. Both may share what Kaldor refers to as "the individualism and anomie that characterizes the current period."[57]

Beyond Nationalism: Relevance to the "New Wars"

If the role of nationalism in the "old wars" was at best complex and at worst mere myth, that may be even more the case when it comes to the "new wars." As we saw in Chapter 1, states like the United Kingdom, classified as democratic, have for some time been very unlikely to engage one another in war. Unlike the two world wars, the role of the state in new wars is different. In fact, as Kaldor sees it, "The new nationalisms that emerged were a new form in the sense that it was associated with the disintegration of the state,"[58] including its monopoly on organized military force within the state.

For a start, nationalism surely played some role in all the conflicts that brought independence from colonialism to countries in Africa, Asia, eastern Europe, and elsewhere during the twentieth century. That is not surprising if "Nationalism as a doctrine asserts that a group of people sharing characteristics that differentiate them, *in their own minds*, from others should be politically autonomous."[59] As Keith Lowe says, "nationalism . . . the very force that had been so discredited by the Second World War was given new life in the war's aftermath by the emerging nations of the world. . . . All over the world, the idea of the nation-state seemed to have been strengthened by the war, rather than weakened by it."[60] The exact form it took and its importance relative to events taking place at the imperial center varied greatly however: independence from the Ottoman, Dutch, British, French, Portuguese, and Soviet empires took different forms, and the parts played by nationalism were different. In the case of Israel, a totally new country took shape, involving a series of wars with its neighbors. Like later "new wars," wars for independence were often complex and difficult to categorize.[61] The Mau Mau rebellion which preceded Kenyan independence, for example, was, Lowe states, "as well as a nationalist uprising and a peasant revolt, a straightforward class struggle"; and the way it was put down had some elements of a civil war between Africans.[62]

The, mostly later, new wars that Kaldor wrote about often took the form of civil wars, having more to do with intrastate ethnic, religious, and regional divides, or what others have referred to as "factions."[63] Not that civil wars are "new." Hugh Thomas' book of the early 1960s, *The Spanish Civil War*, was an early influence, promoting my interest in why people engage in such a horrifying activity as waging war. Nationalism was of central importance: the problem was that different sections of the Spanish population held very different ideas about their nation. The causes of the war, as Thomas so vividly described them, included very long-standing "searing quarrels," between the Church and anti-clerical liberals, between landowners and the working class, and between those demanding regional autonomy for Catalonia, the Basque provinces and elsewhere and those who saw central control from Castile as essential to Spanish nationhood. Spain at the time also had large organized groups of those who were passionate about the restoration of the monarchy and others who were committed anarchists.[64]

Very similar conflicting nationalisms existed in Venezuela immediately after the Second World War, "between conservatives and radicals, between civilians and the military, business and labour, the clergy and educational reformers, and between competing political parties of every colour," giving rise to two military coups separated by three years—the *Trienio*—of radical reform inspired by ideals of liberty, equality, and fraternity before the restoration of "social order" in the early years of the Cold War. Venezuela confronted the same question faced by many emerging countries, how to define the nation: "Was there a common culture in the country and, if so, who was it that decided what that culture was? Was it the traditional elites, or the Church, or the people, or the workers—or the army?"[65]

In her book on new wars, Kaldor recognized the importance of what can sound very much like familiar old-style nationalism. She believed, however, that the nationalism of the new wars was of a new kind, involving *dis*integration of the state and underpinned by political stoking of fear and hatred rather than by a moral narrative. The Congo Wars of 1996–97 and 1998–2003, referred to in Chapter 1, provide an example. Not only was state nationalism weak, we are told, but previously dormant awareness of sub-identities around clan, tribe, or region were heightened, and fear of domination by another group became widespread.[66] Kaldor took the disintegration of the former Yugoslavia as a case study, contrasting that with earlier "modern" nationalisms which aimed at state-building. Nor, as she saw it, is new warfare like revolutionary warfare: "For the revolutionaries, ideology was very important. . . . In contrast, the new warriors establish political control through allegiance to a label rather than an idea." Particular versions of history were being reinvented and hate and fear aroused for purposes of political mobilization. It then becomes important "that the majority of people living in the territory under control must admit to the right label." In Bosnia-Herzegovina, for example, "It was not only members of other ethnic groups who were targeted in the strategy of ethnic cleansing. It was moderates as well, those who refused . . . to be drawn into the mire of 'fear and hate'"[67]

But there is nothing *new* about that. War, in general, "makes those who seek peaceful reconciliation appear to be either naive or unpatriotic and the object of scorn and harassment."[68] Kaldor also made much of the contrast between what she saw as the "exclusivism" of the new wars and the multicultural, universalist values characteristic of cosmopolitanism.[69] But old warriors were hardly champions of cosmopolitanism either.

As the new wars Kaldor has written about have spilled over to impact those in more settled countries, there has been much attention paid to how it is possible for people to be "radicalized" with apparently irrational ideas that are shared with others and provide such a "heroic justification" for "terrorism." Compared to interstate war, this is a quite different type of collective violence. It is more likely to be engaged in by non-state actors, representing ethnic and regional divides within states or religious or ideological persuasions which transcend state boundaries.[70] Some acts of terrorism may in fact be more individual than collective, and there is increasing interest in the role of an individual's mental illness as an explanatory factor.[71] But most acts which attract the label *terrorist* are committed by those who believe themselves to be part of a just war on behalf of a cause bigger than themselves. Those are the values, the causes, for which Mill and Pearse and so many others thought we should be prepared to take up arms against others. Drawing on military historian van Creveld, Mary Kaldor believes engaging in war requires something beyond personal selfishness or mere "individualistic utilitarian calculation." It requires, she says, "a common goal in which the individual ... can believe and ... share[s] with others."[72] To overcome our natural resistance to the use of aggression to solve conflicts, support for war requires for its justification a powerful idea, a form of narrative, or a set of values under threat.

One of the most thoughtful psychological models of radicalization, having considerable empirical support, is Kruglanski and colleagues' *3Ns—need, narrative, network—model* of terrorism.[73] One element of the model is need, more to do with terrorists' own personal motivations, which we looked at from the personal motivation perspective in the last chapter. We shall see in the next chapter the role played by the network, focusing on how terrorism may be encouraged by small, close-knit, informal, radical social groups. The most relevant part of the model for the present chapter is narrative. Collective violence, this part of the model states, requires some "violence-justifying ideology," a set of beliefs, endorsed by some authority and shared by a group, "a narrative around which a group can cohere and which serves to justify its actions, especially actions thought necessary to protect its values and its welfare, even its very existence." The model emphasizes the importance of the shared narrative both for imposing upon its members a basic duty to protect the group's interests by any means necessary and at the same time offering them a path to personal significance as a devoted member of the nation, religion, or group.[74] By embracing the need to commit acts of violence that others find thoroughly immoral, the narrative provides a demand for such action of a virtuous, sacred, one could even say moral kind. The moral justification for supporting war is a topic we shall return to in Chapter 7.

Merely Slumbering: The War-Justifying Potential of Nationalisms and Other Identities

Nationalism, whether of an old or a new variety, may promote interstate or civil war but in itself may not be necessary or sufficient for it, some conclude.[75] It requires arousing or provoking. In *Causes of War*, Levy and Thompson[76] are skeptical about the idea that "ancient hatreds" between rival ethnic or religious groups provide a sufficient explanation for ethnic wars; it may contribute, they acknowledge, but not all such rivalries lead to war. For example, Serbs and Croats fought little until the 1990s and Persians and Arabs little in two centuries until the Iran–Iraq war of the 1980s. Most nationalisms "slumber," suggests James Hughes. Using the example of "the Troubles" in Northern Ireland, he asks whether the rise of aggressive nationalism may be reactive, "where one nationalism evokes or provokes another through a sequence of action and reaction, and where violence may be the catalyst?" He traces how Irish nationalism had been peripheral in Northern Ireland prior to the Troubles and how it had been more infused with leftist ideas, advocating moral not physical force. Only later, as an emotional reaction to "harsh British counterinsurgency tactics" and the end of the "honeymoon" between the British army and the Catholic community, was there a decisive turn toward "a new vibrant form of Irish nationalism" under which violence was promoted.[77] Similarly, one of the more immediate causes of heightened tension in Spain, and "a steady decline into chaos, violence, murder and, finally, war" in the 1930s, was, according to Hugh Thomas' account, the brutal quelling of an attempted revolutionary uprising by miners in the Asturias region in the north of the country.[78]

The Shia–Sunni split within Islam may be a particularly clear example of identities lying dormant and slumbering peacefully until aroused to hatred by events. Certainly, Kim Ghattas, award-winning Lebanese journalist and writer who covered the Middle East for 20 years for the BBC and *Financial Times*, makes that case in her book *Black Wave: Saudi Arabia, Iran and the Rivalry That Unravelled the Middle East*. A prominent theme of her book is how, following the Iranian revolution of 1979 and its clash with Saudi Wahhabism, people across the Middle East, from Pakistan to Egypt, "redefined their identities around sect and Sunni–Shia hatred began to take hold." In Pakistan, for example, Shias were the largest minority but had never felt downtrodden, she claims. Anti-Shia sentiment existed, but, as in the Muslim world generally, it was limited in its expression to a minority of clerics and their followers. Muhammad Jinnah, father of the Pakistan nation, was himself a Shia; and "in the first decades of its existence the sectarian identities of its leaders were of no relevance. . . . The historical, theological Sunni–Shia schism did not preoccupy people in their daily lives." That changed in the 1980s. Saudi charities were encouraged to build hundreds of madrassas along the Afghan border, and sermons in Pakistan's cities grew increasingly angry with words locals had not heard before, such as "kill in the name of God" and Shia "infidels." In 1986, a series of fatwas began to circulate, banning Sunnis from eating food cooked by Shias or attending their funerals. Then came more fatwas explicitly declaring Shias kafir—a true "license to kill." Sunnis began to kill Shias and vice versa: "Sectarianism had been weaponized." Sectarian intolerance and violence then grew exponentially. "By 2012, one in every two Pakistanis did not accept that Shias were Muslims."[79]

The inter-ethnic violence that followed the partition of India at the end of the British colonial era is another case in point. Kavita Puri's book *Partition Voices: Untold British Stories*[80] is based on interviews with now elderly men and women who had lived most of their lives in Britain but had at partition been forced to emigrate out of what became Pakistan into the new India or vice versa before finally coming to Britain. It recounts how people who apparently had lived happily together as neighbors and friends, sometimes for generations, could suddenly become murderous toward each other. At the same time, it is clear that the two communities had long been seen as distinct and that the potential for violent conflict was there to be aroused. Several interviewees remarked that members of the different communities would not, even at the best of times, eat together—even in some cases not eating from vessels touched by the other—or inter-marry—even in some cases ostracizing or inflicting honor killing if such taboos were broken.

Whether in the countries that made up the former Yugoslavia, in the Catholic and Protestant communities in Northern Ireland, among Hindu and Muslims in India at the time of partition, or between Shia and Sunni Islam in the Middle East, or in any one of countless other conflicts that have led to collective violence, intergroup differences of identity may have lain slumbering for decades, even centuries. With the help of a rousing narrative, events can unfold and be interpreted to arouse fear and hatred. Factions can harden remarkably rapidly it seems. Violence can be made to appear justified, even moral. Relationships can be transformed from peaceful coexistence into support for war.

Conclusions

The main conclusions that I draw from the material discussed in this chapter are summarized in Figure 3.1. My first conclusion is that feelings of identity with one's nation state, although remaining the single most important source of war-supporting causes, are not the only ones. Sets of strongly held values based on adherence to a religious faith, an ethnic group, or a region within a state, are prominent examples of identities which share some of the characteristics of nationalism. They may be the more important in the now more common, so-called new wars. Like nationalism, they are complex, multifactorial, contested, fluid, ever-changing.

Of particular importance, I conclude, is a crucial distinction between identities which take a benign form and have only a weak relationship with war support and those meriting the term *chauvinistic*, which are more strongly war-supporting. The more an identity and the values associated with it depart from cosmopolitanism, and the more they carry the elements of exclusivity and superiority over others, the more available they are to be exploited in support of armed hostility. That potential for war may lie dormant for years, even for generations, but given the right circumstances, and stoked by political encouragement, it may harden and escalate rapidly. The development and acceptance of a shared group narrative, imposing upon its members a basic duty to protect the group's interests and justifying collective violence if necessary, always plays an important role in that process. It helps to make war seem virtuous, even moral. Those who decline to support war are then likely to be the subjects of scorn and criticism.

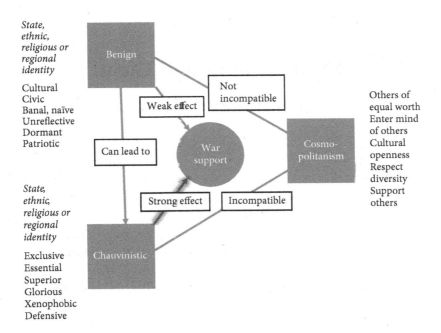

Figure 3.1 War in defense of national and other identities and values: a summary of principal conclusions

Combining these conclusions with those I reached at the end of Chapter 2, a fuller answer to the question of war support is starting to take shape. An integration of the themes that have emerged so far, and that will emerge in the following chapters, will be a task for the concluding Chapter 8. Meanwhile the psychology of war support, and of the attitudes, beliefs, and values that underpin it, requires a further component, which we shall examine in the following chapter. Making war needs an enemy, an out-group in opposition to our in-group. How we mentally construct images of the enemy and how we define our own national, ethnic, religious, regional, or other group in comparison with the enemy's are the subjects we turn to next.

4
Thinking of Us and Them, Enemies and Heroes

The problem with heroes is that they will always need a monster to fight; and the more perfect the hero, the more correspondingly threatening the monster must be.

Keith Lowe, *The Fear and the Freedom:
How the Second World War Changed Us*[1]

Good and Evil are reduced to Us and Them.... They act from a wish for power. We act from self-defense, benevolence, and reasons of common decency and morality. The real problem started with an act of will on the part of the enemy.... Since the enemy is evil, he naturally lies. Communication is not possible. Only force can settle the issue. *We* tell the truth (news, education). *They* lie (propaganda). "We" and "They" are qualitatively different.... There is doubt that we and they really belong to the same species.

Lawrence LeShan, *The Psychology of War*[2]

In the previous two chapters we have examined explanations for war support which have focused on personal and collective beliefs, motivations, values, identities—all about us and why we might decide war is justified, even to be experienced as something positive. But war is not just about "us," it is about "them" as well. War requires an adversary, an "enemy"; if we can be convinced that the enemy is sufficiently bad and we are correspondingly good, then we are up for the fight. This chapter is about how we think about others and ourselves. An area of psychology that can broadly be termed *cognitive-social* comes into its own here. In the context of war it takes on the particular form of how we perceive a potential enemy and how we see ourselves in relation to the enemy. We shall examine the mental processes that it is thought are necessary in order to construct the idea of an enemy and which might justify the use of armed conflict against it. In the process we shall look at a number of relevant areas of psychological theory and research. Two leading theories are examined in some detail: social identity theory and e interpersonal contact theory. The chapter concludes by considering the spiral conflict model and its implications for how cognitions and feelings about the enemy escalate as conflict develops.

This chapter has a key role to perform in the development of the model of war support toward which the book is traveling. It contributes to the core idea of preparedness for war by helping us see how identifying another state or group as a potential enemy is already a retreat from the principle of cosmopolitan humanity, the belief that we are all citizens of the same world. The process hardens once an out-group is believed to constitute a threat to the in-group's identity and position, the more so once the enemy starts to be described in demonizing, even in dehumanizing, terms. Intergroup rivalry, preexisting hostility, and earlier wars are often background factors facilitating threat perception and enemy stigmatization.

Alongside preparedness for war and threat perception, two of the core factors in the model I am developing, the present chapter brings up in stark relief the third factor, mental simplification. Among the variety of well-recognized simplifying cognitive biases contributing to war support that we shall consider, particularly relevant are the fundamental attribution error and the actor–observer discrepancy: the enemy's acts can be attributed to its essential nature, whereas ours are driven by circumstances, not of our making; the enemy is to blame, whereas we were provoked into making an armed response. As we shall see, cognitive simplicity in the perception of a rival or enemy country or group is reinforced by lack of contact. Intergroup negativity and prejudice, as well as reduced ability to critically reflect on one's own group's position in relation to the enemy group, flourish without intergroup contact.

Identifying and Demonizing the Enemy

Is that, then, close to one of the answers to my question, Why do we support war? There is indeed a great deal of evidence to support that theory of the basis for war. Much has been written, for example, about the power of public xenophobia—"a morbid dislike of foreigners"[3]—to push leaders into war.[4]

War, it has often been said, requires identifying a feared, "demonic enemy," magnifying the threats it represents, and casting collective violence against it as being in the national or group interest.[5] The authors of *War and Society* refer to the "other-ization" of the opposing side.[6]

Not all adversaries are seen in the same way. Distinctions have been drawn between different images. They include the barbarian, rogue, and degenerate images, as well as a straightforward enemy image.[7] According to *enemy image theory*, those who fulfill requirements for the simple enemy image are seen as our equals in terms of their culture and their military capability, but they are viewed as threatening. Barbarians—as the Greeks and the Romans called the threatening Germanic tribes to their north—are viewed as superior in capability but inferior culturally. In Britain and France in World War I, the idea of defending "our" civilization against German barbarism was prominent. Exaggerated stories of German atrocities in Belgium and northern France and German spy stories, such as John Buchan's *Thirty-Nine Steps*, emerged. Croatian images of Serbs in the Balkans conflict and some Israeli images of Arabs might also qualify. The rogue image refers to the images of a country or organization held to be inferior in terms of both culture and capability. Examples might be NATO allies' images of countries supported by the Soviet Union during the Cold War. The degenerate image has similarities with the barbarian but is accompanied by feelings of contempt, scorn, hatred, disgust—the Allies' image of the Japanese in World War II is the clearest modern example. Such a categorization system may be too crude. There are many examples of more nuanced images such as the German First World War images of the French as materialistic and corrupt, the British as grasping capitalists, the Russians as decadent.[8] And images can change in a matter of a few years. In World War II, Americans thought Russians had more positive traits than Germans; during the Cold War it was the other way round.[9]

As well as images of the "other," self-images are of as much, if not more, importance. If the enemies or potential enemies are seen as monsters, we need to see ourselves as heroes, to use Lowe's words, or as more moral or resolute.[10] From a psychoanalytic perspective other-images and self-images are intimately linked in ways that we are at best only dimly aware of most of the time. Among the mental mechanisms for explaining the sources of war are said to be splitting and projecting demonized images onto "the enemy" as a response to insecurity and threat to one's own identity.[11] In his book *The Roots of War and Terror*, psychiatrist and psychoanalyst Anthony Stevens refers to our "propensity ... to distinguish 'us' from 'them' ... incit[ing] us to xenophobia, racism, militant nationalism, and to war . . . out-groups make ideal repositories into which the in-group can project the archetype of the enemy."[12]

Dehumanization

Others who have written about war have spoken of an even more extreme violence-justifying mental mechanism variously described as "dehumanization" or "pseudospeciation," when members of the enemy group are thought of as if they were of a different species, less than fully human in fact.[13] The two world wars provide good illustrations. *Untermenschen*—literally "subhumans"—as the Nazi term for Jews,[14] is the example everyone knows about. But others did their share of dehumanizing their enemies. Keith Lowe, writing of World War II, tells us that "The Japanese routinely characterized the Chinese as apes, rats or donkeys, and drew cartoons of them with claws, horns or short, stubby tails. In return, Chinese propaganda routinely characterized their Japanese invaders as dwarves or devils."[15] The Allies' images of the Japanese are among the clearest examples of dehumanization. Racial stigmatization was commonplace among the Allies' leaders and citizens. The Japanese were often perceived as non-human, as animals, reptiles, or insects. A swarm of bees servicing their queen, the emperor, was one popular image. Ants was another: in his memoirs, General Slim, commander in the Burma campaigns, wrote, "We had kicked over the anthill . . . the ants were running about in confusion. Now was the time to stamp on them."[16] Rats was another. The most common caricature was the monkey or ape. There was even a rumor that Japanese troops had achieved their rapid advance down the Malay Peninsula to capture Singapore by swinging from tree to tree. The magazine *Punch* printed a full-page cartoon depicting such in January 1942. John Dower refers to dehumanizing images like these serving a "softening of the killing process," aided by the frequent use of two figures of speech, metaphors of the hunt and of exterminating vermin: "It is, at least for most people, easier to kill animals than fellow human beings."[17] Some of the same dehumanizing metaphors, often in association with the metaphor of the spread of infectious disease, are regularly found being used to justify genocidal warfare: rats, snakes, maggots, lice, viruses, parasites.[18] For example, Hutu politician Léon Mugesera told his supporters, in 1992, two years before Rwanda's civil war, that Tutsis were "cockroaches."[19] Some students of genocide have distinguished between those where the victim group is "dehumanized"—Black Darfuris by Sudanese Muslims and many indigenous peoples by European settlers are suggested examples—and others where the victims are "demonized"—those seen as heretics in the eyes of ideologies or dictatorships, for example. In some cases the two were combined.[20]

Once we look at the idea of dehumanization more closely, as with something like nationalism that we considered in the previous chapter, things rapidly become more complicated. There are finer distinctions to be drawn. A paper in the journal *Peace and Conflict* distinguished between three forms of dehumanization.[21] One was the familiar *animalistic dehumanization* whereby members of the out-group are seen as lacking such traits as "civility, refinement, moral sensibility, rationality, and maturity," a lack normally ascribed to non-human animals, and perhaps also to children before they are fully socialized as adults. Another, *mechanistic dehumanization*, occurs when out-group members are viewed as like machines or automata, deficient in human qualities of "emotional responsiveness, interpersonal warmth, cognitive openness, agency, and depth." The third uses religious language, such as the word *kafir* or unbelievers, or negative religious images such as *Satan* and *demon*.

To examine dehumanization more closely, the same paper reported a study of Muslim–Christian conflicts in southern Mindanao in the Philippines. These are conflicts involving regular armed clashes between the Philippine government and the Moro Islamic Liberation Front (MILF) with tension going back several centuries. One study analyzed conventional and social media reports from both Christian and Muslim sources at the height of one such clash in 2015. Statements in the reports were independently coded for dehumanization by Muslim and Christian coders. The results were interpreted as symptomatic of the asymmetric power structure underlying a conflict of this sort. Media content indicating humanization was found on both sides to be dominated by heroic stories, more often constructed using religious language than in the more secular Western conflicts where animalistic and mechanistic dehumanization strategies were dominant. However, the features of heroism that were described were not identical. Christians were more often depicted as brave heroes, whereas humanity for members of the Muslim group was more often portrayed as full of kindness and compassion. Among the higher-power group, the Christians, "adulation veers toward a tough courage that abets victory in the war," but the low-power group "seek leaders who stand in solidarity with suffering and whose human softness calls out others to endure." Whether or not one agrees with that interpretation of the findings, the general point about the varying semantics of humanization is a valid one. Humanization and dehumanization may be regular features of collective armed conflict, but the form they take and the language in which they are expressed can vary greatly.

A further point of general interest emerging from this study probably shouldn't have surprised the researchers, although they said it did. The data coders, supposedly neutral and objective, turned out not to be so. Muslim and Christian coders classified some of the statements in significantly different, sometimes even opposite, ways. For example, the Christian coder did not see any dehumanization in a story which suggested that the MILF and Muslims were not committed to a peaceful solution to the conflict. The Muslim coder, on the other hand, classified that as dehumanizing Muslims. The claim that "Islam does not promote violence, but we Muslims are always blamed" was classified by the Muslim coder as another example of dehumanizing Muslims but was deemed by the Christian coder not to be, in fact to be an illustration of *humanizing* Muslims. Dehumanization is, at least to some degree it seems, in the eye of the beholder.

Before moving on, I need to raise an issue that lurks in the background to all debates about psychology and war. War requires an enemy. But who, exactly, is the enemy? Anthony Stevens touches on this when he says that the demonization of enemy leaders, such as Slobodan Milošević and Saddam Hussein in modern times, enabled a spreading of the demonization on to their followers. He detects a similar spreading of demonization, under George W. Bush's war rhetoric, from the demonization of terrorists to nation states identified as supporting terrorists.[22] This spreading of demonization, or deliberate confusing or merging of levels to put it another way, is a point that is often overlooked in debates about support for war. We see it now in statements made by public figures in the United Kingdom about Russia and China, often referred to as sources of danger, even as potential, if not actual, "enemies." But the language slips between identifying *President Putin*, the *Russian regime*, and simply *Russia* and between the *Chinese Communist Party* and *China* as the potential villains. Care is usually taken not to demonize the Russian or Chinese people generally, who would of course become chief victims of any war which did ensue, although the same consideration may not extend to their military personnel. Reducing a whole other nation or potentially threatening group to the status of a single entity, as if it were an individual person—the "unitary actor framing" referred to at the close of

Chapter 1—has been shown to increase support for harmful, indiscriminate military actions against the enemy group.[23]

Simplistic Thinking, Cognitive Complexity, the Importance of Language

Those who have studied and thought about the psychological foundations of war have often pointed to the need, if war is to be supported, for a large dose of mental over-simplification. Dividing people into "us" and "them," friend and foe, allies and enemies, heroes and villains, is itself a gross simplification. But there are many other forms of simplistic thinking on which, it has been suggested, war thrives. Around the 1970s a "cognitive revolution" occurred in mainstream psychology. Broadly speaking, it challenged the earlier model of human behavior, in which I was trained, that assumed it was only behavior and the contingencies that maintained it that mattered; what people thought was largely froth, of little account. Since then, there has been an explosion of research and theory about thinking, for example about how we make decisions, how we justify our actions, how we make sense of the world, and the narratives or stories we spin about ourselves and others. The large bulk of this work has concluded that we are not as rational as we might like to think. We are, it seems, prone to multiple biases and distortions of reality.[24] Perhaps this is one place where the truth about war support lies.

Among the cognitive biases which look likely candidates for inclusion in a mental simplification theory of war support are *selective attention*—seeing only what you expect or want to see—and *premature cognitive closure*—stopping searching for more information once a solution is reached that satisfies us. Another is the *availability heuristic*, a kind of cognitive shortcut, whereby judgments are overly influenced by events that are familiar and salient. This can give rise to what has been called *analogical reasoning*, whereby historical events are seen as relevant guidelines for the present. One very familiar example is the "appeasement" of Hitler by the UK Chamberlain government prior to World War II—the Munich analogy. The Vietnam analogy is another, regularly brought out to warn of US military involvement risking a long, drawn-out engagement. Sometimes those advocating a particular action are deliberately selecting a convenient historical analogy to support their position, a "rhetorical use of history."

A particularly relevant cognitive bias is the *fundamental attribution error*. This refers to our tendency to attribute others' behavior to something fundamental, essential, or a more or less permanent disposition of theirs—for example, an adversary's innate hostility or untrustworthiness—whereas we attribute our own behavior to circumstance. Our actions are therefore understandable under the circumstances. In a conflict situation our hostility is excusable as a response to others' actions or perceived intentions—a bias known as the *actor–observer discrepancy*. The "other" is at fault, whereas we were provoked. What was in reality a long action–reaction–action chain of events with no very clear starting point is "parsed" in our minds, such that we believe "they" started it and we were then compelled to respond. They may sometimes appear to act in a good or conciliatory way but only because of our resolute preventive actions, or, worse, it is strategically deceptive on their part—the idea of *inherent bad faith*.

The inherent bad faith model also takes views of oneself or one's group into account. Lack of self-criticism, in this model, is a contributor to an absence of empathy or understanding of others' worldviews and how others may harbor feelings that their interests are being threatened.[25] Beliefs become fixed and difficult to change, particularly if such beliefs occupy a relatively high level in one's hierarchical system of beliefs—for example, if they concern basic values or goals. In his comprehensive review of propaganda (which we shall consider in more detail in Chapter 6) Philip Taylor says that for any public information to be effective it is necessary "to ensure that the information being received is done so by people who have already been sufficiently infused with propaganda over a long period of time so that they perceive it in accordance with a predetermined world-view."[26]

Discussions about the psychology of war are peppered with references to participants adopting a Manichean perspective, whereby what is right and what is wrong are made clear, with little or no room in between.[27] This comes close to an operational definition of *cognitive simplicity*. At the other end of the scale is *cognitive complexity*, a way of thinking about some phenomenon—a group of people perhaps—that is both differentiated and integrated. In other words, it is a style of thinking which takes into account multiple characteristics as well as the connections among those characteristics. If a group of other people is viewed in that relatively nuanced, sophisticated way, particularly if our own group is viewed in a similarly balanced way, Manichean, heroes-and-monsters thinking about our respective strengths and weaknesses is difficult to sustain.[28] Cognitive simplicity is a mental bias that has been applied more to the thinking styles of politicians and military leaders and the press—for example, speeches made by twentieth-century national leaders during political crises showed declining complexity preceding war[29]—than to the large mass of people on whose behalf and with whose support war is waged. This illustrates the point which I come back to time and again, that ordinary people's support for war is a topic that has been relatively neglected in war studies.

Simplified thinking does play a prominent role, however, in the *3Ns model* of radicalization which we have met already in previous chapters. In that model it takes the form of *need for cognitive closure* (NFC), a desire for a firm, unambiguous worldview, a wish for certainty, a "preference for simplistic black-and-white, us-versus-them narratives." Views about one's own self and about one's own group are integral to the 3Ns model. Anything, such as a humiliating experience which contributes to confusion, uncertainty, and self-doubt, arouses an individual's NFC and the need to restore a feeling of certainty. In the process, there is an increased tendency to adopt "imbalanced points of view that privilege the ingroup's narrative and justify aggression against the outgroup. . . . The creation and propagation of . . . Manichean narratives" which contribute to radicalization.[30]

The way language is used is relevant for war support at several points. It will crop up again in later chapters when we look at how weapons are spoken of, its use in war propaganda, and how it functions to distance us from the immorality of inflicting death and injury on others in warfare. Of relevance to the present discussion is the way language can be used to construct a convincing argument—a narrative if you like—that portrays a potential enemy as a legitimate target for violence. One idea is that of the *conspiratorial narrative* that marries the idea of narrative with that of a conspiracy theory. The suggestion is that violence toward members of another group is justified, not only because the other group is identified as "other" but more importantly because of how these others have contributed to one's own group's oppression. It is not just who the potential enemy is but what they are said to be doing or to have done to us. Conspiratorial narratives go hand in hand with negative enemy images, identifying who our enemies are, negatively characterizing them, and explaining what they are doing which is against the in-group's interests, even its survival. They therefore promote strong feelings such as anger and resentment and provide powerful legitimacy for violent retribution, which is therefore seen as virtuous.[31] The very label *terrorist* implies an illegitimate way of waging warfare, even a dehumanizing of those who employ such methods.[32]

Myths and the Distortion of Reality

The notion that the argument for violence against another group might sometimes bear similarity to a conspiracy theory moves us on toward the more general idea that support for war rests on the creation of myths, even on a mental departure from reality. Such ideas have been more easily accommodated by those of a more psychoanalytic persuasion. From his perspective as a Jungian psychoanalyst, Anthony Stevens, for example, talks of "shadow projection." That, he says, distorts people's perception of reality, "making them deeply suspicious of all of the other side's intentions and conceited about their own . . . keeps them effectively unconscious of their own power drives and destructive capacities."[33] Jung, shortly before he died, wrote about Cold War relations as a perfect example: what "Western man . . . fails to see is that it is his own vices . . . that are thrown back in his face. . . . It is the face of our own shadow that glowers at us across the Iron Curtain."[34]

Lawrence LeShan, who served for several years as a psychologist in the US Army and whose book *The Psychology of War* is subtitled *Comprehending Its Mystique and Its Madness*, went further. He draws on Erik Erikson's notion of a "mythic" versus a sensory mode of construing reality. Erikson believed that under certain conditions we could experience a sudden shift in the way we see things. In war, LeShan argued, how we appraise an international situation can shift from a sensory to a mythic reality remarkably rapidly as tensions escalate. Our relationship with the enemy is reduced to a Manichean collection of simplifications, as the quote from LeShan at the beginning of this chapter describes. We start to live in a world more like those of *The Wizard of Oz, Cinderella, Little Red Riding Hood*, or *The Lord of the Rings*. They have U-boats; we have submarines. The bombing of Rotterdam is one thing, that of Hamburg quite another. One sign of the shift is the withdrawal of acknowledgment that the other side consists of individuals: "There are fewer and fewer individual 'Germans' or 'Japanese'; there is only 'Germany' or 'Japan.'"[35]

Another sure sign that a society's mode of thinking about a war has tipped from sensory to mythical is that "it becomes dangerous to challenge the now-accepted wisdom of mythic reality. . . . Contrary ideas become dangerous to express. . . . Those who even *question* the accepted wisdom are condemned, first as 'unpatriotic,' later as 'traitors.'"[36] He gives two examples. From the ancient world was the vote in Athens to drive Euripides into exile after he wrote the great anti-war play *The Trojan Women*. In modern times, John Steinbeck was attacked and vilified for his very human portrayal of German soldiers occupying a Norwegian town during World War II.[37] As Anthony Stevens says, "When a nation goes to war, its citizens close ranks in a shared patriotic identity, and dissenters are stigmatized as traitors for not giving unqualified support to 'our troops on the battlefield.'"[38]

Those ideas might seem fanciful, and out of keeping with most modern academic psychology, if it were not for the fact that some quite similar ideas are expressed by others coming from a very different theoretical background. For example, in 2015 community psychologists Mark Pilisuk and Jennifer Rountree cited LeShan's ideas with approval, although they applied them principally to combatants, "whose ordinary reality contains sharp inhibitions against inflicting violence [but] may switch into an alternative reality that permits killing and even genocide." They refer to a kind of detachment, a "dissociative state," a "distorted reality," almost a parallel, second reality, alongside one's normal reality in which killing others would be unthinkable.[39]

In-Groups and Out-Groups

It is not possible to journey far in the search for understanding support for war without coming across notions of in-groups and out-groups. We already met these theoretical ideas when discussing the role of national and other identities in the previous chapter. The main emphasis there was on collective identity as a powerful example of in-group sentiment. In this chapter the focus is as much on the enemy as an out-group.

One of the best-known and longest-surviving theories in social psychology—*social identity theory* (SIT)[40]—is forever associated with the name of Henri Tajfel, its chief originator. Like a number of other figures prominent in European social psychology, Tajfel was a Jewish emigrant who wanted to apply psychology to understand the origins of Nazism and the Holocaust. He came to Bristol from Poland, where a large number of his family had been killed in the Holocaust.[41] He was to have great influence on a whole generation of social psychologists.

One of the most notable features of SIT is *minimal distinctiveness*. Numerous experiments have shown that in-group favoritism and derogation of an out-group can easily be triggered simply by assigning people to groups on the basis of some arbitrary and quite minimal distinction. An early such study, well known in psychology, was the Robber's Cave experiment. Boys attending summer camps were divided into two groups which then took part in a variety of activities involving competition. In-group cohesion and favoritism, as well as feelings of hostility toward members of the other group, both increased. Role-play it seems, even in the absence of any history of conflicts of interests, is enough to provoke in-group solidarity and out-group negativity.[42] Subsequent experiments have shown that even assigning people to groups on the basis of the toss of a coin can produce a degree of such minimal distinctiveness effects, although assigning competitive roles, such as perpetrator and victim[43] or jailer and prisoner, can be especially powerful. Although the SIT experiments have clearly demonstrated that the simple assignment of individuals into different groups is enough in itself to induce bias toward in-group favoritism and out-group discrimination, it is better appreciated now that care needs to be taken in generalizing to the real world from effects found in experiments carried out under controlled conditions.[44]

In the real world, of course, the groups we identify with have much more than minimal origin and appeal. *Self-categorization theory* (SCT),[45] proposed by John Turner, another name of lasting importance here, has more to do with our identification with certain groups that provide a good fit with our own personal interests and commitments. It is the combination of SIT and SCT which provides a psychological foundation for appreciating why aligning with groups is so important for war support. Most of us may have little choice about which nation to identify with; but SIT shows how very basic are the processes which feed on and augment commitment to an in-group that was assigned to us, and SCT speaks to the scope we have to identify more or less strongly with any group, assigned or chosen—national, religious, or ethnic included—which might contemplate war with a distinct out-group.

SIT is based on acceptance of the Janus-like duality of human nature: our identities have two components, individual and social. We all need affiliation with social groups for the maintenance of our self-esteem. This is especially important when self-esteem is threatened, for example due to suffering economic or social deprivation or being consistently devalued.[46] We have a stake in maintaining or improving the positivity of our group. That can be achieved by increasing the in-group's status or power and/or by derogating or otherwise diminishing the perceived status or power of rival out-groups. We are, in short, motivated to engage in in-group bias in order to protect the relative social status of our in-group and, hence, our personal self-esteem.[47] At the social level, the bolstering of in-group cohesion and solidarity is one outcome. The other side of the same coin, the dark side, is the corresponding perception of out-groups which, by comparison with our own, are bound to be relatively less respected and valued. The crucial insight contained within SIT is that the two go hand in hand. Our in-group's status and our own self-esteem are dependent on there being out-groups against which to contrast ourselves. The *conflict–cohesion hypothesis*, the idea that out-group hostility contributes to in-group cohesion, has a long history going back at least to the late nineteenth century.[48] Arthur Koestler, in his book *Janus*—the two-headed Roman god, simultaneously looking in opposite directions—accepted that idea of a group being strengthened by having an outside enemy as one of the causes of war, a consequence of humankind's social nature and the need to form groups: our "excessive capacity and urge to become identified with a tribe, nation, church or cause, and to espouse its credo uncritically and enthusiastically."[49]

Although the positive, group cohesion–promoting effect of strong in-group identity has its parts to play as well, support for war mostly rests on the dark side of group identity. A distinction has been drawn between "secure" and "defensive" forms of group identity. Solidarity with one's own group is the more dominant when group identity is secure. By contrast, defensive identity is relatively strong on belief that one's own group is exceptional, suspicion of out-groups, sensitivity to being disrespected, and a tendency to react to threats in a hostile fashion. This has been referred to by some as "collective narcissism" and the equivalent at a national level as "national narcissism."[50]

Threat to the In-Group

Perceptions of both in-group and out-groups are likely to be more polarized, and therefore dangerous, if the image of the "other" is that of a threatening "enemy."[51] Perceived threat to one's own group is a central topic in SIT, but its focus remains on what it terms *distinctiveness threat* to the in-group, especially *reflective distinctiveness*. That involves differentiating one's group from the out-group in order to clarify intergroup boundaries. It is threatened if the in-group and out-groups are perceived as being insufficiently distinct. This chimes with the discussion of collective identities in the previous chapter: recall that distinctiveness and exclusivity were found to be characteristics of chauvinistic identities in contrast to the openness and respect toward others that characterize cosmopolitanism.

Realistic conflict theory (RCT) and other variants such as *intergroup threat theory*,[52] on the other hand, are less about the in-group and maintaining its status and distinctiveness and more about how intergroup hostility arises because of objective conflicts of interest and how the actions or intentions of an out-group might be threatening the in-group. Conflicts are primarily driven, it is presumed, by economic competition, by incompatible values, ideologies, and ways of life, and by struggles for power, control, and dominance. Perception of threat plays a key role in the theory, strengthening both in-group solidarity and hostility toward the out-group, especially where there is already a history of antagonism. Destructive conflict is therefore seen as being about real differences, not otherwise managed in a more constructive fashion.[53] RCT can be seen as the psychological equivalent of the theories of the realist school of international relations which we looked at in Chapter 1.

SIT does acknowledge the importance of "status threat" from any out-group which is perceived as a competitor for power, resources or prestige, and it also recognizes *symbolic threat*, which refers to specific threats to the in-group which go beyond pure threats to its distinctiveness, for example threats arising from conflicts in values, norms, culture, or beliefs. Both RCT and SIT are likely to be necessary to explain negative perceptions of out-groups and how they contribute to hostility toward out-group members and the potential for war. Preexisting conflicts of interest and processes that help develop in-group favoritism are both likely to play their parts.

Some theorists have placed as much, if not more, emphasis on emotions that can amplify perceived threat, such as uncertainty, fear, and anger (again there are echoes here of things discussed in Chapters 2 and 3, such as the role of uncertainty, reminders of one's mortality, and other emotions in terror management theory and the 3Ns model, as well as the swift arousal of dormant fear and hatred that can accompany religious, sectarian, and ethnic conflicts). Feelings of uncertainty are found to increase out-group derogation and motivate search for safety and security and have been shown to relate to intergroup violence, including genocide. For instance, public opinion polling indicated that anger and fear were commonly expressed in the United States after the 9/11 attacks; the angrier people were, the more likely it was that they supported overseas military action after the attacks. However, as is the norm for things psychological, there is no inevitable, simple association between such emotions and inclination for a violent response. Fear, for example, although it can in some circumstances promote out-group derogation and opposition to compromise and reconciliation, in other circumstances can have the opposite effect of motivating a search for compromise.[54] Summarizing a large body of research on the consequences of perceived threat for intergroup conflict, a review paper in the *American Psychologist* concluded,

> Generally, perceived threat increases levels of ethnocentrism and xenophobia as well as prejudice. More important, in the context of inter-group conflict, perceived threat leads many people—but not all, to become more politically intolerant, to respond more punitively and to support aggressive retaliatory policies against outgroups.

These effects, the review went on to say, are most pronounced among those who identify more strongly with their groups. Echoing the discussion of chauvinistic identities in the previous chapter, a feeling of in-group superiority was identified as a key factor leading to "heightened perceptions of intergroup threat, increased support and willingness for military engagements, and justification of both anticipated and past violence perpetrated by the ingroup."[55] As examples, the review pointed to stronger support for military action in Iraq and fewer demands for proceedings against those responsible for torture used by US and UK forces against Iraqis, among those with stronger nationalist and in-group superiority beliefs.

Defining the In-Group and the Out-Group

Before we leave the in-group/out-group theories, and just to make matters even more complicated, we need to face the question of whether it is that easy to even define an in-group and an out-group. To take the in-group first, consider one example, the Turkish–Kurdish conflict. That conflict, which has led to as many as 45,000 fatalities since the early 1980s and the displacement of over a million people within Turkey, is still without a clear and agreed solution. As the authors of a report of a piece of research carried out with laypeople, living in one multi-ethnic city in the south of Turkey, put it, "Social psychological research on intergroup conflict (and intergroup relations more generally) has tended to focus on the two parties to a conflict as if they were two homogenous groups," neglecting the possibility of there being subgroups within or even across the parties in conflict.[56]

Participants in that study were more or less equally divided between women and men and between those identifying as Turks, Kurds, and Arabs. Half had been directly affected by the conflict. The political views of the participants ranged across the spectrum. The research method, known as Q-sorting, involved them responding to a set of statements covering the causes, dynamics, and possible solutions related to the conflict. The analysis identified five different viewpoints on the conflict. Two of them were most clearly pro-Turkish and could be seen as different varieties of the "Turkish state discourse" or of a Turkish "master narrative." Providing the most obvious pro-Kurdish viewpoint was one which emphasized long-term oppression of Kurds and asserted Kurdish identity and political rights. The remaining two perspectives were less obviously polarized one way or the other: one expressed an ambivalent view of the Turkish state; the other emphasized the democracy and human rights dimensions of the conflict. Although the most obviously pro-Kurdish viewpoint was endorsed solely by Kurdish participants, all the others were supported by at least some from each of the identity groups. Furthermore, contrary to the "mirror images" notion of the viewpoints of the adversaries in a protracted intergroup conflict—a concept put forward to account for the apparent similarity of US images of the Soviet Union and Soviet images of the United States in the context of the Cold War[57] —there was not the strong inverse correlation between the pro-Turkish and pro-Kurdish attitudes that might have been expected.

Such complications concerning the in-group may be of special significance in the case of the "new wars" and less so in the case of traditional interstate wars. Defining the out-group, however, may also be more complicated than theory suggests in the case of any kind of war. In the context of discussion of the types of "conspiratorial narrative" displayed by Nazi propaganda, Hutu génocidaires' media, and IS propaganda, four types of out-group have been identified.[58] *Far out-groups* are those perceived as responsible for originating a crisis and the ideas behind it, but they are at a distance, geographically or in terms of everyday encounters, and usually out of reach of the in-group. *Close out-groups* play a secondary role and are located closer to hand. They serve the interests of the far out-groups, either in a subordinate position, carrying out the latter's instructions, or collaborating as equals for the benefit of both.

In that model there are then two hybrid groups, lying at the border between in-group and out-group, neither clearly "in" or "out." They are seen as playing a pivotal role in in-group narratives. First, *traitors*, who were or should be loyal in-group members, now promote out-group interests, working for an out-group organization and/or embracing out-group thinking and policies. Second, and perhaps of particular resonance for students of war, there is the *contaminated in-group* whose commitment is less than 100% and whose loyalty is suspect. Their in-group identity may be compromised in any number of ways, including conversion to the out-group's religion or tradition, family relationships which make wholehearted support for the in-group uncomfortable, or simply through contact with out-group members. Commentators on war, whatever perspective they are coming from, have often pointed out that those among the in-group who don't subscribe to the shared image of the enemy may be heavily criticized, even accused of cowardice and treason,[59] as noted earlier in the context of mythical or distorted thinking that can accompany war support.

Interpersonal Contact Theory

That idea, that contact with potential enemies interferes with wholehearted support for taking up arms against them, takes us directly to another theory that has been described as one of the most successful in social psychology.[60] It is sometimes referred to as the *contact hypothesis* or, more appropriately, as the *interpersonal contact theory* (ICT). Its basic tenet is that intergroup contact reduces prejudice and that positive contact can increase trust and improve attitudes between groups in conflict. In modern psychology the theory goes back at least to the 1950s and Gordon Allport's book *The Nature of Prejudice*,[61] now a classic text. Since then, contact research has been conducted in an impressively wide range of contexts around the world. It is now known that contact is associated with many peace-related outcomes such as increased trust, forgiveness, and reconciliation efforts, even in conflict-ridden and segregated settings like Northern Ireland and South Africa.[62] One much quoted meta-analysis included over 500 studies, involving a quarter of a million participants in 38 nations, providing robust evidence, consistent with the theory, that there is a negative association between intergroup contact and prejudice and threat.[63]

The theory is that contact reduces prejudice, but of course the reverse may also be the case. Prejudiced individuals are probably more likely to avoid contact with out-group members or at least be less likely to seek opportunities for contact. As is so often the case in psychology, when longitudinal data are available, they show that causality runs in both directions. Vicious, and virtuous, cycles are more often the rule than simple one-way cause-and-effect relationships. Intergroup contact has a negative effect on prejudice, and prejudice also has a negative effect on contact, providing the possibility of accumulating or spiraling cycles over time.[64]

The one conflict that has perhaps attracted most contact research is the Israeli–Palestinian conflict. One study involved 16- to 18-year-old male and female students studying in 28 different schools in settlements in the Negev area in southern Israel.[65] The background was the ongoing conflict between the majority Jewish-Israelis and the minority Negev-Arabs. Jewish and Negev-Arab adolescents usually lived parallel lives there, the study's authors say, attending separate schools and living in separate settlements, with little or no intergroup contact. The study focused on a yearlong scholastic program that, while not directly addressing intergroup relations in its formal curriculum, did bring majority and minority young people together once a week to study extracurricular courses, giving them an opportunity to interact during classes and breaks. The program was perceived by both groups as facilitating contact, and it demonstrated positive results for the Jewish group. At the beginning of the year, they had perceived their Negev-Arab peers as mainly Bedouins and believed that was how their peers saw them too. By the end of the year, they saw them in a more complex fashion, now more often perceiving of them as Arabs, or Muslims, as living in Israel, or as Israelis. The findings followed those of a number of other studies in finding weaker effects of contact for members of minority groups in comparison to majority group members. The Jewish group reported higher levels of intergroup contact than did the Negev-Arab group, and it was only in the Jewish group that much change in perceptions was recorded.

Another study also involved a yearlong course specially designed to encourage contact between Jewish and Palestinian students studying in the Negev. In this case students were Jewish-Israelis studying at university level, and the program did directly address intergroup relations in its formal curriculum.[66] The course started with 12 weekly meetings, which combined learning about topics such as the nature of conflicts, collective identities and narratives, social power relations, and reconciliation. During meetings held after each lecture, participants were encouraged to reflect on their emotions and thoughts provoked by the topics covered. This was followed by two daytrips to sites connected to historical narratives about the Nakba (the Catastrophe in Arabic, referring to the eviction of Palestinians from their homes in 1948) during which participants met with Palestinians who shared their personal stories. Dialogue sessions were held before and after each day trip. The results were presented in qualitative form, which has the advantage of providing more detailed insight into how perceptions might have changed. The quotations given in the report provide evidence of the way in which the program helped students not only to question their perceptions of Arab Israelis but also to be more critical of their assumptions about Jewish-Israelis—for example realizing how diverse they are, not all European, not all religious—and about the actions of the Israeli military in which many of them had served. Here, for instance, is one quote from a female student:

> The other day I was traveling by bus; all over the bus I saw plugged in phone chargers. It was a scary sight; I felt as if all people were being fed the same stuff. During the course, I thought about the narrative I was brought up to believe, about how much I believe in the narrative or whether it is an outcome of my upbringing, about my position on issues of politics, that I do not want to have things prescribed, I want to make up my mind on my own . . . I want to know, and learn and get as close as possible to things as they are.

The lack of contact, other than relatively superficial contact, between Hindu and Muslim families prior to partition of India, discussed in the context of nationalism in Chapter 3, was probably an important factor allowing violence to break out.[67] Northern Ireland provides another obvious example of how communities can live in apparent harmony for long periods of time while in reality living parallel, segregated lives with limited contact, providing the background for conflict and violence if circumstances change.[68]

For a long time it was assumed that it was working with others, carrying out real tasks requiring cooperation between equals, that was necessary for breaking down prejudice.[69] Although such cooperative working together must surely be a good route to reducing prejudice, it may not be the only way. Direct contact may not be the sole route to a greater understanding of a potential enemy group's experience and position. There have been dialogue groups, informed by contact theory, taking place between Jews and Arabs in Israel since the 1980s. More recently, partly due to constraints on Israeli and Palestinian groups meeting in person, an alternative approach has been tried which offers increased familiarity with the perspective of the "others" but without having actual contact with them. The method works entirely through reading literature, attending lectures, going on tours, and so on. A study that compared the two methods, carried out as semester-long courses at the same university in the Negev, found little difference in effectiveness.[70]

One group, *with* contact, mixed Jewish-Israeli and Palestinian participants. The other, *without* contact, was attended by Jewish-Israeli students only. The former was led by a Jewish and an Arab facilitator, the latter by two Jewish-Israeli facilitators (although some of the course lecturers were Palestinian). The two groups achieved similar results: reduced hatred, fear, and anger and increased trust expressed toward Palestinians and increased acceptance of the legitimacy of their perspective on the conflict.

Even taking part in a one-off experiment might at least kick-start a process of achieving greater understanding of others. One such experiment demonstrated the potential value of e-contact among Catholic and Protestant students in Northern Ireland.[71] First-year university students, half Catholic, half Protestant, joined in discussion with a "student" of the other community (actually a confederate of the experimenter). Their task was to devise a program of help for new students. Compared to controls, those who took part showed an increase in positive out-group attitudes and positive expectations of out-group contact as well as decreased anxiety about meeting those from the other community. There have been other studies suggesting that indirect contact—via family and friends having contact or having remote electronic contact, for example—can also improve intergroup relations. Analysis of five studies from four countries showed that such indirect contact in fact leads to direct contact.[72]

So, if actual contact may not be necessary, what is really going on? The same authors who carried out the large meta-analysis of contact studies, referred to earlier, went on to publish a further paper on the evidence regarding variables that are most likely to be mediating between contact and reduced prejudice. They concluded there was good evidence in support of three mediating mechanisms. They found evidence that contact increases both *knowledge* about the out-group and *empathic ability* to take the perspective of the other group and decreases *threat and anxiety* about intergroup contact.[73]

Many studies from a number of countries, going back to the 1960s[74] have shown that children's knowledge about a group of foreign people is correlated with their feelings toward them: the better-informed express greater friendliness. They also use a greater diversity of descriptive terms and a smaller number of evaluative terms to describe them—in short, they take a more rounded, nuanced, complex view of them. They are tending to see these "foreigners" as less foreign.[75] Is it, therefore, exposure to the complexity of others, learning about and being better able to take the other's perspective, empathizing with others, starting to have some awareness of how they feel, that is the important thing? Contact may be one of the best ways for that to happen, but it is only a means to those ends. The studies already mentioned indicating that contact can take a number of direct and indirect forms suggest that may be the case. Nor is the increased learning confined to learning about the others. The *American Psychologist* review, mentioned above, described two broad psychological contributors to peace. One consisted of factors that increased empathy and understanding of the out-group. But the second, equally important, was made up of factors that increased the capacity of in-group members for *critical evaluation of their own group*.[76] Likewise, in *The Causes of War*, Levy and Thompson conclude that self-criticism is important for changing beliefs to reduce intergroup bias.[77] The conclusion the researchers drew from their findings of the Negev university students' study, described earlier, were also clear on this point. The course the students went on gave an opportunity for them to examine their own "cognitive and emotional responses to contradicting narratives . . . [and] for the exploration of [their own] involvement in collective narratives."[78]

No theory can survive the rigors of close scrutiny and scientific testing for long without being questioned or modified. Contact theory is no exception.[79] One of the questions that has increasingly been raised is, How good is contact theory in providing for the perspectives of both minority and majority status participants? Although research has shown contact, especially cross-group friendships, to be important for the improvement of intergroup attitudes among minority group members, contact effects have generally been shown to be of more influence among majority group members and weaker for members of minority groups.[80] Contact theory research has also come in for criticism for focusing only on positive contact, neglecting the possibility that intergroup contact may often be negative. Although less often studied, negative contact experiences have been shown to undermine positive intergroup attitudes by increasing the perception of threat from the out-group.[81] An alternative way in which the benign effects of contact may be undermined, noted in some studies, is that contact can sometimes lead to the assumption that those contacted are not typical of the group. Thus, stereotypes of the out-group as a whole group remain in place.[82]

We need, as always, to be reflective about the over-enthusiastic and uncritical application of our theories. Possible unintended effects of intergroup contact is another neglected topic according to some critics. One suspicion, for which there is now growing evidence, is that intergroup contact, although it may alter attitudes, may be ineffective in promoting real change.[83]

The suggestion, furthermore, is that contact might actually reduce motivation to engage in collective action for change. In fact, at least one reviewer has concluded that research has consistently demonstrated that contact, by creating false expectancies about intergroup equality, is indeed related to reduced motivation for social change. This has been referred to as contact's "sedative effects."[84] There may also be unintended effects for in-group attitudes. Contact may improve attitudes toward the out-group but at the same time distance individuals from their in-group, an effect which has been called "deprovincialization."[85] Among the many questions that have been posed about the contact hypothesis is another—a crucial one for this book—of how relevant the effects of contact are in settings of high conflict, where collective violence is threatening or has already broken out. It has been suggested that contact may actually become a negative and counterproductive experience in settings already characterized by high levels of hostility and conflict, particularly where conflict seems intractable.[86]

I have spent some time looking at ICT, even though much of what has been written about it is not about war and support for it specifically. But it *is* about prejudice toward members of a group other than one's own. We know how important competition with and perceived threat from other groups is for fostering war support (Chapter 2), how exclusive identities and chauvinism underpin it (Chapter 3), and how dehumanizing and other negative images and lack of nuance generally in thinking about another potential enemy group can strengthen war support (see earlier in this chapter). That makes ICT one of the most relevant ideas in psychology for trying to answer my question, Why support war? Though mostly not about war directly, the contact hypothesis *is* about potential conflict between groups, and it therefore has direct relevance to the prevention of escalation toward war. The way in which events, and attitudes, can escalate, appearing to spiral out of control, in the run-up to war and once war is engaged, has been a recurrent theme in the chapters of this book so far. To close this chapter, let us look at a psychological model which directly addresses it.

How Conflicts Escalate: The Spiral Conflict Model

Wars don't just suddenly happen out of the blue. Nor, once started, do they continue in the same way. One of the most appealing conceptions of war, from a psychologist's point of view, is the spiral conflict model. Most wars, "reflect a process that plays out over time. Conflicts of interest can lead to rivalry, the combination of both can lead to disputes, disputes lead to crises, and crises sometimes escalate to war."[87] Part of the appeal of the model lies in the fact that it derives from a more general understanding of how social interactions of various kinds can spiral out of control, becoming increasingly hostile and damaging. That can happen in all manner of social settings, domestic and work settings included.[88] This was spelled out by Morton Deutsch in the 1970s and 80s. In 1986 he applied his model to the then hot topic of how to prevent a crisis in relations between the superpowers developing into a malignant spiral process of hostile interaction, even to nuclear war.[89] Such a crisis should be seen, according to Deutsch and others since, not as a single event but as the consequence of a long series of exchanges. The key elements were thought to be an anarchic social situation, a win–lose or competitive orientation, inner conflicts (within each of the parties) that express themselves through external conflict, cognitive rigidity, misjudgments and misperceptions, unwitting commitments, self-fulfilling prophecies, vicious escalating spirals, and a gamesmanship orientation which turns the conflict away from issues of what in real life is being won or lost to an abstract conflict over images of power.[90] Most of those elements have already emerged in our exploration of war and war support more generally; for example the international situation characterized by anarchy, conflict, and power games (Chapter 1) and the cognitive simplifications and biases of various kinds that accompany the drift toward war (the present chapter), hardening as conflict spirals out of control.[91]

A chapter in a book, published in 2011 and dedicated to Deutsch's legacy, applied his thinking to trying to fathom the persistence of "intractable" armed conflicts.[92] At the time it was estimated that around 40% of current *intra*state armed conflicts had lasted for 10 years or more. Data on international conflicts in the years between 1945 and 1995 had included 18 cases of intractable *inter*state relationships that had produced 75 separate armed conflicts. These figures in themselves make the point that the outbreak of a war is very often, perhaps almost always, no isolated event and needs to be understood in the longer context of interstate or intergroup conflict, military and otherwise.

The key to understanding the maintenance of intractable conflict, it was argued, was the way in which each party to the conflict becomes stuck in a state of thinking about the other party which is then resistant to change. Once the process of becoming locked into a certain mindset becomes established, it is all too easy for it to escalate and harden due to the operation of positive feedback loops of various kinds. Events and information which might be interpreted as *dis*confirming the antagonistic views of the other party, and its motives, its claims, the history, and other aspects of the conflict (in other words, which could provide negative, conflict-*reducing*, feedback), are increasingly interpreted in such a way as to ossify the conflict-perpetuating mindset. New or discrepant or ambiguous information is discounted or reinterpreted to make it consistent with the group's prevailing view. The chapter used the metaphor of an "attractor," the state of a system that has evolved to the point where the range of mental states and actions now experienced has become so restricted that alternative views are threatening to the system and are resisted. Dysfunctional though such a system is for finding a way to reduce conflict, for those who are bent on seeing a conflict through, it can be argued that it provides a coherent view of the conflict and a clear path for action.

Specialists in conflict resolution more generally have continued to spell this out in more detail. Among the questions that most obviously resonate with war theory is how the parties to conflict reconcile cooperation and competition—those two fundamental axes of social interaction, central to the functioning of all social exchange and all human groups and institutions.[93] Cooperation implies that our activities bring mutual benefit; failure of cooperation implies the opposite, that our needs are incompatible. Competition can be constructive, as people discuss their differences with the aim of clarifying them in attempting to find a solution. Or it can be destructive, involving engaging, as conflict escalates, in a competition or struggle to determine who wins or loses, adopting rigid positions and negative or defensive attitudes and perceptions, after which it is hard to give up a grudge, to maintain any trust in one's adversary, or to disarm without feeling vulnerable.

The spiral conflict model can be seen as the psychological equivalent of the more general steps-to-war theory, popular among international relations experts and mostly applied to the behavior of war leaders or that of countries or organizations. It too speaks of a kind of vicious, cumulative cycle of mutually reinforcing steps that gathers momentum and makes drawing back from war increasingly difficult. Formation of alliances, counter-alliances, military buildups, existing rivalry, territorial disputes, all make escalation to war more likely.[94] The way in which the great powers slid seemingly inexorably into the horrors of the First World War is the example often given, as is that war of so much else. The "declaration" of war is obviously a highly significant step in the spiraling process. Once that threshold is crossed, troops are mobilized, and propaganda (the subject of Chapter 6) intensifies.

Of course, it is not only leaders who are caught up in it. The people are as well. Writing about the Irish War of Independence of 1919-21 and the Irish Civil War of 1922-23 which followed, war correspondent Fergal Keane provides vivid examples of spiraling conflict and its effects on ordinary people in his intriguing and moving book *Wounds: A Memoir of War and Love*, which we have already met in Chapter 2. It focuses on the area of north Kerry where he has family roots. He has much to say about the increasing support for the Irish Volunteers/Irish Republican Army (IRA) around 1918-20. For example, anybody trying to buy milk from the local privately owned creamery faced attack, and when local farmers formed their own vigilance committee and began patrols with the police, the IRA stepped in and disarmed them. In little time, all the farmers in the area had joined the IRA. As he puts it, "a collective view starts to take root and every event that conforms to that view is seized on and added to the weight of evidence, and this evidence becomes the justification for all that is to follow."[95]

The escalation of war preparation and engagement was a theme that emerged early in our exploration (in Chapter 1), and the escalation of support for war has been a recurrent theme since then. Any psychological understanding of why we support war must have a place for it.

Conclusions

In Figure 4.1 I have attempted to summarize the main ideas covered in the chapter.

Going to war can harden attitudes and has often been associated with extreme, dehumanizing images of the enemy. Characterizing the enemy as inferior in some way or other can be seen as a prime example of simplistic thinking, a popular concept in political and cognitive psychology. How we view ourselves and our own group, for example as heroic or as morally superior, is of just as much importance. Common simplifying mental processes, notably the fundamental attribution error, are particularly important in war as ways of interpreting events, including the enemy's and one's own side's actions, in ways that justify pursuing war. The simplified, lack of nuanced thinking about others and ourselves which support for war requires may even be said to amount to a mental departure from reality.

THINKING OF US AND THEM, ENEMIES AND HEROES   123

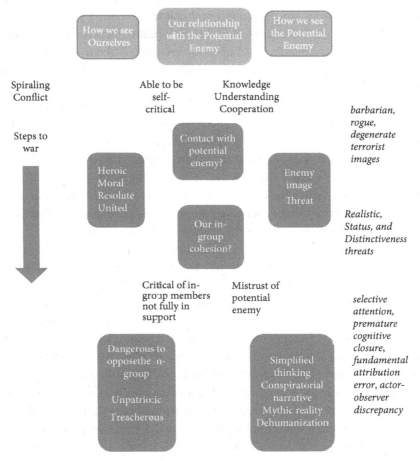

Figure 4.1 Thinking of us and them, enemies and heroes: a summary of the main ideas

Among psychological theories that might help us better understand how that can come about, two stand out as leading candidates. Social identity theory helps explain the importance for our personal and social esteem of identifying with an in-group, believed to be distinct and of good status. Support for the in-group and derogation of the out-group go hand in hand. The balance between the two varies, but both intensify as we progress further along the warpath. Interpersonal contact theory explains how lack of contact with a potential enemy group leads to poorer knowledge about it and an inability to sufficiently take the other group's perspective and understand its view of the world. The perception of threat from another group plays an important role in both the contact and social identity theories. Hostility toward an out-group contributes to in-group cohesion. Solidarity is crucial in the face of an enemy; it becomes unpopular, unpatriotic, even dangerous to oppose the prevailing in-group view.

The cognitive-social processes dealt with in the present chapter can be seen in the context of a dynamic process of perceptions, emotions, pronouncements, and unfolding events spiraling out of control, becoming increasingly hostile and damaging. The chapter concluded with a consideration of the spiral conflict model, which speaks of the kind of vicious, cumulative cycle of mutually reinforcing steps that gathers momentum and makes drawing back from war increasingly difficult. All the cognitive simplifications and distortions that have featured in this chapter harden as the drumbeats of war get louder.

At the halfway point in our exploration of war support, we can begin to see some recurring themes which may serve as core building blocks for a unified model of war support. There are a number of echoes in the material covered in this chapter of themes that emerged in earlier chapters. They include beliefs in a competitive and dangerous world in Chapter 2; the chauvinistic, exclusive adherence to a set of nationalistic or other values discussed in Chapter 3; and the theme of escalation and the steps-to-war theory, popular among experts in international relations, which featured in Chapter 1.

This chapter and the two that preceded it may have given a misleading impression that we are more in control of how we think about war than is really the case. We may be forgiven for thinking that war support is under the influence of our personalities, our values and beliefs, our attitudes toward our own country or group and toward others who are or might become enemies—all things that we should have at least some control over. The next two chapters challenge that perspective. Chapter 6 will consider the possibility that we are, in a sense, persuaded or coerced into supporting war through propaganda. Before that, in the next chapter, we turn to examine the idea that we are prepared, primed, for war support through our immersion in a militaristic culture. The topic is militarism.

5
Embedded Militarism and Readiness for War

> The raising, training and supplying of military forces is a given in almost all states, as if it were as natural as breathing ... result[ing] in an institutionalisation of the idea of war: it is built into the DNA of the society and the economy.
>
> A. C. Grayling, *War: An Enquiry*[1]

> Militarism ... includes a set of attitudes and social practices which regards war and the preparation of war as a normal and desirable social activity.
>
> Michael Mann, "The Roots and Contradictions of Modern Militarism," *New Left Review*[2]

Militarism, and the way we welcome it or at least take it for granted as an integral part of our societies and of our governments' responsibilities, will carry a heavy weight in my final understanding of war support. The fact that things pertaining to military action are so evident in our lives, so deeply embedded in culture and civic society, is the plainest sign of our permanent acceptance of preparedness for war. It is one of the central pillars on which support for war is built. We shall be exploring in this chapter various ways in which militarism is implanted in the lives of children and adults. The role that games, films, and other entertainments have played in the "military–industrial–entertainment complex" will be discussed, as will the militarization of education. We consider the controversial issue of whether war graves and war memorials serve the cause of war support.

The question of how important weapons themselves are as part of militarism and support for war is a complicated one. We are fascinated by, and show admiration for, weapons of war. We often justify them by referring to them in euphemistic terms as "defensive," "precise," even as ethical, humanitarian. We are accepting of a colossal legal arms trade, and we support those who govern us spending large sums on acquiring and maintaining military arsenals necessary for the defense of our group's values and security. The long-term trend of weapon development has been toward ever-more deadly weapons, enabling fighting at a greater distance. Drones are discussed as a controversial modern weapon, a notable example of the continuation of that trend, part of the West's modern preference for "risk-transfer war," limited to distant war zones, heavily reliant on air power, and minimizing casualties to Western troops.

A distinction is often drawn between "militarism" and "militarization," the latter focused more closely on valuing and supporting the nation's or group's military organization and personnel. The chapter will conclude by discussing the possibility of a growing "cultural gap" in some countries between the public and the military and whether militarism in general may be in decline. System justification theory would lead us to expect that support for a set of policies and associated beliefs and values as long and strongly supported as militarism and militarization would not fade easily.

What Is Militarism? Acceptance of Readiness for War

A good definition of *militarism* is "a set of beliefs, values, and assumptions that stress the use of force and threat of violence" as a way of settling conflicts between nations or groups which can be effective and appropriate in certain circumstances and should be prepared for.[3] It is the normalization of these beliefs—the way in which they have become widely accepted, ordinary and unremarkable, unquestioned, even difficult to discern—which many believe is the strongest factor making war more likely. As John Lindsay-Poland, Wage Peace Coordinator of the American Friends Service Committee in San Francisco, says, normalized militarism comes from above, from leaders and elites, but "also occurs from below, in ordinary people's attitudes toward the use of violence and expectations from their governments."[4]

A distinction is often drawn between militarism and militarization, although the two overlap to such an extent that the distinction is difficult to maintain. Militarization goes beyond a belief in the value of force or threat of force to solve political problems by supporting the planning, organizing, arming, and training necessary for threatening or engaging in violent conflict.

It is support for one's country's or organization's military strength and expenditure and attraction to military service.[5] A 2018 study carried out among Turkish university students is of interest here because it broke down the concept of militarization into component parts.[6] It identified five elements: support for the existence of the military, valuing the military, less criticism of the military system, accepting compulsory military service, and supporting an active political role for the military. Each of the five elements was correlated with right-wing political views, military affiliation, and stronger and exclusive Turkish identity, reflecting similar such correlations found in studies carried out with students in the United States and in South Korea.[7]

Although militarism and militarization usually go together, they are not the same. One is a general set of values and beliefs about the importance of threat and force, the other a more specific set of attitudes favoring support for things military. I shall mostly use the general term "militarism," understanding it to embrace "militarization," using the latter term only when referring specifically to support for the military. As we shall see, there are occasions when the distinction is important; for example when debating later the significance of war memorials or when considering present-day attitudes to serving in the military.

Some degree of support for militarism and militarization is widely shared in countries around the world, and democracies are no exception. It has been argued, in an article in the *Online Journal of Peace and Conflict Resolution*, that the inter-democratic peace thesis, that democracies do not fight each other (see Chapter 1), overlooks the continual replenishment of state militarization in which citizens of democratic states are "personally implicated in an anarchic regime of vast international proportions through their loyal and responsible support of their state's independence and security requirements."[8] At the same time citizens are not fully aware of their role—they are "cognitively disarmed" as the article puts it—because "their present political cultures provide only a vague and limited understanding of the salient forces and the moral and substantive implications of their roles in generating these forces."[9] As A. C. Grayling puts it,

> Military personnel are respected, honoured, applauded ... the whole matter of military forces, the money for them, the relationship between the arms industry and the economy at large, the encouragement of positive attitudes to those whose business is war, result in an institutionalisation of the idea of war.[10]

Nor have psychologists failed to recognize the role of militarism and militarization. A number of them have emphasized the importance of preparing for war during times of peace, as did William James, often described as the first peace psychologist, who opined that "preparation for war by nations is the real war, permanent, unceasing."[11] "Wars are not accidents. They are products of a social order that plans for them and then accepts this planning as natural," say the authors of *The Hidden Structure of Violence*. They point to the mythic status afforded a nation's troops, a favoring of war almost amounting to an addiction, aided by militaristic pageantry and a collusive media.[12]

The Role of Games, Films, and Other Entertainments in Supporting the Militarization of Culture and Civic Society

If militarism is culturally embedded, if we are scarcely aware of how we have been conditioned to accept it, how does that happen? How does support for war preparation come to permeate a whole culture and affect us all? Is it the case, as many have argued, that indoctrination in militarism starts in childhood?

George Mosse's book *Fallen Soldiers: Reshaping the Memory of the World Wars*, published in 1990, tells us that during the First World War the kinds of war toys marketed for children included armored vehicles, mines, and camouflage. But it was tin soldiers, mass produced since the second half of the eighteenth century, that were the most popular. Some thought them indispensable for educating young people in warfare. For example, instructions for German boys told them how to play with tin soldiers in a proper warlike manner. Indeed, war and games were not so different; for example in England boys were taught that fighting for the empire was much the same as playing for one's school. The war as an adventure story had great appeal, and war games were particularly interesting to boys: "they combined the joy of playing with a militant spirit."[13]

Joanna Bourke takes up the theme in her 2014 book *Wounding the World*, which provides us with much useful detail on the subject. By the 1980s, she tells us, 10% of toys for sale in the United States were war toys, and in 1986 19 million toy guns were sold there, rising to 33 million in 1997. Technological advances were enabling games to become much more realistic and less lighthearted than they had been: *Brother in Arms: Road to Hill 30* (2005) and

Battlefield Vietnam (2004), for example, required choice of weapons, choice of correct ammunition, and precision to be shown and appropriate tactics to be employed. In *America's Army*, she tells us, novice players go through "basic training" in "barracks." Replicas were carefully created of the US Army post at Fort Benning. There was now an emphasis on accuracy; for example the sounds made when weapons were fired tried to mimic reality. Recent games had included short documentaries about real-life happenings, interviews with veterans, and online visits to battle sites. Game production teams were consulting military experts, and players could expect to be consuming large amounts of technical information about weapons and ballistics.[14]

The increasingly close relationship between the entertainment industry and the military which Bourke describes took a further step forward in 1999 when a $45 million partnership was established between the University of Southern California and the US Army to establish the Institute for Creative Technologies (ICT). This brought together military specialists, computer and social scientists, writers, artists, and cinematographers, aiming to improve military modeling and simulations but also to give the armed services a more modern face. In 2011, ICT estimated that more than 75,000 soldiers had been trained using its technologies. She notes that the military has good evidence that this greatly improves their armed personnel's "lethal effectiveness." This is all part of what she calls "the snowballing militarization of American life."[15]

In September 2004 ICT released the first military training application for a commercial game console: "*Full Spectrum Warrior* was one of many games that served a dual function as training programme for the military and entertainment for a wider (primarily male) public."[16] It was set in a fictional place in the Middle East and based on the "war on terror." *America's Army*, which took three years to produce and initially cost $7.5 million, was designed to help boost flagging recruitment to the armed forces, although military spokespersons frequently claimed it was not designed for that purpose. It was launched on Independence Day 2002, rated T (suitable for teenagers), and won Guinness World Records for its popularity, having been downloaded more than 42 million times. It was reckoned to be saving the US Army between $700 million and $4 billion a year in recruitment costs.[17] In some cases, games appeared to be teaching a particularly sinister form of war; for example, *Conflict: Desert Storm* (2002) announced on its cover "No Diplomats. No Negotiations. No Surrender." Such games also reinforce the masculinization of conflict, Bourke argued: two-thirds of US boys between

12 and 17 were playing first-person shooters competitively but only 17% of girls.[18]

They were also in effect teaching real soldiers how to make war more game-like, making their combat experiences resemble those in the games and vice versa. Bourke cites several examples. One, a 20-year-old serving in Iraq, interviewed for the *Washington Post*, recalled the first time he shot someone: "You just try to block it out . . . see what you need to do, fire what you need to fire. Think to yourself, This is a game, *just do it, just do it*."[19] He and his mates would often play war games until the early hours of the morning and then go on patrol. A similar effect was observed by men who piloted or navigated drones. As one said, it was "a surreal experience. Almost like playing the computer game *Civilisation*, in which you direct units and armies in battle."[20]

Not that war gaming has always been accepted without controversy.[21] In the United Kingdom, Waddington's game *Bombshell*, which involved defusing bombs in Northern Ireland, Ireland, and mainland Britain (after four injuries, you were "out"), so appalled families of bomb disposal experts killed by Irish Republican Army bombs that the game had to be withdrawn. The gaming company Konami discovered the same opposition when they planned to release *Six Days in Fallujah*, only to meet with resistance from members of Military Families Speak Out and Stop the War Coalition. Most controversial were atomic bomb games such as *Atomic Bomb Dexterity Puzzle* produced around 1947 in the United States in which a box was shaken so that two bomb-shaped missiles might come to rest beside cities labeled Hiroshima and Nagasaki on a map of Japan. Bourke reminds us of the protests, notably by feminists between the 1960s and 1980s, which gave rise to a large amount of research exploring the relationship between war games, aggression, and testosterone in young males; periodic bonfires of toy guns and war books; and zero tolerance for such games in many schools and creches. She acknowledges that the research linking specific acts of violence and playing war games is patchy and mixed. But she argues, convincingly in my view, that attempting to find such a link is misguided since it misses the bigger picture, the role games play in reinforcing a culture of militarism and militarization.

Bourke also tells us how the armed forces have used cinema very effectively.[22] Examples have been the *Why We Fight* series of seven films produced during the Second World War, the *Why Vietnam?* film in 1965, *The Unique War* (1966), and *Vietnamese Village Reborn* (1967), which spread a strong anti-communist message and helped US citizens see the war as one of liberation and freedom. But she thinks the link between cinema and the armed forces is much more subtle than that obvious propaganda. *The Green Berets* (1968) benefited from the loan of military airplanes, helicopters, weapons, and troops; the *Transformer* series (2007, 2009, 2011) required the help of military personnel and airbases; and *Behind Enemy Lines* (2001) involved the US Navy loaning the filmmakers a vast array of equipment including a supercarrier, fighter planes, and helicopters, as well as personnel. In return the Navy was allowed to make significant changes to the script, to use clips in a recruitment campaign, and to set up recruiting stations in the lobbies of movie theaters. US Army veteran and diplomatic historian Andrew Bacevich comments that recovery of attitudes toward the armed services after the low point of Vietnam was nowhere seen more clearly than in Hollywood in the Reagan era—as examples he cites *An Officer and a Gentleman*, the *Rambo* series, and *Top Gun*—as well as in popular fiction of that era.[23] Bourke uses J. Der Derian's expression, the "military–industrial–entertainment complex." In summary, she concludes, "Entertainment has become a way of creating militarized citizens.... We are all turned into citizen-soldiers."[24] William Ehrhart, writing in 1980[25] about serving as a Marine in Vietnam, is one who has spoken about being fully conversant with all things military before his basic training because he had been immersed in war games, films, and literature since childhood.

A. C. Grayling and Anthony Stevens join those like George Mosse and Joanna Bourke in believing that the whole entertainment industry plays a role in supporting war. Films, novels, TV programs all give an unrealistic, "cosmeticized" version of war, says Grayling, not showing the blood and guts. Even films showing the horrors "are avidly watched and enjoyed because there is romance even in the horror and danger, and both are vicariously enjoyed."[26] Stevens notes how war movies continued to be popular throughout the second half of the twentieth century. And when it comes to war games, he remembers that toward the end of the Cold War, a popular game involving mock battles was *Splatball*, otherwise known as *The National Survival Game*, which became increasingly realistic with the introduction of a variety of military elements, including an automatic gun, the SMG-60, that fired 600 paint-ball rounds a minute.[27]

But Stevens sees war games' contribution to preparedness for war in the wider context of war and sport. They are both, he says, "different variations on the same archetypal theme—the theme of aggressive conflict between bonded, organized groups of men.... Soldiers love sport, and armies use team games as a training for group morale in combat. Generals are notoriously prone to using sporting metaphors."[28] The war–sport connection persists. The largest US defense contractors spend large amounts on TV advertising with a concentration on public affairs programs, and most insidious, he thinks, is the effort the military exerts to connect militarism with love of sport in the United States. F-35 flybys at football games and troops running into stadiums waving flags before sporting fixtures are examples he gives. Between 2012 and 2015 the US Department of Defense (DOD) supported professional sports teams to the tune of $58 million.[29]

Militarization of Education

There is, however, a more direct route whereby the education of children and young people is militarized. In Britain, from the late nineteenth century onward, military drill in schools was promoted by a wide range of politicians, military leaders, doctors, and writers, on the grounds of both public health and military preparedness.[30] Although drill may be less popular than it once was, the militarization of education continues. Reports produced by ForcesWatch, such as *The New Tide of Militarisation*, refer to visits to schools and colleges by armed forces, numbering in the thousands each year; as well as new initiatives such as university technical colleges, each sponsored by a university and employers, specializing in practical, employment-focused subjects for 14- to 19-year-olds. In 2017 half of such colleges were sponsored or partnered by part of the armed forces and/or an arms company.[31] There are reports of the international arms company BAE Systems offering postgraduate apprenticeships and a master's program and collaboration on drone development at British universities.[32] At secondary school level, the first "military academy" in Britain opened only a few years ago.[33]

Perhaps even more relevant to the issue of militarization, and more troubling to some, is what ForcesWatch describes as an increasing emphasis on "military ethos" in schools. As a statement from the Department of Education in 2012 said, "We associate the military with many positive values, loyalty, resilience, courage and teamwork to name but a few. We recognise that these core values, together adding up to a 'military ethos,' can have a positive impact on pupils." There are signs of a growing theme of the military helping to develop character and solve social problems, it claims. ForcesWatch sees it differently. It suggests that this apparently benign and subtle growing militarism is dangerously misleading. It thinks it discourages critical thinking, dissent, and independence; is not balanced with peace education; encourages uncritical support for military institutions and action; reduces space for alternatives to military approaches to conflict; does not question whether military values including hierarchy, obedience, chain of command, and conformity are good ones; and offers a partial, sanitized view of military careers and activities.[34]

There is no shortage of writers on the military and war who believe that obedience to authority and group cohesion are central to the military ethos. Norman Dixon argued that "bull"—obsessive attention to details of military dress and turnout—is insisted on because it is hostile to diversity: "Militarism is dedicated to the ironing out of differences," as he put it.[35] Anthony Stevens is particularly forthright on the subject of the military ethos: it is "designed to mobilize group loyalty, self-discipline, aggression, and masculinity.... An essential function of drill is to numb critical intelligence and independent thought in order to replace it with instinctive obedience."[36]

Veterans frequently agree about the importance of obedience. One is Griffin, ex-SAS, who refused to return to combat in Iraq. He asks how war is enabled, answering that soldiers are not born but learn as children, from multiple sources including medals, war films, respect shown at the Cenotaph, and in the cadets, and later psychological indoctrination during military training, where the military ethos inculcates obedience without question, enforced by punishment if necessary, loyalty to the gang versus others—especially versus civilians but also versus those in other branches of the services—and removing the natural barrier to kill.[37]

Drill in the military, and military parades more generally, are thought by some to constitute powerful examples of social "synchrony," of multiple bodies moving in unison—rallies of all sorts and displays of strength before sporting events are others. They function, it is believed, to bond participants together, while at the same time promoting obedience and sending a powerful signal to others about in-group cohesion and power.[38]

It is the extended influence of the military ethos in the society from which military personnel are drawn, and especially its extension into education of the young, that is the point here. From the United States, John Lindsay-Poland, in his chapter entitled "The Normalization of Militarism and Propensity for War," writes,

> Voluntary service . . . requires that the military proactively reach into the civilian population for its members, and it seeks young people. It thus has an incentive to support the militarization of the sites of youth culture, especially schools, popular culture, sporting events, and social media.

He notes, as examples, how unremarkable it is in the United States for military recruiters and live-fire rifle ranges to be present in junior high schools.[39] In the same volume, Kathy Barker, in her chapter "The Quiet Military Buyout of Academia,"[40] documents how universities and colleges required loyalty oaths from faculty members during the Cold War and how the Reserve Officers' Training Corps (ROTC), familiar on campuses until student protests in the 1960s caused many units to be closed, were now returning: in 2012 there were 70,000 ROTC cadets on 300 campuses. Among the claims of ForcesWatch[41] is the assertion that military recruitment in the United Kingdom is targeted at disadvantaged schools and pupils. There have been charges that US military recruitment also draws disproportionately from the disadvantaged, for example, from poorer counties in the United States during the Korean War and from those with psychological problems for service in Iraq.[42]

The special issue of the recruitment of child soldiers continues to be important in various parts of the world. A 2016 Medact report drew attention to under-age recruitment to the armed forces in the United Kingdom: 22 of every 100 UK army recruits were under 18, and, although they were not deployed on frontline activity at that age, they were more vulnerable to being casualties later—for example, being twice as likely to have been killed or injured in Afghanistan than those recruited at an older age.[43]

Arguably, militarism and militarization are yet more strongly stimulated in educational establishments by universities' and colleges' enthusiastic acceptance of military financial support for research—amounting, for example, to about $1.75 billion received from the US Department of Defense (DOD) in 2016, which funds things like weapons research, intelligence, data collection and analysis, and cybersecurity. The DOD particularly funds engineering research but also physical sciences, life sciences, and social sciences, with a focus on anthropology and psychology. Since the 2008 recession, US universities are increasingly dependent on federal funds. A decline in tenured positions, with the academic freedom that brings, may mean academics feel less able to speak up about growing militarism. Indeed, Kathy Barker, from the University of Washington, says many academics are now required to have top secret security clearances and are not free to discuss their work. Furthermore, she detects a trend toward campus leaders having backgrounds related to the military or security—former Central Intelligence Agency director Robert Gates is one of several examples she gives.[44]

Professional associations have occasionally stepped in to debate the ethics of specific military actions, but, she complains, militarism itself is seldom questioned. Barker cites, as exceptions, the American Psychological Association's bar on its members from participating in national security interrogations following the revelation, in the 2015 Hoffman report,[45] that its leaders had colluded in torture programs in Guantánamo and elsewhere. The American Anthropological Association and the American Public Health Association had made similarly strong statements about the ethics of embedding social scientists with combat troops and about the stand that health practitioners and academics might take against war as a public health and human rights issue. Individuals, computer scientist Benjamin Kuipers for example, have occasionally made powerful statements too. But, regrettably, "Academics and administrators are paid for their silence about militarism with research money, and it is unusual that administrative or academic participants in military funding will speak against war."[46]

War Memorials: Do They Support War or Peace?

The infusion of militarism in our cultures is by no means limited to education of the young. Throughout our lives we are surrounded by reminders of the prominent position held in our societies by things related to war. Many have noted the prominence of wars in the telling of history in different countries around the world and over the centuries, the much greater weight given to war than to peace in history texts, and the important part that military history has played in militarizing minds.[47] The modern military–entertainment complex, discussed earlier, is really just the latest illustration of something that has a very long history. In his book *Munitions of the Mind*, on the subject of propaganda (for more on this, see Chapter 6), Philip Taylor provides numerous examples of the use of art, images, poetry, and omens in support of militarism and war in the ancient world. An early example was the public use of heroic military hymns and epic poems by Assyrian kings in the 1200s BC to celebrate wars and glorify a king's achievements, and drama, poetry, and song were put to similar purpose in Rome.[48]

Statues and spectacular public monuments, such as the Egyptian pyramids, the Acropolis in Athens, and Rome's triumphal arches and columns, have been used down the centuries to demonstrate military power and victory.[49] War graves and war memorials are monuments that have played a special role in war history, and that role has been much written about, studied, and been the subject of controversy. Nowhere is this better described than in George Mosse's book:

> Those concerned with the image and the continuing appeal of the nation worked at constructing a myth which would draw the sting from death in war and emphasize the meaningfulness of the fighting and sacrifice.... The aim was to make an inherently unpalatable past acceptable, important not just for the purpose of consolation but above all for the justification of the nation in whose name the war had been fought.... The reality of the war experience came to be transformed into what one might call the Myth of the War Experience, which looked back upon the war as a meaningful and even sacred event.[50]

The military cemetery, he argued, played a special role as a symbol in the Myth of the War Experience, helping to sanitize, dramatize, and romanticize war. Earlier war memorials to generals, kings and princes, usually on horseback and in battle dress, already existed. Modern war memorials no longer focused so much on individual generals—although we still had those, as a walk from Trafalgar Square and down Whitehall in London testifies—but now on figures symbolic of the nation and the sacrifice of all of its men. The Tomb of the Unknown Soldier is one such. The return and burial of the Unknown Soldier, accompanied by all the symbolism and mythology of military cemeteries, was pioneered by England and France. A single event, honoring all "the fallen," became the focus of national ceremonies including Armistice Day. In the United Kingdom, the Cenotaph (a Greek word meaning an empty tomb), unveiled as a permanent monument in 1920, is the national war remembrance site. In France, the Arc de Triomphe, built by Napoleon, was the first to honor the army as a whole rather than just its leaders.[51] US sociologist Richard Lachmann notes the "increasingly strenuous . . . efforts to find and recover the bodies of the dead . . . the ever more elaborate and expensive efforts to identify the remains of US troops from past wars, especially in Vietnam" and the importance afforded to comfort and "closure" for families. At the same time, he captures the mixed message about war itself which memorials convey. Like George Mosse, he also comments on how memorials have changed, now more individual and personal, but in the process how they honor the war, "convey[ing] the message that the most, indeed the only, significant fact about each soldier's life worthy of memory was their service and sacrifice in war."[52]

An intriguing modern type of memorial "ceremony," which was popular in the United States in the late 2000s and early 2010s, was the military "reunion" video relayed on YouTube or on cable TV. A typical video would show a returning soldier surprising a family member, usually a spouse or child, at a public event.[53] One analysis, noting how comments on the videos repeated such phrases as "while defending their country" or "serving their country," suggested that their impact was to reinforce the importance of the sacrifices these soldiers and their families make. Their popularity lay in the powerful combining of the military—the only institution besides "small businesses" that still enjoys overwhelming trust in the United States according to surveys—and the home, the one setting where most people feel most in control and secure.[54]

Although it may be considered bad form to voice dissent at the time such events are taking place, they are not uncontroversial. In one of her BBC Reith Lectures, historian Margaret Macmillan reminded listeners that there had been talk in the 1980s of dropping war Remembrance Day celebrations in the United Kingdom. Since then it had become very evident to her that support for war remembrance, far from declining, had been restored and heightened.[55] This raises the question of what purpose is served by the persistence of war commemorations. Do they serve, as popularly espoused, a "preventative" function, decreasing support for war by evoking regret, or an "inspirational" function, by evoking pride and gratitude for soldiers' actions and promoting a willingness to face future suffering for the nation or group when needed? In a nutshell, the question is whether such ceremonies, with their reminders of past sacrifices, serve the cause of peace, as proponents argue, or of militarism. Do they make support for war in the future less or more likely? In the United Kingdom this is symbolized in the red and white poppies. In the days running up to November 11th, the red poppy is on sale widely, and public figures making an appearance are expected to be wearing one—it appears to be de rigeur for anyone appearing on television, for example. The peace poppy, the white one, is scarcely in evidence; but some have taken to wearing both the red, in respect for those who have made war sacrifices, and the white, in recognition that the red variety alone is at best ambivalent in its pro-peace stance.

A study of US residents, reported in 2019, is claimed by its authors to be the first empirical test of whether war remembrance celebrations are more war- or peace-promoting.[56] The study had two parts, one correlational, the second experimental. The first looked for correlations if there were correlations between the degree of participation in the range of separate activities available to take part in on US Memorial Day (of which there were no less than 15 listed) and a number of relevant felt emotions and attitudes. The same set of emotion and attitude questions was used in the experimental part of the study. Participants were randomly assigned to watching one of a number of different 4-minute videos, either a typical Memorial Day video commemorating fallen soldiers or a comparison military display video highlighting US military power or a control condition with no video. Both types of video, we are told, contained military and patriotic imagery accompanied by stirring music, but only the Memorial Day video drew attention to the cost of war in terms of human lives and suffering.

One group of questions asked about feelings of regret over the country's involvement in past and possible future wars (e.g., "I feel bad that the US has been involved in wars in the past": *strongly disagree* to *strongly agree*). Participants were also asked how much "the loss of life suffered by the US during war" aroused in them each of 11 emotions, grouped into positive (pride, admiration, gratitude) and negative (anger, disgust, shame, guilt, anxiety) scales. The final questions were about whether they valued and supported war on behalf of the country (11 items, e.g., "Sometimes my country needs to go to war to make wrongs right": *strongly disagree* to *strongly agree*).

A positive relationship was found between either participating in Memorial Day activities or watching a Memorial Day video and experiencing positive emotions toward the sacrifices made by soldiers, as well as perceiving war to have value. Only in the experimental part of the work was there some support for an increase in feelings of regret for war, but this was inconsistent and limited compared to the positive, pro-war effects. The study's authors concluded they had shown "that although war commemorations inconsistently induce regret for the country's actions, they consistently elicit emotions such as pride and admiration in response to the costly sacrifice of soldiers." Needless to say, no single study like that, suggestive though it might seem, can be at all conclusive. I would agree with Joanna Burke and others, though, that it is the bigger picture that matters here, the way in which a society's life is imbued with so many reminders of war and the military, few of them explicitly and unambiguously anti-war and pro-peace. Another source of militaristic imagery which surrounds us is that of military weapons, a topic to which we must now turn.

Weapons and Their Fascination

Opinions differ markedly on the question of the degree to which the very weapons that are used in fighting are to blame for the costs of war, and indeed for promoting war in the first place. Psychologists Marc Pilisuk and Jennifer Rowntree, at one end of the argument, are clear that the destructiveness caused by war, and indeed the possibility of making war at all, are dependent on weapons being available.[57] Stephen Pinker as usual has a contrary view and puts it rather forcefully: neither armaments nor disarming are important, however much one might like to think they are: "Writers who are engrossed by violence and those who are repelled by it have one thing in common: they are fixated on weaponry." Nor, he concludes, is there any support for the "equally weaponcentric" belief that the invention over time of more and more destructive weapons, such as dynamite, poison gas, or nuclear bombs, would render war unthinkable. He draws an interesting analogy with gun control: "guns don't kill people; people kill people." To which he hurriedly adds, in parentheses, "which is not to endorse the arguments for or against gun control."[58]

Every idea that I started out with in my quest to understand support for war has turned out, on investigation, to be more complicated than I had first thought. My initial bias was certainly toward believing that weapons were very important. One of the observations that got me starting to think, years ago, about war support was the sheer weight of books on weaponry to be found in most bookshops and libraries. Surely, if there is so much interest in weapons of war, that must have something to do with why we continue to support war, so I thought. I continue to hold to that view, although now I recognize that the link is, as I might have predicted, not a simple one.

It is difficult to refute the observation that many people are attracted to and fascinated by weapons of war. Or to deny that some weapons themselves have a special, revered, place in people's minds. Throughout my lifetime, the spitfire and hurricane fighter aircraft have been associated with the Battle of Britain and with Winston Churchill's memorable "never has so much been owed by so many to so few." It is not only the airmen who are still held as heroes of the nation and of the fight against fascism but the aircraft themselves. To this day they appear regularly on British television news as honored icons of national pride, often accompanied by the words of a fighter pilot's descendant and the playing of gentle, romantic music. Fighter aircraft may be special because of the ecstatic image of aerial combat, the "dogfight" duels in the sky, the "ace," death-defying fighter pilots among the chief heroes of the world wars in most of the countries involved, including Germany, France, England, the United States, Russia, and Japan.[59] But the adulation of war weapons extends beyond fighter aircraft. Bomber aircraft share in the glory. The Second World War film *The Dam Busters*, with its accompanying arousing music, is still popular. The more recent first Gulf War was accompanied in the media by sentimentalized images of moonlit bombers.[60] One study conducted shortly after that war found that, while those with pro-war attitudes were more likely to recall images about the technical aspects of war such as the dropping of bombs and the firing of cruise missiles, anti-war respondents more often recalled images of destruction and suffering.[61]

In her book, Joanna Bourke provides ample evidence of what she refers to as our "propensity to aestheticise deadly weapons" as objects of beauty, even charm. When air bombardment of cities was introduced, its proponents described it as both terrible and awe-inspiring. Lord Thomson's encomium of 1925, "the flower of the male youth in each contending state, manipulating marvellous machines, the latest products of invention in the conquest of the air," was an example. Weapons continue to be given genial names including ones from nature such as the Falcon, Hummingbird Warrior, Panda, and Walrus. Even the cluster bombs that caused appalling wounds in Vietnam had tasty nicknames including "pineapples" and "guavas." The relative merits of different armaments are keenly discussed, with weapons even given names with comforting or peaceful connotations. Examples would be the atom bomb referred to as Oppenheimer's "baby," the Cult .45-caliber six-shooter known as the Peacemaker, the MX missile dubbed "The Peacekeeper" by President Reagan, and the twenty-first-century missile called Special K, which blasted out razor-sharp shrapnel to "slice and dice anyone within a 20-foot radius."[62]

Whether weapons and their use are glorified in that way or alternatively spoken of in dry, technical, disembodied military language, the reality that they are designed to kill and maim living people is disguised.[63] This continued glorification of the weapons of war Bourke sees as part of something bigger; "the over-blown, breathless, vivid and carnivalesque language associated with violence." Repeatedly British and US men in combat during the two world wars described their experiences of aggressive acts in sporting terms, she claims, pitting skill against that of an opponent, with hunting or poaching analogies being dominating ones. Popular journals about weapons and war "also waxed lyrical over the thrill of bloodshed." She points to the prominent use of euphemism when weapons are talked about. Examples she gives include emphasizing the defensive rather than offensive functions of armed forces (the UK government in 1963 replaced the War Office with the Ministry of Defence); forces personnel recently becoming "warfighters" or "warriors"; ballistics experts using phrases such as "delivery may be achieved," as though they might be referring to flowers; and fusion bombs referred to as "clean bombs," even though they are several hundred times more powerful than the Hiroshima fission bomb. Mathematical abstraction is used: for example, standardized casualty and killing rates; a weapons designer is not a murderer but scientist and engineer, statistician, metallurgist, seeking neat and elegant solutions to problems. A sleight of hand presents weapons research as lifesaving, and service personnel as peacekeepers, even Hiroshima and Nagasaki as saving thousands of lives. The motto of US Strategic Air Command, she reminds us, is "Peace Is Our Profession."[64]

Nor can there be much doubting the development, over the centuries, of ever-more deadly weapons Many writers on war have summarized that process. A. C. Grayling picks out as especially significant the chariot and the composite bow, the knight on horse, both heavily armored, the appearance of artillery and hand-held firearms, and heavily armed warships which achieved supremacy at the time of the Anglo–Dutch wars in the age of Pepys and "played a key role in all subsequent wars until the Boer War of 1899–1902."[65]

It is not difficult to see what has been the long-term trend, namely "to improve the technology of fighting at a distance."[66] The bow and sling dramatically increased range and accuracy compared to the javelin and "permitted a man to kill from a concealed position."[67] Man-to-man combat had been seen as honorable in the medieval age of chivalry; distance weapons such as the crossbow were deprecated as cowardly.[68] That was the real success of artillery. By the nineteenth century artillery could be fired at up to a mile away from those being killed. By World War I, naval guns and onshore siege guns had ranges up to 10 miles. Air power can be seen as "the epitome of long-distance fighting."[69] The same trend continues into the present time with moves toward ever more high-tech weapon systems: surveillance by aircraft, satellites, or drones, operating thousands of kilometers from the battlefield; infrared sensors; laser targeting; computer analysis of photos and video feed; and advances in communication networks and human–machine coordination.[70] Andrew Bacevich sees this technological advance in how war can be waged—if "advance" is the appropriate word—as being a factor in restoring the image of the military in the eyes of US citizens after the low point of the Vietnam War:

> A new image of war had emerged . . . of high-tech warfare, waged by highly skilled professionals equipped with "smart" weapons . . . low-risk, low-cost . . . [characterized by] speed, control, and choice. Information empowered . . . swiftness, stealth, agility, and precision would characterize the operations of modern armies. . . . This new aesthetic has contributed, in turn, to an appreciable boost in the status of military institutions and soldiers themselves.[71]

The military use of the drone, a type of unmanned aerial vehicle (UAV), is a part of this technological advance which has attracted much attention. Grayling describes drones, able to stay aloft for long periods and hard to detect, as "chillingly effective weapons . . . distancing the killer from the victim at a sanitary remove."[72] He points out that UAVs actually have a long history, as flying bombs in the world wars, as decoys and for surveillance in the Yom Kippur war of 1973, and for over 3,000 reconnaissance missions in Vietnam, becoming central to US operations in the Middle East and Afghanistan after 2001.

In his book *Drone Theory*, Grégoire Chamayou makes the case that the rapid expansion of the use of drones in the twenty-first century has been accompanied by a "theoretical offensive" supporting their justification.[73] The latter includes the declaration that drones are humanitarian, indeed among the most ethical of weapons, "a low-cost, low-risk alternative to big wars."[74] His own view is very different. War, as he sees it, has become as a consequence less like a duel and more like a manhunt, as names given to drones testify. Predator (bird of prey) and Reaper (angel of death) drones operational in 2005 and 2007, respectively, figured in the US drone campaign started under George W. Bush and rapidly increased under Obama. The New

America Foundation estimated that by February 2013 more than 350 drone strikes had claimed between 2,000 and 3,250 lives, civilians including women and children among them. They are a significant part of the globalization of violence in which sovereignty of nations is not respected, Chamayou argues. Their use against terrorism involves a change in the way the enemy is understood, no longer as combatants fighting on behalf of a state but rather as dangerous individuals, hence it "individualizes the problem and reduces its objectives to neutralizing, on a case-by-case basis, as many suspects as possible."[75] The morality of drone warfare is something we take up again in Chapter 7 when considering just war theory.

We need to remind ourselves at this point that many of the most recent wars either have not involved the "advanced militaries" at all or have been non-reciprocal wars between one such country and an enemy whose weapons are not "advanced." In fact the large majority of recent war deaths have been caused by "small arms," the colossal sales of which are relatively unregulated.[76] There were almost 640 million small arms in use or in stockpiles around the world according to the Small Arms Survey in 2006.[77] Mary Kaldor points to the use of light weapons in "new wars"—rifles, machine guns, hand grenades, and, at the upper end, low-caliber artillery and short-range rockets—left over from the Cold War and other wars. They can be used by the relatively unskilled and by children. The huge supply of arms to Afghan guerrilla groups by the United States in the 1980s, which "transformed itself into networks of arms and drug trade covering Afghanistan, Pakistan, Kashmir and Tadjikistan," is an example. The hundreds of thousands of cheap Kalashnikovs which became available in Kosovo after the collapse of the Albanian state is another. The new wars could be seen as "a form of military waste-disposal—a way of using up unwanted surplus arms generated by the Cold War, the biggest military build-up in history." Disarmament had become a never-ending task, owing to the widespread availability of surplus weapons.[78]

The Huge and Shadowy World of Arms Dealing

A big part of the militaristic system we accept and approve is arms sales. Weapons have long been big business. At the time of World War I, it was suggested that capitalist economies might need war to justify high military spending in order to maintain demand and keep unemployment low, and in the 1920s many believed armaments manufacturers had had too much influence on the US decision to enter the war—the "merchants of death" hypothesis.[79] Skeptics believe that military contractors "always lobby for the development of super-expensive, technologically innovative weapons on which they realize the highest profit margins and the longest and largest contracts."[80] According to estimates made by the much respected Stockholm International Peace Research Institute, in 2021 more than $2 trillion was spent on military worldwide. The US share of global military expenditures was a staggering 38%, China second at 14%, followed by India 3.6%, the United Kingdom 3.3%, and Russia 3.1%, with France, Germany, Saudi Arabia, Japan, and South Korea each contributing between 2.5% and 3% of the total.[81]

The biggest spender, the United States, is therefore spending about $800 billion annually on the military (although less than half of that is likely to be spent on military equipment plus research and development[82]). Many US commentators have remarked critically on the colossal commitment their country is making to entrenching militarism, both nationally and globally. Miriam Pemberton, for one, in her chapter "The War Profiteers," points out that, instead of the expected returning of industry to peaceful production after the Second World War, the Cold War provided the rationale for maintaining a "permanent war economy . . . [which] remains fully operational today." In the United States, she says, "the military economy has a foothold in every state . . . has little to do with industrial efficiency and much to do with political protection."[83] She provides examples of poor efficiency, waste, over-charging by contractors, and multiple levels of subcontracting, making it difficult to know how many private military contracts there are. But the number, she is sure, is huge, the contribution to political campaigns massive, and the revolving door of retired military officers then working for defense contractors or consultants much in evidence. The involvement of personnel working for private contractors has ballooned she tells us: in World War II there was one for every seven soldiers; by 2006 in Iraq there were more private contractor employees than there were soldiers. Mark Pilisuk and Jennifer Rowntree highlighted the global role of the United States as the dominant supplier of arms internationally, the concentration of weapon sales and distribution on developing countries, and the worldwide spread of US military bases, some long established, others relatively new. With the addition of new mini-bases, "lily pads," small, secretive, and inaccessible, they say, "the U.S. military easily maintains the largest collection of foreign bases in world history: more than 1,000 military installations" outside the United States.[84]

The arms industry is not only colossal in size; it seems it is also stained with corruption. In his 2011 book *The Shadow World: Inside the Global Arms Trade*, campaigner and former South African Member of Parliament Andrew Feinstein describes the murky world of arms brokers or dealers; the bribery and corruption that have become de rigueur in arms transactions involving even the largest, most respected arms companies; the shadowy relationships with governments; and the "revolving door" through which powerful, well-paid people move between government, the military, and the arms industry. So close but murky had relationships between these supposedly independent sectors of society become, for example under the George W. Bush presidency in the United States, that it is "extremely difficult to critically analyze and hold to account the massive military–industrial complex that drives the country's predisposition to warfare and the increasing militarization of American society."[85] Illustrating the weakness of arms control, Feinstein referred to there having been over 500 documented allegations of violations of the United Nations arms embargoes since their inception but only two instances where these had led to any legal accountability and only one which led to prosecution. The warning given by General Dwight Eisenhower in his farewell address as US president was prescient: "[with] the conjunction of an immense military establishment and a large arms industry. . . . In the councils of government we must guard against the acquisition of unwarranted influence by the military–industrial complex."[86]

Pilisuk and Rowntree enlarge on the "egregious" connections between the US government and the defense industry, picking out Halliburton and the Bechtel and Carlyle Groups for special mention. They refer to the case made by James Risen of the *New York Times* that "the U.S.-led wars in the Middle East . . . have come to be sources of corrupt accumulation of profit and career paths for those who reap the benefits of a war machine." They refer to "the arms trade supermarket . . . a culture of secrecy at the weapons laboratories . . . [and] nuclear weapons and the sprawling government complex that develops and produces them." They too bemoan the roles now played by private companies, not just everything from supplying helicopters to doing the laundry but also recruiting, offering information-technology consultancy, and even acting as combatants. Their greatly increased presence raises many issues to do with the conduct of war; for example, should they carry arms, can they "desert," be POWs, be required to follow the rules of the Geneva Convention? Mercenaries, of which there is a long tradition, now exist, they say, in a newly sanitized form, protected from the reach of international law by their publicly traded private military corporation masters.[87]

Granted, weapons alone do not make war. But again, there is a bigger picture. There is much to convince us that, rather than being horrified at the thought of our country or group possessing destructive weapons, we approve of them, treat them with acclaim, sanction their manufacture, trading, stockpiling and readiness for use. The truth surely is that it is people armed with weapons that can kill, injure, and destroy that makes war and, of most relevance to war support, it is our acceptance and approval of such weapons and the system of which they are part that helps make war possible. Both people and weapons contribute. It is the relationship between the two that is important.

Is Militarism Supported and Has Support Declined in the West?

We saw in Chapter 2 that there are individual differences, such as authoritarianism and belief in a dangerous and competitive world, which are associated with stronger support for war, and some evidence was also cited suggesting that being involved in a conflict or being reminded of one increased militaristic attitudes. The central question for us here, though, is the extent to which militarism, including collective arming *in preparation* for war, is generally supported. Studies of public attitudes toward state foreign policy in Britain and the United States have generally found two dimensions. One such study, based on five British national surveys conducted in 2008, labeled these as "liberal internationalism" and "British militarism."[88] Those relatively high on the latter factor had the stronger tendency to agree with statements such as "Britain needs to spend more money on its armed forces" and "Britain should maintain its overseas military bases." We might note, however, that finding two distinct dimensions means that it is possible to score relatively highly on both cooperative or liberal internationalism, oriented toward peace rather than war, *and* militaristic attitudes. The two should not necessarily be thought of as polar opposites. This tends to support a conclusion reached in Chapter 3 that cosmopolitanism and national identity are compatible and that both can be associated with willingness to go to war for one's country. We cannot say, simply, that people are somewhere on a single spectrum ranging from militaristic to anti-militaristic. Nor, in the light of what we have seen in this chapter about the embeddedness of militarism in society, should it surprise us that public attitudes are more complicated than that. We don't have to be dyed in the wool militarists to subscribe to cultural militarism.

In the search for understanding why we support such a culture of militarism, a theory which sounds as if it should be helpful is *system justification theory* (SJT).[89] According to SJT, there exists a quite basic motivation to justify, legitimize, and defend the social systems, the rules, policies, and norms, which form the status quo within which we live. The idea is that it is uncomfortable, threatening indeed, to keep on thinking that the existing system is wrong and needs changing, particularly if we are partly responsible for how things are. Viewing as undesirable, illegitimate or unfair, the rules, norms, and conventions of a system one can do little to change, gives rise to anxiety. Justifying or rationalizing the system is a way of coping with that anxiety. SJT is one of a number of psychological theories which rest on the idea of us being motivated to reduce the threat and anxiety occasioned by a lack of fit between how we would like to believe things are, and the actual reality. *Terror management theory*, discussed in Chapter 2, is one such. The *theory of cognitive dissonance* is another, but both those theories are more concerned with one's personal mortality or behavior. Another, *belief in a just world theory*, is more oriented, like SJT, toward perceptions about a system but focuses more specifically than SJT does on perceptions of justice.

There now exists a lot of work supporting SJT. It includes research showing that it applies not only to those in powerful positions who stand to gain most from maintaining the system as it is but also to those in positions of lower power.[90] A number of studies have shown that people in low-power or disadvantaged positions often justify a system which has been responsible for putting them in that position and in which they themselves play merely a small and lowly part. The system can be justified, for example, by subscribing to the view that those more privileged within the system are virtuous or deserving and/or that the disadvantaged are less worthy.[91] There is also good evidence that system justification is especially strong when the system has been in existence for longer—an extension of SJT termed *longevity bias*—perhaps because we assume that a system that has endured must have intrinsic worth.[92] Things have long been this way, throughout our lifetimes perhaps, so surely that is how things are meant to be.

Much of the SJT-related research has aimed at understanding the conditions that are especially likely to set off this source of anxiety and therefore to make it even more likely that the motivation to justify the system would be activated. Perceiving oneself to be controlled by the system or dependent on it are among those conditions, and perceiving the system as immutable is another. One factor facilitating system justification which has particular relevance for war support is the perception that the system is under threat. Since system justification, as the theory has it, is motivated by the anxiety-reducing effect of defending the system, if the legitimacy of the system is threatened, the motivation to justify it should be enhanced.[93]

The potential relevance to support for the system of militarism is obvious. Deeply embedded as it is in most countries, of long standing and hardly likely to be seriously challenged let alone to disappear, militarism is part of the system we live with. Any discomfort we might feel about that should, according to SJT, motivate us to defend militarism all the more strongly. As we move further along the warpath, support for militarism is likely to increase. Interestingly enough, SJT would predict a counterintuitive effect on the motivation to support the system: since support for militarism is even less questioned than it was in more peaceful times, there is now *less* urgency to reduce any anxiety caused by it being under threat. The overall, net effect on justifying militarism is not so clear. This may be an example of where the psychology may be very different depending on whether, as war is contemplated, we find ourselves in a situation where our country or group is being attacked or one, perhaps, in which we are asked to give support to a controversial military engagement far away. Under the former circumstances, the feeling of threat from an attacking military is likely to swamp the reduced anxiety occasioned by renewed support for our military system. Under the latter conditions, however, the suggestion of military action and reduction of threat to the system of militarism may be the stronger influence. The net effect in that case might be *reduced* justification for militarism. This just goes to show that, since the circumstances surrounding wars vary so greatly, even a powerful and well-supported theory like SJT can only capture a part of what is going on in the minds of those called on to support them.

Since the United States not only has the biggest military and largest share in world arms trading but also carries out the bulk of the relevant research, it is not surprising that support for militarism in the United States has received a great deal of comment. Several US scholars have attributed the perpetuation of the country as a military–industrial complex since the end of the

Second World War to the conservative political culture of US society, while others have attributed it to the military superiority of the United States and its militarized worldview: "The more a society is militarized, the more its political culture will tend to legitimate the use of violence,"[94] is one view. Although he doesn't use the language of SJT explicitly, Andrew Bacevich, whom we met earlier, might well have done when he says, in *The New American Militarism*,

> The global military supremacy that the United States presently enjoys—and is bent on perpetuating—has become central to our national identity... Americans... have fallen prey to militarism, manifesting itself in a romanticized view of soldiers, a tendency to see military power as the truest measure of national greatness, and outsized expectations regarding the efficacy of force.[95]

Despite situating himself "culturally on the right," Bacevich tells us he has become disenchanted with US militarism. George W. Bush and his policies had been roundly criticized across the political spectrum for their militarism, but Bacevich believes that to blame him would be a case of scapegoating, since current militarism in the United States is deeply rooted in its past. On military matters politicians are allowed no contrarian views, he claims; all have to demonstrate that they are "sound on defense." The one unforgivable sin is to be found guilty of failing to "support the troops." Presidents have made it look as if they are part of the military by, for example, appearing in military clothing when addressing troops.[96] Others, of course, take a different stand. Since Carter, if not further back to the time of Wilson's presidency, the United States has been, says Azar Gat,

> The guarantor of the global order and insurer of last resort for the cause of liberal democracy.... The United States seems to be able to do nothing right, blamed as it is for either intervening or not intervening. In Europe, long habituated to depending on America's hegemonic role for its security while criticizing its excesses—real and imagined—pacifism among the public has become even more deeply entrenched.[97]

Across the pond, a 2012 article in the journal *Armed Forces and Society* addressed the very issue of the relationship between the armed forces and the rest of society in the United Kingdom.[98] What are our armed forces for in the world of today? How strong and durable is public support for the use of force in international relations? Against the backdrop of public sector cuts, what was the United Kingdom willing to spend on defense? What commitments should we be making to service personnel willing to serve their country? The article took as its starting point a part of army doctrine called the British Military Covenant, published in 2000 (actually a specifically Army statement but nevertheless of relevance for all the military services). It addressed the concern that, as a result of changes in society, recruits no longer understood the moral standards and expectations of service in the Army—the military ethos we considered earlier in the context of education generally. As a senior commander noted, "in past generations it was assumed that young men and women coming into the Armed Forces would have absorbed an understanding of the core values and standards of behaviour required by the military from their family or from within their wider community. Such a presumption today cannot be made." With only 7% of all 17- to 24-year-olds having a family member with any military experience at all, the Army felt it was operating in a society that had little understanding of the role of the armed forces or of its culture and values. At the same time, a purpose of the Military Covenant was to defend the right of the Army to be *different* from the society from which it came. In particular, the article's author was concerned that civilians who knew or cared little about the Army would fail to recognize the need for the armed forces to have distinct military codes and laws, supplemented by norms and values to ensure combat effectiveness. As the Chief of the Defence Staff, General Guthrie, had commented in 2001, "One way or another the raft of employment legislation we face today is in danger of breeding a generation averse to taking risks, to making courageous decisions or to operating without the benefit of reams of rules and regulations."

The unpopular wars in Iraq and Afghanistan had brought questions about the relationship between the armed forces and society into even sharper focus. Questions were raised about ineffective and incompetent Ministry of Defence procurement practices, about the adequacy of equipment capable of protecting against improvised explosive devices, and about the provision of medical care for the growing number of injured service personnel and the government's duty of care for those with subsequent long-term health problems. Was the Ministry of Defence being "cavalier with their lives and their safety"? The Covenant had been used to urge the public to support the armed forces even if they did not support the missions in Iraq and Afghanistan. It was important that the Army felt valued and supported by the public. General Dannatt was among the most vocal on that subject, noting "that soldiers returning from Iraq and Afghanistan have been dismayed at the 'indifferent' attitude toward them by the public." The Minister for the Armed Forces expressed concern about "a growing disconnect in the public debate" which needed to be bridged or we would witness diminishing support for the armed forces in combat.

In the United States too there has been recognition of a recently growing civilian–service "cultural gap" of increasing separation between military and non-military families, compounded by reduced service history among Congress representatives.[99] The under-representation of the upper levels of the socioeconomic class hierarchy in the modern US military has become, according to Centano and Enriquez,

> A very contentious issue ... we publicly honor those who have served in uniform while not desiring to know much about their experiences, addressing many of their needs, or considering why their service may have been necessary. ... The US ... has been at war for almost fifteen years, yet it is hard to perceive it in the everyday lives of the vast majority of Americans.[100]

Andrew Bacevich agrees: "since Vietnam, the American elite has largely excused itself from military service. Minority and working class kids might serve; the sons and daughters of those who occupy positions of influence in the corporate, intellectual, academic, journalistic, and political worlds have better things to do . . . the demise of the ancient American tradition of the citizen-soldier." One result of the present gap between the armed services and US society was "a sentimentalized version of the American military." The public now "admire soldiers from a safe distance."[101] From a historical perspective there is perhaps nothing new about the relations between the military and society being problematic. The UK's Military Covenant set out a highly idealized notion of how relations between the armed forces and society should look, but some have argued that, looking across the last two centuries, the British armed forces "have never enjoyed a strong bond of understanding with the public ... [and] have never had those deep ties with their society."[102]

Some blame retreat from universal conscription for what they see as a decline in support for militarism in the United States and elsewhere.[103] Others are more inclined to put the focus on a lowered tolerance of casualties and the general public's reduced willingness to risk their own lives—increased "casualty aversion." Richard Lachmann, for example, cites a 1999 survey which reported the median responses of the general public to hypothetical situations. The results suggested that 100 US deaths would have been an acceptable cost to defend Taiwan or to intervene to bring democracy to the Congo and 500 to remove weapons of mass destruction from Iraq—far smaller numbers than the actual casualties in Vietnam or Korea. He thinks casualty aversion will continue to grow.[104]

In *The New Western Way of War*, published in 2005 following the invasion of Iraq by Western forces, Martin Shaw described this growing casualty aversion as part of something more general, the West's modern preference for what he called "risk-transfer war."[105] Any wars that the Western powers engaged in now had to satisfy a variety of criteria. They should be "quick-fix" wars, time-limited, and also limited to distant war zones. They should rely heavily on air power, on "precision" weapons, and above all minimize casualties to Western troops. Some of Shaw's other criteria for risk-transfer war take us to a consideration of propaganda—for example, those who engage in wars must now anticipate "the problems of global surveillance . . . suffering and death must be unseen, indirect, less visible and less quantifiable" and "media management is essential"—which is the subject of the next chapter. Others chime with long-standing "just war" criteria—for example, the risks of "accidental" civilian casualties should be minimized—which we discuss in Chapter 7.

Are these changes due to our longer life expectancy, smaller families, more years of enjoyable life, or the greater chance of the war-injured surviving, as has been suggested? Or are they just responses to whether wars have been going badly?[106] Or is this greater aversion to casualties, and the civilian-military gap which many in the West have detected, part of a much longer, general "decline of martial culture," thanks, as Steven Pinker believes (see Chapter 1), to a civilizing process, starting long ago in the Middle Ages and given a boost with the horrors of the First World War? That war, he argues, finally put an end to romantic militarism in the Western mainstream and the whole idea that war was in any way desirable or inevitable, glorious or heroic.[107]

As I review the draft of this chapter, the 2022 war in Ukraine has been going on for over 12 months. There is every indication that, when circumstances bring it to the surface, continued support for militarism in the United Kingdom and among Western allies becomes apparent. This is as SJT and longevity bias theories would predict. At the time of writing, it is the Ukraine military that is being praised and supported with additional armaments. Whether militarism, in the sense of support for *our own* military and militarization, remains as strong as ever is not being put to the test.

Conclusions

The present chapter has focused on militarism, the normalization of a set of shared beliefs and practices which support developing and maintaining the means for making war as a valued way of defending one's nation's or group's common interests. At its extreme, it can be manifest as a belief in military power as the pinnacle of national greatness. We explored some of the ways in which militarism is embedded in culture and civic society, summarized in Figure 5.1. We examined the role that games, films, and other entertainments have played in supporting militarism; and we looked at militarism in education, including the influence of the "military ethos."

We considered the controversial issue of whether war graves and war memorials serve the cause of peace or of war and the complicated question

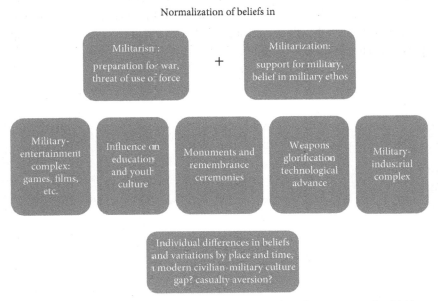

Figure 5.1 A summary of some of the ways in which militarism is embedded within culture and civic society

of how important weapons themselves, and acceptance of the arms trade, are as part of militarism and support for war. The long-term trend of weapon development has been toward ever-more deadly weapons, enabling fighting at a greater distance. Drones are a notable example of the continuation of that trend, which may be part of the West's modern preference for "risk-transfer war," limited to distant war zones, heavily reliant on air power and on "precision" weapons, and minimizing casualties to Western troops.

A distinction is often drawn between "militarism" and "militarization," the latter focused more closely on valuing and supporting the nation's or group's military organization and personnel. Although some concern has been expressed, in both Britain and the United States, that there has been a growing "cultural gap" between the public and the military, *system justification theory* would lead us to expect that support for a set of policies and associated beliefs and values as long and strongly supported as militarism and militarization would not fade easily.

It is the largely unquestioned acceptance of a major role for military preparedness and the ever-present possibility of our country or identity group engaging in war—in a word, militarism—that is the central conclusion of this chapter. Militarism is either actively promoted, seen as benign, or passively taken for granted. Whether at any one time it is waxing or waning may be a matter of dispute, but to one degree or another it is always with us. Support for war rests on it. It will occupy a pivotal position in the model of war support I develop in the final chapter.

6
Engineering Consent
Propaganda and Persuasion

> Naturally, the common people don't want war.... But after all it is the leaders of the country who determine policy, and it is always a simple matter to drag the people along.... All you have to do is to tell them they are being attacked, and denounce the pacifists for lack of patriotism and exposing the country to danger.
> Hermann Göring, Nazi minister of information at the time of the Nuremburg trials[1]

> The injection of the poison of hatred into men's minds by means of falsehood is a greater evil in wartime than the actual loss of life. The defilement of the human soul is worse than the destruction of the human body.
> Lord Ponsonby, writing in 1926[2]

Militarism may be the bedrock on which preparedness for war, if and when required, rests. But for us to support our nation or group preparing for, and actually engaging in, war we need to be convinced that war is or may be necessary. Our personal and collective worldviews, values, and identities and our images of ourselves and of the enemy (among the topics covered in Chapters 2, 3 and 4) are all highly relevant. But to what extent are we the objects of persuasion and coercion by those who want to lead us toward war and to maintain our support during a war? What role does propaganda play? That is the question for this chapter. In the course of trying to answer it, we shall look at topics including the history of propaganda, the role of the media, and the importance of leadership.

The subject of war propaganda, and the psychological issues it raises, will make a major contribution to understanding two of the three factors central to the war support model presented in the final chapter, threat perception and mental simplification. A crucial task for propaganda, and hence for a state's or group's leaders, and for the media that they control or which support them, is to win public consent to a narrative involving perception of threat from an identified enemy. At the same time, propaganda always presents an over-simplified and one-sided account of the circumstances leading to war, omitting the enemy's perspective and the detail of history and context and causes.

In common with all the topics dealt with in this book, propaganda changes with time, as war moves from something unspecified which we are told we must be *prepared* for, to something more specific which is now being *contemplated*, to actions our nation or group is now *engaged* in. Propaganda is important to war support at early and late stages and at all points in between. War-related propaganda arguably begins, long before armed hostilities break out, in the form of messages which have already "regimented our minds" to think in certain ways about a potential enemy and our relationship with it. At a late stage, reports about the progress of a war, once engaged, contain at the least a very selective presentation of the real facts. As the journey along the path to war progresses, departures from the approved, simplified war support narrative become less acceptable, in danger of being seen as unpatriotic, supportive of the enemy, examples of appeasement.

History of Propaganda

In *The Internationalists: And Their Plan to Outlaw War*, by Oona Hathaway and Scott Shapiro, we are told of the long history of "war manifestos," distributed widely among the population.[3] They laid out in detail the case for war, and esteemed writers, scholars, or lawyers often helped draft them. For example, Cromwell commissioned John Milton to write his manifesto when ordering the invasion of Spanish possessions in the Caribbean in 1655. They continued to be issued into the nineteenth and twentieth centuries, though the term "manifesto" became less common. Because there had been few studies of them and none in English, Hathaway and Shapiro compiled more than 400 in various languages dating from the late fifteenth century to the time of the Second World War. Sixty-nine percent used self-defense as justification, 47% enforcing treaty obligations, 42% obtaining compensation for tortious injuries, 35% for violations of the laws of war or law of nations, 33%

stopping those who disrupt the balance of power, 19% protection of trade interests, and 17% humanitarian considerations—the latter something that we had been led to believe was a peculiarly modern justification for states engaging in military action. These manifestos were in effect "propaganda used by sovereigns to sell wars to their subjects."[4]

Philip Taylor, then professor of international communications at the University of Leeds, wrote what remains an outstanding work on the subject of war propaganda. His *Munitions of the Mind: A History of Propaganda from the Ancient World to the Present Day* first appeared in 1990, with the third edition of 2003 bringing it up to date to the first few years of the new century. It was the Vatican, he tells us, that gave us the term "propaganda" early in the seventeenth century, when it was deployed to defend and propagate "the true faith" against Protestantism. Since then it has acquired a poor reputation, seen as something that is being used to control us, playing on our emotions, something *they*, the enemy, says and does, while *we* only tell the truth.[5]

Early on, on his third page in fact, he puts that self-serving bias to rest: it was the British, he says, who set the modern standard for war propaganda during the First World War. We are familiar with the famous "Your King and Country Need You" World War I poster, with Lord Kitchener's outstretched index finger inviting enlistment. And later, as recruitment dwindled, the more aggressive appeals such as "Who's absent—is it You?," "Women of Britain Say Go," and "What did you do in the Great War, Daddy?" Less well known now are the National War Aims Committee set up to sustain the civilian population's will to fight and the secret war propaganda bureau at Wellington House.[6]

Many wartime atrocity stories, circulated in the press during World War I, were found to be false after the war. The sinking of the passenger liner *Lusitania* by a German U-boat—evidence discovered in the 1980s suggested it was carrying illegal armaments—and the execution of Nurse Edith Cavell, as well as alleged German atrocities in Belgium, such as the cutting off of Belgian children's hands, were among the "evidence" that the Germans were living up to the stereotype of the "Beastly Hun" who mutilated babies, violated women, and looted churches.[7] Although, Ferguson believes, there is no question Germans did commit atrocities in Belgium in 1914, he agrees entente propaganda exaggerated them. Most influential was the Bryce Report (*Report of the Committee on Alleged German Outrages*) compiled from depositions of Belgian refugees. At the time it seemed to sustain the Allied claim of a contest between good and evil, but it was discredited years later in the 1930s.[8] One telling incident was British foreign secretary Balfour's response to the rumor that Germans had been using human corpses, for example for boiling down to make soap. Taylor quotes him as saying, "there does not, in view of the many atrocious actions of which the Germans have been guilty, appear to be any reason why it should not be true."[9]

Britain's First World War propaganda machine was so much admired by Hitler that he used it as a model. Nazi Germany saw one of history's most complete propaganda campaigns, with Goebbels head of the Ministry for Propaganda and Public Enlightenment, with its 12 departments for the press, film, radio, culture, education and so on. The pre-war mass rallies held in Nuremberg and elsewhere were one spectacular technique, newsreel clips of which are still regularly replayed in Britain in the twenty-first century. Past German victories and British imperialist oppression and decadence were important themes. Churchill was portrayed as a drunkard.[10] Japan too had its own World War II "thought war," its preferred term for propaganda, with rigorous control of radio and film. Themes included racist brutality by the British in Hong Kong and oppression of the Chinese through the Opium Wars.[11]

All the parties to the Second World War vied to be the best propagandists ever. The Ministry of Information (MOI) in the United Kingdom began with old-fashioned Kitchener-type exhortations but quickly moved to Churchill posters of the "Let Us Go Forward Together" and "We're Going to See It Through" variety, as well as information posters with slogans, quoted to this day, such as "Coughs and Sneezes Spread Diseases," "Make Do and Mend," "A Clean Plate Means a Clear Conscience." The MOI's Crown Film Unit's own "official" short information films about how to plant potatoes, how to wear a gas mask, even how tanks were built, although not obviously propagandist, presented "an illusion of reality," aimed at serving the war effort. In fact, all films shown in Britain were official in the sense that none could be shown without MOI approval or a British Board of Film Censors' certificate.[12] Many surprising names can be listed among those making their contributions to the propaganda machine. Poet Dylan Thomas was one. Between 1942 and 1945 he worked on at least 10 documentary films including *Our Country* for the MOI about wartime Britain, *New Towns for Old* about post-war town planning, and *Balloon Site 568*, encouraging women to join the anti-aircraft balloon service.[13]

But Taylor does not let others off the hook. He devotes several pages to early Bolshevik propaganda, before, during, and after the revolution and the civil war. With limited literacy, newspapers such as *Pravda* ("Truth") had a small circulation. So posters and "education" and agitation via agit-trains and agit-ships were used to take the message into rural areas, as were early radio and films. Lenin's view was that the cinema for them was the most important of the arts. Sergei Eisenstein's *Battleship Potemkin* and *October*, from 1926 and 1927 respectively, were more propaganda than accurate history, in Taylor's opinion. Later, Soviet Cold War Agitprop (the Administration of Agitation and Propaganda of the Communist Party Central Committee) was active, for example jamming western radio broadcasts and orchestrating an international campaign against the US neutron bomb. The editor-in-chief of *Pravda* stated in 1978, "Our aim is propaganda, the propaganda of the party and the state. We do not hide this."[14]

By the time Philip Taylor was writing *Munitions of the Mind* it was the Americans, when it came to propaganda, who, he judged, "today stand as the masters of its art, science and craft."[15] Distortion and cover-up of information have been a big part of it. Taylor and others offer a catalogue of examples. Reports of attacks on two US Navy destroyers, one of which was later revealed not to have taken place, were used to gain congressional approval for the Vietnam War.[16] It has been claimed that later on in that war the US military deliberately underestimated enemy strength in Vietnam because they wanted to see it through and that the Central Intelligence Agency's (CIA's) Bay of Pigs invasion of Cuba was justified by a deliberate overestimation of the likelihood of it triggering a popular uprising on the island. Stories of atrocities committed by Iraqi soldiers in Kuwait were found to have been deliberately fabricated, as was the evidence about Iraq's weapons of mass destruction (WMD), a famous example of what has been called the "politicization of intelligence."[17] The Abu Ghraib prison scandal was repeatedly attributed by the US government to a "few bad apples," whereas a later investigation revealed "the collective wrongdoing and failure of Army leadership at the highest levels."[18]

As the authors of *The Hidden Structure of Violence* see it, the administration learned an important lesson from Vietnam, namely that public opinion had been allowed to interfere with US war aims. That, they argue, is why George W. Bush spent so heavily on engaging private public relations firms—nearly $80 million a year between 2003 and 2005. The White House and the Pentagon, which was reported to have spent over a billion dollars in media contacts over 30 months between 2001 and 2004,[19] engaged in what the *New York Times* referred to as an "information war" carried out by "a host of shadowy disinformation or counter-propaganda units" including the Pentagon's well-endowed Psychological Operations group and the Counter Terrorism Information Strategy Policy Coordinating Committee at the White House.[20] Drawing on Rampton and Stauber's 2003 *Weapons of Mass Deception: The Uses of Propaganda in Bush's War on Iraq*, Marc Pilisuk and Jennifer Rowntree refer to "a shocking world where marketers . . . can sell an entire war to consumers."[21]

War propaganda has not only been used to influence one's own side of course. There is also a long history of "psychological operations" (psyops) directed at the enemy, its combatants, or its civilian population. In World War I, a huge volume of psychological warfare was employed by the Allies, and in the Second World War the United Kingdom's Political Warfare Executive had the aim of lowering the enemy's morale—"The fighting services attack the body, we attack the mind." In Vietnam, use was made of leaflet dropping, radio broadcasts, and even messages in bars of soap and on ping-pong balls dropped over enemy lines; and psyops were used extensively in the 1991 Gulf War. The list of modern psyops targets is a long one, including populations in Vietnam, the Balkans, Somalia, Haiti, North Korea and China via Radio Free Asia, and Afghanistan, where more than 80 million leaflets were dropped.[22] The US Defense Department now refers to psyops using the term "military information support operations."[23] Propaganda might be thought to cross a further moral red line if the recipients are deliberately deceived about where it is coming from. Taylor draws an important distinction between white (source disclosed) and black (undisclosed) propaganda. The Political Warfare Executive set up in Britain in September 1941 was prepared to use both. An example of the use of black propaganda by the United States in the Cold War was the CIA's Radio Swan transmissions to Cuba.[24]

Munitions of the Mind is strongest on propaganda of the twentieth century. But in the final pages of the 2003 edition of Taylor's book he was able to note the continuing use of propaganda; for example, by the Taliban—who warned that the humanitarian food aid being dropped in Afghanistan by the United States was poisoned or was actually cluster bombs; in Rwanda—where Radio Mille Collines called for the massacre of Tutsis; and how Russians tried to exclude the media altogether from the second Chechen war.[25] Nearer to home for Brits like myself, James Hughes, in *Nationalism and War*, has much to say about myth-making propaganda in the context of the Northern Ireland "Troubles." On the British side, politicians and the media painted a false "benign gloss" on their role as a "broker," even-handedly operating to "keep the peace between the communities." On the republican side, the *Republican News* supported a move to the use of physical force, drawing strongly on history and "the heritage of the 1916 Rising, the War of Independence, and the United Irishmen." As tension mounted it consistently drew attention to British Army brutality in Catholic areas and warned Catholics against fraternizing with British forces. Catholic areas "were flooded with republican propaganda, pamphlets, and books as part of the reeducation strategy."[26]

The Role of the Media in Engineering Public Consent to War

Many believe that the media have played a crucial role in supporting war. Philip Taylor wrote of "the enormously jingoistic influence of the press" during the First World War.[27] Niall Ferguson also concluded that World War I "was certainly a media war." He cites an extraordinarily honest statement that Lloyd George made to C. P. Scott of the *Manchester Guardian* at a low point in the war in December 1917: "If the people really knew, the war would be stopped tomorrow. But of course they don't—and can't know. The correspondents don't write and the censorship would not pass the truth." Novelist John Buchan had commented, "So far as Britain is concerned, the war could not have been fought for one month without its newspapers."[28] Not only did vilification of the enemy and exalting of the war's aims bring many substantial increases in newspaper circulation; it also endowed their proprietors with prestigious wartime positions and honors.[29] Prominent examples were Sir Max Aitkin who was a Member of Parliament and controlled the *Daily Express*, appointed Minister for Information, responsible for propaganda in Allied and neutral countries, becoming Lord Beaverbrook, and Alfred Harmsworth (Lord Northcliffe), owner of *The Times*, the *Daily Mail*, and other papers, put in charge of the Department of Enemy Propaganda and subsequently made a viscount. At least 12 press knighthoods were also awarded.

In World War I media censorship was draconian, Ferguson tells us. In Britain, the 1914 Defence of the Realm Act,

> drastically increased the state's power . . . explicitly prohibited reports or statements . . . which were "intended or likely" to undermine loyalty to the King, recruitment or confidence in the currency. The censors also banned

publication of news of troop movements, or even speculation about them.... . Wartime Britain thus became by stages a kind of police state.... Gradually ... all countries went beyond censorship of military information and used their wartime powers in a more overtly political way.[30]

Media censorship was again firm at the beginning of the Second World War, Taylor tells us, to the extent of police occupying Fleet Street offices and seizing offending newspapers. Later the media accepted what he calls "precensorship," with most war news controlled by the censors before it ever reached them.[31]

Despite radio having become established as a major influence by the time of the Spanish Civil War in the late 1930s and World War II,[32] and the growing importance of the internet in conflicts such as the Balkan wars in later years,[33] the print news media continues to be highly influential. Mergers have now resulted in a small number of media mega-corporations dominating US newspapers and television stations. According to Pilisuk and Rowntree, in 1983, 50 companies owned 90% of US media, but by 2011 six owned 90%. The result, they believe, amounts to a "gradual decline of journalistic integrity... [and] corporate domination over current U.S. domestic and foreign policy."[34] A 2020 BBC TV series, *The Rise of the Murdoch Dynasty*, drew attention to the role of the Murdoch media empire in encouraging the Blair government to join the United States in invading Iraq.[35] The *New York Times* and *Washington Post* later made front-page apologies for their absence of scrutiny of the Iraq WMD claims.[36]

The underreporting in the US media of civilian deaths due to US forces' actions, as opposed to atrocities committed by the enemy, is something often commented on. Articles published in the *Lancet*, finding that Iraqi civilian deaths were up 95% due to the US and UK invasion of 2003, were completely dismissed by major US news media, although they did make headlines around Europe. A later *Lancet* article estimated there had been 655,000 excess Iraqi deaths as a result of the war.[37] John Pilger provides other examples of the continuing role of the media in suppressing the truth about wars. The invasion of Somalia was one. The 7,000–10,000 Somali deaths which Operation Restore Hope led to were not to his knowledge reported in the mainstream media, which instead concentrated on the 18 US deaths, later glorified in the film *Black Hawk Down*. The 1991 Gulf War was another: Ken Jarecke's famous picture of a retreating Iraqi burned to a cinder, sitting at the wheel of his vehicle, was suppressed in the US until long after the war, and only the *Observer* in Britain showed it at the time but, even then, not on the front page. "The truth was that the whole US press collaborated in keeping silent about the consequences of the Gulf War," says Pilger.[38] Lawrence LeShan is even more outspoken. He describes the first Gulf War as the most "sanitized" since the Crimean War of the nineteenth century. The media, he concludes, was "magnificently well managed by the military." The public was informed that the enemy had "the fourth largest army in the world" and told about the battle experience of the elite Republican Guard with its modern tanks and artillery, but any criticism of US allies such as Syria and its protection of terrorist groups was carefully avoided.[39]

Pilger sees through the claim of a clear distinction between a free Western press and one that is state-controlled elsewhere. Control in the Western media is often exerted through self-censorship, he claims: "Compliance to institutional and corporate needs is internalised early in a journalist's career. The difference, in authoritarian societies, is that the state makes these demands directly." The result is too often the adopting of double standards and the "repetition of received truths disguised as news." Israel, Kosovo, and Afghanistan are among his examples. In Israel the "regime continues to set the international news agenda. Israelis are 'murdered by terrorists', while Palestinians are 'left dead' after a 'clash with security forces'. . . . The BBC refers to Israel's policy of assassination as 'targeted killing', the euphemism used by Israeli spokesmen." The Western media overwhelmingly supported NATO action in Kosovo as "humanitarian intervention"—a "grotesque" description according to one former senior NATO planner—and did not report deliberate targeting of civilians (referred to as "mistakes," "blunders" only). In Afghanistan, the Taliban were routinely described as evil, and "Although occasional reference was made to the Anglo-American role in the creation of the fanatical *jihadi* groups which spawned the Taliban," little was provided by way of recent history which would have made the easy distinctions between good and evil less clear-cut.[40]

It seems that one of the greatest tasks facing the political body, state or non-state, that declares war is control of the media. Commentators like John Pilger and Lawrence LeShan might be dismissed by some as coming from an extreme position, but the accounts of war propaganda are too ubiquitous and come from such a variety of sources that there is no avoiding the conclusion that support for war depends, much of the time, on distortion of objective truth or at least a very selective presentation of the real facts. Philip Taylor's *Munitions of the Mind* is a careful, detailed study of war propaganda, and it often agrees with the likes of LeShan and Pilger. He acknowledges Vietnam as a uniquely "uncensored war," during which media attitudes became more questioning and critical, a departure from the tight censure that had been the norm since the Crimean War.[41] Lessons, though, were learned by both the UK and US governments. The UK government learned more about media management from the Northern Ireland "Troubles" also. In the 1982 Falklands War, reporters and reporting were tightly controlled. Only a small number of journalists were permitted to accompany the task force, and they were dependent on the Navy in terms of travel, company, and communicating their copy. Back in the United Kingdom, the BBC was criticized by government for being "unacceptably even-handed" if it deviated from unequivocal support.[42]

The tabloid newspapers, notably *The Sun*, adopted a jingoistic tone, phrases such as "horribly burned" were cut out, and report of the loss of *HMS Sheffield* was delayed. When Ministry of Defence official Clive Ponting was arrested and tried under the Official Secrets Act when he released documents showing the government had lied over the sinking of the *Belgrano*, which was actually sailing away at the time—although it was welcomed in *The Sun* with its infamous headline "GOTCHA!"—the jury refused to convict him. The same tight media control was exercised during the US invasion of Grenada in 1983, Taylor tells us. He also agrees with others about the tight control of the media in the United States and United Kingdom in the 1991 Gulf War. Only "smart" bombing was shown, although it turned out later that less than 10% of bombs dropped were of the new smart variety. He agrees with Pilger that the media effectively policed itself. When several hundred civilians were killed in one bomb attack and BBC TV showed images of it—sanitized though they were—the *Daily Mail* accused the BBC of being the Baghdad Broadcasting Corporation.[43]

Throughout the twentieth century and into the twenty-first there have been critics of the press and media generally for their role in supporting war by distorting, or at least presenting a selective version of, the truth. They have included satirists like playwright Karl Kraus who spoke of the "impoverishment of the imagination . . . [and] abuse of language" used by the wartime press in World War I,[44] public relations industry pioneer Edward Bernays who explained how it was possible for the press during both world wars to "regiment the public mind every bit as much as an army regiments their bodies," and famous journalist Walter Lippmann who recognized his profession's ability "to manufacture consent" when it came to war,[45] as well as academics like Noam Chomsky who has written more generally about the role of the media in propaganda and its ability "to dominate ideas through control over the public discussion of issues."[46]

Not that any of this is new. Lawrence LeShan gives us a number of pre–First World War examples: horrific photographs taken during the American Civil War were not shown until long afterward; during the Crimean War, the foreign correspondent William Howard Russell was barred from London gentlemen's clubs after reporting, accurately, on what the war was like at the front; and during the Boer War, *The Times* refused to publish its own correspondent's account of General Baden-Powell's discriminatory food policies which led to starvation among Black inhabitants of Mafeking, the siege of which was depicted as glorious and heroic. As LeShan says, in mythic wars, when perceptions begin to depart further from a balanced assessment of reality, negative information about ourselves or our allies, along with anti-war activists and movements, have to be discouraged or suppressed. In his terms, "In order for a war to retain its mythic aspects, and thus increase the intensity of meaning in our lives and bond us more completely as group members, enough of the real facts of how war is waged must be concealed."[47]

The Role of Social Networks and Social Media

Propaganda of the traditional sort, emanating from prominent political or military figures, with the help of cooperative print and broadcast media, may be of less central importance in modern wars, especially for "new wars" or civil wars. Particularly in the case of paramilitary activity, family and community support, training and traditions may be equally important, as they may have been, for example, among those on the republican side during the Northern Irish Troubles[48] and during the earlier Irish independence and civil wars.[49] The second N in the 3Ns model of terrorism (see Chapter 3) is the social network. Kruglanski and colleagues tell us that social network analysis has been showing how narratives supporting terrorism are encouraged by "charismatic persuaders in Internet chat rooms, via propaganda videos, or through radical sermons" and by "close-knit radical networks" in which family members often play a major role. In general, it is now recognized, they say, "that a growing proportion of violent attacks from political groups were largely orchestrated by small, informal, dynamic social groups, rather than by rigid hierarchal paramilitary organizations."[50] Face-to-face recruitment to a terrorist cause is important but so too is the exploitation of modern social media.

In his book *Information at War: Journalism, Disinformation, and Modern Warfare*, Philip Seib describes the war-related information revolution that has occurred since the beginning of the present century. Internet-based social media, starting with the creation of Facebook as recently as 2004, followed by YouTube and Twitter in 2005 and 2006 and numerous others since, have been of central importance: "In something less than two decades, social media progressed from being a novelty to becoming an essential tool for states and non-state actors involved in conflict." As a consequence, it is now much more difficult for government and military leaders to control the flow of war-related information, including photographic images of the reality of war.[51]

I made the case in Chapter 2 that, although individual terrorist acts may not amount to war, wars often do include acts of terrorism and the distinction between war and terrorism is not clear-cut. The modern use of social media is a common element. "Terrorism is war . . . [and] Sometimes terrorist organizations can take on the trappings of more traditional militaries," says Seib. Islamic State and al-Qaeda are examples of organizations which have recruited "media operatives," skilled in using social media including messaging services such as Instagram. The latter service was used effectively, for example, by the rebel group Ansar Dine in Mali, one of the groups operating in the Sahel region in North Africa which joined al-Qaeda of the Islamic Maghreb.[52] Sub-Saharan Africa generally is a part of the world where social media has made rapid advances and where it has contributed to civil war in several countries, including the conflict with Tigrayans in Ethiopia.[53]

The Hamas–Israel conflict is an example of how the use of social media in war has increased. The 2008–09 Gaza War was an early example of "social media warfare," with Israel using YouTube videos to try to show that only combatants were being targeted and Hamas relying on blogs and websites. By the time of the 2014 Gaza War, the Hamas Twitter hashtag gazaunderattack was used four million times during the month of the war, and Israel was putting civilians to work in the form of up to 400 university students sending computer messages to online forums in 30 languages and lobbying Facebook to remove content inciting anti-Israel violence.[54] As Philip Seib says,

> Virtually every war has narratives driving it. . . . No longer the exclusive domain of bards and presidents and generals, the wartime narrative may now incorporate contributions from millions of individuals using social media to help to shape the cases for and against a conflict's protagonists.[55]

Nor have the world's largest state military powers been slow to take advantage of the information revolution. The US military renamed its longstanding psyops as "military information support operations," designed, as the Department of Defense says, "to influence . . . the behavior of foreign governments, organizations, groups, and individuals in a manner favorable to the originator's objectives." In 2020 the British Army announced Information Manoeuvre, which "involves the use of information in all its forms . . . to ensure the Army's activities and intentions are appropriately recognised by allies, populations and adversaries."[56] Seib describes Russia, as of 2020, as "the most accomplished information warrior." It has its Internet Research Agency, or Glavset, based in St. Petersburg, while NATO has its Strategic Communications Centre of Excellence, based in Riga, of which the United Kingdom was a founder member in 2014.[57] In 2015, Russian Lieutenant General Andrei Kartapolov wrote, "a classical war of the twentieth century consisted usually of 80 percent violence and 20 percent propaganda. New-type wars consist of 80 to 90 percent propaganda and 10 to 20 percent violence."[58]

Seid provides an example of how social media can be used to spread false information and contribute to a spiral toward war. The incident occurred in the Middle East in May 2017. The Qatar News Agency website reported that Qatar's emir had made a speech praising Hamas, Hezbollah, the Muslim brotherhood, and Iran. A quartet of countries—Saudi Arabia, the United Arab Emirates, Bahrain, and Egypt—responded to this disinformation by initiating a physical and economic blockage of Qatar, and at one point Saudi Arabia seemed poised to invade Qatar, a move finally averted by last-minute diplomacy.[59]

In her book *How Civil Wars Start: And How to Stop Them*, Barbara Walter devotes a whole chapter to social media and its ability to function as an "accelerant" in the buildup to collective violence in the modern era. As a prime example she takes the violent inter-ethnic/inter-religious events that unfolded in Myanmar from 2012 onward. The country was an example of the rapid increase in internet access in just a few years and the launch of Facebook, which quickly became "the most popular social media platform—and the primary source of digital news." It was used by a group of charismatic persuaders, "Buddhist ultranationalists" in this case, to target the country's Muslims. Military and government leaders then used it to create fake accounts and spread disinformation (i.e., misinformation which is intentionally misleading) about the Rohingya people—Bengalis as they called them—whom they described as illegal immigrants.[60]

The "like" button was introduced by Facebook in 2009. It turns out, as Walter sees it, "that what people like the most is fear over calm, falsehood over truth, outrage over empathy. People are far more apt to like posts that are incendiary than those that are not." Social media's business model requires it to engage as many users as possible and to keep them engaged for as long as possible. The invention of an algorithm that uses a person's "likes" to determine the posts that are channeled their way contributes to this. As Walter puts it,

> It's this business model of engagement that makes social media so terrifying to those of us who study civil wars. . . . Social media is every ethnic entrepreneur's dream. Algorithms, by pushing outrageous material, allow these nationalist extremists to shape people's toxic views of "the other"— an ideal means of demonizing and targeting racial minorities and creating division.[61]

By January 2018, the estimate was that over 20,000 Rohingya had been killed; over 100,000 raped, assaulted, or beaten; and most of the million Rohingya forced to flee—more genocide than civil war at that stage, since the violence was one-sided, but qualifying as civil war later as resistance to military rule grew.[62] Facebook was criticized for its role by the United Nations, and after having refused to acknowledge the problem for several years, it finally admitted it had contributed to the violence and removed nearly 500 pages and over 150 accounts—too little too late according to human rights groups.[63] Facebook has been contributing to violence in another way too, hosting arms bazaars where weapons ranging from handguns to heavy machine guns and guided missiles are for sale.[64]

Philip Seib views the new importance of social media in supporting war as the latest development in the long history of war propaganda:

> War and information are inseparable. . . . Information helps to shape opinion: let's go to war; let's not go to war; let's escalate and win an existing war; let's disengage from that war. Within the past 100 years, the information on which people rely to develop and sustain those opinions has been transformed by technology—from print and telegraph, to radio,

to television, to internet—with speed of delivery and vividness of content changing from one step to the next.[65]

How Does Propaganda Work? The Importance of Threat Perception

Propaganda of one form or another appears to be a universal accompaniment of war, used to some degree by all parties. How, though, are people persuaded by propaganda to support war? How is "perception management," one of the euphemisms for propaganda,[66] achieved? One of the techniques, according to Pilisuk and Rowntree, is the constant repetition of slogans, stereotypical buzzwords: "A concise message is repeated over and over until it is accepted and integrated seamlessly into our thinking." They draw on psychologists Pratkanis and Aronson who suggested four strategies for successful propaganda: one was "pre-persuasion," creating a climate in which the message will be believed; a second was reference to a credible source, a public figure or likable and/or authoritative speaker; the third, the use of a clear and simple message. But it is the fourth of this list of strategies that seems to capture so much of what we call propaganda in the context of conflict with an enemy: "fear must be evoked and projected upon some target group."[67]

There is general agreement among those who have theorized on the subject of propaganda about the importance of encouraging fear and the perception of threat. Annabel McGoldrick, in *Preventing War and Promoting Peace*, depicts war propaganda as resting on an understanding of "the world as a field of risk and fear, where we should prepare for the worst and punish the guilty."[68] The rhetorical "we are under threat" is heard repeatedly. Jack Levy and William Thompson, in *Causes of War*, point to "existential threat" as an expression, now often used, implying a menace so serious that one's very existence is under threat. Clearly something so hazardous cannot be ignored. Anyone who does so is charged with lack of foresight, of patriotism. Preexisting rivalry is often an important background ingredient, they say: "The alchemy of rivalry . . . emphasizing the threats from a rival works much better than if the target is a state with little history of hostility towards one's own state." They draw on earlier models of violent conflict, emphasizing the way elites promote "strategic myths" about threat, using history for rhetorical purposes, justifying people's fears, and legitimizing a hostile response.[69]

From detailed analyses of the content of newspaper reports, David Winter shows how, as conflicts have escalated, readers have been exposed to increasingly alarming material. He provides examples, from the period immediately before the outbreak of World War I, the weeks following the Nazi invasion of Czechoslovakia in 1939, and the most tense moments of the Cuban Missile Crisis, of the way in which newspapers such as *The Times* and the *New York Times*, when summarizing statements by enemy leaders, have accentuated the latter's "power imagery"—for example how forceful and controlling they appear—and hence how threatening they are perceived to be.[70]

The stoking of the fire of threat perception and fear was never clearer in the modern era than during the Cold War. Of the climate of fear of the Red Bolshevik Menace in the West, says Taylor, "the rhetoric of the free world and the slave ... came to dominate public discourse about international conflict." In the United States, especially from 1947 to 1958, all written, film, and TV material was poured over by "self-appointed watchdog groups of red-hunters" with the effect of creating a climate in which only an image of the Russians as demons was acceptable. The House of Representatives' Un-American Activities Committee and the McCarthyite "witch hunts" are well-known symptoms of those times. It applied to both sides: "The other side had always to be portrayed as aggressive, militaristic and repressive—as a genuine threat to peace and freedom however such concepts were defined." The Soviet Union launched its own propaganda assault, weaponizing the use of words such "peace," "independence," and "liberation" in their own way. Front organizations like the World Peace Council were needed to mask Moscow's central organizing role.[71]

An interesting set of experiments reported in a 2019 edition of the *Cambridge Review of International Affairs* concerned the influence of US media reports on citizens' attitudes to international conflict more recently. The conflict in question was that between the United States and China, a conflict that has increasingly come to the fore in the media while I have been writing this book (see Chapter 8). The report's authors were interested in how the dominant narratives people are offered shape foreign policy sentiments, trust, threat, and anger being especially important. In particular they drew on something they call *social interdependence theory*, which explores the psychology of whether social actors believe their interests and goals are aligned or not—in game theory terms, whether the outcome of interaction is perceived as positive-sum or zero-sum—and when human interaction leads to cooperation and when to competition. US–China relations are, like

ENGINEERING CONSENT 171

all conflicts which could turn nasty, equivalent to mixed-motive games in which either competition or cooperation is possible. The research took the form of randomized online experiments in which the participants—a regional sample in one experiment, a national sample in another—were shown real CNN news video clips. The clips, carefully tested for validity, depicted the transition in the relative power of the United States and China either as positive-sum or as zero-sum. Across both experiments, the latter reduced US citizens' trust in the Chinese people, reduced trust in the Chinese government, and increased anger about China's rise in power. All three of those experimental outcomes in turn increased preference for a tough as opposed to friendly national policy toward China, and in one of the two experiments they also led to increased perceived likelihood of military conflict between the United States and China within the next 10 years.[72]

The concept of cognitive simplicity versus complexity was introduced in Chapter 4 and is highly relevant again here. Several writers have pointed out how government announcements and media reports are often one-sided and simplistic, omitting altogether the other side's perspective.[73] Trauma therapist and peace journalist Annabel McGoldrick provides several recent examples, one of direct relevance to US–China rivalry and potential conflict. She points out that Western journalists are not asking *why* China might be building airstrips in the South China Sea, although the answer to many is obvious: the United States is encircling China with a network of bases. She likens war journalism to sports reporting, focusing on "the fight between two teams, with the death toll and casualties representing the score . . . [and] the tactics, moves, and confrontation on each side." She contrasts that with peace journalism, which is more like health reporting. Unlike war reporting, it "emphasises backgrounds and contexts . . . [and] is committed to revealing . . . the underlying causes, and cures to promote long-term healing."[74]

Communication theorists have long sought to tease out a distinction between the ancient art of rhetoric and the more recent concept of propaganda. Long before Pope Gregory XV invented the latter term in the seventeenth century, Plato sought to distinguish true rhetoric from an abusive use of rhetorical power. Although rhetoric is less often mentioned by communication experts nowadays, while propaganda is a popular topic, some theorists like Beth Bennett and Sean O'Rourke continue to find it helpful to compare and contrast the two. Table 6.1 summarizes some of the main differences that have been noted. This may give a rather too idealistic picture of rhetoric and may draw too sharp a contrast with propaganda. Even Plato recognized that

Table 6.1 The Contrast between Respectful Dialogue and Propaganda

	Respectful dialogue True rhetoric, thoughtful persuasion	Propaganda Manipulative rhetoric, mindless propaganda
Aim	Mutual understanding	Manipulate opinion
In the interests of	Principally the audience	Principally the persuaders
The audience as	Co-participants, thinking "experts"	Targets to be persuaded, otherwise uninformed
Truth	Discovered or constructed through exchange	Already known to the propagandist; may be concealed
Main techniques	Dialogue, debate	The most effective, including emotional arousal
Ethics	Aims for an ethical relationship between persuader and audience	Means justify the ends

the ideal form of "true rhetoric" was only possible when the audience was wise and knowledgeable enough to partake; popular rhetoric required the use of techniques such as flattery in order to appeal to the masses.[75] And propagandists, of course, maintain that the interests their techniques serve are principally those of the people they lead and represent, not just their own. The contrasts shown in the table do serve, however, to make an important point. Propaganda, encouraging us to support war, either as combatants or as civilian non-combatants, is a form of persuasive communication which departs from mutually participative dialogue between equals. Pratkanis and Aronson put it starkly when they depict the one as "mindless" and the other as "thoughtful."[76]

Enemies and Leaders: Who's Who in the Battle for Our Minds?

We have noted a number of times how conflict-related discourse can move seamlessly between referring to an enemy or potential enemy in different terms, sometimes as a unitary state or other political body (Russia, ISIS), sometimes as a symbol of it ("Washington," "Westminster"), sometimes as a component of the state (the Chinese Communist Party, "the regime"), and sometimes as a whole people (the Iranians, the Iraqis). In the academic international relations world, there is a general tendency "to anthropomorphize the state," as the author of the *Cambridge Review of International Affairs* paper put it, treating the state as if it were "a unitary actor," akin to an individual with personal agency. States are spoken of as if they were people. Quite often, especially when referring to states or organizations seen as rivals or adversaries with which we are not presently at war, it is indeed individual political leaders (Putin, Xi) who are held responsible for the threat we are told we should feel.[77]

When it comes to propaganda, these distinctions are of great importance. In the United States during World War I, for example, the Committee on Public Information and US propaganda generally suggested that the country was fighting "for peace, freedom, and justice for *all* peoples ... it also served to warn Americans that their enemy was a regime, not a people, an ideology rather than an army." President Wilson in 1917 stated, "We have no quarrel with the German people. We have no feelings towards them but one of sympathy and friendship. It is not upon their impulse that their government acted in entering this war."[78] In Britain, despite widespread anti-German sentiment, "conscience-stricken Liberals on the *Daily News*," as Ferguson puts it, were able to focus their attacks on German militarism. They claimed their quarrel was not with the German people but with "the 'tyranny which has held them in its vice.'"[79] In the Second World War, according to Taylor, there was an initial attempt in Britain to draw a clear separation between the German people and their leaders, although it proved impossible to maintain that distinction and the war of words descended into vindictiveness against the German people (see Chapter 4). Stalin personally wanted to divide German people from Nazi leaders, but Soviet propaganda overtook any such distinction. In the 1991 Gulf War, with polls in the United Kingdom and United States holding at 70%–80% approval for the war, coalition leaders insisted this was not a war against the Iraqi people and that only "smart" bombing of military targets was to be used, not indiscriminate bombing of the capital. During the NATO psyops campaign in the Balkans, leaflets were dropped over Belgrade and Novi Sad and elsewhere suggesting that NATO was not fighting the civilian population but rather the Milošević regime. "This personalization of the campaign," if anything, backfired and increased support for Milošević: "We are all targets" became a rallying cry.[80]

This is not to say that leadership is not important; it clearly is. But it raises the question of why we seem to be so ready to follow our leaders when they take us into war. Psychological understanding of leadership has changed, as Haslam and colleagues explained in their book *The New Psychology of Leadership*. The old psychology of leadership attributed the influence of leaders to their personalities, their charisma. It was the characteristics they possessed as individuals that conferred on them their ability to lead and our propensity to follow them. One problem with that was that it encouraged an unrealistic personality cult of a glorified, heroic, great leader. It also made the rest of us appear like thoughtless followers.[81]

Drawing on in-group social identity theory (see Chapter 4), Haslam et al.'s new psychology of leadership was as much about "followership" as leadership, we-ness as much as I-ness. Their first rule of leadership was that a leader must be seen as "one of us"; the second that the leader must act as the group's champion; the third that leaders needed to be "skilled entrepreneurs of identity" reflecting who we are and what we want to be; and, fourth, that leaders be "embedders of identity," reinforcing the importance of who we are. Instead of the leader being seen as the one with the power to influence, and the rest of us powerless followers, power is seen as jointly vested in in-group members and their leaders, whose influence is seen as positive, not an imposition to be passively accepted or resisted.

Barbara Walter, writing of the wars in the former Yugoslavia, talks of "opportunistic leaders," the "ethnic entrepreneurs," like the Serbian Milošević and Croatian Tudjman, tapping into dormant but rapidly growing fears and resentments, "mak[ing] the fight expressly about their group's position and status in society." The ethnic propaganda in which such leaders specialize only has minority support to begin with and is readily dismissed, she explains, but average citizens "become willing to show support if they feel a mounting threat—to their lives, livelihoods, families, or futures." Control of the media also played a role in the Serbia–Croatia war, as it has done in so many wars. Milošević and his government gained control of the Politika publishing house, which owned multiple TV and radio stations and newspapers, and Tudjman started the rival Croatian News Agency.[82]

Another good example of a war leader who provided the necessary fit with his followers' preoccupations and sense of identity at a particular moment in history was Patrick Pearse of the 1916 Dublin Easter Rising. In his book *Wounds: A Memoir of War and Love*, BBC war correspondent Fergal Keane, whom we met in earlier chapters, describes Pearse as "my personal idol in those days. He was handsome and proud and gloriously doomed. My father often recited his poems and speeches." Although, as someone who has witnessed a number of wars, Keane recognizes something else in Pearse's writings: "I read them now and shiver. After nearly three decades reporting conflict, I recognise in the words of Pearse a man who spoke of the glory of war only because he had not yet known war."[83]

The new way of viewing leadership in social psychology, consistent with social identity, in-group/out-group theory, predicts that support for a war changes principally in response to being reminded of one's social identity, for example as a patriotic citizen of one's country, and what opinions are expected of a loyal member of one's in-group in the interest of group solidarity in the face of an external threat. Listening to an inspiring leader can remind one of that. So too can seeing the war featuring prominently in the media. Indeed, it has been concluded by some that it is the reminder of one's identity that is more important than any new information media reports may provide, for example about how the war is progressing. The claim is that reminders of social identity are more influential than information updating when it comes to the dynamics of war support. That thesis was supported by an analysis of US news coverage of all major American wars between 1950 and 2010. That included wars in Korea (1950–53), Vietnam (1965–73), the Persian Gulf (1990–91), Kosovo (1999), Afghanistan and Iraq (from early 2000s and still ongoing at the time of the analysis). Opinion change was gauged by questions used in national representative survey samples. The research team found no consistent evidence that levels of war support changed in ways predicted by an information-updating model. Instead, war support went up during periods when wars were prominently featured in the news—for example when coverage of the war was prominent on the front page of the *New York Times*—and reduced when wars slipped out of the headlines and front pages. Although this is just one study and there may be other interpretations, it did look as if a powerful determinant of support for the use of military force might be the reminder that the larger group one identifies with, the nation in this case, is engaged in conflict with another.[84]

Misgivings about Propaganda

In the early parts of this chapter I drew heavily on Philip Taylor's detailed history of war propaganda. His splendid book is also of interest for his reflections on our misgivings about being coerced, deceived even, by propaganda—its morality indeed. He begins, on his very first page, by declaring that there is no point making moral judgments about it. But he acknowledges that we tend to react badly if we don't trust what we are being told or if we feel we are being told what to think—a tendency that psychologists have called "reactance." We may also suspect that propaganda is being used for other, undeclared political purposes. Taylor tells us there was some discomfort after the war had ended, about how it was used in World War I. It left a bad taste in British mouths. Lord Ponsonby caught that prevailing mood about the use of propaganda when in 1926 he wrote the words quoted at the heading of this chapter.[85]

Should we in any case blame governments and other war leaders? Writing about the First World War, Ferguson points out that it was not only governments that produced propaganda; in almost all the combatant countries, journalists, academics, amateur poets, and many others did too, and businesses manufactured it in the form of such products as toys and comics for children.[86] Taylor asked a related question. Can a clear line be drawn between propaganda, on the one hand, with its explicit intent to support the interests of one side in a conflict, and, on the other hand, education and culture, with its more subtle influence? Since we know history tends to be written by the victors, is history education itself just another type of "social and political engineering." In practice, the line between propaganda and education is, in his opinion, a thin one. And what about "cultural propaganda" in the United States, "Coca-Colonialism" or "cultural imperialism" as critics have termed it, or what the British and French preferred to term "cultural diplomacy," or the exercise of "soft power," to use a now popular term? An example from early in the Cold War was the US revitalization of Second World War information services, including an "educational" role for Hollywood, officially designed "to promote a better understanding of the United States in other countries, and to increase mutual understanding between the people of the United States and the people of other countries." Such "influence operations" raised further ethical doubts for Philip Taylor.[87]

It can even be questioned whether propaganda plays any great part in helping to cause war by encouraging the people's support for it. In 1964 a report from the World Rule of Law Centre stated that it does. But in Taylor's opinion that report "missed the point. Wars are not caused solely, or even mainly, by propaganda." It enters the picture and can help escalate conflict but only after a decision to go to war has been made.[88] An alternative conclusion, and the one toward which I lean in the light of the material discussed in earlier chapters—for example, on the important role played by the inculcation of chauvinistic nationalist and other values and identities in Chapter 3—is that propaganda only becomes *identifiable* as such once war is under way. Taylor himself recognized that there was only a thin line between outright propaganda and more subtle softening-up influences such as those imposed by the history we are taught and the cultural militarism we are brought up to accept. The outbreak of war—not always so easy to date exactly—may be a tipping point, beyond which the drumbeats of war becoming deafening; but they were sounding before, often long before. The basic psychology of war support doesn't change.

Conclusions

This chapter has shifted the argument yet further away from an explanation for war support that rests on personal beliefs and inclinations. The chapter's general conclusion is that propaganda has always played an important role and continues to do so. It is difficult to avoid the conclusion that support for war depends on some distortion of objective truth or at least on a very selective presentation of the real facts. If that is to be believed, it is not so much that we genuinely support war but rather that we are mentally coerced into support for wars that our political leaders wish us to support and with which we comply. The print and broadcast media have been crucial in managing the public's perception of war-related events and possibilities, and social media now plays a major role in "new" and civil wars. Are we simply the victims of the "regimenting of the public mind," of the "manufacturing of consent"?

In the course of this chapter a number of themes, already familiar from earlier chapters, have recurred. We need to take special note of these because they will occupy important places in the psychological model of war support which I propose in the concluding Chapter 8. The importance of *in-group identity*, and support for it (see Chapters 3 and 4), encouraged by leaders and by the media, is one of them. Modern ideas about leadership stress the need for an effective leader to be seen as "one of us," to be acting as the nation or group's champion, and to reflect and reinforce the importance of group identity. A main function of the media in encouraging war support may also rest on its capacity as a reminder of group identity and the expectation of support for it.

The centrality, for understanding how we are persuaded to support war, of *threat perception*, is another. This chimes with our discussion of the security dilemma in international relations (Chapter 1) and with beliefs in a dangerous world (Chapter 2). If we can be persuaded that our group is under threat, especially if that amounts to "existential threat," it is difficult to oppose the call for action. To do so would open one up to the charge of disloyalty to one's nation or identity group.

A further theme that has recurred is that of *cognitive simplicity versus complexity*, which was introduced in Chapter 4. It is highly relevant again in the context of war propaganda and persuasion. War-related government announcements and media reports are often one-sided and simplistic, omitting altogether the other side's perspective. They fall well short of the standards set by the best of war journalism, which thoughtfully tries to reveal the background context to a conflict, its underlying causes and possible resolutions.

A closely related theme, echoing the content of Chapter 3, is that of the *causes and values* in the name of which people are called on to support war. A benign way of construing propaganda is that leaders have to market to their public, using whatever means they can, what they consider to be a just cause.

The way in which war and its support can spiral out of control is a theme noted from Chapter 1 onward. There is an argument for saying that wars are not caused solely, or even mainly, by propaganda; that it can contribute to the *escalation of conflict* but that it usually comes after the policy has been decided. I favor an alternative view that propaganda and persuasion—not usually recognized or labeled as such—play a major role in the earlier process of preparing for the possibility of war, only becoming clearly identified once war is under way.

We have seen again when considering propaganda something we noticed first in Chapter 1 and which keeps on cropping up. Discussion of war often conflates and confuses *levels of analysis*, often moving seamlessly between referring to an enemy or potential enemy as a unitary state or other political body, as a component of it, a symbol of it, or as a whole people. We note again in the present chapter a general tendency to anthropomorphize the state or organization, treating it as if it were "a unitary actor," akin to an individual with personal agency. Indeed, it is often individual political leaders who are held responsible for the threat we are told we should feel.

The questionable *morality* of war and of support for it is a further recurrent theme throughout this book's exploration of why we support war. It featured in Chapter 2 and will be a main theme in the next chapter when we look at just war theory. "Propaganda" is a dirty word, implying something of doubtful morality. We don't like the idea of being coerced by it, particularly if we think we may have been deliberately misled by it, by "the injection of the poison of hatred into men's minds by means of falsehood," as Lord Ponsonby put it a century ago.

7

Just War?

War as a Moral Dilemma

When all other means have failed, it is permissible to draw the sword.

Revered guru in Sikh history, Guru Gobind Singh[1]

The concept of the Just War is a contradiction in terms—there may be just motives, but they are corrupted immediately in the prosecution of war.

Reverend Donald Soper, Methodist minister[2]

The fraught question of whether war can ever be considered ethical, moral, is one I have touched on in several places in previous chapters. How can supporting war be justified in the light of the scale and dreadfulness of the harms it causes (Chapter 1)? Is the use of some weapons, perhaps especially those that enable killing or injuring at a great distance, itself immoral (Chapter 5)? When does propaganda cross an ethical red line (Chapter 6)? Perhaps collective violence is morally motivated, and what is immoral is *not* being prepared to fight for a cause such as liberty or one's group's survival (Chapter 3). In this chapter the morality of supporting war is the principal focus. We will need to consider the notion that wars can, under certain circumstances, be considered just—*just war theory*. We shall look at psychological theories of moral justification and their relevance for understanding war support. Along the way we will touch on conscientious objections to engaging in and supporting war, as well as the "moral injury" suffered by veteran combatants who have been required to transgress moral beliefs that forbid the killing or maiming of others.

The belief that war is sometimes necessary and can be morally justified, even positively virtuous, is a final crucial element of war readiness. It is to be found in the war-justifying statements, or at least ambivalence toward war, associated with all world religions, which have supported some wars and weapons as "holy" and often viewed taking up arms to confront evil and injustice as legitimate, even a duty. It is codified in just war theory, a kind of ethical rough guide to war, justifying the decision to go to war under certain conditions and stipulating the ways in which war can be pursued ethically. Justifying war morally also requires a large measure of cognitive simplification, another of the central planks of the model of war support I am constructing. The mental tactics that allow us to justify to ourselves the supporting of actions otherwise considered immoral, such as wounding others, have their parallels in the simplifying language of militarism and propaganda that we have met in earlier chapters. Those "mechanisms of moral disengagement" include calling on right or honorable ends to justify harmful actions and dehumanizing the victims of one's actions by attributing blame to them for bringing harm upon themselves.

Since they offer moral guidance and mostly forbid the taking of human life, we might expect religions to have taken a strong stand against supporting war, so we must consider what they have had to say on the subject. Let us begin there.

The Ambivalent Attitude of World Religions toward War

It hardly needs to be said that the story of religion's support for war and militarism is a long and complex one. In *The Selfish Gene*, Richard Dawkins proclaims, "What a weapon! Religious faith deserves a chapter to itself in the annals of war technology."[3] Religious fervor has been singled out as a factor which has increased war's brutality and casualties over the centuries. Rome's principal god was Mars, the god of war. Some of the most famous wars were quite explicitly holy wars. In Europe, the nearly 100 years up to 1648 when the Treaty of Westphalia ended the Thirty Years War, has been called by one war historian the *Age of Religions*. Religious passion inspired Cromwell's New Model Army. Protestants have fought Catholics, Catholics have fought Russian Orthodox Christians, Sunni and Shiite Muslims have fought one another, and Christian countries have taken arms against Muslim countries. Nor have monotheistic religions had a monopoly on war support; war has been just as prevalent under religions such as Buddhism and Confucianism. Instead of giving us an unequivocal lead *against* supporting war, religions have often done precisely the opposite.[4]

Support for the twentieth century's First World War came from the Christian churches, as Niall Ferguson makes plain. The start of the war saw, he says, "an upsurge in religious observance in nearly all the combatant countries."[5] Many church leaders encouraged the notion that this was a holy war, perhaps the clearest example being the shocking Advent sermon given by the Bishop of London in 1915. The bishop described the war as,

> a great crusade—we cannot deny it—to kill Germans: to kill them, not for the sake of killing, but to save the world; to kill the good as well as the bad, to kill the young men as well as the old . . . and to kill them lest the civilization of the world should itself be killed . . . a war for purity, for freedom, for international honour and for the principles of Christianity.[6]

Religious justification for war was likewise drawn on by politicians and generals. Ferguson believes General Haig's approach to the war cannot be understood without knowing of his membership of the Church of Scotland. Haig is quoted as proclaiming to his wife before the Battle of the Somme, "I feel that every step in my plan has been taken with the Divine help." In Germany, too, the Protestant church, especially in its more radical forms, offered war support. One of the leaders of the Pan-German League, for example, declared, "War is holy to us, since it will awaken all that is great and self-sacrificing and selfless in our people and cleanse our souls of the dross of selfish pettiness."[7] From George Mosse's *Fallen Soldiers: Reshaping the Memory of the World Wars* we know also of the central role of Christian church services and war cemeteries, and their associated symbolism, in the commemoration of those killed in that war (see Chapter 5). The Cross of Sacrifice was central in British cemeteries. Mosse's book contains a photograph of a typical British military cemetery overseas with a sword shown inside the cross—"a stark sword brooding in the bosom of the cross," as Rudyard Kipling put it.[8]

Religion's support for war continues to the present day in the United States, the United Kingdom, and Russia. Andrew Bacevich devotes a whole chapter of his book *The New American Militarism* to the influence especially of evangelical Christians in support of US militarism since the Second World War, notably in the aftermath of the 9/11 attacks.[9] The British Military Covenant, published in 2000, which frames the relationship and expectations between the Army and its soldiers, according to Forster's description, draws heavily on Christian values and ideas and is written in a style with quasi-religious overtones.[10] In Russia in September 2017 an event was reported that speaks volumes about religion's continued support of militarism: a statue of Mikhail Kalashnikov, the inventor of the AK-47 assault rifle, had been unveiled in central Moscow. The 9-meter monument depicts Kalashnikov clutching his automatic weapon. The event was attended by high-ranking officials and religious leaders. The collusion of formal religion in militarism is illustrated by the blessing of the statue by a Russian Orthodox priest, who shrugged off suggestions that it was inappropriate to sprinkle holy water on a statue of a weapons designer. Another religious leader wrote on Facebook, "Our weapon is a holy weapon."[11] Christian thought about war has not just been about mitigating its horrors 'but was just as much a casuistical endeavour to justify war despite the fact that Christianity is manifestly a non-violent and pacifist religion," says A. C. Grayling.[12]

Writing about US Army chaplains in World War II, Jenel Virden says it seems that few clerics felt a particular need to justify the breaking of the sixth commandment, *thou shalt not kill*.[13] Killing was seen as incidental to the goal, the defeat of evil, as long as one killed without hatred or malice. Chaplains' correspondence back to the Chief of Chaplains office in Washington DC was mainly about vice and immoral behavior such as gambling, use of profanity, alcohol consumption, sexuality, problems of discipline, suspect entertainment, indecent literature, and sex of any kind. Rarely if ever mentioned in the files of the Chief of Chaplains were the big issues of the morality of killing and of war itself. Memoirs of chaplains and official histories of various branches of the chaplains' corps discuss war in heroic terms, and chaplains themselves are cited as brave men who made useful and valuable contributions to the war effort.[14]

All religions, without exception it seems, have struggled with this question of how to reconcile their commandments to seek peace with support for war. All are ambivalent, and all have come to an uneasy and unconvincing compromise, as the various chapters of *Just War in Comparative Perspective*, published in 2003, testify. The Catholic Church is one example. Although a constant commitment to strive for justice through non-violent means, and forgiveness, are at the heart of the Catholic faith, many recognize that force may be necessary in a sinful world and that military force may be necessary as a last resort to resist and confront evil and serious injustice, says Paul Dearey in his chapter.[15] In its 1992 catechism the Catholic Church said, "The use of arms must not produce evils and disorders greater than the evil to be eliminated."[16]

There is a lack of moral clarity and consistency in reflections on the morality of war by Orthodox bishops and theologians too. War is considered undesirable but necessary so long as it is pursued in a measured way. Alexander Webster cites the 2000 Jubilee Bishops' Council of the Russian Orthodox Church to the effect that it is not the use of force, nor even the taking of life in the last resort, which is morally deplorable but rather "malice in the human heart and the desire to humiliate or destroy." The Orthodox Church's unconvincing attempts to compromise on war have a long history. Webster cites Saint Basil the Great who suggested in the fourth century that those who kill in the course of war should abstain from Holy Communion for 3 years, as opposed to 20 years for murderers. Later, canonists of the twelfth century thought this unfairly burdensome since wars were so frequent that Christian soldiers, particularly the bravest, would never be able to partake of communion.[17]

Judaism has also struggled with the question of how widely the concept of "defense" should be applied. In modern times, states George Wilkes, "Most of the rabbinic leadership has concluded . . . that the defensive mandate for war applies in a wide sense because of the apparently implacable hostility of Israel's enemies."[18] The question of whether taking up arms can ever be considered a duty under Islam has been highly controversial. John Kelsay refers to the document which appeared in a London paper in February 1998 under the headline "Text of a Declaration by the World Islamic Front with Respect to Jihad against the Jews and the Crusaders." Behind this declaration stands the language of armed struggle as an individual duty, no longer just a communal obligation but a duty in which every Muslim must understand the emergency and do their part. Kelsay points out that none of the five people associated with the document (Osama bin Laden was one) was a recognized scholar of Islam and that the call for direct and intentional strikes at civilian targets is a direct violation of Islamic norms.[19] It is widely understood that Islamic texts, like Christian and Judaic ones, can be interpreted in many different ways and can be used to support totally divergent courses of action.[20]

According to Francis Clooney, pain, and the distinction between pain and harm, plays an important role in Hinduism's fundamental but seemingly complex attitudes toward war. An important distinction is made between, on the one hand, exerting force and causing pain, with killing as an extreme outcome, in order to fulfill a duty or achieve a higher goal and, on the other hand, the causing of harm, which is always condemned. Brahmins and kings would in fact be criticized if they were not willing to cause pain when necessary. Indeed, exerting force and causing pain lessens the overall amount of pain in the long run—a sentiment long echoed by numerous realist international relations experts and politicians, whatever their religious background.[21] Sikhism, Gurharpal Singh explains, also has a clear conception of a justified war as a necessary, defensive act. Guru Gobind, involved in many battles with the local Punjab rajas and the Mogul court, famously enunciated the principle, cited at the heading of this chapter, that the Sikh should never be the first to draw the sword. UK Prime Minister Tony Blair, at a Sikh celebration in Birmingham in 1999, referred to the NATO campaign in Kosovo as consistent with that key element of the Sikh faith that when all other ways of redressing injustice have failed, taking up the sword is right and just.[22]

Although the teachings of Confucius, Thomas Kane tells us, encouraged people to hold military personnel and military concerns in contempt, neither did he forbid warfare. Lao Tzu, founder of Taoism, warns in the *Tao te Ching* that even for the victor, warfare is wasteful and destructive: "Thorn bushes spring up wherever the enemy has passed." But he too was a pragmatist about war. The Taoist might objectively appraise a situation and conclude that fighting is a natural response to the circumstances. Even so, "Though they have armour and weapons, no one displays them," "A good soldier is not violent," "a good fighter is not angry," and "a good winner is not vengeful."[23]

The first essential step in the path of living in Buddhism is *sila*, morality, at the heart of which is the undertaking not to harm any living beings including oneself. Perpetrating or sanctioning the violence of war harms both self and others, according to Buddhist text and tradition. Elizabeth Harris cites Dhammapada v. 5—"Hatred is never appeased by hatred in this world: by non-hatred alone is hatred appeased. This is an eternal law." However, justifications for war can be found, such as the utilitarian argument concerning the greater good, particularly the argument that rulers may be drawn into conflict for the sole purpose of protecting their citizens—fighting between the military and the Liberation Tigers in the Sri Lanka war is one example. It seems that even Buddhism, which can appear to be one of the clearest of religions on the subject of war, is sometimes not so clear after all.[24]

Justification for War: Just War Theory

In recent times, there has been a renewed interest in these dilemmas among philosophers, legal scholars, political scientists, and citizens generally.

A central question, as always, is, How can we explain killing in war being seen as morally permissible, often indeed morally admirable? Just war theory, which proposes that under certain conditions war can be just and that there are moral rules that apply to the fighting, is at the heart of the debate. How can we support the deliberate use of deadly force, a method of trying to win in a situation of conflict, which we abhor in the context of personal encounters with fellow human beings? An idea that is central to just war theory, Helen Frowe tells us in *The Ethics of War and Peace*, is that the "domestic analogy" is of little help since war is an activity that has no equivalent in a settled civil society. The rules of war are sui generis; there is nothing else like it. It is by living in the state and forming a common life within it that citizens agree to their state using force for protection of them. That collectivist account suggests that in war we move beyond what individual rights can tell us. War is essentially political. Actions as a collective cannot be reduced to the actions of individuals because sovereignty is necessarily group-based. Indeed, current laws of armed conflict hold that combatants do not act illegally simply by fighting, even if they fight on the unjust side. Combatants have "an essentially *political* permission to do violence."[25] This is in line with the truism that "war made the state, and the state made war" that featured prominently in Chapter 1. Also discussed in that opening chapter was the idea that states are required to act to protect their citizens within an international field of forces which is essentially anarchic and amoral, a situation quite unlike that operating within the constraints of the domestic law within a well-functioning country. Depending on one's point of view, this either can be seen as offering permission for collective violence or can be construed as allowing state actors to "abdicate moral responsibility for their military decisions."[26] It is even less obvious that it exonerates those who plan and support civil wars or other types of "new war" (see Chapter 1).

The expression "just war" is attributed to Saint Augustine, in his *The City of God*. Aquinas quoted him extensively in *Epistle to Marcellus* and developed his own ideas further in *Summa Theologica*, where he said three things were necessary for a war to be just. One, that the war has "the authority of the sovereign by whose command the war is to be waged." Two, that it has "just cause . . . namely that those who are attacked, should be attacked because they deserve it on account of some fault." Three, that "the belligerents should have a rightful intention, so that they intend the advancement of good, or the avoidance of evil . . . [citing Augustine] 'not for motives of aggrandisement, or cruelty.' "[27]

The other key figure was the Dutch jurist Hugo Grotius, whose *On the Laws of War and Peace* was part of the wider debate in moral philosophy in the seventeenth and eighteenth centuries following the horrors of the 1618–48 Thirty Years War.[28] He is generally considered to be the "father of international law" and, according to some, the preeminent philosopher of war.[29] Grotius said that a sovereign state, in the absence of any higher authority, had the right to go to war if it could claim to have been wronged. His view of war was therefore based on rights, and he did not limit this to Christians, which perhaps explains his positive reputation since then. But it is the case that he worked for the Dutch East India Company, and his ideas were congenial to them. The world he described in 1625 is full of the rights of individuals, states, native peoples, and trading companies, one of the rights being the right to wage war to defend all the other rights. It would become the foundation for all further treaties on international law. He relied on the long tradition of just war theory, building these ideas and rules together into a system that formed the basis for global commerce and international relations for the next several centuries—what Hathaway and Shapiro call the "Old World order"—the right of sovereigns and their chartered trading companies to wage war to enforce their rights against one another. Kant called him a "sorry comforter" of warmongers, and Rousseau thought his ideas were favorable to tyrants. However, as well as seeking to legitimize just wars, Hathaway and Shapiro believe he helped to delegitimize others, such as holy wars, land grabs, "regime change" as we would now call it, and wars of annihilation, none of which should qualify as wars aimed at remedying a wrong.

There are two parts to modern just war theory. The first, *jus ad bellum*, following Augustine's lead, talks of the conditions required in order to decide to wage a just war. The present list of criteria varies slightly from one theorist to another, but there is general agreement about the inclusion of at least the six criteria shown in Table 7.1.[30] All, needless to say, are matters of judgment and can be challenged in relation to almost all wars. There is, understandably, much skepticism about leaders' claims regarding their war intentions. The just cause, right intention, proportionality, and last resort criteria are especially open to challenge. Proportionality and last resort in particular are notoriously subjective and ambiguous. It was those two criteria which Archbishop Pilarczyk, president of the National Conference of Catholic Bishops, thought might be violated when he wrote to President George H. W. Bush about the first Gulf War.[31] The president claimed, "We went halfway round the world to do what is moral, just, and right." But, as Joanna Bourke

Table 7.1 Our Moral Rough Guide to Making War: The Jus ad Bellum Just War Criteria and Some of the Reasons Why Their Application Is Problematic

Jus ad bellum criterion	The grounds for a war being just	Why the application of the criterion is problematic
Just cause	Attack or imminent threat of attack	Imminent threat is hard to judge. Must the threat be to territory? Might it be directed at religion or other values?
Right intention	To repel invasion, not in revenge or to inflict punishment, to gain territory, or to bring about regime change	Intentions can be mixed. Can war to preempt or prevent future attack be just? Is war engaged on humanitarian grounds justified?
Competent authority	Authorized by an internationally recognized government or international organization and properly declared	Wars are increasingly complicated. For example, can war undertaken by a non-state group to overthrow a tyrannical government be justified?
Reasonable chance of success	Confidence in a short, decisive engagement	That is a necessary claim in order to reduce the costs of war and to ensure support, but it is often not achieved in practice.
Proportionality	A judgment that the costs of not engaging in war outweigh the likely costs of engaging	This involves a very difficult calculation, weighing unpredictable costs of different kinds.
Last resort	All reasonable efforts at a non-military solution have been tried	There are always further efforts at diplomacy or other methods which could be tried.

Sources: Based on H. Frowe, *The Ethics of War and Peace: An Introduction* (London: Routledge, 2011) and B. Howe, "Conflicting Normative Dimensions of Justification: The Gulf War," in *Just War in Comparative Perspective*, ed. P. Robinson (Burlington, VT: Ashgate, 2003), 200–217.

says, "It is difficult to find a single example of armed intervention carried out by the Americans, Europeans and their allies in the past century that has not been justified on benevolent grounds."[32]

The second part of just war theory, *jus in bello*, is all about the ways in which wars, once under way, may be justly prosecuted. This is where, according to

Brendan Howe, just war theory now places a greater emphasis.[33] To start with, there is a realist position which is that the nature of war defies legal or moral constraint on how it is pursued.[34] The absence of rules is better, it is argued, because without rules war, although brutal, would be shorter and in the long run less costly. A second, more defeatist, position is that we cannot regulate war and are fooling ourselves if we think that we can impose rules; it is futile to try and restrain actions in the midst of war, which puts soldiers in some of the most dire situations imaginable.[35] Nevertheless, most contemporary just war theorists reject both those realist and defeatist positions, believing that it is possible to formulate rules about how war can legitimately be prosecuted.

Civilian Immunity?

The in bello rules are legally enshrined in the Hague Conventions of 1899 and 1907, the Geneva Convention of 1949, and the Geneva Protocols of 1977. The distinction between combatants and civilians is central. To qualify as a combatant, a person must be part of a hierarchical group with a recognizable chain of command, wear a distinctive emblem that is visible from a distance, bear arms openly, and obey the rules of jus in bello as laid out in the Convention. The Convention forbids all intentional violence toward non-combatants (and toward members of the armed forces who are *hors de combat* through surrender, capture, or injury). Nor are members of the military such as doctors and clergy legitimate targets as they are deemed to be performing civilian roles. The rule about attacking non-personal targets such as buildings is that they can be struck if they have a military function, including telephone exchanges and research centers used for military purposes. Anything serving a civil rather than military function is an illegitimate target unless taken over for military purposes during the war. Bombing a purely or largely residential area is not permissible—hence the firebombing of German cities such as Dresden in the Second World War would not have been within the rules. Schools and hospitals cannot be attacked but can permissibly be destroyed in the course of targeting something else such as a power plant or military base. Military commanders, therefore, must be firmly focused upon the opposing military force. Actions must be proportionate, the least harmful means of achieving the aims.[36]

The main harm in war may be the taking of life; but not all lives count equally in war, and most accounts of proportionality do not count the deaths of enemy combatants as a harm to be weighed in the balance—by enlisting, combatants waive their right not to be killed in battle. Nearly all just war theorists think that one must, on the other hand, include the lives of enemy non-combatants in proportionality calculations. The Geneva Convention prohibits the targeting of non-combatants but not their killing as an unforeseen side effect of an offensive aimed at gaining some military advantage. Most would think that the lives of enemy non-combatants count equally with the lives of our own non-combatants, but some argue that states have an obligation to prefer the interests of their own citizens.[37] Even less obvious is how the death of one of our combatants is weighed in the cost–benefit equation against the death of an enemy non-combatant. The in bello just war rules turn out to be little more unambiguous than the ad bellum ones.

Does the idea that civilians are immune from attack in war imply, then, that they are innocent, that those of us who support a war are free of guilt for causing it or engaging in it? This strikes me as being a rather important question, fundamental to the issue of war support. As we saw in Chapter 4, negative, even dehumanizing images of the enemy are often applied well beyond enemy combatants. Furthermore, to restate a point I have had cause to make several times, debates and discussions about war and its support regularly conflate political leaders, military personnel, and general citizens, without distinction. In fact, the principle of non-combatant immunity in war was notably absent in the writings of Saint Augustine, who argued that all members of aggressing states are guilty. War tactics in his time often included things like sieges of towns or cities, which would predictably result in non-combatant deaths.

The shift from his "collective guilt" view to the endorsing of non-combatant immunity came with Hugo Grotius' writings on international law. Even then, while it is combatants who seem to pose the threat, it can be said that not all combatants are engaged in frontline fighting and that those who provide technical support can count as posing just as much of a threat.[38] Hence, in some eyes, legitimate wartime targets include many people such as army drivers who could not reasonably be described as threats in ordinary life.[39] They mark themselves out as acting on behalf of a guilty collective even if they are morally innocent as individuals. Some say that munitions workers count as posing a threat because, if those driving guns to the front are included as threats, why would one exclude those making the guns. Michael

Walzer, in *Just and Unjust Wars*, tried to distinguish between the things that soldiers need as soldiers—armaments, parachutes, reconnaissance equipment, armored vehicles, and so on—and things they need more generally as human beings, such as food, shelter, appropriate clothing, and medical care. Munitions workers and drivers might therefore be counted as guilty parties but not chefs.[40]

The doctrine of "double effect," first formulated by Thomas Aquinas in the thirteenth century, tries to make a distinction between intending harm as an end or means and doing something that it is foreseen will cause harm but merely as a side effect. All the doctrine says is that combatants should *not try to* harm civilians rather than *try not to*. It also promotes the view of intention as an interior mental act: actions are legitimate so long as a person believes they do not intend evil. That sounds like a difficult distinction to draw, perhaps little more than a playing with words. In *Just and Unjust Wars*, Walzer modified that doctrine to include "double intention": "combatants must act with an intention to reduce the risk of harm to civilians." It is not enough that combatants do not *intend* to kill non-combatants; what is required is a "positive commitment to save civilian lives."[41]

Walzer accepted that there could be exceptions to non-combatant immunity in "extreme emergency" where defeat is imminent and might result in the annihilation of a people or way of life, under which circumstances the ordinary limitations are temporarily suspended.[42] But when is an emergency "extreme" enough to justify going against his principle that risk to non-combatants must be reduced as much as possible? Some of the West's leaders have gone so far as to claim that committing atrocities against civilians is sometimes the only option. This gives comfort to defenders of twentieth- and twenty-first-century bombing. For example, Winston Churchill wrote to Lord Beaverbrook, "there is one thing that will bring him [Hitler] down, and that is an absolutely devastating, exterminating attack by very heavy bombers from this country upon the Nazi homeland."[43] Military officers proclaimed at the time that it would have been immoral not to kill as many as possible. As the chaplain to the bombers who dropped the bombs on Hiroshima and Nagasaki said, "Gosh, it's horrible, but gosh, it's going to end the war. Finally the boys will get home."[44]

Even when non-combatants are not directly targeted by bombing, there are reasons to be skeptical about whether Walzer's principle is really honored in practice. As we saw in Chapter 1, civilian casualties increased throughout the twentieth century as a proportion of all war casualties.[45] Joanna Bourke is among the skeptics. Bombing, she points out, was hardly precise during the Second World War, nor has it been since. In the first of the two Gulf Wars fewer than 8% of bombs dropped were precision-guided. In the second, two-thirds of weapons were capable of precise targeting, many delivered by drones; but the United States defined a "combatant" as any male of military age living in areas in which the United States was conducting military operations,[46] and furthermore bombing usually relies on human intelligence, which is anything but precise. As guided munitions used in Iraq had an average "circular error probable" of 8 meters, some non-targeted casualties were certain. Adding in human failure, informant error or malice, bad weather, dust, and technical malfunctions all makes it worse; but "the illusion of precision" allowed Western militaries and governments to attribute non-combatant casualties to inadvertent mistakes and to refer to them as "collateral damage." Increased domestic aversion to their own combatants returning home in "body bags" only made this worse.[47] There is the further assumption that when civilians are not killed directly, but rather by hunger or illness following bombardment, as in the case of Iraq, "we" are not responsible.

Has Just War Now Been Abandoned?

Those, then, are the basic rules, imprecise, ambiguous, and controversial though they may be, about when wars are thought to be just and how they should be justly prosecuted. Whether or not, as individuals, we are aware of them, they roughly correspond to what most thinking people who lend a particular war their support would consider a just way of deciding and proceeding. For war supporters, they are their rough guide to making war. For others, it is merely a set of justifications, excuses for supporting war.

In any case, is our ethical rough guide to war, imperfect as it is, now in danger of being abandoned? There has been a growing number of voices warning that the trends are not encouraging. Not only has war not been effectively outlawed, despite the between-the-wars Paris Peace Pact and the post–World War II United Nations (UN) Charter (see Chapter 1),[48] but the very basis of the just war principles are being undermined, some say. Both state actions and justifications and those of non-state actors in the "new wars" are to blame. Veteran war reporter David Wood; Andrew Bacevich, US soldier turned academic; and academics and writers including Mark Pilisuk and Jennifer Rowntree, A. C. Grayling, Brendan Howe, and Joanna Bourke are among those concerned voices. The greatest alarm expressed by these authors and others is that the jus in bello principle that non-combatants should be protected in the face of modern military technology is being widely flouted.

Andrew Bacevich charts in detail what he sees as the abandonment of the jus ad bellum rules by the world's largest military power in the late twentieth century. US Secretary of Defense Caspar Weinberger in 1984 proposed a series of tests for going to war which came to be known as the *Weinberger doctrine*. They were more or less in line with jus ad bellum. Chief among them were "to restrict the use of force to matters of vital national interest; to specify concrete and achievable objectives, both political and military; to secure assurances of popular and congressional support; to fight to win; and to use force only as a last resort." The *Powell doctrine*, following the views of General Colin Powell and supporting the Desert Storm invasion of the first Gulf War, added two: having an "exit strategy," "a clear idea of when and how to extract US forces even before intervening"; and an emphasis on "overwhelming force," sufficient to do the job quickly. Those two doctrines combined would, Bacevich argues, have limited US involvement in war to engagements that were "brief, economical, operationally (if not politically) decisive, and, above all, infrequent."[49]

Following 9/11, President George W. Bush told the nation that, "this country must go on the offense and stay on the offense." The *Bush doctrine* of offensive war abandoned the Weinberger–Powell principles, as did the second Gulf War and the Kosovo campaign, Bacevich believes. Importantly for us, he adds, "The American public's ready acceptance of the prospect of war without foreseeable end and of a policy that abandons even the pretence of the United States fighting defensively or viewing war as a last resort shows clearly how far the process of militarization has advanced."[50] David Wood agrees. Three days after the 2001 9/11 terrorist attacks, he reminds us, the US Congress enacted the Authorization for the Use of Military Force, which sanctified killing of alleged terrorists anywhere on the globe. President Bush then invoked concepts of good and evil to justify the invasion of Iraq: "Fifteen centuries after Augustine, we have returned to the idea that if you are fighting evil, you are excused from the biblical commandment *Thou shalt not kill*. Your cause has to be just a bit less evil than the enemy's."[51] There was no serious anti-war movement in the United States and very little questioning of the moral justification of the wars. Others join the long queue of those who have questioned the justification for US military engagements in the modern era. Pilisuk and Rowntree remind us that the first Guantánamo detainees were described by Rumsfeld as "unlawful combatants" thus precluding them from protection as prisoners of war under the Geneva Convention.[52]

In 2014 the United States justified its air campaign against IS claiming it was acting to defend Iraq. That may have been justifiable according to Hathaway and Shapiro but not if measured against the requirement to be acting in self-defense. The UN Charter allows self-defense only in cases of "armed attack": "If states can always invoke self-defense as a justification to use force, then the prohibition on war becomes meaningless," and if the United States does that, it cannot stop others from arguing the same.[53] In fact, the UN itself in a report in 2004 revisited the issue of jus ad bellum, asking, "What should the Security Council consider as sufficient to persuade it to endorse the use of military force?" They answered with five "basic criteria... the seriousness of the threat, the purpose of the military action, whether there is no other remedy for or means to resolve the problem, whether the force to be used is proportional, and whether the likely consequences are acceptable." These are mostly reiterations of the traditional jus ad bellum criteria. But two changes are notable. The last of the five UN criteria substitutes, in place of "likely success," the more general and inclusive "consequences." The first is even more expanded from the original. No longer is threat to one's own security necessary; going to war is justified "if genocide, ethnic cleansing and major violations of humanitarian law were occurring or imminent." If the list of threats that can justify war is so expanded, Grayling wonders—perhaps including terrorism, transnational organized crime, environmental threats, pandemics, mass migrations, and misuses of technology—maybe just war theory is now irrelevant, even misleading, and no longer serves a useful purpose.[54]

Much depends upon how widely "threat" to one's nation, group, allies, or ideology is interpreted. Highly influential in promoting an enlarged conception of what constitutes defense in the United States, according to Bacevich, has been the right-wing media such as the Rupert Murdoch–supported *Weekly Standard*. Equally, if not more, important, he believes, has been the "enormous clout" wielded by the approximately 100 million US citizens who define themselves as evangelicals and who hold "a highly permissive interpretation of the just war tradition," and neo-conservatives generally. In the run-up to the 2003 Iraq War, the National Association of Evangelicals declared "most evangelicals regard Saddam Hussein's regime—by allegedly aiding and harbouring terrorists—as already having attacked the United States."[55]

One way, favored by some, of maintaining jus ad bellum as our rough guide to deciding when war should be supported is to add a seventh criterion to the generally agreed basic six criteria. This is the *goal of peace*. It claims that, while war can be considered evil in itself, it is not so if waged to put an end to an existing conflict or to ensure that war is less likely to take place in the future.[56] That justification for war is not one that is universally ascribed to by just war theorists. It has come to the fore as a controversial issue in recent times in the form of preventive or preemptive war. Preventive war is usually thought to be impermissible, but the 2002 National Security Strategy of the United States insisted that new kinds of threat posed by terrorism required revising what counts as preemptive war:

> America will act against such emerging threats before they are fully formed. We cannot defend America and our friends by hoping for the best. So we must be prepared to defeat our enemies' plans, using the best intelligence and proceeding with deliberation. History will judge harshly those who saw this coming danger but failed to act. In the new world we have entered, the only path to peace and security is the path of action.[57]

This emphasis on what an enemy state could or might like to do rather than what it *is* doing represents a quite radical departure from contemporary understanding of preemptive war.[58] A further challenge for those who make and support war in the twenty-first century, suggest Centano and Enriquez, is "the apparent contradiction between our technologically driven destructive capacity and the normative constraints placed upon its exercise and use."[59] Technological advances—if "advances" is the appropriate word in the context of war—challenge the in bello rules as well. Drone warfare, discussed in Chapter 5, has brought up these ethical questions in a stark modern form. Grégoire Chamayou takes up such questions in his book *Drone Theory*. He argues that "remoteness" and distance—the very advantages of remote operation—are morally problematic: while the physical distance that separates the assassin and the assassinated may be colossal, the former may be able to witness what happens to the latter very clearly, although the former's actions are not witnessed by the latter. That, he speculates, might be an important factor in reducing the resistance to killing and may promote psychological "distancing" or "compartmentalizing" (see later), which can make doing harm to others easier. Drone warfare, he suggests, is contrary to the principle of reciprocity in warfare, that each party has an equal right to kill the enemy without committing a crime and that each party can see what is happening and has a right to fight back. Willingness to die, he reminds us, is at the heart of traditional military morality with its central virtues of courage, sacrifice, and heroism. Killing by drones without risking one's own life—dropping bombs from a safe height is similar—would be seen in those terms as "the highest degree of cowardice and dishonor."[60]

The contrary argument is that killing without danger to one's own troops is to be commended since it is an imperative to preserve the lives of one's own soldiers as far as is possible. The "ethic of heroic sacrifice" has been replaced, he argues, by the "ethic of vital self-preservation" in an increasingly risk-averse military.[61] Not that this kind of reasoning is new. For example, attempts were made in 1899 to outlaw the particularly vicious dum-dum bullet, designed and manufactured at the British East India Company's ammunition factory in Dum Dum near Kolkata. Their use was defended by recourse to the familiar "comparative cruelty" argument, used to this day to defend controversial weapons on the grounds that the more effective they are, the more their use prevents our own combatants being killed (see Chapter 5).[62] Later, the same argument was used to defend strategic bombing of civilian areas, used sparingly at first in World War I and used against colonial subjects by Italy, France, Spain, and Britain. A. C. Grayling likens the instinctive reaction many have to remote drone killing—that operators are at no physical risk and that it appears sinister, unfair, improper—to the reaction in the press—outrage, "unsporting"—to the very first use of aerial bombing, by the Italian military throwing grenades out of a monoplane onto Ottoman troops in North Africa.

Grayling's pessimistic conclusion is that all attempts to limit the harm threatened by new war technologies have been futile: "Whoever has had the superior technology in a war has always had the better chance of winning it."[63] It might even appear that a general principle was operating: that "a weapon will be restricted in inverse proportion . . . to its effectiveness . . . the more efficient a weapon or method of warfare, the less likelihood there is of its being restricted in action by rules of war."[64] Joanna Bourke too sees a huge asymmetry between states with and those without the most advanced war technology: "Humanitarian law . . . comes down hard and unremittingly on 'murdered by machete' yet turns a benign face to mass murder by atomic bomb or targeted assassinations by drones."[65]

Psychological Models of War and Personal Morality

The religions of the world, and the just war tradition with its Christian roots, have tried to give political leaders and those they represent an ethical guide to war-making. But it is so full of platitudes and ambiguities, and so easy for political leaders to interpret in ways that suit their purposes, that it leaves us now without a clear moral guide on the matter. As potential supporters—or resisters—of war, we may feel powerless faced with new technologically "sophisticated" ways of war. Adding prospects of chemical, nuclear, cyber, and autonomous weapons makes decisions appear even further beyond our control.

There is, however, no shortage of writers on the subject of war who see it in terms of a personal moral dilemma for all of us. A. C. Grayling is clear about the immorality of war and its supposed justifications. Nowhere, he declares, are the human "spiritual gifts" to be found in just war theory: "love, joy, kindness, goodness, gentleness, self-control and peace," and forgiveness. Like so many others, he believes that violence, including the collective violence we call war, distorts human experience by promoting attitudes which degrade us.[66] Hathaway and Shapiro express the moral dilemma just as starkly when they write,

> The licence to kill in wartime is amongst the strangest ever recognised by human beings. Mass murder is morally monstrous and obviously criminal. But, somehow, when the slaughter took place after a formal declaration of war, it suddenly became legal. . . . They also had the licence to trespass, break and enter, steal, assault, maim, kidnap, extort, destroy property, and commit arson . . . to perform acts that would be crimes if committed in peacetime.[67]

At the individual psychological level, a number of models of moral thought and behavior are relevant. Hannah Arendt, in her study of Nazi stormtroopers, was impressed by how ordinary, like the rest of us, these evildoers seemed. That gave rise to her controversial concept of the "banality of evil."[68] Since then, psychologists have started to understand how we justify, to ourselves and others, ideas and actions which might otherwise appear to be contrary to moral principles, which might even be held to be evil. Leon Festinger's idea of *cognitive dissonance*, of finding ways to accommodate to an otherwise uncomfortable mismatch between one's conduct and one's ethical beliefs, became a prominent theory in psychology from the 1950s onward' and the notion of "psychic numbing," or slowly learning to live with moral inconsistency, deceiving ourselves, avoiding self-reproof, compartmentalizing, was introduced by Sissela Bok in the 1970s.[69]

More recently Jonathan Haidt's typology of five "moral foundations" or virtues has become popular. The five are: *care*—protecting others from harm; *fairness*—a desire to see justice, in contrast to cheating; *in-group loyalty*—to family, group or nation, the opposite of betrayal; *respect for legitimate authority*—opposite to subversion; and *purity or sanctity*—abhorrence for uncleanliness, decay, or defilement. He saw these as intuitions, examples of what Kahneman called System 1–type thinking—pre-reflective, fast, effortless—in contrast to slower, thoughtful, System 2 thought, requiring reflection. Although *moral foundations theory* (MFT) has not, to my knowledge, been directly applied to understanding war support, it has relevance for two reasons. For one thing, at least two of the foundational virtues remind us of some of the war support–related psychological factors we have already met. Respect for legitimate authority sounds very like the deference to authority and support for conformity which constitute authoritarianism discussed in Chapter 2 and in-group loyalty featured prominently in Chapter 4 as a major factor underpinning war support. Furthermore, Haidt's typology has relevance in the United States for political allegiance, which we know is related to war support. In his 2012 book *The Righteous Mind*, Haidt showed how US Democrats and Republicans equally value fairness and care but that respect for authority and in-group loyalty (along with purity) are more important to Republican supporters, who are the more militaristic.[70]

A second reason for including MFT here is the counterbalance it provides to an otherwise heavy reliance on theories of war-related morality based on religious teachings. It offers a strong rationalization for the belief that morality need not depend on religion. According to MFT, these universally approved moral foundations take the form of intuitions we are all familiar with and grow up with, owing to the joint influence of natural selection and social learning (though societies vary in the exact combinations in which their customs, laws, and institutions draw upon them).[71]

Another eminent psychologist, Albert Bandura, who died in 2021, has made one of the most pertinent contributions to a psychological understanding of justification for harmful actions generally and for war specifically, including terrorism and drone warfare.[72] He outlined a number (for

Table 7.2 Six Mechanisms of Moral Disengagement

Moral justification	Justifying harmful means in terms of what are believed to be righteous or honorable ends such as national protection against terrorism threat
Advantageous comparison	Rendering harmful conduct as benign through comparison with something worse, for example arguing that precision targeting spares lives
Euphemistic labeling	Sanitizing harmful behavior by the use of euphemistic and innocuous language
Diffusion and displacement of responsibility	Dispersing responsibility so widely that no one is held responsible; evading personal responsibility by displacing it on to others such as those higher up the chain of command
Minimizing, denying, or distorting consequences	Disputing the harmful outcomes of actions by, for example, minimizing civilian casualties or referring to them as "enemies" until proved otherwise
Disparaging, denigrating, and blaming victims and critics	Weakening moral qualms about actions by dehumanizing the victims of one's actions and blaming them for bringing harm upon themselves; demonizing those who criticize our actions

Sources: Based on A. Bandura, "The Role of Selective Moral Disengagement in Terrorism and Counterterrorism," in *Understanding Terrorism: Psychosocial Roots, Consequences, and Interventions*, ed. F. Moghaddam and A. Marsella (Washington, DC: American Psychological Association, 2004), 121–150; A. Bandura, *Moral Disengagement: How People Do Harm and Live with Themselves* (New York: Worth Publishers, 2016); and A. Bandura, "Disengaging Morality from Robot War," *The Psychologist* (February 2017): 39–43.

convenience I have combined them into six) principal *mechanisms of moral disengagement* shown here in Table 7.2. Of particular relevance to the argument developed in the present book are the evident connections of each of Bandura's justificatory mechanisms with themes that have been emerging in our explorations of war support over the course of this and earlier chapters. The first, moral justification—the perceived ends justify using violent means—corresponds to the jus ad bellum criterion of just cause. Much of Chapter 4 was also about exactly this. There we identified threat perception as a crucial element in reinforcing our images of a potential enemy and of our own group in relation to the enemy. Countering such a threat can serve to provide the moral justification for supporting action which would in other circumstances be viewed as immoral. Basic ideas of righting wrongs, even of good versus evil, are put to use. The use of advantageous comparison—justifying harmful conduct such as supporting those who serve our nation or group killing others as part of war, on the grounds that this avoids something far worse—chimes, to give just one example, with our discussion in Chapter 5 on militarism and the justifications that have so often been given for the development and use of ever more effective ways of attacking and killing enemies at a distance. The use of euphemistic language—Bandura's third means of justification—has been a feature of war support rhetoric touched on in several chapters, perhaps most obviously in the context of propaganda in Chapter 6.

The fourth way of justifying our support for war—avoiding feelings of personal responsibility for supporting deliberate aggression toward others by offloading the responsibility onto others or sharing it widely with others—was a theme especially in Chapters 3 and 4 where issues of national or group identity came to the fore. Since war is a collective undertaking, indeed if war can serve to enhance group cohesion in the face of threat from an out-group, then individual personal responsibility is effectively diluted. Personal responsibility can be evaded by displacing it on to the enemy and its leaders or, depending on one's position regarding a particular war, onto one's own political or military leaders. Putting the harmful consequences of war out of sight and out of mind, as Bandura puts it, by minimizing, denying, distorting, or disputing them—mechanism number five—is relevant at many points in war support, notably over the issue of civilian casualties discussed in Chapters 1, 5 and 6 and touched on elsewhere. The final justificatory mechanism—amounting to throwing the blame onto the victim—is inherent in the idea of war and support for it, as has been clear throughout. War support requires a mindset that sees competition and danger, conceives of one's own group in chauvinistic terms, and perceives a threat from another (among the foci of Chapters 2, 3 and 4). Our susceptibility to being persuaded by our leaders to see things that way formed the substance of Chapter 6. The use of demonization and dehumanization was highlighted. In addition, the denigrating of those who fail to support the dominant war narrative, whether such critics are "enemies within" or outwith our group, is part of what Bandura had in mind here and has been a theme that we have touched on a number of times, particularly in Chapter 6.

Powerful and highly relevant though Bandura's model of moral disengagement is for understanding war support, it perhaps does not do sufficient justice to the *positive* arguments that are always produced to justify a particular war. If a war's positive "cover story," as it might be called,[73] is accepted, it is not merely a question of how to justify wrong behavior. The question can now be reversed: how can we justify *not* "doing something," including taking up arms if necessary, in order to do the honorable thing, to combat wrongdoing perpetrated by others. Indeed, one could go further and assert, as has so often been claimed, that war serves the cause of peace: "If you want peace, prepare for war" (see Chapter 1). As arch-realist Azar Gat says, "A strategy of conflict concerns not only the object presently in dispute but also the whole pattern of future relations. Standing up for one's own might in fact mean lessening the occurrence of conflict in the future. Conflict is about deterrence no less than it is about actual fighting."[74]

Bandura's model is based on the premise that harming others is immoral: the mentally simplifying tactics he identified are justifications, rationalizations. I believe he had a fundamental dislike, a feeling of revulsion, toward violence of any kind. That, I must admit, is my starting point too. I am motivated in writing this book by my horror of war, a desire to understand support for it and to contribute my penny's worth toward the prevention of it. There is, however, a psychological perspective which views violence through a very different lens. I have in mind something called *relational models theory* (RMT). This has been developed by University of California anthropologist Alan Fiske and his colleagues, and its application to war support is spelled out in *Virtuous Violence: Hurting and Killing to Create, Sustain, End, and Honor Social Relationships*.[75] Fiske and his co-author, Tage Rai, start by debunking the common notion that violence is all bad, evil, the antithesis of good social relations. In fact, they say, their appraisal of violent acts and practices across history and different cultures suggests quite the opposite. When people inflict violence on others, even to the point of killing them, they usually do it because they feel it is the morally right thing to do. That is because they are motivated to put right something that is wrong in their relationship with the victim of their violence (or in the victim's relationship with an important third party). The impulse to violence is not immoral. Quite the reverse: "most violence is morally motivated. Morality is about regulating social relationships, and violence is one way to regulate relationships." This I find hard to accept. But let's examine their theory a bit more closely.

RMT, which has a large body of work behind it, is about how people generate and conduct their relationships with others. We all do this, nearly all the time, it is claimed, by making sense of our relationships and evaluating them in terms of four criteria, termed "relational models." RMT names these: communal sharing (CS), authority ranking (AR), equality matching (EM), and market pricing (MP, not the happiest of expressions to my eyes). The four criteria are motivated, respectively, by the need for unity, hierarchy, equality, and proportionality in our relationships. Sometimes violence is used to manage relationships, which is what Fiske and Rai's book is specifically about. One chapter is devoted to war.

They give AR a prime role when it comes to the moral basis for making war. How a nation or other war-making group is seen to stand in hierarchical terms, and the related questions of honor and humiliation, matter greatly. Hence, "decision-makers and public opinion are motivated to declare war to maintain or raise the rank" of their nation or group in relation to others. EM may also play a prominent role in deciding on war, morally motivated by retaliation or vengeance for wrongs committed by others. Equality needs to be restored—the principle of an eye for an eye, a tooth for a tooth. Sometimes EM and AR motives combine and may be difficult to distinguish. CS also has an important but different role to play in the form of "mutual care and sacrifice, working together communally to achieve the mission . . . ahead of individual welfare or survival" (although in feudal societies, the AR morality of loyalty and obedience, in the form of vassalage and commitment to follow one's lord into battle, was the more important). What the theory calls "market pricing" (MP), but I would prefer to call "maximizing benefits–minimizing harms," has its part to play too but is more relevant when it comes to the conduct of a war once war is engaged (a similar distinction to that drawn between the just war criteria for deciding to wage war and for how to prosecute it). We expect our political and military leaders to wage war in a proportionate manner, maximizing the collective good and minimizing the harm; "it is the morality of doing the greatest good for the greatest number at the least cost in lives and suffering," say Fiske and Ray.

Moral Injury

The last few years have seen the whole question of morality and war come up in yet another way. In *What Have We Done: The Moral Injury of Our Longest Wars*, David Wood focuses attention on the moral dilemmas facing those who actually do the war fighting. However well and professionally trained, it cannot be easy for a soldier to kill another human being, if faced with the requirement to do so. An influential report, about Allied soldiers fighting the Japanese in the South Pacific in World War II, claimed that many soldiers who found themselves in that situation could not or would not go ahead and kill. Although that claim was never backed up with data, according to Wood, its conclusion has now generally been accepted.[76]

For those who do kill an enemy combatant, there may be lasting psychological consequences. A highly relevant development since the 1990s has been a number of works drawing attention to what has come to be known as "moral injury," suffered by veteran combatants.[77] They include Wood's own book, which is rather remarkable for a number of reasons. First of all is how the author describes himself, as a veteran war reporter, raised as a pacifist, and accorded the US government-certified status of conscientious objector. He has spent over 30 years covering military conflicts in Somalia and elsewhere in Africa, then at the Pentagon and later "embedded" with US troops in Iraq and Afghanistan. He says he got to know personally men and women, "the blue-collar, working class of the military," mostly young, enlisted.[78] It is his admiration for those on the frontline of warfare, and an understanding of their traumas, combined with his criticism of war and of those who decide upon it, which shines through and which is not untypical of the best war reporters.

One of his main themes is the distinction between moral injury and post-traumatic stress disorder (PTSD): "Someone with PTSD is a victim. A moral injury is a self-accusation."[79] Wood cites with approval the following definition of moral injury: "The lasting psychological, biological, spiritual, and social impact of perpetrating, failing to prevent, or bearing witness to acts that transgress deeply held moral beliefs and expectations."[80] He has comments to make about the conditions US combatants found themselves facing in Iraq and Afghanistan. The new counterinsurgency concept, mixing killing and protecting the civilian population, is disorienting, he says, and was not popular, requiring "moral decision-making" that current military training does not prepare people for. He refers to the grief, even many years later, at the loss of a good comrade and the guilt at not having spotted the explosive device that killed a buddy. But it was the "killing that lies at the heart of their moral injury" but which is rarely discussed. The conflict was chaotic and extremely violent, and the increasingly strict rules of engagement were resented. It was up to soldiers and marines to figure out how to interpret them, unsure whether one might win a medal or a court-martial. Responsibility for making life-affecting choices almost always fell on the most junior of soldiers. None of their training prepared them to manage "the moral challenges of warfare."[81]

Not that moral injuries are only a function of very modern sensibilities. Fergal Keane touches on this in his book *Wounds: A Memoir of War and*

Love, which I have had reason to cite more than once already. He tells of the lasting effect on individuals such as his grandmother's Irish republican and civil war pro-treaty comrade Con Brosnan, of killing, among others, a local district police inspector who was also a neighbor. This was something he did not speak about later, although "We know that he prayed, every day, for the men he killed." As Keane says, like other combatants in wars, old and new, "None of the men tasked with killing the District Inspector had fired at a living target before." Keane also writes, in the same book, about his own depression and guilt due to his exposure to war as a reporter and has since talked movingly on British TV about his own PTSD.[82]

Conscientious Objection

Although this book is about *support* for war and how to understand it, and not about resistance to war, this chapter would not be complete without at least brief mention of conscientious objection, focusing on Britain. After military conscription was introduced, for the first time in its history, in January 1916, conscientious objectors (COs), popularly known as "conchies," started to be arrested. Tribunals were set up to hear their claims to exemption from service. COs fell into two groups: "alternatives," who were willing to accept non-military service, whether as non-combatants in the Army or undertaking civilian or humanitarian relief work outside the military, and "absolutists," who would accept nothing less than the absolute exemption from service which was one of the options tribunals could award. Very few absolute exemptions were offered. Over 6,000 were arrested, at first kept under guard in a military camp or barracks and, once their lack of cooperation became clear, sent to prison. There they were put to punishing physical work, many suffering physically and mentally, in some cases dying in prison and in many cases never fully recovering their health. As well as being ostracized and rejected by neighbors and relatives and often facing loss of employment, conchies were often denied voting rights after the war.[83]

The No More War Movement was founded in 1921, as was War Resisters' International, and the Peace Pledge Union followed in 1935. One of the latter's founders was the Reverend Dick Sheppard, who had served as an army chaplain during the First World War but had decided that support for the military was incompatible with his religion. But the widespread anti-war sentiment following World War I dissipated quickly in the face of the rise of fascism as the 1930s went on. Even Fenner Brockway, a founder of the No-Conscription Fellowship in 1914, who drew attention to conditions in British prisons and probably thereby contributed to reform of the prison system, was influenced to abandon his absolute pacifist position by what he saw during the Spanish Civil War. A. A. Milne, who wrote *Peace with Honour*, was one of a number of well-known writers who inspired pacifists in the 1930s, only to disappoint them when they changed their position later.[84]

The tribunals that heard COs' claims during the Second World War were organized differently; for example, military representation was not mandatory, and a greater diversity of alternative types of service acceptable to COs was offered. Fewer were imprisoned for more than a year than had been the case during the First World War. But the stigma and rejection, job loss, in some instances brutality experienced during incarceration, and for some the lasting effects on health, remained.[85]

After World War II, from 1949 to 1960, there was compulsory military service for 18- to 20-year-old males (I just escaped it), and there continued to be conscientious objections, although at a lower rate than during the war. The story of objections to war has gone on unabated since. The formation of the Campaign for Nuclear Disarmament in 1958, the six Aldermaston marches between 1958 and 1963, the anti-war campaigns against the wars in Vietnam and later in Iraq, and the British Withdrawal from Northern Ireland Campaign at the height of the "Troubles" there, are among the highlights during my lifetime.[86]

Conclusions

The overall conclusion that I draw from this chapter is that whether or not to support war—both the idea generally that war is conscionable and specifically that a certain war is supportable—is a moral minefield, for ordinary folk, politicians, military leaders, combatants, international relations experts, and jurists alike. We might expect religion to be a guide, but all the world's major religions have struggled with the question of how to reconcile their commandments to seek peace with support for war. All, even Buddhism, are ambivalent, and all have come to an uneasy and unconvincing compromise. Just war theory, updated with the Geneva

Conventions and UN Charter, is central to the moral debate. It should give us all a rough guide about what is ethical and what is not. In fact, though, its conditions for supporting going to war, and for how war should then be ethically conducted, are all to a degree subjective and ambiguous, leaving room for them to be challenged in relation to specific wars. That war should be a "last resort," should be a "proportional" response and conducted in a proportionate fashion, and that civilians must have immunity are especially problematic. Concern has been growing that increased flouting of the principle of civilian immunity, coupled with an enlarged conception of what constitutes threat to a nation or group's security, may be undermining the just war principles.

Facing the fact that engaging in war poses a moral dilemma is sometimes inescapable for those required to take part. The "moral injury," suffered by veteran combatants who have been required to transgress deeply held moral beliefs in the course of fighting, particularly after killing another human, is one example. Another is the moral stand against war taken by non-combatant conscientious objectors, for example in Britain in the two world wars, and in anti-war campaigns since. But how far does responsibility for war extend? Who is to blame for war's horrors and should bear some of the guilt? If war is a moral dilemma, whose dilemma is it? As we have repeatedly found in earlier chapters, it is usually left unspecified whether we as supporters of war should be held accountable, or only combatants, or only political leaders. What about those who manufacture and sell armaments or who service an army? When our country or group makes war, are we all part of a guilty collective, as Saint Augustine argued?

Among a number of psychological models and theories aiming at understanding how we justify ideas and actions which might otherwise be thought to flout moral principles, the model of moral disengagement is one of the most applicable to war support. It posits a number of justifying mechanisms including displacement and dispersal of responsibility, attributing blame to others, disputing the harmful outcomes, and dehumanizing the victims of one's own or one's side's actions. Each of these mental tactics that enable war support resonates with themes, such as adherence to in-group narratives and negative out-group stereotypes and the perception of threat and danger, which have recurred throughout earlier chapters. The time has come to attempt an integration of what we have learned into some kind of whole—a unified psychological model of war support. That is the main object of the next, final, chapter.

8
An Answer
Toward a Unified Understanding of War Support

> For too long, students of peace . . . have abandoned the understanding of war . . . to . . . [the] disciplines of political science, security studies, and international relations . . . [they] spend much time trying to conceptualize peace while avoiding the very real problems of war.
>
> Barash and Webel, *Peace and Conflict Studies*[1]

> Datta, Dayadhvam, Damyata/Shantih, Shantih, Shantih (Giving, Showing compassion, Restraining oneself/Peace, Peace, Peace)
>
> The last two lines, based on "The Voice of Thunder" in the sacred Hindu text the Upanishads, of T. S. Eliot's poem *The Waste Land*[2]

This has been a personal exploration, seeking an answer to a question that has bugged me all my adult life. In this final chapter I shall present my conclusions. The result will be presented in the form of a psychological *war support model* (WSM). That will constitute the centerpiece of the chapter. It will be bookended with an introduction and a finale. The former will serve to make the point that fathoming the mystery of why wars happen, including understanding war support, continues to be one of the most pressing intellectual tasks humanity faces. The war problem has not gone away. Indeed, arguably, it is now more urgent than ever. Because I have studied and worked as a psychologist for over 50 years, and because the WSM I am developing is a psychological one, I also need to say something about why psychology has not done more to address the war support question. After presenting the model, by way of a finale I shall illustrate the model with specific reference to the war in Ukraine, ongoing as I write, and to the future of relations between the "Western alliance" and Russia and China.

Wars and Readiness for War Continue

For better or worse, I rely for most of my news on the BBC and the weekly *Guardian* magazine, *The Guardian Weekly*. During the writing of this book, I have continued to hear and read about wars taking place in various parts of the world. Despite advances in international law, despite the reluctance of democracies to fight each other, despite any further civilizing of our natures which may have occurred, it seems we have not eradicated the possibility of war nor expunged it from our consciousness. War, and the possibility that we may support it, remains on our agendas. It continues to be part of our psychology.

"New," civil or intrastate wars appear to be permanently with us—although none of those three terms used to describe them do justice to their chaotic complexity. The Sahel region of North Africa has featured in the news, although rarely headline news in the United Kingdom and then not for long. Across the region, from west to east, I learn that intrastate wars have continued, often spilling over across country borders. In Senegal the army has been engaged with separatist rebels of the Casamance area off and on for 40 years. In March 2022 a new attack on the rebels was reported to have resulted in several hundred Senegalese being displaced, fleeing north into The Gambia, where over 5,000 Gambians were also displaced. Farther east, the abducting of schoolchildren in northern Nigeria as part of hostilities between Islamist fighters and the Nigerian government has been in the news spasmodically. Widespread starvation and malnourishment in South Sudan have followed the years of fighting by rival groups since that country became independent from Sudan in 2011, and in 2023 a viscious intrastate war of complex origins erupted in Sudan. Farther east still, a third of a million Tigrayans in the breakaway region of Tigray in the northwest of Ethiopia were reported in 2021 to be suffering famine conditions, up to five million are experiencing food insecurity, and over 50,000 are reported to have fled across the border into Sudan, following Ethiopian government attacks on and blockade of the region, supported by forces from neighboring Eritrea. This war, described by the World Health Organization as "out of sight and out of mind" compared to the war in Ukraine, has resulted in thousands of reported civilian deaths, over 20,000 incidents of sexual violence, concentration camps housing ethnic Tigrayans, and mass arrest of Tigrayans in the Ethiopian capital.[3]

Farther south in Africa, there is an even less-well-known English-speaking regional secessionist movement engaged in hostilities with the

French-speaking majority government in Cameroon.[4] The remote area on the border of the Democratic Republic of the Congo and Uganda is another African war zone where a typically complex and confused war, with an estimated more than 100 armed groups, continues (see also Chapter 1), recently in the form of fighting between Congolese forces and the Allied Democratic Forces, a rebel group originally from Uganda with a radical religious-militant agenda. At least 1,000 civilians had been killed and an estimated 40,000 displaced.[5]

Meanwhile old conflicts break out again or threaten to do so, and some of these receive better coverage in mainstream news sources in my country. Take the Israel–Palestine conflict for example. In May 2021, 12 people, all but one civilians, were reported killed by attacks from Gaza, and 248 Palestinians, including 66 children, were reported killed in Gaza, over 50 schools destroyed, and 80,000 people displaced from their homes. One report tells me that, unlike in earlier bad years, violence extended beyond Gaza and the occupied territories, into Israel's mixed towns where Jewish and Arab citizens have lived side by side for decades. Some blame this reigniting of the dormant Israel–Palestine conflict on repressive, racist Israeli government policies. Others place the blame on Hamas and Islamic Jihad militants and weak Palestinian leadership. Others blame Iranian interference.[6] Like most armed conflicts, this, needless to say, has a history. One key date was the founding of Israel in 1948. The displacement of an estimated 700,000 Palestinians, who fled or were expelled, is celebrated on May 15, Nakba Day, each year, although the government denies funds to any institution commemorating the day and teachers have been reprimanded for mentioning it in class. Peter Beinart, editor of *Jewish Currents* and professor of journalism and political science at the City University of New York, with others, has presented a "Jewish case for Palestinian refugee return," something which the Israeli government and its allies claim is impossible and without legal or historical justification.[7]

Elsewhere the legacy costs of war continue to be felt. Armenian refugees and prisoners of war are a big issue following the Armenian–Azerbaijan war of 2020, and the location of landmines planted during that war and continuing to cause casualties was a major concern for the Azeris. That short outbreak of war over the disputed region of Nagorno-Karabakh followed the much longer war of 1988 to 1994 which resulted in over half a million Azeri refugees. The long civil war in Syria, with the involvement of foreign powers and militant groups not confined to country borders, is not over as I write. Among its legacies is the plight of "ISIS brides" still held in detention camps and the flourishing of an illicit trade in stimulant drugs. The threat of famine and starvation on a large scale is one of the most costly effects of the war in Yemen, where Saudi Arabia has supported the government in its fight with Houthi rebels, as has the UK government by allowing arms sales to the region. As so often in war-torn countries, suspicion, mistrust, and insecurity are the results of years of armed conflict in Iraq. In Afghanistan, 2021 saw the final withdrawal of US troops and the complete takeover of the country by the Taliban. A poll taken in August that year suggested that the internationally controversial US withdrawal had the support of the majority of the US public, weary of the 20 years of engagement there which had cost over 2,000 US military deaths and a trillion dollars.[8]

To me most of those wars seem far away from home. That changed early in 2022. War is now nearer at hand for me and my fellow UK residents than it has been for a long time. The news bulletins and current affairs programs on my beloved BBC have have continued to be dominated by the war in Ukraine . Not only is this war "close to home," but it can also be read as threatening the return of old-style wars between nation states. This is not a "new war" of the kind Mary Kaldor described (see Chapter 1), although, appearing in a BBC Radio discussion program in late January 2022, she pointed out that the fighting that had been going on in the Donbass area of Ukraine since 2014, already costing, it is reported, more than 13,000 lives by 2021, *had* been such a new-style war.[9] I shall have more to say later on about the Ukraine war, in the light of the presentation of the WSM.

A consequence of the war in Ukraine has been commitment by a number of countries to increase their military spending in response to what is seen as the threat of Russian aggression. A speech made by the new German chancellor a few days after Russia's invasion, promising a massive increase in defense spending, is especially significant in view of Germany's post–Second World War reluctance to join the club of countries with the largest military budgets and its preferred role as a Western nation that maintained a closer relationship than others did with Russia. Equally significant is the move by Sweden and Finland to join NATO, in the process abandoning decades of military non-alignment.[10]

More generally, it seems we are now witnessing widespread increased readiness for war in the form of enhanced acquisition of armaments. Major powers have continued to invest in their nuclear arsenals. In 2021 the UK government announced an increase in its nuclear weaponry, and the United States has done the same. In 2022 the Stockholm International Peace

Research Institute reported that the world stock of nuclear weapons was expected to increase for the first time since the end of the Cold War. The Doomsday Clock—the iconic motif of the *Bulletin of the Atomic Scientists*, founded 75 years ago by Albert Einstein and scientists from the Manhattan Project—stood at 100 seconds to midnight when I was writing this chapter (reduced to 90 seconds during its final drafting), closer than it was at any time during the Cold War. The non-governmental British–American Security Information Council has been warning for some time that the need for nuclear disarmament through multilateral diplomacy is greater now than it has been at any stage since the end of the cold war.[11]

The arms race, the perceived need by governments to ensure potential enemy states don't get ahead in terms of weapon development and capacity, continues. There are new developments in the offing. One is the specter of the militarization of space. The United States, Russia, and China are each reported to be experimenting with new weapons including orbiting hypersonic vehicles capable of launching nuclear weapons from space. Other activities in space may be presented to the public as having non-military intentions, but there are likely to be military applications in mind as well.[12] Another sinister feature of the arms race is the development of lethal autonomous weapons (LAWs). Stuart Russell discussed these and their dangers in his Reith Lecture in December 2021, as part of his lecture series *Living with Artificial Intelligence*. Now available for purchase on the web, such weapons use artificial intelligence to "locate, select and engage" targets. Among future likely developments, he anticipated that LAWs, which can be minute in size—tiny quadcopters, for example—could be produced cheaply and in very large quantities. Restrictions on their use have been resisted, he told us, by the United States and Russia, with the United Kingdom, Israel, and Australia in support of their position.[13] The familiar argument that these new weapons would reduce civilian casualties is being used once again. The dangers are all too evident: intensification of the international arms race, acquisition of such weapons by non-state actors, and the prospect of "flash wars" in which control of autonomous weapons is lost.[14]

Psychology Has Neglected War Support

My aims in writing this book go beyond exploring the drivers of war support and offering a model that summarizes my findings. In the process I hope to have contributed to establishing a new area within my own discipline of psychology. The latter, I believe it fair to say, either has been relatively silent on the question of war support, has taken an ambiguous position on the subject, or has positively contributed to war support rather than clearly opposing it.

Although I have cited psychologists who have had insightful and important things to say on the subject of war or who have carried out valuable relevant research, they are few. The subject of war psychology, let alone war support, can scarcely be said to exist. It figures in political psychology but is not mainstream even there. Peace psychology is one well-established subdiscipline to which one might look for contributions on war support. But its focus is mostly elsewhere, for example concerned with conflict resolution, peace-making interventions, reconciliation after conflict, peace education, and peace movements.[15] Although it also deals with the origins of violent ways of solving disputes, including possible psychological causes, war support per se is not a clear focus. Furthermore, its starting point for a consideration of war is different from mine. Peace psychology has not taken an unambiguous position on war, often speaking of peace in the absence of social justice as "negative peace," implying that armed conflict may be justified as a means of obtaining social justice. Mere peace without justice, equity, or harmony is downplayed as a relatively conservative goal, even a passive state in the face of slavery or gross political or economic oppression, as in the Pax Romana.[16] The distinction between negative and positive peace is associated with the distinction between direct violence, as in war, and indirect or structural violence, built into the structure of social, cultural, and economic institutions, killing people indirectly and slowly. For example, psychologists Pilisuk and Rowntree's excellent book, which I have cited a number of times, is called *The Hidden Structure of Violence*; and much of it is devoted to exposing networks of power and forms of brutality and exploitation including sexual and forced or bonded labor, inequality, and debt in the United States and beyond. Of war they say, "Military violence is our most profound threat but is not, at this time, our most lethal killer ... patterns of investment and exploitation already contribute to a loss of life greater than all wars."[17]

Discussions about war and militarism can easily get diverted into discussions about inequality, neoliberalism, or climate change. Needless to say, such topics are themselves of monumental importance to psychologists and everyone else. But at the very least this has the effect of diverting attention from war and militarism on to a range of other humanitarian issues. This may be one of the reasons why there is not a more clearly defined subdiscipline within psychology focusing on war and support for war. Outside psychology, there are those who recognize that war and other urgent problems such as climate change and inequality are inseparable. Patrick Hiller, director of the War Prevention Initiative in the United States, who describes himself as a conflict transformation scholar, is one such: "Most ongoing civil wars and violent conflicts are experienced by some of the world's poorest countries. Poverty is associated with the onset of violent conflict.... Countries can be caught in the so-called conflict trap, where conflict leads to the reversal of economic development, which in turn increases the likelihood of violent conflict."[18] In short, psychologists have for the most part left it to others to attend specifically to war and its causes.[19]

The argument that war may, under certain circumstances, be better than putting up with oppression, might be seen as a variety—the most persuasive perhaps—of the general theme, discussed in Chapter 1, that we are ambivalent about war because it may bring benefits as well as costs. There are other ways, too, whereby psychologists have avoided taking on war support wholeheartedly as a problem to be understood. Support for the war-is-in-decline thesis is one way. US psychologist Steven Pinker's book *The Better Angels of Our Nature: A History of Violence and Humanity* provides one of the best examples of how psychology has failed to take a clear stand against war. It can be read, so I have concluded, as a subtle argument in defense of war, or at least as a failed opportunity to oppose conditions and policies which support war. To be fair, Pinker is clear about the unmitigated horrors of war. Near the end of his magisterial book, he writes, "To review the history of violence is to be repeatedly astounded by the cruelty and waste of it all, and at times to be overcome with anger, disgust, and immeasurable sadness ... with deepening horror as it comes to realize just how much suffering has been inflicted by the naked ape upon its own kind." But, as I described in Chapter 1, it is the *decline* of violence that is his main theme and which he celebrates. Hence, Pinker is dismissive of always asking, Why is there war? rather than, Why is there peace?: "We can obsess not just over what we have been doing wrong but also over what we have been doing right." He refers to an unwarranted new pessimism about war. For example, instead of relief at the decline of organized violence, the "innumeracy of our journalistic and intellectual culture" has led pundits to talk about a return to great power rivalry or the world being a more dangerous place than ever, he says.[20] Since that was written, the public argument that the world is a dangerous place has, if anything, strengthened. The war in Ukraine has occurred, with its hardening of hostility between the world's superpowers, and great power rivalry between China and the United States and its allies has only intensified.[21]

Psychologists Working for the Military: Professional Co-option

There is, however, another side to psychologists' lack of contribution to the study of war support.[22] The fact is that many have worked for the military in one way or another, as psychologists, either explicitly promoting militarism or at best struggling to avoid being co-opted. They are not alone in facing that dilemma. Chaplains are an obvious case in point, as I discussed in Chapter 7. Lawyers provide another example. In her book *Wounding the World: How Military Violence and War-Play Invade Our Lives*, historian Joanna Bourke pointed out that the importance of the international laws of war (see Chapter 1) necessitated integrating lawyers into military systems. Lawyers were now playing an increasing role in decisions about whether or not to use military force and about the conduct of conflict once underway. The 1990–91 Gulf War, during which US forces employed over 400 lawyers, is often thought to have been decisive in that respect. But, she points out, like embedded journalists and medical professionals interacting closely with the military, lawyers found it difficult to distinguish "cooperation" and "co-optation."[23] Others have stressed the need for doctors and other health workers to see themselves as primarily health workers when working in the military, not primarily as officers, and to work at their own professions' highest ethical standards.[24]

Bourke also describes the militarization of science and what some have called the military–industrial–academic complex. Scientists generally have been keen to engage in work of military application, work which is usually thought of as "cutting-edge, intellectually rewarding and, of course, lucrative." Academic researchers may not even be aware of the military applications of their findings. In 1971 students published a two-volume report listing over 100 research contracts, held by academics at Stanford University, which were fully or partially funded by the US Department of Defense, constituting a quarter of all contracts or grants held by the university. While the academics described their research as improving traffic, reducing pollution, and so on, the Defense Documentation Center (DDC) gave a very different account of the military potential of the research. The contract for the famous prison role-play study carried out by psychologist Philip Zimbardo, for example, described it as being about "Individual and group variables influencing emotional arousal, violence, and behavior," but the DDC title referred to "Personnel Technology Factors Influencing Disruptive Behavior among Military Trainees."[25]

Four decades ago, Peter Watson's book *War on the Mind: The Military Uses and Abuses of Psychology* exposed "the extent to which the military potential of psychology had been ruthlessly exploited," taking off in his estimation in the early 1960s. Much of the work was secret—Watson obtained access to a large amount of classified information—covering a shocking range of matters including selection and training of service personnel, improving the efficiency with which soldiers used armaments, the effectiveness of military leadership, improving military performance under stress, understanding the enemy, and torture and other interrogation techniques, including techniques used during internment in Northern Ireland. The latter involved hooding, exposure to noxious noise, and being forced to stand with hands above heads against the wall for several hours at a time, as well as periods of sleep deprivation and diet restriction.[26] Rereading this book now is chilling, not just because of the evidence it gives of the widespread use of psychology to support militarism but because of its failure to take any kind of stand against war and militarism. Interestingly, Watson himself took no such stand either. The abuses of psychology which he appears to have been most concerned about were largely due to the clandestine nature of much military psychology, and therefore its poor quality, rather than the bigger issue of the questionable use of psychology in supporting militarism.

The ethical conflict for psychologists, and for others too, is well illustrated by a more recent debate in the pages of *Peace and Conflict: Journal of Peace Psychology* regarding "operational psychology" (OP) in the United States, the psychology specialty applied to national security and defense. Arrigo et al. have argued that OP should be split into what they call "collaborative operational psychology" (COP), concerned with such things as the selection of service personnel, health assessments, and trauma therapy, and "adversarial operational psychology" (AOP). The latter "engages psychologists in direct support of deception, coercion, and assault in military and intelligence operations and in covert operations research. It encompasses the tasks of identification and manipulation of adversaries in counterintelligence and counterterrorism operations and of overt behavioral and weapons research on human subjects." They argue that, despite the collusion of the American Psychological Association in justifying such applications of psychology, it should be beyond the pale for psychologists because their work is not subject to ethical oversight by anybody outside the national security establishment, and the targets of their interventions are unable to provide informed consent, may be harmed in stipulated ways, and have little or no recourse to complain or redress.[27] One of the most notorious examples of psychologists playing a key role in military-related procedures deliberately inflicting harm on others (referred to when discussing militarism in Chapter 5) was the involvement in torture programs, for example in Guantánamo.[28]

Quite apart from the consequences of AOP for those who are directly harmed by it, the unintended consequences include, according to Arrigo et al., the undermining of trust in COP and in psychology generally and the militarization of psychology. Staal and Greene, operational psychologists at US Special Operations Command and both then current or retired colonels in the US Air Force, objected to the distinction that was being drawn between COP and AOP and the negative characterization of the latter. One of their main arguments was that OP was not alone in posing such dilemmas and requiring ultimate loyalty to the institution for which psychologists work; for example, those working in areas of law enforcement, police, public safety, forensic science, and market research were all in similar situations.[29]

New weapons and new ways of making war are only likely to inflate these ethical dilemmas. Grégoire Chamayou provides interesting examples of the use of academics in the justification of using unmanned aerial vehicles (UAVs), otherwise known as drones (see Chapter 5). For example, Bradley Strawser was hired as a professor of philosophy at the US Naval Postgraduate School in Monterey, California. His thesis was that, according to a "principle of unnecessary risk," there is a duty to use UAVs to protect from harm "an agent engaged in a justified act," so long as that act accords with principles of discrimination and proportionality (among the jus in bello just war principles discussed in Chapter 7). Chamayou gives several examples of how psychological knowledge and expertise has been drawn on. Just one involves the use of social network analysis and cognitive science in the panopticon-like surveillance systems used to identify, study, follow, and in some cases ultimately target suspected individuals.[30]

The War Support Model: Three Recurring Themes

When I began to compile the present book, I didn't know where it would take me. One thing I have become more and more convinced of during its writing is the importance of the topic. How it is that ordinary folk support their leaders in engaging in the hugely costly (in so many senses) and morally questionable (if not repugnant) activity of taking up lethal arms against another group of our own species is a question that psychology has neglected. Meanwhile wars and the accumulation of increasingly dangerous weapons of war have continued unabated. To try and fathom why we support war is, I would argue, one of the most urgent tasks my discipline of psychology is faced with. With no more ado, then, let me present, in the form of a War Support Model (WSM), my conclusions. I do so, I must add, with a good degree of uncertainty and humility.

For one thing, the WSM owes a debt to a number of existing psychological theories, hypotheses, models, and concepts which I have drawn on in earlier chapters. They include realistic conflict theory, social identity theory, interpersonal contact theory, the theory of moral disengagement, system justification theory, the 3Ns model of terrorism, relational models theory, the spiral conflict model, power theory, and concepts such as the authoritarian personality, social dominance orientation, masculinity, and cognitive complexity versus simplicity. Because war support has not been a main subject within the discipline of psychology, I have also found myself drawing on sources beyond my discipline. I have never thought that psychologists have a monopoly on psychology, very far from it, and that is certainly the case when it comes to war studies and war support.

Models attempt to organize and simplify what is otherwise a muddled and complicated set of ideas. The WSM is obviously preliminary, but if taken up by others, it could lead to refinement, to a consideration of how it might apply to different types of war, and to the generation of specific, testable hypotheses, and hence to a growing body of productive research. Although it is, of course, for the reader to judge whether my exploration of the topic of war support has borne fruit, I am personally reassured by what I have found, that it has.

The material I found, of psychological relevance to war support, fell into the six domains covered in Chapters 2 to 7, supported by the lines of thinking about war more generally which I dealt with in Chapter 1. The attempt to produce a summary model was made possible, I concluded, by the regular occurrence of themes cross-cutting those domains. I have signaled those cross-cutting themes as the chapters have progressed. For example, it was apparent early on that *threat perception* was going to be a contender for inclusion in any model that might emerge. It came up in Chapter 2 in the form of the war-supporting personal disposition, for some people more than others, to believe that the world is basically a dangerous, threatening one. It recurred in the context of attitudes toward an out-group and in the content of war propaganda in Chapters 4 and 6, respectively. Furthermore, these are the psychological reflections of a theme familiar to international relations and war studies. The "realist" school of thought, as we had discovered already in Chapter 1, also views the world as "anarchic," insecure, threatening, and dangerous, a world in which military preparedness is necessary for security. The same recurrence throughout the core chapters of this book applies to the other two dominant themes, *acceptance of readiness for war* and *over-simplification*.

I conclude, therefore, that these three are leading candidates for providing a provisional answer to the question I set myself at the outset. Why have we, the ordinary people of the world, so often supported the wars that our political and military leaders have decided upon? Since wars continue to be fought, the question can equally be phrased in the present tense: Why *do* we so often support war? The model summarizes my three leading answers: we are ready for war, we are susceptible to the perception that we are being threatened, and we are easily prone to a mental simplification of the issues involved.

Theme #1 Acceptance of Readiness for War

My first conclusion is that we support war because we are primed for it, socialized to believe that it is a possibility, that it is sometimes necessary, even to expect it. In my understanding there are at least the following five components of our acceptance of readiness for war. They have been touched on in most of the foregoing chapters but particularly in Chapters 2, 3, 5 and 7.

Embedded militarism and militarization (see Chapter 5) Our readiness for war takes its plainest form in acceptance of the militarism which is so deeply embedded in a state or other war-making group's culture, its history, its heroes, its memorials, the socialization of its young, along with people's support for its military and for the military ethos that accompanies it. My life, like that of others, has been infused with reminders of the importance of militarism, including everything from the ubiquity of war films to universities' acceptance of military funding.

Admiration for weapons, support for the arms trade (see Chapter 5) We are fascinated by, and show admiration for, weapons of war. We often justify them by referring to them in euphemistic terms as "defensive," "clean," "precise," "low-cost, low-risk," even as ethical, humanitarian. We are accepting of a colossal legal arms trade, and we support those who govern us spending large sums on acquiring and maintaining military arsenals necessary for the defense of our group's values and security. Along with toys, games, and other forms of leisure time diversion which prominently feature weapons, that has been called "the military–industrial–entertainment complex."

War-supporting masculinity that values power and dominance (see Chapter 2) Military establishments, and the design, manufacture, and dealing in armaments, are dominated by men and are imbued with traditional male gender values of strength and competitiveness. Men are on average more supportive of and less negative about war. War fighting itself continues to be largely a male activity, associated with gendered characteristics such as aggression, bravado, emotional detachment, feelings of being "a real man," and loyalty to a male group.

Exclusive, superior national or group identity versus cosmopolitanism and respect for diversity (see Chapter 3) Strongly held values based on identity with one's nation state, or with a religious faith, an ethnic group, or a region, constitute one of the most important elements contributing to acceptance of readiness for war. Though it may lie dormant during peaceful times, the more our feelings of nationalism, or other kind of identity, take an exclusive, chauvinistic form in contrast to a cosmopolitan worldview grounded in inclusive, universalist values, the more it contributes to our acceptance of preparedness for war.

Belief that war is sometimes necessary and just (see Chapter 7) The belief that war is sometimes necessary and can be morally justified, even positively virtuous, is a final crucial element of war readiness. It is to be found in the war-justifying statements, or at least ambivalence toward war, associated with all world religions which have supported some wars and weapons as "holy" and often viewed taking up arms to confront evil and injustice as legitimate, even a duty. It is codified in just war theory, a kind of ethical rough guide to war, justifying the decision to go to war under certain conditions and stipulating the ways in which war can be pursued ethically. At a more personal level, a number of mental mechanisms are readily available to us, enabling the justification of supporting war and distancing from responsibility for its harms.

Those five elements together provide a powerful backdrop to war support. They are the foundation upon which support for a specific war is based. They constituted, as William James had it, preparation for war. Wars were not accidents, he stated, since we lived in a world that accepted planning for war as natural. We still do. It is the largely unquestioned acceptance of this war planning and preparedness which is so influential. It is always with us and mostly taken for granted. Such a dominating combination of elements contributing to acceptance of war preparedness is hard to counter and unlikely to be easily dismissed.

Theme #2 Threat Perception

Perception of a threat from an identified source, a potential enemy, is central to the second recurring theme. I see it as being composed of at least the following five elements. They have recurred throughout the foregoing exploration of war support but were especially prominent in Chapters 2, 3, 4 and 6.

- *General beliefs in a dangerous, threatening world* (see Chapter 2) There are individual differences between people in how generally threatening and dangerous the world is understood to be. Authoritarianism, a positive orientation toward hierarchy, and a preference for competition rather than cooperation are related personal beliefs which make some people more inclined to perceive threat and support preparation for armed action to counter it. A personal sense of meaninglessness and being reminded of one's own mortality are further factors influencing personal support for war.
- *Identification of an enemy or potential enemy* (see Chapter 4) General readiness for war and personal beliefs in a threatening world become more focused when there is perceived to be threat from a specified potential enemy. The named threatening out-group may be a unitary state or other political body, its leader, or a component or symbol of it, and less often (at least while war remains a possibility only) its whole

people. Earlier war or wars, preexisting hostility, or at least rivalry with the now-threatening state or group is often a background factor reinforcing threat perception.

Lack of contact with and understanding of a potential enemy group (see Chapter 4) Perception of threat from another country or group is reinforced by lack of contact. Intergroup contact is associated with better knowledge about and ability to appreciate the perspective of another group. Intergroup negativity and prejudice are reduced by sharing a common goal and cooperating together. Ability to critically reflect on one's own group's beliefs and position in relation to a potential enemy group is equally important.

A specific narrative justifying war (see Chapter 3) Support for war requires a powerful ideology or set of values about one's nation or identity group, which is believed to be under threat, providing a narrative around which the group can cohere and which serves to justify collective armed action and sacrifice. Such a threat-laden narrative may *demand* violence and sacrifice to protect the group's welfare or values, even its very existence.

Leaders and the media encourage feelings of threat (see Chapter 6) National or group leaders, in their role as group champions, reflecting and reinforcing group identity, play a key role in encouraging perception of threat from an identified source, arousing fear and mobilizing support for military action. The media, and increasingly social media, are also a vital influence in spreading alarm and threat perception. Governments try to ensure media messages are consistent with the approved position.

That is my second conclusion: threat perception is a major driver of war support. As individuals who identify as members of a nation state or an ethnic, religious, or regional group, we are prone to feeling threatened by other groups. Such feelings of threat, and the associated feelings of fear and anger, are more easily aroused under certain conditions. Threat perception flourishes more strongly the more we believe the world is a threatening one; the more threat is perceived to be coming from an identified out-group, especially if there is a history of hostility or rivalry between us; the less contact we have with that group and the less understanding we have of its members; the more we believe a narrative about that group and our relationship with it which encourages threat perception; and the more that narrative is reinforced by our leaders and the media.

Theme #3 Over-Simplification

The third theme, which has recurred throughout earlier chapters, I shall call over-simplification. It links with a long-standing area of psychological theorizing and research usually referred to as *cognitive simplicity versus complexity*. It has come up consistently but in varying forms while considering the origins of support for war. It can be conveniently summarized in terms of the following five components. These aspects of over-simplification were found in all chapters but especially in Chapters 4, 6 and 7.

Negative, demonizing images of the enemy (see Chapter 4) As focused threat hardens, and a potential enemy begins to be perceived as an actual one, there is a retreat from acknowledgment that the enemy consists of individuals just like us, all citizens of the same world, the idea central to the concept of cosmopolitan humanity. The enemy starts to be seen in negative, demonizing terms, inferior in culture, in capability, or in some other way. It may even be described in dehumanizing terms, likened to insects or other non-human species.

Lack of criticism of one's in-group; criticism focused on in-group members not in support (see Chapter 6) Absence of criticism of one's own nation or war-making group contributes to an over-simplification of the relationship with the enemy and a failure to understand the latter's perspective. As perceptions harden, it becomes unacceptable, even dangerous, to challenge the accepted wisdom and to express contrary ideas. Those who refuse to subscribe to the mainstream narrative or who favor seeking peaceful reconciliation are said to be giving support to the enemy and may be deemed as appeasers, unpatriotic, traitors to the group's cause. Even formerly moderate opinion may be condemned and those unwilling to relinquish such opinion scorned and harassed.

Mentally biased versus more considered, complex thinking about circumstances (see Chapter 4) A variety of well-recognized cognitive biases contribute to the mental simplification upholding war support. They include selective attention, premature cognitive closure, and use of the availability heuristic—a kind of mental shortcut, whereby judgments are overly influenced by events that are familiar and easily brought to mind. A particularly relevant cognitive bias is the fundamental attribution error, which refers to the tendency to attribute others' behavior to a relatively fixed and essential disposition such as an enemy's innate hostility or untrustworthiness, in contrast to our own behavior, which we believe is driven by circumstances not of our making. Closely related is the actor–observer discrepancy: *our* hostility is excusable as a response to *their* actions or perceived intentions—the enemy is at fault, whereas we were provoked.

Propaganda, truth distortion (see Chapter 6) Wars require "regimenting the public mind," "manufacturing consent." Propaganda and war are bedfellows. Support for war necessitates, to some degree, distortion of objective truth or at least a very selective presentation of the real facts about the origins and progress of the war. Support for war depends on dis- or at least mis-information. Control of the media during wartime is common on all sides. Announcements by governments and war leaders, as well as media reports, are often over-simplified and one-sided, omitting the enemy's perspective and the background context and causes. The effectiveness of wartime propaganda often rests on a long period of "pre-persuasion" which has already provided us with a pre-formed understanding of a potential enemy, its leader(s), and our relationship with them.

Moral disengagement (see Chapter 7) A number of mental tactics have been identified which enable us to justify to ourselves engaging in or supporting actions, such as killing other human beings, which we would otherwise think of as immoral. Principal among these "mechanisms of moral disengagement" are justifying harmful action in the belief that it is the means to achieve right or honorable ends or by thinking of it as benign in comparison with something worse or by using euphemistic and innocuous language to describe it and evading personal blame by dispersing responsibility so widely that no one is held responsible or displacing it on to political or military leaders or by minimizing, denying, distorting, or disputing the harmful outcomes of actions or by dehumanizing the victims of one's actions or by attributing blame to them for bringing harm upon themselves. Each has clear relevance to the ways in which wars are justified and killing excused.

Hence my third conclusion: all wars are "thought wars." War support thrives in an atmosphere characterized by simplified thinking about, and representations of, what is happening and of those who are involved. It rests on an over-simplification of the threats and dangers, of the enemy or potential enemy, and of ourselves and our position in the world. This is to be found

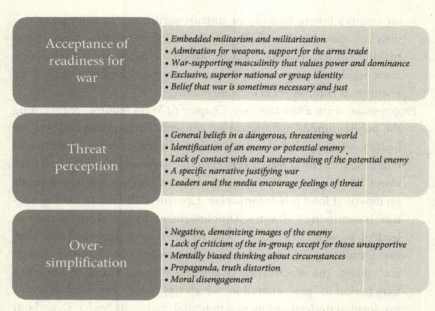

Figure 8.1 The war support model: a summary of three factors driving support for war

in the form of cognitively biased versus more considered, complex thinking about the circumstances surrounding war or potential war, demonizing images of an enemy, relative lack of criticism of one's own group, coupled with criticism of in-group members who are not fully in support, the ubiquity of propaganda and truth distortion prior to and during war, and the mental mechanisms of moral justification for war whereby we distance ourselves morally from responsibility for war and the killing of others which it involves.

It was this recurrence of the major themes which made possible the construction of the model of war support summarized in Figures 8.1 and 8.2. The three themes, as I have termed them, appear in the WSM as three factors driving support for war. A number of points of clarification need to be made about these three factors and how they operate. First of all, they function at both individual and collective levels. Because war is a collective activity, it is no surprise that the WSM's three factors are principally collective; it is *we* who accept readiness for war, *we* who perceive threat, *we* who collectively think in over-simplified ways. At the same time, however, there are individual and socio-demographic differences in each case. Belief in a dangerous

Figure 8.2 The war support model: the three factors form a system of interacting and mutually reinforcing parts

world, for example, is a variable, distributed on a continuum. Women are less fascinated by weapons than men, to give another example. Just war beliefs vary; some people are committed pacifists.

Secondly, the three themes are not independent of one another but rather interact with each other constantly and feed off one another. For example, dominance orientation and an exclusive patriotism, elements of the first theme, contribute to threat perception. Equally, causation is likely to run in the other direction, with perceived threat from a specific out-group strengthening war preparedness. The three themes operate together and cannot easily be separated. Similarly, lack of contact with members of an enemy out-group and misunderstandings of that group make acceptance of propaganda messages more likely and vice versa.

Time: The Fourth Factor in War Support

The WSM is completed by a fourth factor which is of a different order than the three factors so far described. From Chapter 1 onward we were regularly reminded that conflicts can spiral out of control and that support for war can escalate, often remarkably rapidly. The spiral conflict model (see Chapter 4) addressed this directly. Support for war is part of a process that develops over time, as Figure 8.3 attempts to illustrate. The danger of war, and the breaking out of war itself which sometimes follows, is a developing process. It can be hypothesized that each of the model's three factors strengthens the further we pursue the path toward war. Acceptance of readiness for war is the most evident of the three at the *preparing* for the possibility of war stage, the model proposes, when arming is accompanied by hope that hostilities will not break out—"hoping for the best while preparing for the worst." But elements of threat perception and mental simplification are always present in some form and to some degree, and each is likely to intensify as the danger of war grows, as war becomes something to be seriously *contemplated*, and once armed conflict is *engaged*. By the time war is engaged, the perception that one's country or group is under threat and the personal and collective move toward a simplification and hardening of beliefs and opinions and images have both grown. By that stage the three factors of readiness, threat perception, and over-simplification play equal parts in a mutually reinforcing spiral of support for war. Adding complexity, different components of the factors are likely to be more evident at different stages in the "steps to war" process. Support for one's country or group's military may show particularly strong growth as war spirals into conflict and the first casualties are reported, and popular images of the enemy may become much more negative and less exclusively focused on its leader or leaders.

It is important to be clear that all three war support factors are present at all stages to some degree. It is the intensity of expression of each factor which grows as war approaches. For example, take the feelings of being at

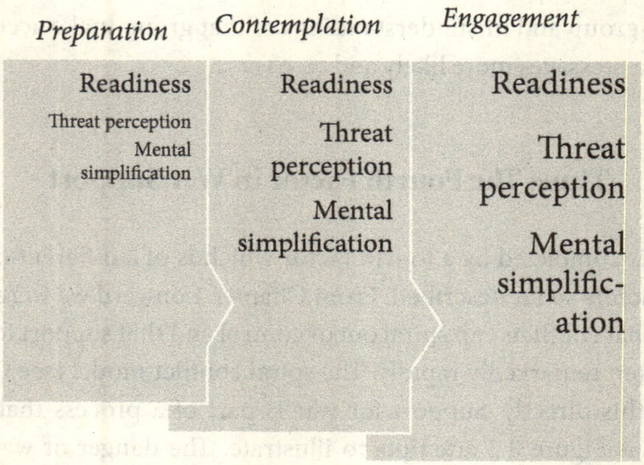

Preparation	Contemplation	Engagement
Readiness	Readiness	Readiness
Threat perception	Threat perception	Threat perception
Mental simplification	Mental simplification	Mental simplification

Figure 8.3 The war support model: the three war support factors grow in strength as we tread the path to war

war that both civilians and combatants have so often described, such as the feeling of purpose and of taking part in a collective enterprise, contributing to something greater than the self (see Chapter 2). Times when one's group is at war have been described as among the most exciting, memorable, ecstatic, even happiest of people's lives. There is "meaning" to be found in conflict. We can feel we are, with others, fulfilling a "mission." But such feelings, although much more intense during war itself, are not completely absent even at times of settled peace. The embeddedness of militarism in most societies, including the glorification of past war successes (see Chapter 5), is depicted in the model as a component of acceptance of readiness for war, the strongest component of war support at the *preparedness-for-war* stage. The acceptance of society's militarism and pride in its military, including valuing military strength and the acquiring of armaments, is the forerunner of the heightened feelings of purpose and significance experienced later, when war has been engaged.

Further along the trajectory toward war, at the stage I have called *contemplation-of-war*, these positive war-related sentiments become more focused on the need to stand up for the group's position and values. The prospect of war takes on enhanced meaning in the face of growing awareness that there is something threatening about one's national, ethnic, religious, or regional group's position in relation to that of another group which is increasingly being perceived as a potential enemy—experienced as direct military threat, humiliation or disrespect, loss or the threat of loss of control, or in some other way. Once war is in prospect, the bases for supporting a possible war begin to be more closely identified and articulated, including naming a specific potential enemy and the specific causes for which a war might need to be fought. The perception of threat moves from the general to the more specific. At an earlier stage it may still be relatively unfocused, for example an acceptance that "we are living in an increasingly threatening world." Later it has become more focused: "country (or group) X is a threat to our way of life (values or territory)."

Questions regarding the morality of war, including questions about the attribution of responsibility and blame for war, have never been far away during our exploration of the bases of war support. Such issues arise at all stages in the growth of support for war. At the preparedness stage they are present in the form of widespread acceptance that there are circumstances which render as "just" engaging in war. As the reality of a possible war becomes something to be contemplated, the moral argument for a war begins to gain ground. Perhaps we will need to defend "our way of life," our values—assumed to be superior—even our group's very existence. The justificatory mental "mechanisms" that allow us to support killing others are more available to us—we share the responsibility, casualties are minimized, it is for the greater good, and so on.

Over-simplification is a growing part of the picture as war support moves from preparedness to contemplation to engagement. But, as with acceptance of readiness for war and the perception of threat, it is there from the beginning. Even quite specific justifications are very often present in quiescent form at the early, preparedness stage. An exclusive, chauvinistic nationalism, of the kind that contributes to war support, can long exist in partial or dormant form until such time as it is aroused in support of a particular war. Intergroup differences of identity, previously "slumbering," have often been aroused, sometimes remarkably rapidly, and used to support collective violence. As war support moves through its stages, becoming more intense and more focused, beliefs supporting war become more fixed and difficult to change, particularly if they are central to one's group's values or identity.

Reduced intergroup contact and negative views of the other group are mutually reinforcing, providing just one example of the many vicious cycles which can contribute to war support spiraling over time. Increasingly, our and their interests are perceived as in conflict, and interaction between us is viewed in terms of competition rather than cooperation—we are now, in game theory terms, parties to a zero-sum rather than a positive-sum "game." Lack of exposure to, and understanding of, the other's perspective may be at its worst in the midst of war, when there is, instead, maximum exposure to one's own side's war-supporting propaganda. But it begins in less extreme form at a much earlier stage. Lack of self-criticism contributes to an absence of empathy or understanding of others' views. Our ways of thinking about "them" and "us" become further simplified as our relationship moves from being perceived as that of rivals to one between potential enemies to that of groups engaged in war against each other. At its height, our perception of the relationship is Manichean in form, almost one of "mythic" proportions, of heroes and villains.

Propaganda plays an important role in the model, but it is there from the preparedness stage onward, long before it is at all likely to be identifiable as such. We are prepared, "infused," with ideas over a long period of time that prepare us for the possibility of war and, increasingly, for war with a specific enemy. Over time, as war support mounts from preparedness to specific contemplation to actual engagement, the window of acceptable opinion—the so-called Overton window—narrows. It becomes unpopular, unacceptable, then even dangerous to challenge or even to express views alternative to the increasingly simplified collective view. History is replete with examples of those who have been condemned, imprisoned, some forced into exile on account of their views that were unsupportive of a popular war. They are examples of the "contaminated in-group." In the process our group's leaders become war leaders, either becoming increasingly war-supporting themselves or being replaced by those who better reflect the move from unfocused preparedness to contemplation of war to active war-making. They change, as the rest of us do, in another vicious cycle of increasing war support.

Nor does time stop moving on once war is engaged. The intense mix of feelings and thoughts associated with being at war may serve to support the continuation of conflict and provide a barrier to bringing it to an end, at least while optimism about the success and short duration of the war last. Although the dynamics of war duration are beyond the scope of the model as currently presented, it recognizes that the pinnacle of war support, with readiness for continued war still strong and threat perception and oversimplification at their zeniths, never lasts forever—although it can last for years. War support eventually declines from its peak because one's side has won, or has lost, or because "war fatigue" has set in. What has been called the *Iraq syndrome* refers to the rapid fall in US public support for their country's engagement in the second Iraq War as American casualties mounted. A similar, though less rapid, loss of public support occurred in the earlier US wars in Korea and Vietnam, as it did in the case of wars to defend colonial interests, for example, that fought by the French in Indochina in the 1950s.[31] From the public's perspective, these were wars being fought "far from home," and their perception of having a stake in the outcome could not be taken for granted. That is very different from a war being fought by a nation or group directly under attack, but in all cases, once war-related losses (see Chapter 1) begin to accumulate, the war-supporting and war-escalating factors that have been the subject of this book and which constitute the core of the WSM are now pitted against calls for the war to be brought to an end.[32] Such calls may not be heard so soon, may be more difficult to voice, and receive less support when the stakes are higher; but they will be there.

Are There Implications of the WSM for the Prevention of War?

Attempting to draw implications of the WSM for war prevention is a further step, deserving more thought and probably another book, or for others to take up. What is more, unless and until the model is tested for validity in the marketplace of academic scrutiny, it remains a set of untested ideas, however well-grounded they might be. But some will very reasonably argue that unless there are such implications to be drawn, the model is little more than an academic exercise, unlikely to be of any practical real-world use. Let me try, then, to say something about possible implications for two related conflicts. I choose these because both are generally considered to be of the utmost importance, both now and for the future. Hence, both have been featuring prominently in mainstream news as I have been writing. But more than that, they both concern me personally. My support, or lack of it, for potential war is salient in both cases. It is *my and my country's* own readiness for war, *our* perception of the threats involved, and the simplicity or complexity of *our* thinking about the issues involved which constitute the very substance of the matter in these two cases. I, and my fellow countrymen and -women, are the subjects here. This is personal. The two conflicts or potential conflicts I have in mind are my country's involvement in the Ukraine war and our relationship with Russia and the relationship between the United States and its allies and China. For completion I might have also chosen a "new" or civil war example, but none currently feels so "close to home" or so urgent for me as the two I have opted for.

The War in Ukraine

Although my country is not officially at war in Ukraine, I can remember no war in my lifetime that feels so personal for us. My local premiership football team, Brighton and Hove Albion, turned out for at least one game in a new strip in the blue and yellow Ukrainian national colors. Flags in those colors appeared all over the place, and some van owners painted their vehicles blue and yellow. Individual families have offered their own homes for Ukrainian refugees. Our former prime minister finally resigned in July 2022 after repeated calls for him to quit, which were resisted on several grounds, including the argument that it would be a bad time to change leader "while a war is on." The clear implication was that we were on one side in this war against the other: we were all Ukrainians now, at least in spirit. Russia is the enemy. This feels like the nearest to my country actually being at war that I can remember. We experienced a "rally around the flag," although the flag was the Ukrainian one in this case.

How do the three factors identified in the WSM figure for me and my fellow UK citizens in the context of the war in Ukraine? Let us take the *acceptance of readiness for war* first. We have in a number of ways accepted readiness for this war for a long time. Throughout my lifetime Russia has been presented to me as our potential enemy. That was clearest during the Cold War; but that image has never gone away since then, and it has been intensifying in the statements made by many UK politicians and in the mainstream media in the last few years. For some time now we have been told that the world is increasingly dangerous for us. Sometimes the sources of that danger are left unspecified. But, as often, it is the threat posed by an "aggressive Russia" (and a "rising China"—see later) that is named.

The role of *threat perception*—in this case the perception of a wider threat Putin's Russia poses for all of us—has been very evident in the British media. The present threat is often attributed to President Putin personally, sometimes more generally to the Russian leadership, and very often to Russia collectively. Frequently that threat is described, even more generally, as a threat to the liberal, democratic, Western way of life. Ukrainian President Zelensky has used that argument repeatedly, that his country is fighting not just for its own freedom but as much for all of us in the West. A variation is the view that the Russian leadership is engaged in an attempt to restore the country's empire and that Ukraine's defense is part of "the great anticolonial struggle of our times."[33] There has been reference to Putin's "ethnic nationalism."[34] The perception of threat from Russia is evidently shared by a number of countries bordering or close to Russia. It appears that public support for increased security in the face of a focused threat from a neighboring country has intensified.

Notably, at least from a British perspective, distant from the frontline of conflict, the threat is never seen as emanating from the Russian people themselves. If the Russian public is referred to at all, it is usually cast as uninformed, misinformed, or simply unaware, due to an autocratic political system that allows them little access to information and little say.[35] Whether any of us have much say about going to war, whatever the political system we live under, is a moot point I will take up at the end of the chapter.

The role of threat perception in relation to the war in Ukraine assists in underlining my claim that the three pillars upholding the WSM, of which threat perception is one, are universal to war support whatever the nature of the threat. It might be argued, very reasonably, that being directly and very violently attacked, as Ukraine has been, is quite different in kind from a country or group's values being under threat, as many in the United Kingdom and elsewhere in the West believe theirs are. The intensity of the experience, its central importance to one's very existence, and the time course of its growth or recession are indeed very different. But the model's contention is that the perception of threat, and its core elements—a narrative, continuously purveyed by leaders and the media, that stresses the dangerousness of the world, identifies and demonizes an enemy, and discourages the contact that might enable a more nuanced understanding—are, in essence, the same. Its effect is also the same: to promote support for war, whether that is support to continue to defend despite huge sacrifices or support for one side in an ongoing war, including providing military and other forms of aid, knowing that there is a risk of our country or group being drawn closer to actual engagement in war. What distinguishes Ukraine and the United Kingdom, as I write, is *time*, the WSM's fourth factor. Ukrainians are engaged in war, when all aspects of war support, including perception of threat, are at their most intense. My country is somewhere between preparedness-for-war and contemplation-of-war. Threat perception, though much less intense, is the same. It is a feature, the model claims, of all wars and potential wars, most of which do not fit so easily into a picture of one country suddenly, unprovoked, invading another. Nor is the experience of the war in Ukraine, and the threat it poses, identical for all Ukrainians, wherever in the country they are living.

Over-simplification has been as evident in the dominant UK and Western narrative about the war in Ukraine as it is in all wars. The prevailing understanding of the war has been a Manichean one, populated by heroes and monsters, heinous actions on one side, noble and fully understandable reactions on the other. For a few weeks at least, my country experienced the kind of rapid "tightening up" in terms of acceptable views which usually accompanies war, even in countries like the United Kingdom that pride themselves on being tolerant of individual deviations from the norm. Those who spoke out against the simplified narrative, academics and supporters of the Stop the War Coalition among them, were quickly branded as aiding the aggressor's cause.[36]

We can see the relevance of the WSM's first three factors for my country's stance on the war in Ukraine. The fourth factor, *time*, is crucial in this case, as it always is when considering war support. The United Kingdom has been hovering on the brink of contemplating war. It is, however, not only prepared for war but also well on in the contemplation-of-war stage. There has been much media debate over the question of whether we should be more directly engaged in Ukraine's defense. Our politicians have wisely drawn the line at sending troops, using the argument that Ukraine is not a NATO member. But other countries bordering Russia are members, and if attacked, my country should be obligated to engage militarily. Since that would mean war between two nuclear powers, this public debate has inevitably led to renewed media discussion about the dangers of the use of nuclear weapons.[37] I have heard it said more than once that we are nearer to nuclear war than at any time since the Cuban Missile Crisis of 1962.

I hope that by the time this book is published that danger will have receded. But my point is this. My country's position over the war in Ukraine provides us with a perfect example of what this book has been all about. We are living the processes of war support as I write. Should events unfold in a different direction, and we find ourselves at war with Russia, we will be able to look back and trace our support for war through our acceptance of readiness for it, our perception that we and our allies were under threat, and our over-simplification of the issues and actors involved. It is those factors, the WSM proposes, which will have driven us from preparedness for war to contemplation of a specific war to actual engagement in war. We will, I argue, be able to understand how we supported it happening. Meanwhile, my country has played the role of a committed ally—the most committed in Europe, our leaders proudly proclaim—of one side in the war, and the majority view has supported that position.

It was not long, however, before cracks appeared in the dominant wall of approved opinion. Questions started to be asked in the mainstream media about whether supporting Ukrainian defense by supplying more weapons was prolonging the war and helping to increase war casualties and might be contributing to the threat of wider escalation. The negative economic consequences of the war, not just for the main protagonists, as well as the effectiveness of sanctions against Russia were other debatable issues as the war lengthened from weeks to months.[38]

What then might we have done differently? How might the contemplation of war with Russia have been avoided? Since it is argued by many that

Ukraine is fighting on our behalf as well as its own, how might we have helped avoid the Ukraine war engagement? Might we have been more alert to the danger of over-simplification which hardens as war approaches? Should we have been more critical of our leaders and of the media, feeding us a dominant threat-filled narrative? Could we have been better at recognizing how our consent was being manufactured by propaganda, as it is in all wars? Why didn't we argue for maintaining contact with a potential enemy, seeking fuller knowledge and understanding of the other's perspective, looking for opportunities for cooperation rather than competition? Shouldn't we have been suspicious of the use of the kinds of demonizing images which are such a feature of war? The roots of readiness for war with Russia are deep, but at least we might have put up a stronger resistance to increasing the supply of armaments into a war zone.

I have been party to accepting, or at least failing to resist, an over-simplified, one-sided account of the circumstances that have preceded the current situation. One note of dissension has been sounded from time to time by those who have pointed to the role of NATO expansion in the long chain of events leading up to the February 2022 Russian invasion. Thomas Meaney of the Max Planck Institute in Göttingen, Germany, has summarized some of the relevant history. He tells us that early on after NATO came into being in 1949 it was unpopular with the public, both in the war-weary United States and in western Europe where there were significant anti-NATO protests in several countries. But, he says, NATO has since then "won a long war of public relations." According to his account, US presidents, including Clinton and later to be president Biden, were skeptical about NATO expansion eastward but were won round to the idea. When the Soviet Union collapsed many assumed NATO had become redundant. There was certainly a widespread view among international relations strategists at the time that NATO expansion was a bad idea and that a pan-European defense force was preferable. There are those who have maintained that position and who believe that Russia has been humiliated since then. Rather than disbanding, NATO expanded, changing in the process, as Meaney sees it, "from being a primarily defensive organization to a brazenly offensive one."[39] According to journalist Neal Ascherson, "many Russians believe that their country was swindled in its hour of weakness."[40] In the wake of Russian protests at the continual expansion of NATO eastward, many are of the opinion that the president who followed Yeltsin "was almost certain to have been a nationalist authoritarian."[41] By such accounts, it was as much as anything else the NATO expansion issue which finally came to a head in Ukraine.

Perhaps, writes Keith Gessen, Russian-born US novelist, journalist, and translator, "we should have thought more deeply about how to create a security arrangement, and an economic one" more conducive to good relations with Russia and one which did not put Ukraine in the position of having to make "a fateful choice" between sides in a conflict between great powers. In WSM language, he regrets the lack of more considered, complex thinking at an earlier stage. Author and radio and TV broadcaster Martin Sixsmith is another who has argued that our politicians have rejected "more thoughtful analyses" of relations with Russia in favor of a perpetuation of the paranoia and "mutual incomprehension" that has "clouded rational judgement" ever since the end of the Second World War.[42]

Let me inject a personal observation at this point. It involves my own professional association, the British Psychological Society (BPS). In March 2022, the month following the invasion of Ukraine, the BPS voted to support the expulsion of Russia from the European Federation of Psychologists' Associations, "as a demonstration of solidarity with Ukraine."[43] It was following, and lending support to, the United Kingdom's approved position on the war. In the light of the WSM, that could be construed as a mistake since it cut UK psychologists off from contact with their Russian colleagues. A more thoughtful response might have helped maintain dialogue—not necessarily agreement about everything—and could have made a contribution to a more considered, complex understanding of events.

It may appear that I am critical of the prevailing UK view of the war in Ukraine, even that I have sympathies with Russia and am unsupportive of those who are suffering in Ukraine. That would be to misunderstand what I am trying to say. My exploration for this book has led me to identify what I believe are the major sources of people's support for war. In the light of the resulting WSM, it is possible to see where the government and alliances that claim to act on my behalf have, if war is to be avoided, made mistakes. But, of course, such mistakes are never confined to one side. It needs to be said that there is nothing but outright criticism of the Russian leadership's 2022 invasion, and of the existence of disinformation and control of the media in Russia, even by those who are clear that the West's attitudes and actions over decades have contributed. There are always two sides to war (sometimes more than two). Criticizing the other side for its acceptance of readiness for war, for falsely perceiving that we are a threat to them, and for adopting a prejudiced, simplified view of us and our relationship with them is easy. Being more thoughtful about our own position is much more problematic. As more and more steps are taken toward war, speaking out and criticizing the dominant view becomes increasingly uncomfortable.

Contemplating War between the United States, the United Kingdom and Their Allies, and China

The dangers of war between the United States and China, and ways it can be prevented, are thoroughly examined in Graham Allison's 2017 book *Destined for War: Can America and China Escape Thucydides's Trap?* Thucydides was the ancient Greek historian who famously explained, about the Peloponnesian War that engulfed the city state of Athens in the fifth century BCE, "It was the rise of Athens and the fear that this instilled in Sparta that made war inevitable." Sparta's accustomed position as the dominant power in the area was threatened. The Harvard Thucydides's Trap Project identified 16 similar cases that have occurred in the last 500 years, each examples of threat to an established major power from a rising power. Twelve of them led to war, ranging from the threat to France from the Hapsburgs in the early sixteenth century to the threat from Japan to the United States in the mid-twentieth. The present-day changing balance of power between the United States and China is both military and economic. The current threat to the economic dominance of the United States was clear to Allison. For example, since the end of the Second World War the US share of the global economic market had declined from about 50% to 16%, while China's had risen phenomenally from 2% to 18%. Rapid Chinese technological development, including military, was "rapidly undercutting America's status as a global hegemon and ... forcing US leaders to confront ugly truths about the limits of American power." Areas of tension between China and the United States which Allison describes as potential trigger points for escalation to war include the South China Sea, Taiwan, the Japanese Senkaku Islands, North Korea, and even economic competition itself.[44]

There are a number of features common to the two cases I have chosen to discuss. Response to humiliation is one common theme. China is principally motivated, Allison believes, by the wish to be great again, to recover its historic sphere of influence in Asia, and thereby to receive the world's recognition and respect. All Chinese high school students learn of the country's shame and humiliation at the hands of Japan and Western powers, he says, and reclaiming international standing and national pride is important to most Chinese people—"The greatest Chinese dream is the great rejuvenation of the Chinese nation," as Xi Jinping has said.[45] A strong military is a vital part of this. Critics have termed this stance one of "belligerent, defensive nationalism."[46] At the same time, "rivalry with the US is exacerbated by deep cultural differences"[47]: the Confucian values of hierarchy, public service, social order, and harmony versus Western values of individualism, liberalism, equality, liberty, and free markets. Even Azar Gat, mostly an apologist for US hegemony, recognizes much of this. He acknowledges the legitimacy of different cultural values, of opposition to what is seen as US cultural imperialism, and the "deep and widespread aversion . . . to being lectured by the West."[48] As Graham Allison puts it, the United States prides itself on being a "benign hegemon," as lawmaker, policeman, judge, and jury; but to Chinese the acceptance of US-made rules provokes resentment.[49]

The three factors central to the WSM are each in evidence in the case of the China versus the West rivalry. I am regularly exposed to the prevailing UK government view that the threat from China—mostly unspecified although economic threat, threat to our way of life and political system, and potential military threat are all implied—is increasing. Simplified thinking is there in the form of regular demonization of China—for example, on human rights grounds—and failure to acknowledge the Western allies' equally unacceptable policies in the not so distant past and their roles in aggravating the relationship with China. While in the Russia case, in terms of the WSM's fourth factor, time, the United Kingdom could be seen as having been poised at entry to the contemplation-of-war stage, with threat perception and oversimplification growing, in the China case we are thankfully still at the stage of preparedness.

But Allison finds plenty of evidence of escalation. There has been recent revival of the Quad alliance of the United States, Japan, India, and Australia; and attitudes toward China in the West are hardening. In 2021 the United Kingdom announced it would have a permanent military presence in the Indo-pacific. One British international affairs correspondent goes so far as to say, "The slide towards confrontation appears inexorable."[50] On the media front, in 2020–21 China and the United States authorized tit-for-tat expulsions of the other's journalists.[51] As I write, tension has been increased due to the controversial visit to Taiwan of the speaker of the US House of Representatives, Nancy Pelosi, during which she addressed the Taiwan parliament and spoke to former

Chinese political prisoners as well as the country's leaders. This was bound to be seen as provocative in China. In response, Chinese military exercises in the area were increased, and Chinese–US climate coordination as well as discussions aimed at reducing military tension were suspended.[52] Allison warns that if the United States keeps on its present path of increasing hostility toward, and misunderstanding of, China, future historians may find themselves comparing the US position with that of British, German, and Russian leaders as they sleepwalked into World War I.[53]

The Future of War Support

There are ample grounds for feeling pessimistic about the future of war support. Great power rivalry has not gone away, quite the contrary. Meanwhile, wars continue to be concentrated in the poorer parts of the world in the form of chaotic intrastate, civil wars of various kinds. Nonetheless, I want to conclude on a more positive note. I suggest that if we can better understand why it is that we so often support war, *Homo sapiens* might, by being less inclined to support collective political violence, do more to deserve that name.

A doubt at the back of my mind while working on this book is whether we, as ordinary citizens, have much say, at all, in whether and when our countries or groups engage in war. Indeed, can it reasonably be said that we ever support war? Perhaps ordinary folk are never much in support of war. Rather, it is imposed on us by our political leaders, who themselves are not as much in control as they like to think. This nagging doubt surfaced again following the events in Ukraine early in 2022 and my government's actions against Russia and in support of Ukraine. It occurred to me at the time that no one in power had asked for my opinion. If things escalated and I found myself at war with a nuclear power, would I have had any say? Would I simply have been a bystander? So, when it comes to war, is the hard truth that we have little or no agency in the matter. My basic premise might be misplaced. In fact, that was what one anonymous early reviewer of the book proposal thought—I was misguided to suppose people supported war. I think he or she was wrong for two reasons.

First, we *do* actively support war in the many ways I have touched on in this book. We are not innocent. We do accept militarism and militarization on a large scale and applaud it. We do subscribe to the notion of a just war and glorify past war engagements. We do thoughtlessly repeat the simplifying messages about our rivals and enemies, and about ourselves, that our governments and much of the media feed us. Many of us believe it is better to be tough in standing up to opponents than to try and understand where they are coming from. And if war comes, we mostly do not resist; rather, we rally around the flag, make the most of it, even sometimes finding it life-enhancing. Second, we *do* have agency in the matter. There *are* actions we can take to resist rather than support war. The following is merely a brief sketch of some of those actions, assuming the validity of the WSM.

It will be argued that this is all very well for those living under democratic governance; that the more common intrastate wars take place predominantly in poorer countries with autocratic or anocratic regimes, where people have far less agency. There is no doubt truth in that, but the difference can be exaggerated; and, harder though it may be for those in non-democratic countries to resist supporting war, the same principles derived from the WSM apply.

Not Supporting War by Resisting Our Readiness for It

Because the WSM supposes that readiness for war is the most significant of the three drivers of war support at the long, early stage of preparation for war, war support–resisting actions in this category are fundamental. They include working to change some deeply engrained ways of thinking and being. Changing our collective adherence to the assumption that war can be a just, effective, and honorable way of solving conflicts, and the chauvinistic forms of national and group identities and hyper-masculinity which reinforce it, is a demanding, long-term project. But without those changes we will continue to be susceptible to the perception of threat and the over-simplified thinking which lurk, ready to grow to dangerous proportions when circumstances are favorable to them. Support for militarization and our complacent attitude toward armaments and the arms trade are also deeply embedded in our cultures. But they might be more amenable to change in the short term. Military spending, at least, is always on the political agenda.

Not Supporting War by Resisting Threat Assumptions

For war to be avoided, the messages from governments, military leaders, and the media, encouraging us to believe we are under threat from a potential enemy, have to be resisted. That need not be by blanket denial that nothing is amiss but by reframing the problem as one that needs to be solved in ways that resist the language of enemies and threats and the sounding of the drumbeats of war. Contact and cooperation with the other party must be encouraged rather than closed down. The narrative which seeks to depict us as a victim threatened by the other must be resisted and an alternative story promoted. The belief that the world is a dangerous, threatening one, although more general, can also be reduced if the most salient current conflicts can be reinterpreted in less threatening terms.

Not Supporting War by Resisting Simplified Thinking

Over-simplified thinking attends war at all stages but intensifies the more closely a war approaches. If the WSM is to be believed, challenging it with more complex, considered thinking is one of the most important ways of resisting support for war. The circumstances that have led to a current problem should be understood in less biased and predetermined ways. The other side to a conflict needs to be viewed in a less stereotypical, prejudiced, blaming, and mistrusting fashion. Demonizing language in particular is to be avoided. Justifications and ways of distancing ourselves from responsibility for the harms inflicted by war should be recognized and countered with more nuanced reflection. Propaganda and misleading information need to be seen for what they are and called out. We need to be more reflective about the position of our own group and maintain tolerance for the expression of views which are contrary to any war-supporting consensus which is developing.

Most of those ideas, deriving from the WSM, have appeared before, in the sentiments expressed by writers on war, whom I have cited as we went along, when they have speculated on how war might be avoided. A. C. Grayling, for example, recommends maintaining mutual linkages of a practical and beneficial kind with potential adversaries.[54] Keith Lowe advocates adopting a more complex view of human nature and putting an end to dividing the world into "heroes who can do no wrong, and monsters who are the irredeemable embodiment of evil."[55] Mary Kaldor would like to see us all taking a more humanist, universalist, cosmopolitan outlook, seeking the truth, recognizing propaganda, and introducing more separation between our national, ethnic, and religious identities and our governments and leaders who claim to represent them.[56] Graham Allison identified a number of clues as to why rivalry between dominant and rising world powers did not always result in war. One was support for wise, more thoughtful leaders and policies. He believes new thinking is required in the context of present US–Chinese relations. That might involve accommodation, negotiation, and redefining the relationship in terms of cooperation in facing common threats, for example from nuclear anarchy, global terrorism, and climate change.[57]

What the WSM has tried to do is to bring those ideas, and others, together in one place in the form of a unified model to explain why we have so often supported going to war and why we continue to do so. The risks that we share globally, including poverty and inequality, the effects of climate change, and the displacement caused by past and current wars, threaten to make wars more likely in the future. At the same time, the proliferation of nuclear weapons and the invention of further means of delivering death and injury remotely make the potential costs of future war to the whole of humankind and the planet unthinkable. I earnestly hope that a better understanding of why war has our support will assist in bringing us to our senses.

Notes

Introduction

1. L. LeShan, *The Psychology of War: Comprehending Its Mystique and Its Madness* (New York: Helios Press, 2002).

Chapter 1

1. C. Von Clausewitz, *On War*, ed. and trans. M. Howard and P. Paret (1832; repr., Princeton, NJ: Princeton University Press, 1976); see, for example, *The Penguin Dictionary of Quotations* (Harmondsworth, UK: Penguin, 1960), 112.
2. D. Wood, *What Have We Done: The Moral Injury of Our Longest Wars* (New York: Little, Brown and Company, 2016), 264–265.
3. J. S. Levy and W. R. Thompson, *Causes of War* (Chichester, UK: Wiley-Blackwell, 2010), 5.
4. Ibid., 5–6.
5. For example, A. C. Grayling, *War: An Enquiry* (New Haven, CT: Yale University Press, 2017).
6. Levy and Thompson, *Causes of War*, 6.
7. W. H. Wiist and S. K. White, eds., *Preventing War and Promoting Peace: A Guide for Health Professionals* (New York: Cambridge University Press, 2017), 38.
8. Citings in this paragraph are from Levy and Thompson, *Causes of War*, 10.
9. Levy and Thompson, *Causes of War*, 6.
10. Grayling, *War*, 231.
11. For example, A. Stevens, *The Roots of War and Terror* (London: Continuum, 2004).
12. M. Centano and E. Enriquez, *War and Society* (Cambridge: Polity Press), 147.
13. L. LeShan, *The Psychology of War: Comprehending Its Mystique and Its Madness* (New York: Helios Press, 2002), 102, 104.
14. C. Tilly, "Reflections on the History of European State-Making," in *The Formation of National States in Western Europe*, ed. C. Tilly (Princeton, NJ: Princeton University Press, 1975), 3–83; cited, for example, by I. Morris, *War: What Is It Good For? The Role of Conflict in Civilisation, from Primates to Robots* (London: Profile Books, 2015), 18.
15. M. Kaldor, *New and Old Wars: Organized Violence in a Global Era*, 2nd ed. (Cambridge: Polity Press, 2006) 15–19.
16. M. van Creveld, *The Transformation of War* (New York: Free Press, 1991); cited by Kaldor, *New and Old Wars*, 19.

17. B. Miller, "The State-to-Nation Balance and War," in *Nationalism and War*, ed. J. A. Hall and S. Malešević (Cambridge: Cambridge University Press, 2013), 76.
18. Kaldor, *New and Old Wars*, 20. The Balkan states, later the site of the wars of the 1990s, are a good, relatively modern, example of the process of development of state militarization. This happened relatively late there, during the nineteenth and early twentieth centuries, in comparison with most other parts of Europe (see also S. Malešević, "Obliterating Heterogeneity through Peace: Nationalisms, States and Wars, in the Balkans," in *Nationalism and War*, ed. J. A. Hall and S. Malešević [Cambridge: Cambridge University Press, 2013], 262–267).
19. Centano and Enriquez, *War and Society*, 120–121.
20. Ibid., 120; A. Gat, *The Causes of War and the Spread of Peace: But Will War Rebound?* (Oxford: Oxford University Press, 2017), 66.
21. For example, R. Lachmann, "Mercenary, Citizen, Victim: The Rise and Fall of Conscription in the West," in *Nationalism and War*, ed. J. A. Hall and S. Malešević (Cambridge: Cambridge University Press, 2013), 44–70.
22. Morris, *War: What Is It Good For?*, 210.
23. Centano and Enriquez, *War and Society*, 80, 82.
24. Kaldor, *New and Old Wars*, 17, 23.
25. Ibid., 25.
26. Cited by Stevens, *Roots of War*, 81.
27. Gat, *Causes of War*, 49; Grayling, *War*, 142, 145.
28. Kaldor, *New and Old Wars*, 18.
29. Levy and Thompson, *Causes of War*, 29.
30. Ibid., 39.
31. Gat, *Causes of War*, 52, 53.
32. Levy and Thompson, *Causes of War*, 59.
33. Ibid., 36, 60–63.
34. Vegetius, fourth century AD, *Penguin Dictionary of Quotations* (Harmondsworth, UK: Penguin Books, 1960), 403; Levy and Thompson, *Causes of War*, 30.
35. Cited by Gat, *Causes of War*, 242.
36. Cited by M. Naím, *The End of Power: From Boardrooms to Battlefields and Churches to States, Why Being in Charge Isn't What It Used to Be* (New York: Basic Books, 2013).
37. Morris, *War: What Is It Good For?*, 16.
38. Ibid., 238, 273.
39. Levy and Thompson, *Causes of War*, 44.
40. For example, Stevens, *Roots of War*; Gat, *Causes of War*; Levy and Thompson, *Causes of War*.
41. Levy and Thompson, *Causes of War*, 208.
42. B. F. Walter, *How Civil Wars Start: And How to Stop Them* (New York: Penguin Random House, 2022), chap. 1.
43. O. Hathaway and S. Shapiro, *The Internationalists: And Their Plan to Outlaw War* (London: Penguin, 2017).
44. Ibid., 98.
45. For example, S. Casey-Maslen, "The Role of International Law in Preventing War and Promoting Peace," in Wiist and White, *Preventing War*, 180–191.

46. Hathaway and Shapiro, *Internationalists*, xii.
47. For example, Casey-Maslen, "Role of International Law," 180.
48. Ibid., 185.
49. Naím, *End of Power*.
50. J. Bourke, *Wounding the World: How Military Violence and War-Play Invade Our Lives* (London: Virago, 2014), 67, 69.
51. J. A. Arquilla, *Insurgents, Raiders and Bandits: How Masters of Irregular Warfare Have Shaped Our World* (Lanham, MD: Ivan R. Dee, 2011); cited by Naím, *End of Power*.
52. Levy and Thompson, *Causes of War*, 12.
53. Kaldor, *New and Old Wars*, 96.
54. Ibid., 5.
55. Ibid., ix, 75–79.
56. Ibid., 2.
57. Ibid., 95.
58. Ibid., ix, 117, 169.
59. Ibid., chap. 3.
60. Ibid., 47; and see, for example, 51, 100.
61. Ibid., 49, 97–102, 113, 166; and see, for example, 100–101, 166.
62. Naím, *End of Power*, 123.
63. R. Lemarchand, "War and Nationalism: The View from Central Africa," in *Nationalism and War*, ed. J. A. Hall and S. Malešević (Cambridge: Cambridge University Press, 2013), 309.
64. Ibid., 310.
65. Ibid., 314.
66. M. Mann, "The Role of Nationalism in the Two World Wars," in *Nationalism and War*, ed. J. A. Hall and S. Malešević (Cambridge: Cambridge University Press, 2013), 172–173.
67. Gat, *Causes of War*, 216–217.
68. Ibid., 217.
69. For instance in Guatemala, Colombia, Cambodia, Iran, Dominican Republic, Guatemala, Chile, Iraq, East Timor, see M. Pilisuk and J. A. Rowntree, *The Hidden Structure of Violence: Who Benefits from Global Violence and War* (New York: Monthly Review Press, 2015), 42–48, 190–202; see also M. Shaw, *The New Western Way of War: Risk-Transfer War and Its Crisis in Iraq* (Cambridge: Polity Press, 2005).
70. Gat, *Causes of War*, 217.
71. For example, Levy and Thompson, *Causes of War*; Gat, *Causes of War*.
72. D. Duriesmith, *Masculinity and New War: The Gendered Dynamics of Contemporary Armed Conflict* (London: Taylor and Francis, 2016), chap. 2.
73. Kaldor, *New and Old Wars*, 16, 30–31.
74. Levy and Thompson, *Causes of War*, 7.
75. P. Collier, et al., *The Second World War* (Oxford: Osprey Publishing, 2018).
76. Levy and Thompson, *Causes of War*, 2–3.
77. Ibid., 1.
78. K. Lowe, *The Fear and the Freedom: How the Second World War Changed Us* (London: Penguin, 2018), 20, 56–57.

79. Ibid., 382, 384.
80. Morris, *War: What Is It Good For?*, 279.
81. Pilisuk and Rowntree, *Hidden Structure of Violence*, 10, 16, 30.
82. Centano and Enriquez, *War and Society*, 34.
83. E. Kanter, "The Effects of War on Combatants, Veterans and Their Families," in Wiist and White, *Preventing War*, 19–20, 22.
84. Mann, "Role of Nationalism."
85. Kanter, "Effects of War," 7–8; Pilisuk and Rowntree, *Hidden Structure of Violence*, 31–33; Wood, *What Have We Done*, 81–82, 94–95.
86. Kanter, "Effects of War," 29.
87. Kaldor, *New and Old Wars*, 9, 107; K. Khoshnood, B. X. Lee, and C. Marin, C., "The Health Effects of War on Civilians," in Wiist and White, *Preventing War*, 34; C. Holland et al., "Weapons of War and Mass Destruction," in Wiist and White, *Preventing War*, 61.
88. Centano and Enriquez, *War and Society*, 90; Gat, *Causes of War*, 139–140.
89. Khoshnood et al., "Health Effects of War," 35–39.
90. Lowe, *Fear and the Freedom*, 104, 391–394.
91. Centano and Enriquez, *War and Society*, 92–95, 100–101; Morris, *War: What Is It Good For?*, 226.
92. Kanter, "Effects of War," 25–26; Morris, *War: What Is It Good For?*, 220, 255; Wood, *What Have We Done*, 276.
93. Pilisuk and Rowntree, *Hidden Structure of Violence*, 37–38, 74, citing also Mozambican political leader Graça Machel's report for the UN *The Impact of War on Children*.
94. Ibid., 39.
95. Holland et al., "Weapons of War."
96. Wiist and White, *Preventing War*, xxiii.
97. Ibid., chaps. 1–4.
98. Lowe, *Fear and the Freedom*, 103, 240.
99. Wiist and White, *Preventing War*, 49.
100. Lowe, *Fear and the Freedom*, 168–173.
101. Kaldor, *New and Old Wars*, 113–116.
102. Wiist and White, *Preventing War*, 37–43, 49–54.
103. Morris, *War: What Is It Good For?*, quotes in this paragraph from 18, 93, 111, 322, 334.
104. Ibid., quotes in this paragraph from 167–168, 202, 225, 203, 232, 234, 271.
105. Review of Morris 2015. Azar Gat, *War in Human Civilization* (New York: Oxford University Press, 2006), Shephard, *The Guardian Weekly*, May 9, 2014.
106. Gat, *Causes of War*, 71–73.
107. Centano and Enriquez, *War and Society*, 124.
108. Ibid., 136.
109. Ibid., 137.
110. T. Piketty, *Capital in the Twenty-First Century*, trans. A. Goldhammer (Cambridge, MA: Belknap Press of Harvard University Press, 2017), 32 and following, 399 and following.

111. M. Macmillan, "The Mark of Cain," the BBC Reith Lectures, broadcast on BBC Radio 4, June–July 2018. This and the following three paragraphs are an edited version of J. Orford, "Psychology, History and War: Two Examples of Academic Discourses Which Fail to Oppose War and Militarism," *The Journal of Critical Psychology, Counselling and Psychotherapy* 19 (2019): 48–59.
112. For example, D. P. Barash and C. P. Webel, *Peace and Conflict Studies*, 2nd ed. (Los Angeles: Sage, 2009).
113. Stevens, *Roots of War*, 4–5, 78.
114. LeShan, *Psychology of War*, 111.
115. S. Pinker, *The Better Angels of Our Nature: A History of Violence and Humanity* (London: Penguin Books, 2012), xxv (emphasis in original).
116. Ibid., 28–31, citing M. van Creveld, *The Culture of War* (New York: Ballantine, 2008).
117. Ibid., 86, drawing on N. Elias, *The Civilizing Process: Sociogenic and Psychogenic Investigations* (1939; repr., Cambridge, MA: Blackwell, 2000).
118. Ibid., 88.
119. Levy and Thompson, *Causes of War*, 69–76, quote from 75.
120. Pinker, *Better Angels*, 57, 62, 66.
121. Ibid., 460, quote from 841.
122. Gat, *Causes of War*, 166–167, 171.
123. Other declinists include Morris, *War: What Is It Good For?*; J. S. Goldstein, *Winning the War on War: The Decline of Armed Conflict Worldwide* (London: Penguin, 2011); J. Diamond, *The World Until Yesterday: What Can We Learn from Traditional Societies?* (New York: Penguin, 2012).
124. Gat, *Causes of War*, 134.
125. Hathaway and Shapiro, *Internationalists*, 316, 329.
126. Ibid., 333, 334.
127. Centano and Enriquez, *War and Society*, 29.
128. Ibid., 83, 85.
129. Grayling, *War*, 114; citing J. S. Levy and W. R. Thompson, *The Arc of War* (Chicago: University of Chicago Press, 2011).
130. M. Altier and J. Kane, "Framing States: Unitary Actor Language and Public Support for Coercive Foreign Policy," *International Studies Quarterly* 67 (2023): sqac080.

Chapter 2

1. C. Hedges, *War Is a Force That Gives Us Meaning* (New York: Anchor, 2003), 3; cited by D. R. Rovenpor et al., "Intergroup Conflict Self-Perpetuates via Meaning: Exposure to Intergroup Conflict Increases Meaning and Fuels a Desire for Further Conflict," *Journal of Personality and Social Psychology* 116 (2019): 119–140.
2. A. Stevens, *The Roots of War and Terror* (London: Continuum, 2004), 7.
3. J. A. Hall and S. Malešević, "Introduction: Wars and Nationalisms," in *Nationalism and War*, ed. J. A. Hall and S. Malešević (Cambridge: Cambridge University Press, 2013), 2–3.

4. S. Freud, "Why War," in *Collected Papers*, vol. 4 (London: Hogarth Press, 1949); cited by M. Pilisuk and J. A. Rowntree, *The Hidden Structure of Violence: Who Benefits from Global Violence and War* (New York: Monthly Review Press, 2015), 78; Stevens, *Roots of War*, 11. Still in the 1970s and 80s, existential psychologist Rollo May thought there was a "daimonic" human quality, the source of both destructiveness and creativity (Pilisuk and Rowntree, *Hidden Structure of Violence*, 78). N. F. Dixon (*On the Psychology of Military Incompetence* [London: Futura, 1979]; cited by Stevens, *Roots of War*, 9) was writing of war propensity being repressed or sublimated during times of peace, when he claimed that reading books and watching films dealing with war become increasingly popular as substitutes for the real thing.
5. For example, K. Lorenz, *On Aggression* (New York: Bantam, 1966); cited by L. LeShan, *The Psychology of War: Comprehending Its Mystique and Its Madness* (New York: Helios Press, 2002), 14.
6. R. Ardrey, *The Hunting Hypothesis* (New York: Atheneum, 1976); cited by LeShan, *Psychology of War*, 13–14. Anthropologist Lionel Tiger (*Men in Groups* [London: Panther, 1971]; cited by Stevens, *Roots of War*, 48) was another, writing in the 1970s, who saw hunting as "the master pattern of the human species," a paradigm for all human inclination toward violence.
7. Stevens, *Roots of War*, 54.
8. R. B. Ferguson, "Pinker's List: Exaggerating Prehistoric War Mortality," in *War, Peace and Human Nature: The Convergence of Evolutionary and Cultural Views*, ed. D. Fry (Oxford: Oxford University Press, 2013); cited by A. C. Grayling, *War: An Enquiry* (New Haven, CT: Yale University Press, 2017).
9. Hall and Malešević, "Introduction," 3.
10. Pilisuk and Rowntree, *Hidden Structure of Violence*, 56.
11. LeShan, *Psychology of War*, 117.
12. A. Gat, *The Causes of War and the Spread of Peace: But Will War Rebound?* (Oxford: Oxford University Press, 2017), chaps. 1, 2, and 4.
13. S. Pinker, *The Better Angels of Our Nature: A History of Violence and Humanity* (London: Penguin Books, 2012), chap. 2, quote on 48.
14. L. M. Bagby, *Hobbes's Leviathan: Reader's Guide* (London: Continuum, 2007).
15. J.-J. Rousseau, *A Discourse upon the Origin and the Foundation of the Inequality among Mankind*, Project Gutenberg, https://www.gutenberg.org/ebooks/11136 (first published 1755).
16. Gat, *Causes of War*, 3; J. S. Levy and W. R. Thompson, *Causes of War* (Chichester, UK: Wiley-Blackwell, 2010), 29, 63, 79.
17. Stevens, *Roots of War*; Grayling, *War*; Levy and Thompson, *Causes of War*, 20–21.
18. M. L. Cottam et al., eds., *Introduction to Political Psychology*, 2nd ed. (New York: Psychology Press, 2010).
19. LeShan, *Psychology of War*, 15.
20. N. Ferguson, *The Pity of War* (London: Penguin Books, 1999), quotes from 343, 357, 359, 360, 361, 447 (emphasis in original).
21. G. Mosse, *Fallen Soldiers: Reshaping the Memory of the World Wars* (New York: Oxford University Press, 1990), 55, 25–26, citing P. Stansky and W. Abrahams, *Journey to the Frontier* (Boston: Atlantic Monthly Press, 1966), 330 (re John Cornford).

NOTES   249

22. G. Gray, *The Warriors: Reflections on Men in Battle* (1959; repr., Lincoln: University of Nebraska Press, 1998); cited by Stevens, *Roots of War*, 5.
23. Ferguson, *Pity of War*, 362.
24. Ibid., 361 (emphasis in original).
25. B. Ehrenreich, *Blood Rites: Origins and History of the Passions of War* (New York: Henry Holt, 1997), 13–15, 238.
26. W. James, "The Moral Equivalent of War," *Peace and Conflict: Journal of Peace Psychology* 1 (1910; repr., 1995): 17–26; cited by Pilisuk and Rowntree, *Hidden Structure of Violence*, 73.
27. Stevens, *Roots of War*, 5.
28. R. J. Evans, *Eric Hobsbawm: A Life in History* (London: Little, Brown, 2019).
29. LeShan, *Psychology of War*, 85–86.
30. Ibid., 16.
31. Mosse, *Fallen Soldiers*, 55–56.
32. F. Keane, *Wounds: A Memoir of War and Love* (London: William Collins, 2017), 10 (quoting from J. Lee, *Ireland 1912–1985* [Cambridge: Cambridge University Press, 1989], 27).
33. LeShan, *Psychology of War*, 89 (emphasis in original).
34. Hedges, *War Is a Force*, 10; cited by Rovenpor et al., "Intergroup Conflict Self-Perpetuates."
35. Rovenpor et al., "Intergroup Conflict Self-Perpetuates" (emphasis in original).
36. Pilisuk and Rowntree, *Hidden Structure of Violence*, 64–65; D. G. Winter, *Roots of War: Wanting Power, Seeing Threat, Justifying Force* (New York: Oxford University Press, 2018), 287; N. Caspi-Berkowitz et al., "To Die for a Cause but not for a Companion: Attachment-Related Variations in the Terror Management Function of Self-Sacrifice," *Journal of Personality and Social Psychology* 117 (2019): 1105–1126.
37. J. Anson et al., "Political Ideology in the 21st Century: A Terror Management Perspective on Maintenance and Change of the Status Quo," in *Social and Psychological Bases of Ideology and System Justification*, ed. J. Jost, A. Kay, and H. Thorisdottir (New York: Oxford University Press, 2009).
38. T. Pyszczynski, J. Greenberg, and S. Solomon, "A Dual Process Model of Defense against Conscious and Unconscious Death-Related Thoughts: An Extension of Terror Management Theory," *Psychological Review* 106 (1999): 835–845; cited by Winter, *Roots of War*, 287–289; G. Brock and Q. Atkinson, "What Can Examining the Psychology of Nationalism Tell Us about Our Prospects for Aiming at the Cosmopolitan Vision?" *Ethical Theory and Moral Practice* 11, no. 2 (2008): 165–179; A. Kruglanski, J. J. Bélanger, and R. Gunaratna, *The Three Pillars of Radicalization: Needs, Narratives, and Networks* (New York: Oxford University Press, 2019), 49–50; Anson et al., "Political Ideology in the 21st Century."
39. T. Pyszczynski et al., "Mortality Salience, Martyrdom, and Military Might: The Great Satan versus the Axis of Evil," *Personality and Social Psychology Bulletin* 32 (2006): 525–537; cited by Caspi-Berkowitz et al., "To Die for a Cause."
40. C. Routledge and J. Arndt, "Self-Sacrifice as Self-Defence: Mortality Salience Increases Efforts to Affirm a Symbolic Immortal Self at the Expense of the Physical

Self," *European Journal of Social Psychology* 38 (2008): 531–541; cited by Caspi-Berkowitz et al., "To Die for a Cause."
41. A. W. Kruglanski et al., "The Psychology of Radicalization and Deradicalization: How Significance Quest Impacts Violent Extremism," *Political Psychology* 35 (2014): 69–93.
42. A. W. Kruglanski et al., "Fully Committed: Suicide Bombers' Motivation and the Quest for Personal Significance," *Political Psychology* 30 (2009): 331–357.
43. N. Uexkull, M. d'Errico, and J. Jackson, "Drought, Resilience, and Support for Violence: Household Survey Evidence from DR Congo," *Journal of Conflict Resolution* 64, no. 10 (2020): 1994–2021.
44. J. Adam-Troian et al., "Positive Associations between Anomia and Intentions to Engage in Political Violence: Cross-Cultural Evidence from Four Countries," *Peace and Conflict: Journal of Peace Psychology* 26 (2020): 217–223.
45. H. P. Smith and R. M. Bohm, "Beyond Anomie: Alienation and Crime," *Critical Criminology* 16 (2008): 1–15; cited by Adam-Troian et al., "Positive Associations."
46. T. W. Adorno et al., *The Authoritarian Personality* (New York: Harpers, 1950); cited by P. T. Dunwoody and D. L. Plane, "The Influence of Authoritarianism and Outgroup Threat on Political Affiliations and Support for Antidemocratic Policies," *Peace and Conflict: Journal of Peace Psychology* 25 (2019): 198–210.
47. B. Altemeyer, *Right-Wing Authoritarianism* (Winnipeg, Canada: University of Manitoba Press, 1981); cited by Dunwoody and Plane, "Influence of Authoritarianism."
48. J. Duckitt and C. G. Sibley, "The Dual Process Motivational Model of Ideology and Prejudice," in *The Cambridge Handbook of the Psychology of Prejudice*, ed. C. G. Sibley and F. K. Barlow (New York: Cambridge University Press, 2016), 188–221; cited by Dunwoody and Plane, "Influence of Authoritarianism."
49. B. Altemeyer, *Enemies of Freedom: Understanding Right-Wing Authoritarianism* (San Francisco: Jossey-Bass, 1988) and *The Authoritarian Specter* (Cambridge, MA: Harvard University Press, 1996); cited by O. Gulevich, A. Nevruev, and I. Sarieva, "War as a Method of Conflict Resolution: The Link between Social Beliefs, Ideological Orientations, and Military Attitudes in Russia," *Peace and Conflict: Journal of Peace Psychology* 26 (2020): 192–201.
50. Gulevich, Nevruev, and Sarieva, "War as a Method of Conflict Resolution."
51. F. Pratto, J. Sidanius, and S. Levin, "Social Dominance Theory and the Dynamics of Intergroup Relations: Taking Stock and Looking Forward," *European Review of Social Psychology* 17 (2006): 271–320; cited by Gulevich, Nevruev, and Sarieva, "War as a Method of Conflict Resolution."
52. J. Duckitt, "A Dual-Process Cognitive-Motivational Theory of Ideology and Prejudice," *Advances in Experimental Social Psychology* 33 (2001): 41–113 and "Differential Effects of Right Wing Authoritarianism and Social Dominance Orientation on Outgroup Attitudes and Their Mediation by Threat from and Competitiveness to Outgroups," *Personality and Social Psychology Bulletin* 32 (2006): 684–696; cited by Gulevich, Nevruev, and Sarieva, "War as a Method of Conflict Resolution."
53. Winter, *Roots of War*, 152.
54. For example, LeShan, *Psychology of War*, 7–8.
55. A. Wolfers, *Discord and Collaboration: Essays on International Politics* (Baltimore: John Hopkins University Press, 1962); cited by Gat, *Causes of War*, 112.

56. For example, Cottam et al., *Introduction to Political Psychology*; D. D. N. Winter et al., "Understanding Militarism: Money, Masculinity, and the Search for the Mystical," in *Peace, Conflict and Violence: Peace Psychology for the 21st Century*, ed. D. J. Christie, R. V. Wagner, and D. A. Winter (Englewood Cliffs, NJ: Prentice-Hall, 2001), 139–148.
57. M. Centano and E. Enriquez, *War and Society* (Cambridge: Polity Press, 2016), 13; Pinker, *Better Angels*, chap. 8.
58. Centano and Enriquez, *War and Society*, 13.
59. Ehrenreich, *Blood Rites*, 125, 127 (emphasis in original).
60. Winter et al., "Understanding Militarism," quote from 144.
61. J. Bourke, *Dismembering the Male: Men's Bodies, Britain and the Great War* (Chicago: University of Chicago Press, 1996); cited by Pilisuk and Rowntree, *Hidden Structure of Violence*, 65.
62. S. Humphries and P. Gordon, *A Man's World: From Boyhood to Manhood 1900–1960* (London: BBC Books, 1996), chap. 3, see 68, 69, 73–74, 97.
63. Mosse, *Fallen Soldiers*, quotes from 60, 61, 166.
64. D. Duriesmith, *Masculinity and New War: The Gendered Dynamics of Contemporary Armed Conflict* (London: Taylor and Francis, 2016), chap. 3, see 30.
65. Ibid., 29.
66. Pilisuk and Rowntree, *Hidden Structure of Violence*, 76–77.
67. Stevens, *Roots of War*, 47, 79.
68. Winter, *Roots of War*, table 8.1, 308, 312, 325.
69. Pilisuk and Rowntree, *Hidden Structure of Violence*, 74.
70. Gat, *Causes of War*, 180.
71. Cécile Allegra. How male rape is weapon of war in Libya. *The Guardian Weekly* (reprinted from *Le Monde*) November 10, 2017.
72. J. Sidanius and F. Pratto, *Social Dominance: An Intergroup Theory of Social Hierarchy and Oppression* (Cambridge Cambridge University Press, 1999).
73. Cottam et al., *Introduction to Political Psychology*; Gat, *Causes of War*; N. Van der Linden et al., "Social Representational Correlates of Attitudes towards Peace and War: A Cross-Cultural Analysis in the United States and Denmark," *Peace and Conflict: Journal of Peace Psychology* 17 (2011): 217–242.
74. Pinker, *Better Angels*, chap. 8, citing J. Goldstein, *War and Gender: How Gender Shapes the War System and Vice Versa* (Cambridge: Cambridge University Press, 2001).
75. Winter, *Roots of War*, 242–245.
76. Van der Linden et al., "Social Representational Correlates."
77. Pinker, *Better Angels*, chap. 8.
78. C. Gilligan, *In a Different Voice: Psychological Theory and Women's Development* (Cambridge, MA: Harvard University Press, 1982), 16–17; cited by R. van den Toorn, "Just War and the Perspective of Ethics of Care," in *Just War in Comparative Perspective*, ed. P. Robinson (Burlington, VT: Ashgate, 2003), 218–229.
79. A. C. Baier, *Moral Prejudices: Essays on Ethics* (Cambridge, MA: Harvard University Press, 1995); cited by van der Toorn, "Just War."
80. Pinker, *Better Angels*, chap. 8.
81. L. Smith, *Voices against War: A Century of Protest* (Edinburgh: Mainstream, 2010).

82. M. Kaldor, *New and Old Wars: Organized Violence in a Global Era*, 2nd ed. (Cambridge: Polity Press, 2006), 128, 131, 171, 173.
83. Stevens, *Roots of War*, 187.
84. Pinker, *Better Angels*, chaps. 8 and 10, see 636, 637; citing M. Potts and T. Hayden, *Sex and War: How Biology Explains Warfare and Terrorism and Offers a Path to a Safer World* (Dallas, TX: Benbella Books, 2008).
85. LeShan, *Psychology of War*, 90.
86. J. Bourke, *An Intimate History of Killing: Face-to-Face Killing in Twentieth-Century Warfare* (New York: Basic Books, 1999); cited by Centano and Enriquez, *War and Society*, 15.
87. Ehrenreich, *Blood Rites*; R. Lachmann, "Mercenary, Citizen, Victim: The Rise and Fall of Conscription in the West," in *Nationalism and War*, ed. J. A. Hall and S. Malešević (Cambridge: Cambridge University Press, 2013), 54.
88. William Shakespeare, *Coriolanus*, act 3, scene 2.
89. Mosse, *Fallen Soldiers*, 61.
90. Gat, *Causes of War*, 55.
91. Centano and Enriquez, *War and Society*, 16.
92. Ehrenreich, *Blood Rites*, 126, 128.
93. Gat, *Causes of War*, 55.
94. Ehrenreich, *Blood Rites*; A. Basevich, *The New American Militarism: How Americans Are Seduced by War*, updated ed. (New York: Oxford University Press, 2013), 144; Centano and Enriquez, *War and Society*, 166–167.
95. India to allow women in combat roles. *The Guardian Weekly*, March 4, 2016; E. Rhodes, "The Unique Needs of Female Veterans," *The Psychologist*, July 12, 2021, https://www.bps.org.uk/psychologist/unique-needs-female-veterans.
96. Basevich, *New American Militarism*, 144.
97. Centano and Enriquez, *War and Society*, 15.
98. Ehrenreich, *Blood Rites*, 230, 231.
99. E. Porter, "Women, Political Decision-Making, and Peace-Building," *Global Change, Peace & Security* 15, no. 3 (2003): 245–262; cited by C. DiRienzo, "The Effect of Women in Government on Country-Level Peace," *Global Change, Peace and Security* 31 (2019): 1–18.
100. K. Cowell-Meyers, "Gender, Peace, and Power," *Women and Politics* 23, no. 3 (2001): 57–90; cited by DiRienzo, "Effect of Women in Government."
101. E. Melander, "Gender Equality and Intrastate Armed Conflict," *International Studies Quarterly* 49 (2005): 695–714.
102. Gat, *Causes of War*, 184.
103. P. Fussell, *Wartime* (Oxford: Oxford University Press, 1989); cited by LeShan, *Psychology of War*, 90.

Chapter 3

1. R. J. Evans, *Eric Hobsbawm: A Life in History* (London: Little, Brown, 2019), 551.
2. J. S. Mill, cited by A. C. Grayling, *War: An Enquiry* (New Haven, CT: Yale University Press, 2017), 164.

3. M. Centano and E. Enriquez, *War and Society* (Cambridge: Polity Press, 2016), 88.
4. J. Black, *English Nationalism: A Short History* (London: Hurst, 2018), 9.
5. H. C. Kelman, "The Role of National Identity in Conflict Resolution: Experiences from Israeli–Palestinian Problem-Solving Workshops," in *Social Identity, Intergroup Conflict, and Conflict Reduction*, ed. R. Ashmore, L. Jussim, and D. Wilder (New York: Oxford University Press, 2001), chap. 8, 191.
6. J. Citrin, C. Wong, and B. Duff, "The Meaning of American National Identity: Patterns of Ethnic Conflict and Consensus," in *Social Identity, Intergroup Conflict, and Conflict Reduction*, ed. R. Ashmore, L. Jussim, and D. Wilder (New York: Oxford University Press, 2001), chap. 4, 74.
7. J. Hughes, "State Violence in the Origins of Nationalism: British Counterinsurgency and the Rebirth of Irish Nationalism, 1969–1972," in *Nationalism and War*, ed. J. A. Hall and S. Malešević (Cambridge: Cambridge University Press, 2013), 104.
8. M. Billig, *Banal Nationalism* (London: Sage, 1995); M. Mann, "The Role of Nationalism in the Two World Wars," in *Nationalism and War*, ed. J. A. Hall and S. Malešević (Cambridge: Cambridge University Press, 2013), 17–56, 192; C. H. Burgos, "Nationalisation, Banal Nationalism and Everyday Nationhood in a Dictatorship: The Franco Regime in Spain," *Nations and Nationalism* 27 (2021): 690–704.
9. M. L. Cottam, et al., eds. *Introduction to Political Psychology*, 2nd ed. (New York: Psychology Press, 2010), 235, 237.
10. R. K. Herrmann, P. Isernia, and P. Segatti, "Attachment to the Nation and International Relations: Dimensions of Identity and Their Relationship to War and Peace," *Political Psychology* 30 (2009): 721–754.
11. Evans, *Eric Hobsbawm*.
12. S. Feshbach, "Psychology, Human Violence, and the Search for Peace: Issues in Science and Social Values," *Journal of Social Issues* 46 (1990): 133–198; cited by D. Druckman, "Nationalism and War: A Social-Psychological Perspective," in *Peace, Conflict and Violence: Peace Psychology for the 21st Century*, ed. D. J. Christie, R. V. Wagner, and D. A. Winter (Englewood Cliffs, NJ: Prentice Hall/Pearson Education, 2001), chap. 4, 52.
13. For example, A. Bacevich, *The New American Militarism: How Americans Are Seduced by War*, updated ed. (New York: Oxford University Press, 2013).
14. M. Kemmelmeier and D. Winter, "Sowing Patriotism, but Reaping Nationalism? Consequences of Exposure to the American Flag," *Political Psychology* 29 (2008): 859–879.
15. M. Pilisuk and J. A. Rowntree, *The Hidden Structure of Violence: Who Benefits from Global Violence and War* (New York: Monthly Review Press, 2015), 281.
16. Citrin, Wong, and Duff, "Meaning of American National Identity," quote from 81.
17. D. Lieven, "Empire, Ethnicity and Power: A Comment," in *Nationalism and War*, ed. J. A. Hall and S. Malešević (Cambridge: Cambridge University Press, 2013), chap. 8; Citrin, Wong, and Duff, "Meaning of American National Identity," 75.
18. J. Sidanius and J. R. Petrocik, "Communal and National Identity in a Multiethnic State: A Comparison of Three Perspectives," in *Social Identity, Intergroup Conflict, and Conflict Reduction*, ed. R. Ashmore, L. Jussim, and D. Wilder (New York: Oxford University Press, 2001), chap. 5.

19. M. A. Centano et al., "Internal Wars and Latin American Nationalism," in J *Nationalism and War*, ed. J. A. Hall and S. Malešević (Cambridge: Cambridge University Press, 2013), 280–281.
20. Pilisuk and Rowntree, *Hidden Structure of Violence*, 298.
21. Herrmann, Isernia, and Segatti, "Attachment to the Nation."
22. Ibid.
23. Ibid.
24. R. Collins, "Does Nationalist Sentiment Increase Fighting Efficacy? A Skeptical View from the Sociology of Violence," in *Nationalism and War*, ed. J. A. Hall and S. Malešević (Cambridge: Cambridge University Press, 2013), 36.
25. C. Bauer and B. Hannover, "Changing 'Us' and Hostility towards 'Them'—Implicit Theories of National Identity Determine Prejudice and Participation Rates in an Anti-Immigrant Petition," *European Journal of Social Psychology* 50 (2020): 810–826.
26. K. Lowe, *The Fear and the Freedom: How the Second World War Changed Us* (London: Penguin, 2018), 182–187.
27. A. Bayram, "Nationalist Cosmopolitanism: The Psychology of Cosmopolitanism, National Identity, and Going to War for the Country," *Nations and Nationalism* 25 (2019): 757–781.
28. D. Goodhart, *The Road to Somewhere: The New Tribes Shaping British Politics* (London: Penguin, 2017).
29. M. Kaldor, *New and Old Wars: Organized Violence in a Global Era*, 2nd ed. (Cambridge: Polity Press, 2006), 7, 73; G. Brock and Q. Atkinson, "What Can Examining the Psychology of Nationalism Tell Us about Our Prospects for Aiming at the Cosmopolitan Vision?" *Ethical Theory and Moral Practice* 11, no. 2 (2008): 165–179.
30. J. H. Liu et al., "Empirical Correlates of Cosmopolitan Orientation: Etiology and Functions in a Worldwide Representative Sample," *Political Psychology* 41 (2020): 661–678, citing M. Nussbaum, "Kant and Stoic Cosmopolitanism," *Journal of Political Philosophy* 5 (1997): 1–25.
31. W. G. Sumner, *Folkways: A Study of Mores, Manners, Customs and Morals* (1906; repr., New York: Cosimo, 2007); cited by Brock and Atkinson, "What Can Examining."
32. Brock and Atkinson, "What Can Examining."
33. Ibid.
34. Liu et al., "Empirical Correlates"; Kaldor, *New and Old Wars*, 92; citing K. A. Appiah, "Cosmopolitan Patriots," *Critical Inquiry* (Spring 1997): 619; A. Tryandafyllidou, "Nationalism in the 21st Century: Neo-tribal or Plural?," *Nations and Nationalism* 26 (2021): 792–806, citing T. Modood, "A Multicultural Nationalism?" *Brown Journal of World Affairs*, 25, no. 2 (2019): 233–246.
35. Bayram, "Nationalist Cosmopolitanism"; R. Ashmore et al., "Conclusion: Toward a Social Identity Framework for Intergroup Conflict," in *Social Identity, Intergroup Conflict, and Conflict Reduction*, ed. R. Ashmore, L. Jussim, and D. Wilder (New York: Oxford University Press, 2001), chap. 9.
36. Bayrum, "Nationalist Cosmopolitanism."
37. Ibid.

NOTES 255

38. For example, M. Sherif et al., *Intergroup Conflict and Cooperation: The Robber's Cave Experiment* (Norman, OK: University Book Exchange, 1961).
39. Brock and Atkinson, "What Can Examining" (emphasis in original).
40. I. Morris, *War: What Is It Good For? The Role of Conflict in Civilisation, from Primates to Robots* (London: Profile Books, 2015), 10–12, 114; J. A. Hall and S. Malešević, "Introduction: Wars and Nationalisms," in *Nationalism and War*, ed. J. A. Hall and S. Malešević (Cambridge: Cambridge University Press, 2013), 8.
41. Cottam et al., *Introduction to Political Psychology*, 235, 237, 238; A. Gat, *The Causes of War and the Spread of Peace: But Will War Rebound?* (Oxford: Oxford University Press, 2017), 82–84.
42. J. S. Levy and W. R. Thompson, *Causes of War* (Chichester, UK: Wiley-Blackwell, 2010), 83.
43. Hall and Malešević, "Introduction"; Collins, "Does Nationalist Sentiment Increase"; Mann, "Role of Nationalism"; S. Malešević, "Obliterating Heterogeneity through Peace: Nationalisms, States and Wars, in the Balkans," in *Nationalism and War*, ed. J. A. Hall and S. Malešević (Cambridge: Cambridge University Press, 2013), intro., chaps. 1, 7, 10.
44. Morris, *War*, 25.
45. Centano and Enriquez, *War and Society*, 52, 88.
46. Druckman, "Nationalism and War," quote from 61.
47. Malešević, "Obliterating Heterogeneity," 262.
48. Mann, "Role of Nationalism," 172–176, 193–194.
49. N. Ferguson, *The Pity of War* (London: Penguin Books, 1999), 201–202.
50. M. Hollis, *Now All Roads Lead to France: The Last Years of Edward Thomas* (London: Faber and Faber, 2011), 161, 164–165, 174, 257–258.
51. E. Thomas, "This Is No Case of Petty Right or Wrong," Poetry Foundation, www.poetryfoundation.org/poems/57205/this-is-no-case-of-petty-right-or-wrong.
52. Lowe, *Fear and the Freedom*, 393.
53. Centano and Enriquez, *War and Society*, 124, 131, citing B. Strauss, "The Dead of Arginusae and the Debate about the Athenian Navy," *Nautiki Epithewrisi [Naval Review]* 545 (2004): 40–67.
54. S. P. Huntington, *Who Are We? The Challenge to America's National Identity* (New York: Simon and Schuster, 2004); cited by Herrmann, Isernia, and Segatti, "Attachment to the Nation."
55. M. Walzer, "The New Tribalism: Notes on a Difficult Problem," in *Theorizing Nationalism*, ed. R. Beiner (Albany: State University of New York Press, 1999), 205–217; cited by Herrmann, Isernia, and Segatti, "Attachment to the Nation."
56. BBC Radio 4, *The Moral Maze: D-Day 75th Anniversary* www.bbc.co.uk/programmes/b006qk11/episodes, June 5, 2019.
57. Kaldor, *New and Old Wars*, 29, 79, citing R. Reich, *The Work of Nations: Preparing Ourselves for 21st Century Capitalism* (London: Simon & Schuster, 1993).
58. Ibid., 41.
59. Pilisuk and Rowntree, *Hidden Structure of Violence*, 67 (emphasis in original).
60. Lowe, *Fear and the Freedom* 266, 347.

61. W. Hiers and A. Wimmer, "Is Nationalism the Cause or Consequence of the End of Empire?," in *Nationalism and War*, ed. J. A. Hall and S. Malešević (Cambridge: Cambridge University Press, 2013), 249–250.
62. Lowe, *Fear and the Freedom*, 297, 300.
63. B. F. Walter, *How Civil Wars Start: And How to Stop Them* (London: Penguin Random House, 2022), chap. 2.
64. H. Thomas, *The Spanish Civil War* (London: Readers' Union, 1962).
65. Lowe, *Fear and the Freedom*, 315–316, 322.
66. R. Lemarchand, "War and Nationalism: The View from Central Africa," in *Nationalism and War*, ed. J. A. Hall and S. Malešević (Cambridge: Cambridge University Press, 2013), 306–315.
67. Kaldor, *New and Old Wars*, 37, 44, 59, 104.
68. Pilisuk and Rowntree, *Hidden Structure of Violence*, 175.
69. Kaldor, *New and Old Wars*, 11, 80, 81.
70. Ibid.; Mann, "Role of Nationalism," 174; A. Stevens, *The Roots of War and Terror* (London: Continuum, 2004), 115.
71. BBC Radio 4, "The Mental Health Frontline," *Terrorism and the Mind*, March 31, 2022.
72. M. van Creveld, *The Transformation of War* (New York: Free Press, 1991); cited by Kaldor, *New and Old Wars*, 28.
73. A. W. Kruglanski et al., "The Psychology of Radicalization and Deradicalization: How Significance Quest Impacts Violent Extremism," *Political Psychology* 35 (2014): 69–93.
74. A. Kruglanski, J. J. Bélanger, and R. Gunaratna, *The Three Pillars of Radicalization: Needs, Narratives, and Networks* (New York: Oxford University Press, 2019), 48–49.
75. M. Lange, "When Does Nationalism Turn Violent? A Comparative Analysis," in *Nationalism and War*, ed. J. A. Hall and S. Malešević (Cambridge: Cambridge University Press, 2013), chap. 5.
76. Levy and Thompson, *Causes of War*, 21.
77. Hughes, "State Violence," 98, 101–102, 115.
78. Thomas, *Spanish Civil War*.
79. K. Ghattas, *Black Wave: Saudi Arabia, Iran and the Rivalry That Unravelled the Middle East* (London: Wildfire, 2020), 148, 157–161, 229, 236, 260, 271–273.
80. K. Puri, *Partition Voices: Untold British Stories* (London: Bloomsbury, 2019).

Chapter 4

1. K. Lowe, *The Fear and the Freedom: How the Second World War Changed Us* (London: Penguin, 2018), 36.
2. L. LeShan, *The Psychology of War: Comprehending Its Mystique and Its Madness* (New York: Helios Press, 2002), 35–36 (emphasis in original).
3. J. B. Sykes, ed., *The Concise Oxford Dictionary*, 6th ed. (Oxford: Oxford University Press, 1976).

4. J. S. Levy and W. R. Thompson, *Causes of War* (Chichester, UK: Wiley-Blackwell, 2010), 212.
5. M. Pilisuk and J. A. Rowntree, *The Hidden Structure of Violence: Who Benefits from Global Violence and War* (New York: Monthly Review Press, 2015), 217.
6. M. Centano and E. Enriquez, *War and Society* (Cambridge: Polity Press, 2016), 114.
7. M. L. Cottam et al., eds., *Introduction to Political Psychology*, 2nd ed. (New York: Psychology Press, 2010), 57.
8. M. Mann, "The Role of Nationalism in the Two World Wars," in *Nationalism and War*, ed. J. A. Hall and S. Malešević (Cambridge: Cambridge University Press, 2013), 177, 179, 185–186; P. M. Taylor, *Munitions of the Mind: A History of Propaganda from the Ancient World to the Present Day*, 3rd ed. (Manchester: Manchester University Press, 2003), chap. 21.
9. S. Pinker, *The Better Angels of Our Nature: A History of Violence and Humanity* (London: Penguin Books, 2012), chap. 6.
10. Levy and Thompson, *Causes of War*, 139–140.
11. W. R. Caspary, "New Psychoanalytic Perspectives on the Causes of War," *Political Psychology* 14 (1993): 417–446.
12. A. Stevens, *The Roots of War and Terror* (London: Continuum, 2004), 45, 42–46, 61.
13. D. P. Barash and C. P. Webel, *Peace and Conflict Studies*, 2nd ed. (Los Angeles: Sage, 2009), 128, 138; Pilisuk and Rowntree, *Hidden Structure of Violence*, 62; I. Eibl-Eibesfeldt, *The Biology of War and Peace* (New York: Viking, 1979); cited by Stevens, *Roots of War*, 4, 113, 197.
14. I. Morris, *War: What Is It Good For? The Role of Conflict in Civilisation, from Primates to Robots* (London: Profile Books, 2015), 267.
15. Lowe, *Fear and the Freedom*, 38.
16. J. Dower, "Apes and Others," in *Making War Making Peace: The Social Foundations of Violent Conflict*, ed. F. M. Cancion and J. W. Gibson (Belmont, CA: Wadsworth, 1990), 100–110, quote from 104.
17. Ibid., quote from 106.
18. Pinker, *Better Angels*, chap. 6.
19. B. F. Walter, *How Civil Wars Start: And How to Stop Them* (London: Penguin Random House, 2022), 45.
20. Pinker, *Better Angels*, chap. 6.
21. C. J. Montiel, E. de la Paz, and Z. I. Cerafica, "(De)Humanization and Trust in an Asymmetric Muslim–Christian Conflict: Heroes, Kafirs, and Satanas," *Peace and Conflict: Journal of Peace Psychology* 25 (2019): 300–311.
22. Stevens, *Roots of War*, 200, 202.
23. M. Altier and J. Kane, "Framing States: Unitary Actor Language and Public Support for Coercive Foreign Policy," *International Studies Quarterly* 67 (2023): sqac080.
24. Ibid., 143; Cottam et al., *Introduction to Political Psychology*, 297.
25. Levy and Thompson, *Causes of War*, 144.
26. Taylor, *Munitions of the Mind*, 11.
27. Centano and Enriquez, *War and Society*, 53.
28. Cottam et al., *Introduction to Political Psychology*, 157; Lowe, *Fear and the Freedom*.

29. Pinker, *Better Angels*, chap. 9.
30. A. Kruglanski, J. J. Bélanger, and R. Gunaratna, *The Three Pillars of Radicalization: Needs, Narratives, and Networks* (New York: Oxford University Press, 2019), 47.
31. S. Baele, "Conspiratorial Narratives in Violent Political Actors' Language," *Journal of Language and Social Psychology* 38 (2019): 706–734.
32. Montiel, de la Paz, and Cerafica, "(De)Humanization and Trust"; N. Bassil, "A Critique of Western Representations of ISIS: Deconstructing Contemporary Orientalism," *Global Change, Peace and Security* 31 (2019): 81–94.
33. Stevens, *Roots of War*, 219.
34. Ibid., 221.
35. LeShan, *Psychology of War*, 35.
36. Ibid., 41, 114–115 (emphasis in original).
37. Ibid., 65, 72.
38. Stevens, *Roots of War*, 224.
39. Pilisuk and Rowntree, *Hidden Structure of Violence*, 62–63.
40. H. Tajfel and J. C. Turner, "An Integrative Theory of Intergroup Conflict," in *The Social Psychology of Intergroup Relations*, ed. W. G. Austin and S. Worchel (Monterey, CA: Brooks/Cole, 1979), 33–48; Cottam et al., *Introduction to Political Psychology*, 46.
41. BBC Radio 4, "The Science of Evil," *Archive on 4*, January 25, 2020.
42. M. Sherif et al., *Intergroup Conflict and Cooperation: The Robber's Cave Experiment* (Norman, OK: University Book Exchange, 1961); G. Brock and Q. Atkinson, "What Can Examining the Psychology of Nationalism Tell Us about Our Prospects for Aiming at the Cosmopolitan Vision?," *Ethical Theory and Moral Practice* 11, no. 2 (2008): 165–179; P. T. Coleman, M. Deutsch, and E. C. Marcus, eds., *Handbook of Conflict Resolution: Theory and Practice*, 3rd ed. (San Francisco: Jossey-Bass, 2014).
43. Pinker, *Better Angels*, chap. 8.
44. Brock and Atkinson, "What Can Examining."
45. Tajfel and Turner, "An Integrative Theory"; Cottam et al., *Introduction to Political Psychology*.
46. Brock and Atkinson, "What Can Examining"; Cottam et al., *Introduction to Political Psychology*.
47. M. Rubin and M. Hewstone, "Social Identity Theory's Self-Esteem Hypothesis: A Review and Some Suggestions for Clarification," *Personality and Social Psychology Review* 2 (1998): 40–62.
48. Levy and Thompson, *Causes of War*, 100–101; Stevens, *Roots of War*, 42, 72.
49. A. Koestler, *Janus: A Summing Up* (London: Pan Books, 1979), 14, 78–83, 93, quote from 14; cited by LeShan, *Psychology of War*, 7.
50. M. Główczewski et al., "National Narcissism and Group-Enhancing Historical Narratives," *Social Psychology* 53 (2022): 357–387.
51. Brock and Atkinson, "What Can Examining."
52. A. Awale, "The Influence of Perceived Warmth and Competence on Realistic Threat and Willingness for Intergroup Contact," *European Journal of Social Psychology* 49 (2019): 857–870; K. Rios, "An Experimental Approach to Intergroup Threat Theory: Manipulations, Moderators, and Consequences of Realistic vs. Symbolic

Threat," *European Review of Social Psychology* 29 (2018): 212–255; B. Leidner, L. R. Tropp, and B. Lickel, "Bringing Science to Bear—On Peace not War: Elaborating on Psychology's Potential to Promote Peace," *American Psychologist* 68 (2013): 514–526.
53. Coleman, Deutsch, and Marcus, *Handbook of Conflict Resolution*.
54. Leidner, Tropp, and Lickel, "Bringing Science to Bear."
55. Ibid.
56. Ö. M. Uluğ and J. C. Cohrs, "Examining the Ethos of Conflict by Explaining Lay People's Representations of the Kurdish Conflict in Turkey," *Conflict Management and Peace Science* 36 (2019): 169–190, citing S. Reicher, "The Context of Social Identity: Domination, Resistance, and Change," *Political Psychology* 25 (2004): 921–945.
57. U. Bronfenbrenner, "The Mirror Image in Soviet–American Relations: A Social Psychologist's Report," *Journal of Social Issues* 16 (1961): 45–56.
58. Baele, "Conspiratorial Narratives."
59. For example, Cottam et al., *Introduction to Political Psychology*.
60. S. McKeown and C. Psaltis, "Intergroup Contact and the Mediating Role of Intergroup Trust on Outgroup Evaluation and Future Contact Intentions in Cyprus and Northern Ireland," *Peace and Conflict: Journal of Peace Psychology* 23 (2017): 392–404.
61. G. W. Allport, *The Nature of Prejudice* (Reading, MA: Addison-Wesley, 1954); cited by A. Mana, "Knowledge about the 'Others', Perspective Taking, and Anxiety about Intergroup Contact in a Natural Intergroup Setting," *Peace and Conflict: Journal of Peace Psychology* 25 (2019): 276–286.
62. M. Hewstone et al., "Intergroup Contact, Forgiveness, and Experience of 'The Troubles' in Northern Ireland," *Journal of Social Issues* 62 (2006): 99–120; L. R. Tropp et al., "Intergroup Contact and the Potential for Post-Conflict Reconciliation: Studies in Northern Ireland and South Africa," *Peace and Conflict: Journal of Peace Psychology* 23 (2017): 239–249; both cited by S. C. Bagci and A. Turnuklu, "Intended, Unintended, and Unknown Consequences of Contact: The Role of Positive–Negative Contact on Outgroup Attitudes, Collective Action Tendencies, and Psychological Well-Being," *Social Psychology* 50 (2019): 7–23.
63. T. F. Pettigrew and J. R. Tropp, "A Meta-Analytic Test of Intergroup Contact Theory," *Journal of Personality and Social Psychology* 90 (2006): 751–783; cited by Awale, "Influence of Perceived Warmth."
64. Awale, "Influence of Perceived Warmth."
65. Mana, "Knowledge about the 'Others.'"
66. M. Sternberg, H. T. Litvak, and S. Sagy, "'Nobody Ever Told Us': The Contribution of Intragroup Dialogue to Reflective Learning about Violent Conflict," *Peace and Conflict: Journal of Peace Psychology* 24 (2018): 127–138.
67. K. Puri, *Partition Voices: Untold British Stories* (London: Bloomsbury, 2019).
68. J. Dixon et al., "Parallel Lives: Intergroup Contact, Threat and the Segregation of Everyday Activity Spaces," *Journal of Personality and Social Psychology* 118 (2020): 457–480.
69. Cottam et al., *Introduction to Political Psychology*; Allport, *Nature of Prejudice*; cited by Mana, "Knowledge about the 'Others.'"

70. E. Zigenlaub and S. Sagy, "Encountering the Narrative of the 'Other': Comparing Two Types of Dialogue Groups of Jews and Arabs in Israel," *Peace and Conflict: Journal of Peace Psychology* 26 (2020): 88–91.
71. F. A. White, "Improving Intergroup Relations between Catholics and Protestants in Northern Ireland via E-Contact," *European Journal of Social Psychology* 49 (2019): 429–438.
72. R. Wölfer et al., "Indirect Contact Predicts Direct Contact: Longitudinal Evidence and the Mediating Role of Intergroup Anxiety," *Journal of Personality and Social Psychology* 116, no. 2 (2019): 277–295.
73. T. F. Pettigrew and L. R. Tropp, "How Does Intergroup Contact Reduce Prejudice? Meta-Analytic Test of Three Mediators," *European Journal of Social Psychology* 38 (2008): 922–934; cited by Mana, "Knowledge about the 'Others.'"
74. W. E. Lambert and O. Klineberg, *Children's Views of Foreign Peoples: A Cross-National Study* (New York: Appleton-Century-Crofts, 1967).
75. D. Druckman, "Nationalism and War: A Social-Psychological Perspective," in *Peace, Conflict and Violence: Peace Psychology for the 21st Century*, ed. D. J. Christie, R. V. Wagner, and D. A. Winter (Englewood Cliffs, NJ: Prentice-Hall, 2001), 46–65.
76. Leidner, Tropp, and Lickel, "Bringing Science to Bear."
77. Levy and Thompson, *Causes of War*, 100–101.
78. Sternberg, Litvak, and Sagy, "'Nobody Ever Told Us.'"
79. T. F. Pettigrew and M. Hewstone, "The Single Factor Fallacy: Implications of Missing Critical Variables from an Analysis of Intergroup Contact Theory," *Social Issues and Policy Review* 11 (2017): 8–37; L. R. Tropp, A. Mazziotta, and S. C. Wright, "Recent Developments in Intergroup Contact Research: Affective Processes, Group Status, and Contact Valence," in *Cambridge Handbook of the Psychology of Prejudice*, ed. F. Barlow and C. Sibley (Cambridge: Cambridge University Press, 2016), 463–480; both cited by Bagci and Turnuklu, "Intended, Unintended, and Unknown Consequences"; Z. Erasmus, "Contact Theory: Too Timid for 'Race' and Racism," *Journal of Social Issues* 66 (2010): 387–400; cited by Z. Gross and R. Maor, "Is Contact Theory Still Valid in Acute Asymmetrical Violent Conflict: A Case Study of Israeli Jewish and Arab Students in Higher Education," *Peace and Conflict: Journal of Peace Psychology* (2020). https://doi.org/10.1037/pac0000440.
80. For example, L. R. Tropp and T. F. Pettigrew, "Relationships between Intergroup Contact and Prejudice among Minority and Majority Status Groups," *Psychological Science* 16 (2005): 951–957; cited by Bagci and Turnuklu, "Intended, Unintended, and Unknown Consequences."
81. Bagci and Turnuklu, "Intended, Unintended, and Unknown Consequences."
82. Cottam et al., *Introduction to Political Psychology*.
83. For example, J. Dixon, K. Durrheim, and C. Tredoux, "Beyond the Optimal Contact Strategy: A Reality Check for the Contact Hypothesis," *American Psychologist* 60 (2005): 697–711; cited by Bagci and Turnuklu, "Intended, Unintended, and Unknown Consequences"; N. Reimer and N. Sengupta, "Meta-Analysis of the 'Ironic' Effects of Intergroup Contact," *Journal of Personality and Social Psychology* 124 (2023): 362–380.
84. Bagci and Turnuklu, "Intended, Unintended, and Unknown Consequences."

85. T. F. Pettigrew, "Secondary Transfer Effect of Contact: Do Intergroup Contact Effects Spread to Noncontacted Outgroups?," *Social Psychology* 40 (2009): 55–65; cited by Bagci and Turnuklu, "Intended, Unintended, and Unknown Consequences."
86. T. F. Pettigrew, "Intergroup Contact Theory," *Annual Review of Psychology* 49 (1998): 65–85; cited by Bagci and Turnuklu, "Intended, Unintended, and Unknown Consequences"; Gross and Maor, "Is Contact Theory Still Valid."
87. Levy and Thompson, *Causes of War*, 211.
88. J. Orford, "The Rules of Interpersonal Complementarity: Does Hostility Beget Hostility and Dominance, Submission?," *Psychological Review* 93 (1986): 365–377.
89. M. Deutsch, "The Prevention of World War III: A Psychological Perspective," *Political Psychology* 4 (1983): 3–31; cited by J. Thompson, *Psychological Aspects of Nuclear War* (London: The British Psychological Society/John Wiley, 1985); see also Cottam et al., *Introduction to Political Psychology*, 304–305.
90. R. K. White, ed., *Psychology and the Prevention of Nuclear War* (New York: New York University Press, 1986), 131–154; M. Deutsch, "Cooperation, Competition, and Conflict," in Coleman, Deutsch, and Marcus, *Handbook of Conflict Resolution*, chap. 1.
91. Coleman, Deutsch, and Marcus, *Handbook of Conflict Resolution*, chap. 8.
92. R. Vallacher et al., "Rethinking Intractable Conflict: The Perspective of Dynamical Systems," in *Conflict, Interdependence, and Justice: The Intellectual Legacy of Morton Deutsch*, ed. P. Coleman (New York: Springer, 2011), chap. 4.
93. Coleman, Deutsch, and Marcus, *Handbook of Conflict Resolution*; J. Orford, "The Interpersonal Circumplex: A Theory and Method for Applied Psychology," *Human Relations* 46 (1994): 1347–1375.
94. Levy and Thompson, *Causes of War*, 61.
95. F. Keane, *Wounds: A Memoir of War and Love* (London: William Collins, 2017), 94, quote from 231.

Chapter 5

1. A. C. Grayling, *War: An Enquiry* (New Haven, CT: Yale University Press, 2017), 231–232.
2. M. Mann, "The Roots and Contradictions of Modern Militarism," *New Left Review* 162 (1987): 35–50; cited by J. Lindsay-Poland, "The Normalization of Militarism and Propensity for War," in *Preventing War and Promoting Peace: A Guide for Health Professionals*, ed. W. H. Wiist and S. K. White (New York: Cambridge University Press, 2017), 78.
3. P. Kraska, "Militarization and Policing—Its Relevance to 21st Century Police," *Policing* 1 (2007): 501–513; cited by Lindsay-Poland, "Normalization of Militarism," 79.
4. Lindsay-Poland, "Normalization of Militarism," 79.
5. Kraska, "Militarization and Policing"; K. Grundy, *Soldiers without Politics: Blacks in the S.A. Armed Forces* (Berkeley: University of California Press, 1983); both cited by Lindsay-Poland, "Normalization of Militarism," 79.

6. F. Özdemir and N. S. Uğurlu, "Development of Militaristic Attitudes Scale and Its Associations with Turkish Identity and Uninational Ideology," *Peace and Conflict: Journal of Peace Psychology* 24 (2018): 175–187.
7. S. L. Bliss, E. J. Oh, and R. L. Williams, "Militarism and Sociopolitical Perspectives among College Students in the U.S. and South Korea," *Journal of Peace and Conflict: Journal of Peace Psychology* 13 (2007): 175–199; cited by Özdemir and Uğurlu, "Development of Militaristic Attitudes Scale."
8. B. Solomon, "Kant's Perpetual Peace: A New Look at This Centuries-Old Quest," *The Online Journal of Peace and Conflict Resolution* 5 (2015): 106–126, quote from 116.
9. Ibid., quote from 109–110.
10. Grayling, *War*, 231–232.
11. W. James, "The Moral Equivalent of War," *Peace and Conflict: Journal of Peace Psychology* 1 (1910; repr., 1995): 17–26; cited by D. D. N. Winter et al., "Understanding Militarism: Money, Masculinity, and the Search for the Mystical," in *Peace, Conflict and Violence: Peace Psychology for the 21st Century*, ed. D. J. Christie, R. V. Wagner, and D. A. Winter (Englewood Cliffs, NJ: Prentice-Hall, 2001), 140.
12. M. Pilisuk and J. A. Rowntree, *The Hidden Structure of Violence: Who Benefits from Global Violence and War* (New York: Monthly Review Press, 2015), 54, 67.
13. G. Mosse, *Fallen Soldiers: Reshaping the Memory of the World Wars* (New York: Oxford University Press, 1990), 141–143, citing M. Cadogan and P. Craig, *Women and Children First. The Fiction of Two World Wars* (London: Gollancz, 1978), 95.
14. J. Bourke, *Wounding the World: How Military Violence and War-Play Invade Our Lives* (London: Virago Press, 2014), 196, 199.
15. Ibid., 169, 202.
16. Ibid., 203.
17. American Civil Liberties Union, *Soldiers of Misfortune. Abusive US Military Recruitment and Failure to Protect Child Soldiers* (New York: ACLU, 2008); cited by Bourke, *Wounding the World*.
18. Bourke, *Wounding the World*, 214, 215.
19. *Washington Post*, February 14, 2006; cited in Ibid., 215.
20. M. J. Martin and C. W. Sasser, *Predator: The Remote-Control Air War over Iraq and Afghanistan: A Pilot's Perspective* (Minneapolis: Zenith Press, 2010), 30; cited by Bourke, *Wounding the World*, 216.
21. Bourke, *Wounding the World*, 215–216.
22. Ibid.
23. A. Bacevich, *The New American Militarism: How Americans Are Seduced by War*, updated ed. (New York: Oxford University Press, 2013), 111–117.
24. J. Der Derian, *Virtuous War: Mapping the Military–Industrial–Media–Entertainment Network* (Boulder: Westview Press, 2001); cited by Bourke, *Wounding the World*, 216–217.
25. W. D. Ehrhart, "Why I Did It," *VQR* (Winter 1980). https://www.vqronline.org/essay/why-i-did-it; cited by Bourke, *Wounding the World*, 155.
26. Grayling, *War*, 232.
27. A. Stevens, *The Roots of War and Terror* (London: Continuum, 2004), 197, 193.

28. Ibid., 195.
29. M. Pemberton, "The War Profiteers: Defense Contractors Driving the Permanent War Economy," in Wiist and White, *Preventing War*, 123.
30. Bourke, *Wounding the World*, 176.
31. ForcesWatch, https://www.forceswatch.net/resources/the-new-tide-of-militarisation (e.g., *The New Tide of Militarisation*, report updated 2018).
32. Campaign Against the Arms Trade *(CAAT)* What UK Universities Need: Funding Not Arms Dealers, February 6, 2018. https://caatunis.net/what-uk-unis-need
33. A. Feinstein, *The Shadow World: Inside the Global Arms Trade* (London: Hamish Hamilton, 2011).
34. ForcesWatch. https://www.forceswatch.net/resources/the-new-tide-of-militarisation
35. N. F. Dixon, *On the Psychology of Military Incompetence* (London: Futura, 1979); cited by Stevens, *Roots of War*, 109.
36. Stevens, *Roots of War*, 101, 109.
37. B. Griffin, speaking in the symposium "War, Conflict and Militarisation as Global Health Issues," as part of the conference *Health through Peace*, organized by Medact, Friends' House, London, November 13–14, 2015.
38. J. Von Zimmermann and D. Richardson, "Synchrony and the Art of Signalling," *The Psychologist* (June 2018): 32–36.
39. Lindsay-Poland, "Normalization of Militarism," 81.
40. K. Barker, "The Quiet Military Buyout of Academia," in Wiist and White, *Preventing War*, 141–152.
41. ForcesWatch. https://www.forceswatch.net/resources/the-new-tide-of-militarisation
42. Pilisuk and Rowntree, *Hidden Structure of Violence*, 69–70.
43. Medact, *The Recruitment of Children by the UK Armed Forces: A Critique from Health Professionals* (London: Medact, 2016).
44. Barker, "Quiet Military Buyout," 141–142, 146–147.
45. D. Hoffman, et al., *Independent Report Relating to APA Ethics Guidelines, National Security, Interrogations, and Torture* (Washington, DC: American Psychological Association, 2015); cited by M. Noor, "Can Psychology Find a Path to Peace?" *The Psychologist* (February 2015).
46. Barker, "Quiet Military Buyout," 148–149.
47. J. H. Liu, & C. Sibley, "Culture, social representations, and peacemaking: A symbolic theory of history and identity," in *Peace psychology in Asia*, eds. C. J. Montiel and N. M. Noor (New York, NY: Springer-Verlag, 2009), 21–39; cited by N. Van den Linden et al., "Social Representational Correlates of Attitudes towards Peace and War: A Cross-Cultural Analysis in the United States and Denmark," *Peace and Conflict: Journal of Peace Psychology* 17 (2011): 217–242; A. Vagts, *A History of Militarism* (New York: Free Press, 1959); cited by R. Holmes, *Acts of War: The Behaviour of Men in Battle* (1985; repr., London: Cassell, 2004), 6.
48. P. M. Taylor, *Munitions of the Mind: A History of Propaganda from the Ancient World to the Present Day* (Manchester: Manchester University Press, 2003), 22, 38–39, 46.
49. Ibid.
50. Mosse, *Fallen Soldiers*, 6–7.

51. Ibid., 46, 59.
52. R. Lachmann, "Mercenary, Citizen, Victim: The Rise and Fall of Conscription in the West," in *Nationalism and War*, ed. J. A. Hall and S. Malešević (Cambridge: Cambridge University Press, 2013), 51–53.
53. B. Steele, "Welcome Home! Routines, Ontological Insecurity and the Politics of US Military Reunion Videos," *Cambridge Review of International Affairs* 32 (2019): 322–343.
54. L. Silvestri, "Surprise Homecomings and Vicarious Sacrifices," *Media, War & Conflict* 6 (2013): 101–115.
55. M. Macmillan, "War and Humanity," the BBC Reith Lectures, broadcast on BBC Radio 4, June–July 2018, lecture 5 "War's Fatal Attraction."
56. H. Watkins and B. Bastion, "Lest We Forget: The Effect of War Commemorations on Regret, Positive Moral Emotions, and Support for War," *Social Psychology and Personality Science* 10 (2019): 1084–1091.
57. Pilisuk and Rowntree, *Hidden Structure of Violence*, 21.
58. S. Pinker, *The Better Angels of Our Nature: A History of Violence and Humanity* (London: Penguin Books, 2012), chap. 10, 813, 814.
59. R. Collins, "Does Nationalist Sentiment Increase Fighting Efficiency? A Skeptical View from the Sociology of Violence," in *Nationalism and War*, ed. J. A. Hall and S. Malešević (Cambridge: Cambridge University Press, 2013), 38–39.
60. Bourke, *Wounding the World*, 152.
61. M. Herrera and S. Reicher, "Making Sides and Taking Sides: An Analysis of Salient Images and Category Constructions of Pro- and Anti-Gulf War Respondents," *European Journal of Social Psychology* 28 (1998): 981–993; cited by Van den Linden et al., "Social Representational Correlates."
62. Lord Thomson, "Aerial Warfare and Disarmament," *Survey* 53 (1925): 503–506; Martin and Sasser, *Predator*; both cited by Bourke, *Wounding the World*, 25, 38.
63. Pilisuk and Rowntree, *Hidden Structure of Violence*, 66.
64. Bourke, *Wounding the World*, 17, 22, citing E. Prokosch, *The Technology of Killing: A Military and Political History of Antipersonnel Weapons* (London: Zed Books, 1995).
65. Grayling, *War*, 72.
66. Collins, "Does Nationalist Sentiment Increase Fighting Efficiency?," 37.
67. Stevens, *Roots of War*, 63.
68. Grayling, *War*.
69. Collins, "Does Nationalist Sentiment Increase Fighting Efficiency?," 38.
70. Ibid., 41.
71. Bacevich, *New American Militarism*, 20–21, 23.
72. Grayling, *War*, 220–221.
73. G. Chamayou, *Drone Theory*, trans. J. Lloyd (London: Penguin, 2015).
74. Pilisuk and Rowntree, *Hidden Structure of Violence*, 213.
75. Chamayou, *Drone Theory*, 68.
76. Winter et al., "Understanding Militarism," 139–148.
77. Pilisuk and Rowntree, *Hidden Structure of Violence*, 53.
78. M. Kaldor, *New and Old Wars: Organized Violence in a Global Era*, 2nd ed. (Cambridge: Polity Press, 2006), 102, 115, 146.

79. J. S. Levy and W. R. Thompson, *Causes of War* (Chichester, UK: Wiley-Blackwell, 2010), 72, 88–89.
80. Lachmann, "Mercenary, Citizen, Victim," 64.
81. Campaign Against the Arms Trade *(CAAT)* What UK Universities Need: Funding Not Arms Dealers, February 6, 2018. https://caatunis.net/what-uk-unis-need
82. Pemberton, "War Profiteers," 118.
83. Ibid., 117.
84. Pilisuk and Rowntree, *Hidden Structure of Violence*, 21, 93, 185–186, 213.
85. Feinstein, *Shadow World*, 304.
86. Ibid., xxvi.
87. Pilisuk and Rowntree, *Hidden Structure of Violence*, 26–28, 142–144, 145, 212, 230.
88. J. Reifler, T. J. Scotto, and H. D. Clarke, "Foreign Policy Beliefs in Contemporary Britain: Structure and Relevance," *International Studies Quarterly* 55 (2011): 245–266.
89. J. Jost, M. Banaji, and B. Nosek, "A Decade of System Justification Theory: Accumulated Evidence of Conscious and Unconscious Bolstering of the Status Quo," *Political Psychology* 25 (2004): 881–919.
90. A. Kay et al., "Inequality, Discrimination, and the Power of the Status Quo: Direct Evidence for a Motivation to See the Way Things Are as the Way They Should Be," *Journal of Personality and Social Psychology* 97 (2009): 421–434
91. A. Kay, J. Banfield, and K. Laurin, "The System Justification Motive and the Maintenance of Social Power," in *The Social Psychology of Power*, ed. A. Guinote and T. Vescio (New York: Guilford Press, 2010), 313–340.
92. J. C. Blanchar and S. Eidelman, "Everything in Its Right Place: Tradition, Order, and the Legitimation of Long-Standing Inequality," in *The Social Psychology of Inequality*, ed. J. Jetten and K. Peters (Cham, Switzerland: Springer, 2019), 349–364.
93. A. Kay and M. Zanna, "A Contextual Analysis of the System Justification Motive and Its Societal Consequences," in *Social and Psychological Bases of Ideology and System Justification*, ed. J. Jost, A. Kay, and H. Thorisdottir (New York: Oxford University Press, 2009), 158–181.
94. Van den Linden et al., "Social Representational Correlates."
95. Bacevich, *New American Militarism*, 1–2.
96. Ibid., 1–5, 10–14, 15, 24, 30–33.
97. A. Gat, *The Causes of War and the Spread of Peace: But Will War Rebound?* (Oxford: Oxford University Press, 2017), table 7.6, 242.
98. A. Forster, "The Military Covenant and British Civil–Military Relations: Letting the Genie out of the Bottle," *Armed Forces and Society* 38 (2012): 273–290.
99. M. Centano and E. Enriquez, *War and Society* (Cambridge: Polity Press), 171–172.
100. Ibid., 173, 176.
101. Bacevich, *New American Militarism*, 26, 28, 97–98.
102. Forster, "Military Covenant," 273–290.
103. For example, Centano and Enriquez, *War and Society*.
104. Lachmann, "Mercenary, Citizen, Victim," 57–58, 67; citing P. Feaver and C. Gelpi, *Choosing Your Battles: American Civil–Military Relations and the Use of Force* (Princeton, NJ: Princeton University Press, 2004).

105. M. Shaw, *The New Western Way of War: Risk-Transfer War and Its Crisis in Iraq* (Cambridge: Polity Press, 2005); a similar idea has been referred to as "virtual war," in which Western aircraft operated without fear of being shot down, with death removed, in conditions of impunity (M. Ignatieff, *Virtual War: Kosovo and Beyond* [New York: Henry Holt, 2000]; cited by L. Freedman, *Command: The Politics of Military Operations from Korea to Ukraine* [New York: Penguin/Random House, 2022]).
106. Lachmann, "Mercenary, Citizen, Victim," 55–57.
107. Pinker, *Better Angels*, 28.

Chapter 6

1. D. G. Winter, *Roots of War: Wanting Power, Seeing Threat, Justifying Force* (New York: Oxford University Press, 2018), 233 (see also M. Pilisuk and J. A. Rowntree, *The Hidden Structure of Violence: Who Benefits from Global Violence and War* [New York: Monthly Review Press, 2015], 243).
2. P. M. Taylor, *Munitions of the Mind: A History of Propaganda from the Ancient World to the Present Day*, 3rd ed. (Manchester: Manchester University Press, 2003), 196–197.
3. O. Hathaway and S. Shapiro, *The Internationalists: And Their Plan to Outlaw War* (London: Allen Lane, 2017), xi.
4. Ibid., 42.
5. Taylor, *Munitions of the Mind*, 2.
6. Ibid., 3, 193, 177.
7. Ibid., 179–180, 197.
8. N. Ferguson, *The Pity of War* (London: Penguin Books, 1999), 246; Taylor, *Munitions of the Mind*, 178; Pilisuk and Rowntree, *Hidden Structure of Violence*, 221–222.
9. Taylor, *Munitions of the Mind*, 181.
10. Ibid., 241–245.
11. Ibid., 238–239.
12. Ibid., 208, 216, 218–219.
13. P. Ferris, *Dylan Thomas* (London: Hodder and Stoughton, 1977), 181–183.
14. Taylor, *Munitions of the Mind*, 198–205, 264, 266, 275.
15. Ibid., 3.
16. Pilisuk and Rowntree, *Hidden Structure of Violence*, 30.
17. Taylor, *Munitions of the Mind*, 293; Pilisuk and Rowntree, *Hidden Structure of Violence*, 280; J. S. Levy and W. R. Thompson, *Causes of War* (Chichester, UK: Wiley-Blackwell, 2010), 174.
18. S. Hersh, "Torture at Abu Ghraib," 2004/05/10. *New Yorker*; cited by Pilisuk and Rowntree, *Hidden Structure of Violence*, 256.
19. Pilisuk and Rowntree, *Hidden Structure of Violence*.

20. J. Gerth, *New York Times*, December 11, 2005; cited by A. McGoldrick, "News as Entertainment: The Ultimate War Propaganda Machine, or Opportunity to Promote Peace?," in *Preventing War and Promoting Peace: A Guide for Health Professionals*, ed. W. H. Wiist and S. K. White (New York: Cambridge University Press, 2017), 133.
21. Pilisuk and Rowntree, *Hidden Structure of Violence*, 243, drawing on S. Rampton and J. Stauber, *Weapons of Mass Deception: The Uses of Propaganda in Bush's War on Iraq* (New York: Tarcher/Penguin, 2003).
22. Taylor, *Munitions of the Mind*, 189, 226, 267, 303–307, 312, 316.
23. Winter, *Roots of War*, 232.
24. Taylor, *Munitions of the Mind*, 222–226, 265, 311.
25. Ibid., 316, 321.
26. J. Hughes, "State Violence in the Origins of Nationalism: British Counterinsurgency and the Rebirth of Irish Nationalism, 1969–1972," in *Nationalism and War*, ed. J. A. Hall and S. Malešević (Cambridge: Cambridge University Press, 2013), 100, 117–119.
27. Taylor, *Munitions of the Mind*, 193.
28. Ferguson, *Pity of War*, 213.
29. Ibid.
30. Ibid., 219, 221.
31. Taylor, *Munitions of the Mind*, 213.
32. H. Thomas, *The Spanish Civil War* (London: Readers' Union, 1962), 181, 485, 512; Taylor, *Munitions of the Mind*, 222–225.
33. Taylor, *Munitions of the Mind*, 309.
34. Pilisuk and Rowntree, *Hidden Structure of Violence*, 226, 221.
35. BBC2 TV series, *The Rise of the Murdoch Dynasty*, July 14, 2020.
36. McGoldrick, "News as Entertainment," 137.
37. Pilisuk and Rowntree, *Hidden Structure of Violence*, 253–254; R. Lachmann, "Mercenary, Citizen, Victim: The Rise and Fall of Conscription in the West," in *Nationalism and War*, ed. J. A. Hall and S. Malešević (Cambridge: Cambridge University Press, 2013), 59.
38. J. Pilger, *The New Rulers of the World* (London: Verso, 2002), 125.
39. L. LeShan, *The Psychology of War: Comprehending Its Mystique and Its Madness* (New York: Helios Press, 2002), 63, 93–94.
40. Pilger, *New Rulers of the World*, 132, 137, 139, 142–152.
41. Taylor, *Munitions of the Mind*, 269.
42. Ibid., 277.
43. Ibid., 277–280, 289–290, 295.
44. Ferguson, *Pity of War*, 240–241, citing E. Timms, *Karl Krauss: Apocalyptic Satirist* (New Haven, CT: Yale University Press, 1986).
45. Pilisuk and Rowntree, *Hidden Structure of Violence*, 223.
46. Ibid., 322.
47. LeShan, *Psychology of War*, 50–61, 67.
48. R. W. White, "Social and Role Identities and Political Violence: Identity as a Window on Violence in Northern Ireland," in *Social Identity, Intergroup Conflict, and Conflict*

Reduction, ed. R. Ashmore, L. Jussim, and D. Wilder (New York: Oxford University Press, 2001), chap. 6.
49. F. Keane, *Wounds: A Memoir of War and Love* (London: William Collins, 2017).
50. A. Kruglanski, J. J. Bélanger, and R. Gunaratna, *The Three Pillars of Radicalization: Needs, Narratives, and Networks* (New York: Oxford University Press, 2019), 51.
51. P. Seib, *Information at War: Journalism, Disinformation, and Modern Warfare* (Polity Press, 2021), 96–103, quote from 114.
52. Ibid., 103–104, 112, quote from 112.
53. B. F. Walter, *How Civil Wars Start: And How to Stop Them* (London: Penguin Random House, 2022), 108.
54. Seib, *Information at War*, 110.
55. Ibid., 111.
56. Ibid., 113, 126.
57. Ibid., 116, 129, 134.
58. Ibid., 126, citing O. Jonsson, *A Russian Understanding of War: Blurring the Lines between War and Peace* (Washington, DC: Georgetown University Press, 2019), 118.
59. Seib, *Information at War*, 151–153.
60. Walter, *How Civil Wars Start*, 104–105, 109.
61. Ibid., 110–111, 121.
62. Ibid., 106.
63. Walter, *How Civil Wars Start*, 112; S. Hare, *Guardian Weekly*, June 10, 2022.
64. Facebook Groups Act as Weapons Bazaars for Militias, *New York Times*, April 6, 2016; cited by Walter, *How Civil Wars Start*, 125; Hare.
65. Seib, *Information at War*, 185–186.
66. Taylor, *Munitions of the Mind*, 310.
67. Pilisuk and Rowntree, *Hidden Structure of Violence*, 237–238, citing A. R. Pratkanis and E. Aronson, *Age of Propaganda*, 2nd ed. (New York: W. H. Freeman, 2001).
68. McGoldrick, "News as Entertainment," 133–134.
69. Levy and Thompson, *Causes of War*, 59; J. Snyder, *Myths of Empire: Domestic Politics and International Ambition* (Ithaca, NY: Cornell University Press, 1991); S. J. Kaufman, *Modern Hatreds: The Symbolic Politics of Ethnic War* (Ithaca, NY: Cornell University Press, 2001); both cited by Levy and Thompson, *Causes of War*, 94, 200.
70. Winter, *Roots of War*, 103, 191–198, 348.
71. Taylor, *Munitions of the Mind*, 252, 259, 253, 255.
72. P. Gries and Y. Jing, "Are the US and China Fated to Fight? How Narratives of 'Power Transition' Shape Great Power War or Peace," *Cambridge Review of International Affairs* 32 (2019): 456–482, citing M. Deutsch, "Cooperation and Trust: Some Theoretical Notes," in *Nebraska Symposium on Motivation*, ed. M. R. Jones (Lincoln: University of Nebraska Press, 1962), 275–319.
73. Pilisuk and Rowntree, *Hidden Structure of Violence*, 243; McGoldrick, "News as Entertainment," 129–140.
74. McGoldrick, "News as Entertainment," 129–140.
75. B. S. Bennett and S. P. O'Rourke, "A Prolegomenon to the Future Study of Rhetoric and Propaganda: Critical Foundations," in *Readings in Propaganda and Persuasion: New

and Classic Essays, ed. G. S. Jowett and V. O'Donnell (Thousand Oaks, CA: Sage, 2006), 51–72.
76. Pratkanis and Aronson, *Age of Propaganda*; cited by Bennett and O'Rourke, "A Prolegomenon," 62.
77. Gries and Jing, "Are the US and China Fated to Fight?"
78. Taylor, *Munitions of the Mind*, 184.
79. Ferguson, *Pity of War*, 233.
80. Taylor, *Munitions of the Mind*, 211, 235, 288, 307.
81. S. A. Haslam, S. Reicher, and M. Platow, *The New Psychology of Leadership* (London: Taylor and Francis, 2010), 15.
82. Walter, *How Civil Wars Start*, 38, 44–47.
83. Keane, *Wounds*, 10.
84. S. Althaus and K. Coe, "Priming Patriots: Social Identity Processes and the Dynamics of Public Support for War," *Public Opinion Quarterly* 75 (2011): 65–88.
85. Taylor, *Munitions of the Mind*, 1, 187, 196–197.
86. Ferguson, *Pity of War*, 229.
87. Taylor, *Munitions of the Mind*, 13–14, 256 (citing the 1948 Smith-Mundt Act), 313–314, 319, 322.
88. Ibid., 268.

Chapter 7

1. Cited by G. Singh, "Sikhism and Just War," in *Just War in Comparative Perspective*, ed. P. Robinson (Burlington, VT: Ashgate, 2003), 126–136.
2. Cited in L. Smith, *Voices against War: A Century of Protest* (Edinburgh: Mainstream, 2010), 110.
3. R. Dawkins, *The Selfish Gene* (Oxford: Oxford University Press, 1989), 331; cited by A. Gat, *The Causes of War and the Spread of Peace: But Will War Rebound?* (Oxford: Oxford University Press), 86.
4. S. Pinker, *The Better Angels of Our Nature: A History of Violence and Humanity* (London: Penguin Books, 2012), chap. 5; M. Kaldor, *New and Old Wars: Organized Violence in a Global Era*, 2nd ed. (Cambridge: Polity Press, 2006), 21; Gat, *Causes of War*, 87.
5. N. Ferguson, *The Pity of War* (London: Penguin Books, 1999), 207.
6. Ibid., 208.
7. Ibid., quotes from 209 and 18, respectively.
8. G. Mosse, *Fallen Soldiers: Reshaping the Memory of the World Wars* (New York: Oxford University Press, 1990), 49, 83.
9. A. Bacevich, *The New American Militarism: How Americans Are Seduced by War*, updated ed. (New York: Oxford University Press, 2013), chap. 5.
10. A. Forster, "The Military Covenant and British Civil–Military Relations: Letting the Genie out of the Bottle," *Armed Forces and Society* 38 (2012): 273–290.
11. M. Bennetts, "30-foot High Statue of Mikhail Kalashnikov unveiled in Moscow," *The Guardian* 19 September 2017.

12. A. C. Grayling, *War: An Enquiry* (New Haven, CT: Yale University Press, 2017), 189.
13. J. Virden, "Justifying Killing: US Army Chaplains of World War II," in *Just War in Comparative Perspective*, ed. P. Robinson (Burlington, VT: Ashgate, 2003), 187–199.
14. Ibid.; J. Bourke, *An Intimate History of Killing: Face-to-Face Killing in Twentieth Century Warfare* (New York: Basic Books, 1999).
15. P. Dearey, "Catholicism and the Just War Tradition: The Experience of Moral Value in Warfare," in *Just War in Comparative Perspective*, ed. P. Robinson (Burlington, VT: Ashgate, 2003), 24–39.
16. Cited by D. Wood, *What Have We Done: The Moral Injury of Our Longest Wars* (New York: Little, Brown and Company, 2016), 106.
17. A. Webster, "Justifiable War in Eastern Orthodox Christianity," in *Just War in Comparative Perspective*, ed. P. Robinson (Burlington, VT: Ashgate, 2003), 40–61.
18. G. Wilkes, "Judaism and Justice in War," in *Just War in Comparative Perspective*, ed. P. Robinson (Burlington, VT: Ashgate, 2003), 9–23.
19. J. Kelsay, "War, Peace and the Imperatives of Justice in Islamic Perspective: What Do the 11 September 2001 Attacks Tell Us about Islam and the Just War Tradition?," in *Just War in Comparative Perspective*, ed. P. Robinson (Burlington, VT: Ashgate, 2003), 76–89.
20. G. Salines and A. Amimour, *We Still Have Words*, trans. J. Hensher (New York: Scribner, 2020).
21. F. Clooney, "Pain but not Harm: Some Classical Resources towards a Hindu Just War Theory," in *Just War in Comparative Perspective*, ed. P. Robinson (Burlington, VT: Ashgate, 2003), 109–125.
22. Singh, "Sikhism and Just War."
23. T. Kane, "Inauspicious Tools: Chinese Thought on the Morality of Warfare," in *Just War in Comparative Perspective*, ed. P. Robinson (Burlington, VT: Ashgate, 2003), 139–152.
24. E. Harris, "Buddhism and the Justification of War: A Case Study from Sri Lanka," in *Just War in Comparative Perspective*, ed. P. Robinson (Burlington, VT: Ashgate, 2003), 93–108.
25. H. Frowe, *The Ethics of War and Peace: An Introduction* (London: Routledge, 2011).
26. B. Solomon, "Kant's Perpetual Peace: A New Look at This Centuries-Old Quest," *The Online Journal of Peace and Conflict Resolution* 5 (2003): 106–126, quote from 112.
27. Aquinas, *Summa Theologica*, Part II, Question 40, cited by Grayling, *War*, 192.
28. Hugo Grotius, *On the Laws of War and Peace* (1625), cited by Grayling, *War*, 198–199.
29. O. Hathaway and S. Shapiro, *The Internationalists: And Their Plan to Outlaw War* (London: Penguin, 2017).
30. B. Howe, "Conflicting Normative Dimensions of Justification: The Gulf War," in *Just War in Comparative Perspective*, ed. P. Robinson (Burlington, VT: Ashgate, 2003), 200–217; Frowe, *Ethics of War and Peace*.
31. Howe, "Conflicting Normative Dimensions."
32. J. Bourke, *Wounding the World: How Military Violence and War-Play Invade Our Lives* (London: Virago, 2014), 67.
33. Howe, "Conflicting Normative Dimensions."

34. Frowe, *Ethics of War and Peace*.
35. Ibid.
36. Ibid.
37. Ibid.
38. D. Rodin, *War and Self-Defense* (Oxford: Oxford University Press, 2002), 115; cited by Frowe, *Ethics of War and Peace*, 55.
39. Frowe, *Ethics of War and Peace*.
40. M. Walzer, *Just and Unjust Wars* (New York: Basic Books, 1977); cited by Frowe, *Ethics of War and Peace*.
41. Ibid.
42. Kelsay, "War, Peace."
43. W. Churchill, *Their Finest Hour. The Second World War*, vol. 2 (New York: Rosetta Books, 1949), 567; cited by Bourke, *Wounding the World*, 121.
44. S. Terkel, *The Good War. An Oral History of World War Two* (New York: Vintage, 1985); cited by Bourke, *Wounding the World*, 118.
45. Kaldor, *New and Old Wars*; W. H. Wiist and S. K. White, eds., *Preventing War and Promoting Peace: A Guide for Health Professionals* (New York: Cambridge University Press, 2017).
46. *New York Times*, May 29, 2012; cited by Bourke, *Wounding the World*. 125.
47. Bourke, *Wounding the World.*, 125, 128.
48. Hathaway and Shapiro, *Internationalists*; S. Casey-Maslen, "The Role of International Law in Preventing War and Promoting Peace," in Wiist and White, *Preventing War*, 180–191.
49. Bacevich, *New American Militarism*, 48, 51–52.
50. Ibid., 19.
51. Wood, *What Have We Done*.
52. M. Pilisuk and J. A. Rowntree, *The Hidden Structure of Violence: Who Benefits from Global Violence and War* (New York: Monthly Review Press, 2015), 257.
53. Hathaway and Shapiro, *Internationalists*, 416.
54. Grayling, *War*, quotes from 201.
55. Bacevich, *New American Militarism*, 123, 145.
56. Howe, "Conflicting Normative Dimensions."
57. Cited by Frowe, *Ethics of War and Peace*, 76.
58. Ibid.
59. M. Centano and E. Enriquez, *War and Society* (Cambridge: Polity Press), 90–91.
60. G. Chamayou, *Drone Theory*, trans. J. Lloyd (London: Penguin, 2015), 98.
61. Ibid., 86.
62. A. Feinstein, *The Shadow World: Inside the Global Arms Trade* (London: Hamish Hamilton, 2011), 389–390.
63. Grayling, *War*, 219.
64. M. W. Royse, *Aerial Bombardment and the International Regulation of Warfare* (New York: H. Vinal, 1928), 131–132; cited by Bourke, *Wounding the World*, 71.
65. Bourke, *Wounding the World*, 71.
66. Grayling, *War*.

67. Hathaway and Shapiro, *Internationalists*, xi, 63.
68. Pilisuk and Rowntree, *Hidden Structure of Violence*, 59–61.
69. P. J. Adams, *Moral Jeopardy: Risks of Accepting Money from the Alcohol, Tobacco and Gambling Industries* (Cambridge: Cambridge University Press, 2016), 66.
70. J. Haidt, *The Righteous Mind: Why Good People Are Divided by Politics and Religion* (London: Penguin, 2013), drawing on, for example, D. Kahneman and A. Tversky, "Prospect Theory: Analysis of Decision under Risk," *Econometrica* 47 (1979): 263–291; Z. Zwald and J. Berejikian, "Is There a Public-Military Gap in the United States? Evaluating Foundational Foreign Policy Beliefs," *Armed Forces and Society* 48, no. 4 (2022): 982–1002.
71. J. Haidt and J. Graham, "Planet of the Durkheimians, Where Community, Authority, and Sacredness Are Foundations of Morality," in *Social and Psychological Bases of Ideology and System Justification*, ed. J. Jost, A. Kay, and H. Thorisdottir (New York: Oxford University Press, 2009), 371–401.
72. A. Bandura, "The Role of Selective Moral Disengagement in Terrorism and Counterterrorism," in *Understanding Terrorism*, ed. F. Moghaddam and A. Marsella (Washington, DC: American Psychological Association, 2004); A. Bandura, *Moral Disengagement: How People Do Harm and Live with Themselves* (New York: Worth Publishers, 2016); A. Bandura, "Disengaging Morality from Robot War," *The Psychologist* (February 2017): 39–43.
73. Pilisuk and Rowntree, *Hidden Structure of Violence*, 60.
74. Gat, *Causes of War*, 43–44.
75. A. P. Fiske and T. S. Rai, *Virtuous Violence: Hurting and Killing to Create, Sustain, End, and Honor Social Relationships* (Cambridge: Cambridge University Press, 2015).
76. Wood, *What Have We Done*, citing S. L. A. Marshall, *Men against Fire: The Problem of Battle Command in Future War* (Brand: University of Oklahoma Press, 1947).
77. Including J. Shay, *Achilles in Vietnam: Combat Trauma and the Undoing of Character* (New York: Scribner, 1994) and D. Grossman, *On Killing: The Psychological Cost of Learning to Kill in War and Society* (New York: Back Bay Books, 1996).
78. Wood, *What Have We Done*, 41.
79. Ibid., 18.
80. W. P. Nash and B. T. Litz, "Moral Injury: A Mechanism for War-Related Psychological Trauma in Military Family Members," *Clinical Child and Family Psychological Review* 16 (2013): 365–375; cited by Wood, *What Have We Done*.
81. Wood, *What Have We Done*, 34, 58, 85, 143–148, 189.
82. F. Keane, *Wounds: A Memoir of War and Love* (London: William Collins, 2017), 293, 159 (Keane also writes, in the same book, about his own depression and guilt due his exposure to war as a reporter, see 295).
83. Smith, *Voices against War*, 21–23, 29–30, 41–42, 45, 55; R. Lachmann, "Mercenary, Citizen, Victim: The Rise and Fall of Conscription in the West," in *Nationalism and War*, ed. J. A. Hall and S. Malešević (Cambridge: Cambridge University Press, 2013), 54.
84. Smith, *Voices against War*, 75, 60, 81, 98.
85. Ibid., 104, 111–112, 116–118, 128.
86. Ibid., 177, 179, 190, 192.

Chapter 8

1. D. Barash and C. Webel, *Peace and Conflict Studies*, 2nd ed. (Los Angeles: Sage, 2009), 91–92.
2. J. Wain, ed., *The Oxford Library of English Poetry*, vol. 3, *George Darley to Seamus Heaney* (London: Guild Publishing, 1986), 342.
3. Re Senegal: N. Roll, Senegal's 40-year war spills over the border, April 8. 2022, 28–29. Re South Sudan: J. Burke, Hunger, raiders and ethnic rivalries ravage South Sudan, June 30, 2017, 12–13. Re Sudan (my new inserted bit): N. Malik, The tragedy of Khartoum, July 28, 2023, 36–39. Re Tigray: S. Tisdall, Mass rape in Tigray is ignored as west wants to keep Abiy on side, May 14, 2021, 48–49; Global report, Famine takes hold in the Tigray region, says UN, June 18, 2021, 8; M. Abraha, The world is ignoring Tigray's year-long nightmare of war, November 26, 2012, 47; Opinion, A glimpse of hope in Ethiopia's hidden war that has claimed 500,000 lives, April 8, 2022, 49.
4. BBC World Service, *From Our Own Correspondent*, Football, power and conflict in Cameroon, January 17, 2022.
5. As of May 2021, at least H. K.Cunningham, Welcome to Semuliki; on the trail of Islamic militants, May 21, 2021, 28–29. *The Guardian Weekly*, May 21, 2021.
6. O. Holmes and S. Taha, "Jerusalem seethes as rockets are fired and tension rises," *Guardian Weekly*, May 21, 2021, 22; O. Holmes and H. Balousha, "Everyone is saying it should not be business as usual," *Guardian Weekly*, May 28, 2021, 15–16.
7. P. Beinart, "A Jewish case for Palestinian refugee return," *Guardian Weekly*, May 28, 2021, 34–39.
8. *The Guardian Weekly*; Re Nagorno-Karabakh: M. Safi, Armenia's diaspora feels the pull of yet another war, October 9, 202, 19; M. Safi, Exile and elation for the two sides of a bloody conflict, December 4, 2020 (I have no record of the page nos.); Re Syria: M. Chulov, The "poor man's cocaine" creating a narco state, May 14, 2021, 23; B. McKernan, V. Mironova and E. Graham-Harrison, Isis brides: how women in Syrian camps are marrying for freedom, July 16, 2021, 13–15; Re Yemen: Global report, Millions marching towards starvation in war-torn state, October 1, 2021, 9; Re Iraq: G. Abdul-Ahad, In the lowlands near Kirkuk, special forces look for hideouts where militants make plans to rebuild the caliphate, July 16, 2021, 11–12; Re Afghanistan: Guardian reporters, The chaos at Kabul airport showed how ill prepared the US was for the speed of the Taliban advance, August 20, 2021, 11–15.
9. BBC Radio 4 The Moral Maze January 26, 2022; O. Grytsenko, "Border line: as Russian forces mass, citizens fear return of war," *The Guardian Weekly*, April 23, 2021, 15–16.
10. Re Germany, P. Olterma, "A new coalition government in Berlin has been reluctant to spell out plans for sanctions against aggression by Moscow," *The Guardian Weekly*, February 4, 2022, 19–20; BBC Radio 4, *Analysis*, Germany and Russia: its complicated, June 20, 2022; re Sweden and Finland, J. Hemley and J. Rankin, "Historic move as Nordic nations seek to join Nato," *The Guardian Weekly*, May 20, 2022, 17.
11. Stockholm International Peace Research Institute, Global nuclear arsenals are expected to grow as nations continue to modernize, press release, Stockholm, June 13, 2022; J. Berger, Tick, tick... boom? Why we're closer to midnight than ever, *The*

Guardian Weekly, January 28, 2022, 23; for example, written evidence to the UK's Defence Select Committee by the British-American Security Information Council, Jauary 4, 2018.
12. House of Commons Library, Research briefing: The militarisation of space, June 14, 2021.
13. BBC Radio 4, December 12, 2021. S. Russell, BBC Reith Lecture, December 2021, as part of his lecture series *Living with Artificial Intelligence*.
14. BBC Radio 4, "AI in Warfare," *Rutherford and Fry on Living with AI*, December 12, 2021; see also L. Freedman, *Command: The Politics of Military Operations from Korea to Ukraine* (New York: Penguin/Random House, 2022), 504–505.
15. H. H. Blumberg, A. P. Hare, and A. Costin, *Peace Psychology: A Comprehensive Introduction* (Cambridge: Cambridge University Press, 2006); Barash and Webel, *Peace and Conflict Studies*; *The Psychologist*, February and September 2016; and see the contents of *Peace and Conflict: Journal of Peace Psychology*.
16. Barash and Webel, *Peace and Conflict Studies*.
17. M. Pilisuk and J. Rowntree, *The Hidden Structure of Violence: Who Benefits from Global Violence and War* (New York: Monthly Review Press, 2015), 10; see also Blumberg, Hare, and Costin, *Peace Psychology*.
18. P. T. Hiller, "Structural Violence and War: Global Inequalities, Resources, and Climate Change," in *Preventing War and Promoting Peace: A Guide for Health Professionals*, ed. W. H. Wiist and S. K. White (New York: Cambridge University Press, 2017), 93.
19. Barash and Webel, *Peace and Conflict Studies*, 91–92.
20. S. Pinker, *The Better Angels of Our Nature: A History of Violence and Humanity* (London: Penguin Books, 2012), quotes from 841, xxv, 356.
21. Some of the foregoing paragraph is closely based on J. Orford, "Psychology, History and War: Two Examples of Academic Discourses Which Fail to Oppose War and Militarism," *The Journal of Critical Psychology, Counselling and Psychotherapy* 19 (2019): 48–59.
22. Some of the following is closely based on J. Orford, "Turning Psychology against Militarism," *Journal of Community & Applied Social Psychology* 27 (2017): 287–297.
23. J. Bourke, *Wounding the World: How Military Violence and War-Play Invade Our Lives* (London: Virago, 2014), 93.
24. For example, V. Nathanson, "Symposium on Responding to War, Conflict and Militarisation as a Health Community," *Health through Peace Conference*, Medact: Health Professionals for a Safer, Fairer and Better World, London, November 14, 2015.
25. Bourke, *Wounding the World*, 130, 148.
26. P. Watson, *War on the Mind: The Military Uses and Abuses of Psychology* (Harmondsworth, UK: Penguin, 1980), 22, 206.
27. J. Arrigo, R. Eidelson, and R. Bennett, "Psychology under Fire: Adversarial Operational Psychology and Psychological Ethics," *Peace and Conflict: Journal of Peace Psychology* 18 (2012): 384–400, quote from 386; J. Arrigo, R. Eidelson, and L. Rockwood, "Adversarial Operational Psychology Is Unethical Psychology: A Reply to Staal and Greene (2015)," *Peace and Conflict: Journal of Peace Psychology* 21 (2015): 269–278.

28. D. Hoffman et al., *Independent Report Relating to APA Ethics Guidelines, National Security, Interrogations, and Torture* (Washington, DC: American Psychological Association); cited by M. Noor, "Can Psychology Find a Path to Peace?," *The Psychologist* (February 2016).
29. M. Staal and C. Greene, "An Examination of 'Adversarial' Operational Psychology," *Peace and Conflict: Journal of Peace Psychology* 21 (2015): 264–268.
30. B. Strawser, "Moral Predators: The Duty to Employ Uninhabited Aerial Vehicles," *Journal of Military Ethics* 9 (2010): 342; cited by G. Chamayou, *Drone Theory*, trans. J. Lloyd (London: Penguin, 2015), 137.
31. J. Mueller, "The Iraq Syndrome," *Foreign Affairs* 84 (2005): 44–54; Freedman, *Command*, 16–17.
32. Pinker, *Better Angels*, chap. 5.
33. N. Cohen, *The Guardian Weekly*, April 29, 2022, 46.
34. BBC Radio 4, *The Moral Maze*, January 26, 2022.
35. A. Roth, *The Guardian Weekly*, February 18, 2022, 12–13, and August 5, 2022, 11–12.
36. J. Gaskarth, "Appeasement and the Ukraine Crisis: The Whiff of Munich?," UK in a Changing Europe, February 22, 2022, https://ukandeu.ac.uk/appeasement-and-the-ukraine-crisis/.
37. For example, BBC Radio 4, *Sideways*, July 13, 2022.
38. For example, P. Wintour, *The Guardian Weekly*, July 1, 2022, 10–12.
39. T. Meaney, *The Guardian Weekly*, May 13, 2022, 36–39, quotes from 36, 38; BBC Radio 4, *The Moral Maze*, January 26 and June 29, 2022.
40. N. Ascherson, *The Guardian Weekly*, March 11, 2022, 23.
41. K. Gessen, *The Guardian Weekly*, March 25, 2022.
42. Ibid.; BBC Radio 4, "*The War of Nerves: Inside the Cold War Mind* by Martin Sixsmith (Welcome Collection, 2021)," *Book of the Week*, July 11–15, 2022.
43. *The Psychologist*, April 2022, 10–11.
44. G. Allison, *Destined for War: Can America and China Escape Thucydides's Trap?* (London: Scribe, 2017), esp. xiv–xvii, 160, 176–184, quotes from xiv, 20.
45. Ibid., 107.
46. S. Tisdall, *The Guardian Weekly*, June 11, 2022.
47. Allison, *Destined for War*, 132.
48. A. Gat, *The Causes of War and the Spread of Peace: But Will War Rebound?* (Oxford: Oxford University Press, 2017).
49. Allison, *Destined for War*, 147.
50. Tisdall, *The Guardian Weekly*, June 11, 2021, 14.
51. V. Ni, *The Guardian Weekly*, August 6, 2021.
52. H. Davidson and O. Milman, *The Guardian Weekly*, August 12, 2022, 11–13.
53. Allison, *Destined for War*, 214.
54. A. C. Grayling, *War: An Enquiry* (New Haven, CT: Yale University Press, 2017).
55. K. Lowe, *The Fear and the Freedom: How the Second World War Changed Us* (London: Penguin, 2018).
56. M. Kaldor, *New and Old Wars: Organized Violence in a Global Era*, 2nd ed. (Cambridge: Polity Press, 2006), esp. chap. 6.
57. Allison, *Destined for War*, 221–229.

Bibliography

Adam-Troian, J., E. Bonetto, M. Araujo, O. Baidada, E. Celebi, M. D. Martin, et al. "Positive Associations between Anomia and Intentions to Engage in Political Violence: Cross-Cultural Evidence from Four Countries." *Peace and Conflict: Journal of Peace Psychology* 26 (2020): 217–223.

Adams, P. J. *Moral Jeopardy: Risks of Accepting Money from the Alcohol, Tobacco and Gambling Industries*. Cambridge: Cambridge University Press, 2016.

Adorno, T. W., E. Frenkel-Brunswik, D. Levinson, and N. Sanford. *The Authoritarian Personality*. New York: Harpers, 1950.

Allison, G. *Destined for War: Can America and China Escape Thucydides's Trap?* London: Scribe, 2017.

Allport, G. W. *The Nature of Prejudice*. Reading, MA: Addison-Wesley, 1954.

Altemeyer, B. *Right-Wing Authoritarianism*. Winnipeg, Canada: University of Manitoba Press, 1981.

Altemeyer, B. *Enemies of Freedom: Understanding Right-Wing Authoritarianism*. San Francisco: Jossey-Bass, 1988.

Altemeyer, B. *The Authoritarian Specter*. Cambridge, MA: Harvard University Press, 1996.

Althaus, S., and K. Coe. "Priming Patriots: Social Identity Processes and the Dynamics of Public Support for War." *Public Opinion Quarterly* 75 (2011): 65–88.

Altier, M., and J. Kane. "Framing States: Unitary Actor Language and Public Support for Coercive Foreign Policy." *International Studies Quarterly* 67 (2023): sqac080.

American Civil Liberties Union. *Soldiers of Misfortune. Abusive US Military Recruitment and Failure to Protect Child Soldiers*. New York: ACLU, 2008.

Anson, J., T. Pyszczynski, S. Solomon, and J. Greenberg. "Political Ideology in the 21st Century: A Terror Management Perspective on Maintenance and Change of the Status Quo." In *Social and Psychological Bases of Ideology and System Justification*, edited by J. Jost, A. Kay, and H. Thorisdottir, 210–240. New York: Oxford University Press, 2009.

Appiah, K.A. "Cosmopolitan Patriots." *Critical Inquiry* (Spring 1997): 619.

Ardrey, R. *The Hunting Hypothesis*. New York: Atheneum, 1976.

Arquilla, J. A. *Insurgents, Raiders and Bandits: How Masters of Irregular Warfare Have Shaped Our World*. Lanham, MD: Ivan R. Dee, 2011.

Arrigo, J. M., R. J. Eidelson, and R. Bennett. "Psychology under Fire: Adversarial Operational Psychology and Psychological Ethics." *Peace and Conflict: Journal of Peace Psychology* 18 (2012): 384–400.

Arrigo, J. M., R. J. Eidelson, and L. P. Rockwood. "Adversarial Operational Psychology Is Unethical Psychology: A Reply to Staal and Greene (2015)." *Peace and Conflict: Journal of Peace Psychology* 21 (2015): 269–278.

Ashmore, R., L. Jussim, D. Wilder, and J. Heppen. "Conclusion: Toward a Social Identity Framework for Intergroup Conflict." In *Social Identity, Intergroup Conflict, and Conflict Reduction*, edited by R. Ashmore, L. Jussim, and D. Wilder, chap. 9, 213–249. New York: Oxford University Press, 2001.

Awale, A. "The Influence of Perceived Warmth and Competence on Realistic Threat and Willingness for Intergroup Contact." *European Journal of Social Psychology* 49 (2019): 857–870.

Bacevich, A. *The New American Militarism: How Americans Are Seduced by War*. Updated ed. New York: Oxford University Press, 2013.

Baele, S. "Conspiratorial Narratives in Violent Political Actors' Language." *Journal of Language and Social Psychology* 38 (2019): 706–734.

Bagby, L. M. *Hobbes's Leviathan: Reader's Guide*. London: Continuum, 2007.

Bagci, S. C., and A. Turnuklu. "Intended, Unintended, and Unknown Consequences of Contact: The Role of Positive–Negative Contact on Outgroup Attitudes, Collective Action Tendencies, and Psychological Well-Being." *Social Psychology* 50 (2019): 7–23.

Baier, A. C. *Moral Prejudices: Essays on Ethics*. Cambridge, MA: Harvard University Press, 1995.

Bandura, A. "The Role of Selective Moral Disengagement in Terrorism and Counterterrorism." In *Understanding Terrorism: Psychosocial Roots, Consequences, and Interventions*, edited by F. Moghaddam and A. Marsella, 121–150. Washington, DC: American Psychological Association, 2004.

Bandura, A. *Moral Disengagement: How People Do Harm and Live with Themselves*. New York: Worth Publishers, 2016.

Bandura, A. "Disengaging Morality from Robot War." *The Psychologist* (February 2017): 39–43.

Barash, D. P., and C. P. Webel. *Peace and Conflict Studies*. 2nd ed. Los Angeles: Sage, 2009.

Barker, K. "The Quiet Military Buyout of Academia." In *Preventing War and Promoting Peace: A Guide for Health Professionals*, edited by W. H. Wiist and S. K. White, 141–152. New York: Cambridge University Press, 2017.

Bassil, N. "A Critique of Western Representations of ISIS: Deconstructing Contemporary Orientalism." *Global Change, Peace and Security* 31 (2019): 81–94.

Bauer, C., and B. Hannover. "Changing 'Us' and Hostility towards 'Them'—Implicit Theories of National Identity Determine Prejudice and Participation Rates in an Anti-Immigrant Petition." *European Journal of Social Psychology* 50 (2020): 810–826.

Bayram, A. "Nationalist Cosmopolitanism: The Psychology of Cosmopolitanism, National Identity, and Going to War for the Country." *Nations and Nationalism* 25 (2019): 757–781.

Bennett, B. S., and S. P. O'Rourke. "A Prolegomenon to the Future Study of Rhetoric and Propaganda: Critical Foundations." In *Readings in Propaganda and Persuasion: New and Classic Essays*, edited by G. S. Jowett and V. O'Donnell, 51–72. Thousand Oaks, CA: Sage, 2006.

Billig, M. *Banal Nationalism*. London: Sage, 1995.

Black, J. *English Nationalism: A Short History*. London: Hurst, 2018.

Blanchar, J. C., and S. Eidelman. "Everything in Its Right Place: Tradition, Order, and the Legitimation of Long-Standing Inequality." In *The Social Psychology of Inequality*, edited by J. Jetten and K. Peters, 349–364. Cham, Switzerland: Springer, 2019.

Bliss, S. L., E. J. Oh, and R. L. Williams. "Militarism and Sociopolitical Perspectives among College Students in the U.S. and South Korea." *Journal of Peace and Conflict: Journal of Peace Psychology* 13 (2007): 175–199.

Blumberg, H. H., A. P. Hare, and A. Costin. *Peace Psychology: A Comprehensive Introduction*. Cambridge: Cambridge University Press, 2006.

Bourke, J. *Dismembering the Male: Men's Bodies, Britain and the Great War*. Chicago: University of Chicago Press, 1996.
Bourke, J. *An Intimate History of Killing: Face-to-Face Killing in Twentieth-Century Warfare*. New York: Basic Books, 1999.
Bourke, J. *Wounding the World: How Military Violence and War-Play Invade Our Lives*. London: Virago, 2014.
Brock, G., and Q. Atkinson. "What Can Examining the Psychology of Nationalism Tell Us about Our Prospects for Aiming at the Cosmopolitan Vision?" *Ethical Theory and Moral Practice* 11, no. 2 (2008): 165–179.
Bronfenbrenner, U. "The Mirror Image in Soviet–American Relations: A Social Psychologist's Report." *Journal of Social Issues* 16 (1961): 45–56.
Burgos, C. H. "Nationalisation, Banal Nationalism and Everyday Nationhood in a Dictatorship: The Franco Regime in Spain." *Nations and Nationalism* 27 (2021): 690–704.
Cadogan, M., and P. Craig. *Women and Children First. The Fiction of Two World Wars*. London: Gollancz, 1978.
Casey-Maslen, S. "The Role of International Law in Preventing War and Promoting Peace." In *Preventing War and Promoting Peace: A Guide for Health Professionals*, edited by W. H. Wiist and S. K. White, 180–191. New York: Cambridge University Press, 2017.
Caspary, W. R. "New Psychoanalytic Perspectives on the Causes of War." *Political Psychology* 14 (1993): 417–446.
Caspi-Berkowitz, N., M. Mikulincer, G. Hirschberger, T. Ein-Dor, and P. R. Shaver. "To Die for a Cause but not for a Companion: Attachment-Related Variations in the Terror Management Function of Self-Sacrifice." *Journal of Personality and Social Psychology* 117 (2019): 1105–1126.
Centano, M. A., J. M. Cruz, R. Flores, and G. S. Cano. "Internal Wars and Latin American Nationalism." In *Nationalism and War*, edited by J. A. Hall and S. Malešević, 279–305. Cambridge: Cambridge University Press, 2013.
Centano, M., and E. Enriquez. *War and Society*. Cambridge: Polity Press, 2016.
Chamayou, G. *Drone Theory*. Translated by J. Lloyd. London: Penguin, 2015.
Churchill, W. *Their Finest Hour. The Second World War*, vol. 2. New York: Rosetta Books, 1949.
Citrin, J., C. Wong, and B. Duff. "The Meaning of American National Identity: Patterns of Ethnic Conflict and Consensus." In *Social Identity, Intergroup Conflict, and Conflict Reduction*, edited by R. Ashmore, L. Jussim, and D. Wilder, 71–100. New York: Oxford University Press, 2001.
Clooney, F. "Pain but not Harm: Some Classical Resources towards a Hindu Just War Theory." In *Just War in Comparative Perspective*, P. Robinson, edited by 109–125. Burlington, VT: Ashgate, 2003.
Coleman, P. T., M. Deutsch, and E. C. Marcus, eds. *Handbook of Conflict Resolution: Theory and Practice*. 3rd ed. San Francisco: Jossey-Bass, 2014.
Collier, P., A. Finlan, M. J. Grove, P. D. Grove, R. A. Hart, S. A. Hart, et al. *The Second World War*. Oxford: Osprey Publishing, 2018.
Collins, R. "Does Nationalist Sentiment Increase Fighting Efficacy? A Skeptical View from the Sociology of Violence." In *Nationalism and War*, edited by J. A. Hall and S. Malešević, 31–43. Cambridge Cambridge University Press, 2013.
Cottam, M. L., B. Dietz-Uhler, E. Mastors, and T. Preston, eds. *Introduction to Political Psychology*. 2nd ed. New York: Psychology Press, 2010.

Cowell-Meyers, K. "Gender, Peace, and Power." *Women and Politics* 23 (2001): 57–90.
Dawkins, R. *The Selfish Gene*. Oxford: Oxford University Press, 1989.
Dearey, P. "Catholicism and the Just War Tradition: The Experience of Moral Value in Warfare." In *Just War in Comparative Perspective*, edited by P. Robinson, 24–39. Burlington, VT: Ashgate, 2003.
Der Derian, J. *Virtuous War: Mapping the Military–Industrial–Media–Entertainment Network*. Boulder: Westview Press, 2001.
Deutsch, M. "Cooperation and Trust: Some Theoretical Notes." In *Nebraska Symposium on Motivation*, edited by M. R. Jones, 275–319. Lincoln: University of Nebraska Press, 1962.
Deutsch, M. "The Prevention of World War III: A Psychological Perspective." *Political Psychology*, 4 (1983): 3–31.
Deutsch, M. "Cooperation, Competition, and Conflict." In *Handbook of Conflict Resolution: Theory and Practice*, edited by P. T Coleman, M. Deutsch, and E. C. Marcus, 3–28. 3rd ed. San Francisco: Jossey-Bass, 2014.
Diamond, J. *The World Until Yesterday: What Can We Learn from Traditional Societies?* New York: Penguin, 2012.
DiRienzo, C. "The Effect of Women in Government on Country-Level Peace." *Global Change, Peace and Security* 31 (2019): 1–18.
Dixon, J., Durrheim, K., and Tredoux, C. "Beyond the Optimal Contact Strategy: A Reality Check for the Contact Hypothesis." *American Psychologist* 60 (2005): 697–711.
Dixon, J., C. Tredoux, G. Davies, J. Huck, B. Hocking, B. Sturgeon, et al. "Parallel Lives: Intergroup Contact, Threat and the Segregation of Everyday Activity Spaces." *Journal of Personality and Social Psychology* 118 (2020): 457–480.
Dixon, N. F. *On the Psychology of Military Incompetence*. London: Futura, 1979.
Dower, J. "Apes and Others." In *Making War Making Peace: The Social Foundations of Violent Conflict*, edited by F. M. Cancion and J. W. Gibson, 100–110. Belmont, CA: Wadsworth, 1990.
Druckman, D. "Nationalism and War: A Social-Psychological Perspective." In *Peace, Conflict and Violence: Peace Psychology for the 21st Century*, edited by D. J. Christie, R. V. Wagner, and D. D. N. Winter, 49–65. Englewood Cliffs, NJ: Prentice Hall/Pearson Education, 2001.
Duckitt, J. "A Dual-Process Cognitive-Motivational Theory of Ideology and Prejudice." *Advances in Experimental Social Psychology* 33 (2001): 41–113.
Duckitt, J. "Differential Effects of Right Wing Authoritarianism and Social Dominance Orientation on Outgroup Attitudes and Their Mediation by Threat from and Competitiveness to Outgroups." *Personality and Social Psychology Bulletin* 32 (2006): 684–696.
Duckitt, J., and S. G. Sibley. "The Dual Process Motivational Model of Ideology and Prejudice." In *The Cambridge Handbook of the Psychology of Prejudice*, edited by C. G. Sibley and F. K. Barlow, 188–221. New York: Cambridge University Press, 2016.
Dunwoody, P. T., and D. L. Plane. "The Influence of Authoritarianism and Outgroup Threat on Political Affiliations and Support for Antidemocratic Policies." *Peace and Conflict: Journal of Peace Psychology* 25 (2019): 198–210.
Duriesmith, D. *Masculinity and New War: The Gendered Dynamics of Contemporary Armed Conflict*. London: Taylor and Francis, 2016.
Ehrenreich, B. *Blood Rites: Origins and History of the Passions of War*. New York: Henry Holt, 1997.

Ehrhart, W. D. "Why I Did It." *VQR* (Winter 1980). https://www.vqronline.org/essay/why-i-did-it.
Eibl-Eibesfeldt, I. *The Biology of War and Peace*. New York: Viking, 1979.
Elias, N. *The Civilizing Process: Sociogenic and Psychogenic Investigations*. Cambridge, MA: Blackwell, 2000. First published 1939.
Erasmus, Z. "Contact Theory: Too Timid for 'Race' and Racism." *Journal of Social Issues* 66 (2010): 387–400.
Evans, R. J. *Eric Hobsbawm: A Life in History*. London: Little, Brown, 2019.
Feaver, P., and C. Gelpi. *Choosing Your Battles: American Civil–Military Relations and the Use of Force*. Princeton, NJ: Princeton University Press, 2004.
Feinstein, A. *The Shadow World: Inside the Global Arms Trade*. London: Hamish Hamilton, 2011.
Ferguson, N. *The Pity of War*. London: Penguin Books, 1999.
Ferguson, R. B. "Pinker's List: Exaggerating Prehistoric War Mortality." In *War, Peace and Human Nature: The Convergence of Evolutionary and Cultural Views*, edited by D. Fry, 112–131. Oxford: Oxford University Press, 2013.
Ferris, P. *Dylan Thomas*. London: Hodder and Stoughton, 1977.
Fiske, A. P., and T. S. Rai. *Virtuous Violence: Hurting and Killing to Create, Sustain, End, and Honor Social Relationships*. Cambridge: Cambridge University Press, 2015.
Forster, A. "The Military Covenant and British Civil–Military Relations: Letting the Genie out of the Bottle." *Armed Forces and Society* 38 (2012): 273–290.
Freedman, L. *Command: The Politics of Military Operations from Korea to Ukraine*. New York: Penguin/Random House, 2022.
Freud, S. "Why War." In *Collected papers*. Vol. 4. London: Hogarth Press, 1949.
Frowe, H., *The Ethics of War and Peace: An Introduction*. London: Routledge, 2011.
Fussell, P. *Wartime*. Oxford: Oxford University Press, 1989.
Gat, A. *War in Human Civilization*. New York: Oxford University Press, 2006.
Gat, A. *The Causes of War and the Spread of Peace: But Will War Rebound?* Oxford: Oxford University Press, 2017.
Ghattas, K. *Black Wave: Saudi Arabia, Iran and the Rivalry That Unravelled the Middle East*. London: Wildfire, 2020.
Gilligan, C. *In a Different Voice: Psychological Theory and Women's Development*. Cambridge, MA: Harvard University Press, 1982.
Główczewski, M., A. Wojcik, A. Cichocka, and A. Cislak. "National Narcissism and Group-Enhancing Historical Narratives." *Social Psychology* 53 (2022): 357–387.
Goldstein, J. *War and Gender: How Gender Shapes the War System and Vice Versa*. Cambridge: Cambridge University Press, 2001.
Goldstein, J. S. *Winning the War on War: The Decline of Armed Conflict Worldwide*. London: Penguin, 2011.
Goodhart, D. *The Road to Somewhere: The New Tribes Shaping British Politics*. London: Penguin, 2017.
Gray, G. *The Warriors: Reflections on Men in Battle*. Lincoln: University of Nebraska Press, 1998. First published 1959.
Grayling, A. C. *War: An Enquiry*. New Haven, CT: Yale University Press, 2017.
Gries, P., and Y. Jing. "Are the US and China Fated to Fight? How Narratives of 'Power Transition' Shape Great Power War or Peace." *Cambridge Review of International Affairs* 32 (2019): 456–482.

Gross, Z., and R. Maor. "Is Contact Theory Still Valid in Acute Asymmetrical Violent Conflict: A Case Study of Israeli Jewish and Arab Students in Higher Education." *Peace and Conflict: Journal of Peace Psychology* (2020). https://doi.org/10.1037/pac0000440.

Grossman, D. *On Killing: The Psychological Cost of Learning to Kill in War and Society.* New York: Back Bay Books, 1996.

Grundy, K. *Soldiers without Politics: Blacks in the S.A. Armed Forces.* Berkeley: University of California Press, 1983.

Gulevich, O., A. Nevruev, and I. Sarieva. "War as a Method of Conflict Resolution: The Link between Social Beliefs, Ideological Orientations, and Military Attitudes in Russia." *Peace and Conflict: Journal of Peace Psychology* 26 (2020): 192–201.

Haidt, J. *The Righteous Mind: Why Good People Are Divided by Politics and Religion.* London: Penguin, 2013.

Haidt, J., and J. Graham, "Planet of the Durkheimians, Where Community, Authority, and Sacredness Are Foundations of Morality." In *Social and Psychological Bases of Ideology and System Justification*, edited by J. Jost, A. Kay, and H. Thorisdottir, 371–401. New York: Oxford University Press, 2009.

Hall, J. A., and S. Malešević. "Introduction: Wars and Nationalisms." In *Nationalism and War*, edited by J. A. Hall and S. Malešević, 1–28. Cambridge: Cambridge University Press, 2013.

Harris, E. "Buddhism and the Justification of War: A Case Study from Sri Lanka." In *Just War in Comparative Perspective*, edited by P. Robinson, 93–108. Burlington, VT: Ashgate, 2003.

Haslam, S. A., S. Reicher, and M. Platow. *The New Psychology of Leadership.* London: Taylor and Francis, 2010.

Hathaway, O., and S. Shapiro. *The Internationalists: And Their Plan to Outlaw War.* London: Penguin, 2017.

Hedges, C. *War Is a Force That Gives Us Meaning.* New York: Anchor, 2003.

Herrera, M., and S. Reicher. "Making Sides and Taking Sides: An Analysis of Salient Images and Category Constructions of Pro- and Anti-Gulf War Respondents." *European Journal of Social Psychology* 28 (1998): 981–993.

Herrmann, R. K., P. Isernia, and P. Segatti. "Attachment to the Nation and International Relations: Dimensions of Identity and Their Relationship to War and Peace." *Political Psychology* 30 (2009): 721–754.

Hewstone, M., E. Cairns, A. Voci, J. Hamberger, and U. Niens. "Intergroup Contact, Forgiveness, and Experience of "The Troubles" in Northern Ireland." *Journal of Social Issues* 62 (2006): 99–120.

Hiers, W., and A. Wimmer. "Is Nationalism the Cause or Consequence of the End of Empire?" In *Nationalism and War*, edited by J. A. Hall and S. Malešević, 212–254. Cambridge: Cambridge University Press, 2013.

Hiller, P. T. "Structural Violence and War: Global Inequalities, Resources, and Climate Change." In *Preventing War and Promoting Peace: A Guide for Health Professionals*, edited by W. H. Wiist and S. K. White, 90–102. New York: Cambridge University Press, 2017.

Hoffman, D., D. Carter, C. Viglucci Lopez, H. Benzmiller, A. Guo, Y. Latifi, et al. *Independent Report Relating to APA Ethics Guidelines, National Security, Interrogations, and Torture.* Washington, DC: American Psychological Association, 2015.

Holland, C., M. Cohn, I. Helfand, and J. Grassman. "Weapons of War and Mass Destruction." In *Preventing War and Promoting Peace: A Guide for Health Professionals*, edited by W. H. Wiist and S. K. White, 61-74. New York: Cambridge University Press, 2017.

Hollis, M. *Now All Roads Lead to France: The Last Years of Edward Thomas*. London: Faber and Faber, 2011.

Holmes, R. *Acts of War: The Behaviour of Men in Battle*. London: Cassell, 2004. First published 1985.

Howe, B. "Conflicting Normative Dimensions of Justification: The Gulf War." In *Just War in Comparative Perspective*, edited by P. Robinson, 200-217. Burlington, VT: Ashgate, 2003.

Hughes, J. "State Violence in the Origins of Nationalism: British Counterinsurgency and the Rebirth of Irish Nationalism, 1969-1972." In *Nationalism and War*, edited by J. A. Hall and S. Malešević, 97-123. Cambridge: Cambridge University Press, 2013.

Humphries, S., and P. Gordon. *A Man's World: From Boyhood to Manhood 1900-1960*. London: BBC Books, 1996.

Huntington, S. P. *Who Are We? The Challenge to America's National Identity*. New York: Simon and Schuster, 2004.

Ignatieff, M. *Virtual War: Kosovo and Beyond*. New York: Henry Holt, 2000.

James, W. "The Moral Equivalent of War." *Peace and Conflict: Journal of Peace Psychology* 1 (1995): 17-26. First published 1910.

Jonsson, O. *A Russian Understanding of War: Blurring the Lines between War and Peace*. Washington, DC: Georgetown University Press, 2019.

Jost, J., M. Banaji, and B. Nosek. "A Decade of System Justification Theory: Accumulated Evidence of Conscious and Unconscious Bolstering of the Status Quo." *Political Psychology* 25 (2004): 881-919.

Kahneman, D., and A. Tversky. "Prospect Theory: Analysis of Decision under Risk." *Econometrica* 47 (1979): 263-291.

Kaldor, M. *New and Old Wars: Organized Violence in a Global Era*. 2nd ed. Cambridge: Polity Press, 2006.

Kane, T. "Inauspicious Tools: Chinese Thought on the Morality of Warfare." In *Just War in Comparative Perspective*, edited by P. Robinson, 139-152. Burlington, VT: Ashgate, 2003.

Kanter, E. "The Effects of War on Combatants, Veterans and Their Families." In *Preventing War and Promoting Peace: A Guide for Health Professionals*, edited by W. H. Wiist and S. K. White, 19-33. New York: Cambridge University Press, 2017.

Kaufman, S. J. *Modern Hatreds: The Symbolic Politics of Ethnic War*. Ithaca, NY: Cornell University Press, 2001.

Kay, A., J. Banfield, and K. Laurin "The System Justification Motive and the Maintenance of Social Power." In *The Social Psychology of Power*, edited by A. Guinote and T. Vescio, 313-340. New York: Guilford Press, 2010.

Kay, A., D. Gaucher, J. Peach, K. Laurin, J. Friesen, M. Zanna, et al. "Inequality, Discrimination, and the Power of the Status Quo: Direct Evidence for a Motivation to See the Way Things Are as the Way They Should Be." *Journal of Personality and Social Psychology* 97 (2009): 421-434.

Kay, A., and M. Zanna. "A Contextual Analysis of the System Justification Motive and Its Societal Consequences." In *Social and Psychological Bases of Ideology and System Justification*, edited by J. Jost, A. Kay, and H. Thorisdottir, 158-181. New York: Oxford University Press, 2009.

Keane, F. *Wounds: A Memoir of War and Love*. London: William Collins, 2017.

Kelman, H. C. "The Role of National Identity in Conflict Resolution: Experiences from Israeli–Palestinian Problem-Solving Workshops." In *Social Identity, Intergroup Conflict, and Conflict Reduction*, edited by R. Ashmore, L. Jussim, and D. Wilder, 187–212. New York: Oxford University Press, 2001.

Kelsay, J. "War, Peace and the Imperatives of Justice in Islamic Perspective: What Do the 11 September 2001 Attacks Tell Us about Islam and the Just War Tradition?" In *Just War in Comparative Perspective*, edited by P. Robinson, 76–89. Burlington, VT: Ashgate, 2003.

Kemmelmeier, M., and D. Winter. "Sowing Patriotism, but Reaping Nationalism? Consequences of Exposure to the American Flag." *Political Psychology* 29 (2008): 859–879.

Khoshnood, K., B. X. Lee, and C. Marin. "The Health Effects of War on Civilians." In *Preventing War and Promoting Peace: A Guide for Health Professionals*, edited by W. H. Wiist and S. K. White, 34–47. New York: Cambridge University Press, 2017.

Koestler, A. *Janus: A Summing Up*. London: Pan Books, 1979.

Kraska, P. "Militarization and Policing—Its Relevance to 21st Century Police." *Policing* 1 (2007): 501–513.

Kruglanski, A. W., X. Chen, M. Dechesne, S. Fishman, and E. Orehek. "Fully Committed: Suicide Bombers' Motivation and the Quest for Personal Significance." *Political Psychology* 30 (2009): 331–357.

Kruglanski, A. W., J. J. Bélanger, and R. Gunaratna. *The Three Pillars of Radicalization: Needs, Narratives, and Networks*. New York: Oxford University Press, 2019.

Kruglanski, A.W., M. J. Gelfand, J. J. Bélanger, A. Sheveland, A., M. Hetiarachchi, and R. Gunaratna. "The Psychology of Radicalization and Deradicalization: How Significance Quest Impacts Violent Extremism." *Political Psychology* 35 (2014): 69–93.

Lachmann, R. "Mercenary, Citizen, Victim: The Rise and Fall of Conscription in the West." In *Nationalism and War*, edited by J. A. Hall and S. Malešević, 44–70. Cambridge: Cambridge University Press, 2013.

Lambert, W. E., and O. Klineberg. *Children's Views of Foreign Peoples: A Cross-National Study*. New York: Appleton-Century-Crofts, 1967.

Lange, M. "When Does Nationalism Turn Violent? A Comparative Analysis of Canada and Sri Lanka." In *Nationalism and War*, edited by J. A. Hall and S. Malešević, 124–144. Cambridge: Cambridge University Press, 2013.

Lee, J. *Ireland 1912–1985*. Cambridge: Cambridge University Press, 1989.

Leidner, B., L. R. Tropp, and B. Lickel. "Bringing Science to Bear—On Peace not War: Elaborating on Psychology's Potential to Promote Peace." *American Psychologist* 68 (2013): 514–626.

Lemarchand, R. "War and Nationalism: The View from Central Africa." In *Nationalism and War*, edited by J. A. Hall and S. Malešević, 306–320. Cambridge: Cambridge University Press, 2013.

LeShan, L. *The Psychology of War: Comprehending Its Mystique and Its Madness*. New York: Helios Press, 2002.

Levy, J. S., and W. R. Thompson. *Causes of War*. Chichester, UK: Wiley-Blackwell, 2010.

Levy, J. S., and W. R. Thompson. *The Arc of War*. Chicago: University of Chicago Press, 2011.

Lieven, D. "Empire, Ethnicity and Power: A Comment." In *Nationalism and War*, edited by J. A. Hall and S. Malešević, 197–211. Cambridge: Cambridge University Press, 2013.

Lindsay-Poland, J. "The Normalization of Militarism and Propensity for War." In *Preventing War and Promoting Peace: A Guide for Health Professionals*, edited by W. H. Wiist and S. K. White, 77–89. New York: Cambridge University Press, 2017.

Liu, J. H., R. J. Zhang, A. K. Leung, H. G. Zúñiga, C. Gastardo-Conaco, V. Vasuitynskyi, et al. "Empirical Correlates of Cosmopolitan Orientation: Etiology and Functions in a Worldwide Representative Sample." *Political Psychology* 41 (2020): 661–678.

Lorenz, K. *On Aggression*. New York: Bantam, 1966.

Lowe, K. *The Fear and the Freedom: How the Second World War Changed Us*. London: Penguin, 2018.

Malešević, S. "Obliterating Heterogeneity through Peace: Nationalisms, States and Wars, in the Balkans." In *Nationalism and War*, edited by J. A. Hall and S. Malešević, 262–267. Cambridge: Cambridge University Press, 2013.

Mana, A. "Knowledge about the 'Others', Perspective Taking, and Anxiety about Intergroup Contact in a Natural Intergroup Setting." *Peace and Conflict: Journal of Peace Psychology* 25 (2019): 276–286.

Mann, M. "The Role of Nationalism in the Two World Wars." In *Nationalism and War*, edited by J. A. Hall and S. Malešević, 172–196. Cambridge: Cambridge University Press, 2013.

Marshall, S. L. A. *Men against Fire: The Problem of Battle Command in Future War*. Brand: University of Oklahoma Press, 1947.

Martin, M. J., and C. W. Sasser. *Predator: The Remote-Control Air War over Iraq and Afghanistan: A Pilot's Perspective*. Minneapolis: Zenith Press, 2010.

McGoldrick, A. "News as Entertainment: The Ultimate War Propaganda Machine, or Opportunity to Promote Peace?" In *Preventing War and Promoting Peace: A Guide for Health Professionals*, edited by W. H. Wiist and S. K. White, 129–140. New York: Cambridge University Press, 2017.

McKeown, S., and C. Psaltis. "Intergroup Contact and the Mediating Role of Intergroup Trust on Outgroup Evaluation and Future Contact Intentions in Cyprus and Northern Ireland." *Peace and Conflict: Journal of Peace Psychology* 23 (2017): 392–404.

Medact. *The Recruitment of Children by the UK Armed Forces: A Critique from Health Professionals*. London: Medact, 2016.

Melander, E. "Gender Equality and Intrastate Armed Conflict." *International Studies Quarterly* 49 (2005): 695–714.

Miller, B. "The State-to-Nation Balance and War." In *Nationalism and War*, edited by J. A. Hall and S. Malešević, 73–96. Cambridge: Cambridge University Press, 2013.

Modood, T. "A Multicultural Nationalism?" *Brown Journal of World Affairs*, 25, no. 2 (2019): 233–246.

Montiel, C. J., E. de la Paz, and Z. I. Cerafica. "(De)Humanization and Trust in an Asymmetric Muslim–Christian Conflict: Heroes, Kafirs, and Satanas." *Peace and Conflict: Journal of Peace Psychology* 25 (2019): 300–311.

Morris, I. *War: What Is It Good For? The Role of Conflict in Civilisation, from Primates to Robots*. London: Profile Books, 2015.

Mosse, G. *Fallen Soldiers: Reshaping the Memory of the World Wars*. New York: Oxford University Press, 1990.

Mueller, J. "The Iraq Syndrome." *Foreign Affairs* 84 (2005): 44–54.

Naím, M. *The End of Power: From Boardrooms to Battlefields and Churches to States, Why Being in Charge Isn't What It Used to Be*. New York: Basic Books, 2013.

Nash, W. P., and B. T. Litz. "Moral Injury: A Mechanism for War-Related Psychological Trauma in Military Family Members." *Clinical Child and Family Psychological Review* 16 (2013): 365–375.

Noor, M. "Can Psychology Find a Path to Peace?" *The Psychologist* 29 (February 2016): 108.

Nussbaum, M. "Kant and Stoic Cosmopolitanism." *Journal of Political Philosophy* 5 (1997): 1–25.

Orford, J. "The Rules of Interpersonal Complementarity: Does Hostility Beget Hostility and Dominance, Submission?" *Psychological Review* 93 (1986): 365–377.

Orford, J. "The Interpersonal Circumplex: A Theory and Method for Applied Psychology." *Human Relations* 46 (1994): 1347–1375.

Orford, J. "Turning Psychology against Militarism." *Journal of Community & Applied Social Psychology* 27 (2017): 287–297.

Orford, J. "Psychology, History and War: Two Examples of Academic Discourses Which fail to Oppose War and Militarism." *The Journal of Critical Psychology, Counselling and Psychotherapy* 19 (2019): 48–59.

Özdemir, F., and N. S. Uğurlu. "Development of Militaristic Attitudes Scale and Its Associations with Turkish Identity and Uninational Ideology." *Peace and Conflict: Journal of Peace Psychology* 24 (2018): 175–187.

Pemberton, M. "The War Profiteers: Defense Contractors Driving the Permanent War Economy." In Wiist, W.H., and White, S.K. (eds.), *Preventing War and Promoting Peace: A Guide for Health Professionals*, edited by W. H. Wiist and S. K. White, 116–128. New York: Cambridge University Press, 2017.

Pettigrew, T. F. "Intergroup Contact Theory." *Annual Review of Psychology* 49 (1998): 65–85.

Pettigrew, T. F. "Secondary Transfer Effect of Contact: Do Intergroup Contact Effects Spread to Noncontacted Outgroups?" *Social Psychology* 40 (2009): 55–65.

Pettigrew, T. F., and M. Hewstone. "The Single Factor Fallacy: Implications of Missing Critical Variables from an Analysis of Intergroup Contact Theory." *Social Issues and Policy Review* 11 (2017): 8–37.

Pettigrew, T. F., and L. R. Tropp. "A Meta-Analytic Test of Intergroup Contact Theory." *Journal of Personality and Social Psychology* 90 (2006): 751–783.

Pettigrew, T. F., and L. R. Tropp. "How Does Intergroup Contact Reduce Prejudice? Meta-Analytic Test of Three Mediators." *European Journal of Social Psychology* 38 (2008): 922–934.

Piketty, T. *Capital in the Twenty-First Century*. Translated by A. Goldhammer. Cambridge, MA: Belknap Press of Harvard University Press, 2017.

Pilger, J. *The New Rulers of the World*. London: Verso, 2002.

Pilisuk, M., and J. A. Rowntree. *The Hidden Structure of Violence: Who Benefits from Global Violence and War*. New York: Monthly Review Press, 2015.

Pinker, S. *The Better Angels of Our Nature: A History of Violence and Humanity*. London: Penguin Books, 2012.

Porter, E. "Women, Political Decision-Making, and Peace-Building." *Global Change, Peace & Security* 15, no. 3 (2003): 245–262.

Potts, M., and T. Hayden. *Sex and War: How Biology Explains Warfare and Terrorism and Offers a Path to a Safer World*. Dallas, TX: Benbella Books, 2008.

Pratkanis, A. R., and E. Aronson. *Age of Propaganda*. 2nd ed. New York: W. H. Freeman, 2001.

Pratto, F., J. Sidanius, and S. Levin. "Social Dominance Theory and the Dynamics of Intergroup Relations: Taking Stock and Looking Forward." *European Review of Social Psychology* 17 (2006): 271–320.

Prokosch, E. *The Technology of Killing: A Military and Political History of Antipersonnel Weapons*. London: Zed Books, 1995.

Puri, K. *Partition Voices: Untold British Stories*. London: Bloomsbury, 2019.
Pyszczynski, T., A. Abdollahi, S. Solomon, J. Greenberg, F. Cohen, and D. Weise. "Mortality Salience, Martyrdom, and Military Might: The Great Satan versus the Axis of Evil." *Personality and Social Psychology Bulletin* 32 (2006): 525–537.
Pyszczynski, T., J. Greenberg, and S. Solomon. "A Dual Process Model of Defense against Conscious And Unconscious Death-Related Thoughts: An Extension of Terror Management Theory." *Psychological Review* 106 (1999): 835–845.
Rampton, S., and J. Stauber. *Weapons of Mass Deception: The Uses of Propaganda in Bush's War on Iraq*. New York: Tarcher/Penguin, 2003.
Reich, R. *The Work of Nations: Preparing Ourselves for 21st Century Capitalism*. London: Simon & Schuster, 1993.
Reicher, S. "The Context of Social Identity: Domination, Resistance, and Change." *Political Psychology* 25 (2004): 921–945.
Reifler, J., T. J. Scotto, and H. D. Clarke. "Foreign Policy Beliefs in Contemporary Britain: Structure and Relevance." *International Studies Quarterly* 55 (2011): 245–266.
Reimer, N., and N. Sengupta. "Meta-Analysis of the "Ironic" Effects of Intergroup Contact." *Journal of Personality and Social Psychology* 124 (2023): 362–380.
Rhodes, E. "The Unique Needs of Female Veterans." *The Psychologist* (July 12, 2021). https://www.bps.org.uk/psychologist/unique-needs-female-veterans.
Rios, K. "An Experimental Approach to Intergroup Threat Theory: Manipulations, Moderators, and Consequences of Realistic vs. Symbolic Threat." *European Review of Social Psychology* 29 (2018): 212–255.
Rodin, D. *War and Self-Defense*. Oxford: Oxford University Press, 2002.
Rousseau, J.-J. *A Discourse upon the Origin and the Foundation of the Inequality among Mankind*. Project Gutenberg. https://www.gutenberg.org/ebooks/11136. First published 1755.
Routledge, C., and J. Arndt. "Self-Sacrifice as Self-Defence: Mortality Salience Increases Efforts to Affirm a Symbolic Immortal Self at the Expense of the Physical Self." *European Journal of Social Psychology* 38 (2008): 531–541.
Rovenpor, D. R., T. C. O'Brian, A. Roblain, L. De Guissme, P. Checkroun, and B. Leidner. "Intergroup Conflict Self-Perpetuates via Meaning: Exposure to Intergroup Conflict Increases Meaning and Fuels a Desire for Further Conflict." *Journal of Personality and Social Psychology* 116 (2019): 119–140.
Royse, M. W. *Aerial Bombardment and the International Regulation of Warfare*. New York: H. Vinal, 1928.
Rubin, M., and M. Hewstone. "Social Identity Theory's Self-Esteem Hypothesis: A Review and Some Suggestions for Clarification." *Personality and Social Psychology Review* 2 (1998): 40–62.
Salines, G., and A. Amimour. *We Still Have Words*. Translated by J. Hensher. New York: Scribner, 2020.
Seib, P. *Information at War: Journalism, Disinformation, and Modern Warfare*. Cambridge: Polity Press, 2021.
Shaw, M. *The New Western Way of War: Risk-Transfer War and Its Crisis in Iraq*. Cambridge: Polity Press, 2005.
Shay, J. *Achilles in Vietnam: Combat Trauma and the Undoing of Character*. New York: Scribner, 1994.
Sherif, M., O. Harvey, J. White, W. Hood, and C. Sherif. *Intergroup Conflict and Cooperation: The Robber's Cave Experiment*. Norman, OK: University Book Exchange, 1961.

Sidanius, J., and J. R. Petrocik. "Communal and National Identity in a Multiethnic State: A Comparison of Three Perspectives." In *Social Identity, Intergroup Conflict, and Conflict Reduction*, edited by R. Ashmore, L. Jussim, and D. Wilder, 101–132. New York: Oxford University Press, 2001.

Sidanius, J., and F. Pratto. *Social Dominance: An Intergroup Theory of Social Hierarchy and Oppression*. Cambridge: Cambridge University Press, 1999.

Silvestri, L. "Surprise Homecomings and Vicarious Sacrifices." *Media, War & Conflict* 6 (2013): 101–115.

Singh, G. "Sikhism and Just War." In *Just War in Comparative Perspective*, edited by P. Robinson, 126–136. Burlington, VT: Ashgate, 2003.

Smith, H. P., and R. M. Bohm. "Beyond Anomie: Alienation and Crime." *Critical Criminology* 16 (2008): 1–15.

Smith, L. *Voices against War: A Century of Protest*. Edinburgh: Mainstream, 2010.

Snyder, J. *Myths of Empire: Domestic Politics and International Ambition*. Ithaca, NY: Cornell University Press, 1991.

Solomon, B. "Kant's Perpetual Peace: A New Look at This Centuries-Old Quest." *The Online Journal of Peace and Conflict Resolution* 5 (2015): 106–126.

Staal, M. A., and C. H. Greene. "An Examination of 'Adversarial' Operational Psychology." *Peace and Conflict: Journal of Peace Psychology* 21 (2015): 264–268.

Stansky, P., and W. Abrahams. *Journey to the Frontier*. Boston: Atlantic Monthly Press, 1966.

Steele, B. "Welcome Home! Routines, Ontological Insecurity and the Politics of US Military Reunion Videos." *Cambridge Review of International Affairs* 32 (2019): 322–343.

Sternberg, M., H. T. Litvak, and S. Sagy. "'Nobody Ever Told Us': The Contribution of Intragroup Dialogue to Reflective Learning about Violent Conflict." *Peace and Conflict: Journal of Peace Psychology* 24 (2018): 127–138.

Stevens, A. *The Roots of War and Terror*. London: Continuum, 2004.

Strauss, B. "The Dead of Arginusae and the Debate about the Athenian Navy." *Nautiki Epithewrisi [Naval Review]* 545 (2004): 40–67.

Strawser, B. J. "Moral Predators: The Duty to Employ Uninhabited Aerial Vehicles." *Journal of Military Ethics* 9 (2010): 342–368.

Sumner, W. G. *Folkways: A Study of Mores, Manners, Customs and Morals*. New York: Cosimo, 2007. First published 1906.

Tajfel, H., and J. C. Turner. "An Integrative Theory of Intergroup Conflict." In *The Social Psychology of Intergroup Relations*, edited by W. G. Austin and S. Worchel, 33–48. Monterey, CA: Brooks/Cole, 1979.

Taylor, P. M. *Munitions of the Mind: A History of Propaganda from the Ancient World to the Present Day*. 3rd ed. Manchester, UK: Manchester University Press, 2003.

Terkel, S. *The Good War. An Oral History of World War Two*. New York: Vintage, 1985.

Thomas, H. *The Spanish Civil War*. London: Readers' Union, 1962.

Thompson, J. *Psychological Aspects of Nuclear War*. London: The British Psychological Society/John Wiley, 1985.

Thomson, Lord. "Aerial Warfare and Disarmament." *Survey* 53 (1925): 503–506.

Tiger, L. *Men in Groups*. London: Panther, 1971.

Tilly, C. "Reflections on the History of European State-Making." In *The Formation of National States in Western Europe*, edited by C. Tilly, 3–83. Princeton, NJ: Princeton University Press, 1975.

Timms, E. *Karl Krauss: Apocalyptic Satirist*. New Haven, CT: Yale University Press, 1986.

Tropp, L. R., D. R. Hawi, T. C. O'Brien, M. Gheorghiu, A. Zetes, and D. A. Butz. "Intergroup Contact and the Potential for Post-Conflict Reconciliation: Studies in Northern Ireland and South Africa." *Peace and Conflict: Journal of Peace Psychology* 23 (2017): 239-249.

Tropp, L. R., A. Mazziotta, and S. C. Wright. "Recent Developments in Intergroup Contact Research: Affective Processes, Group Status, and Contact Valence." In *Cambridge Handbook of the Psychology of Prejudice*, edited by F. Barlow and C. Sibley, 463-480. Cambridge: Cambridge University Press, 2016.

Tropp, L. R., and T. F. Pettigrew. "Relationships between Intergroup Contact and Prejudice among Minority and Majority Status Groups." *Psychological Science* 16 (2005): 951-957.

Tryandafyllidou, A. "Nationalism in the 21st Century: Neo-tribal or Plural?" *Nations and Nationalism* 26 (2021): 792-806.

Uexkull, N., M. d'Errico, and J. Jackson. "Drought, Resilience, and Support for Violence: Household Survey Evidence from DR Congo." *Journal of Conflict Resolution* 64, no. 10 (2020): 1994-2021.

Uluğ, Ö. M., and J. C. Cohrs. "Examining the Ethos of Conflict by Explaining Lay People's Representations of the Kurdish Conflict in Turkey." *Conflict Management and Peace Science* 36 (2019): 169-190.

Vagts, A. *A History of Militarism*. New York: Free Press, 1959.

Vallacher, R., P. Coleman, A. Novak, and L. Bui-Wrzosinska. "Rethinking Intractable Conflict: The Perspective of Dynamical Systems." In *Conflict Interdependence, and Justice: The Intellectual Legacy of Morton Deutsch*, edited by P. Coleman, 65-94. New York: Springer, 2011.

Van Creveld, M. *The Transformation of War*. New York: Free Press, 1991.

Van Creveld, M. *The Culture of War*. New York: Ballantine, 2008.

Van den Toorn, R. "Just War and the Perspective of Ethics of Care." In *Just War in Comparative Perspective*, edited by P. Robinson, 218-229. Burlington, VT: Ashgate, 2003.

Van der Linden, N., B. Bizumic, R. Stubager, and S. Mellon. "Social Representational Correlates of Attitudes towards Peace and War: A Cross-Cultural Analysis in the United States and Denmark." *Peace and Conflict: Journal of Peace Psychology* 17 (2011): 217-242.

Virden, J. "Justifying Killing: US Army Chaplains of World War II." In *Just War in Comparative Perspective*, edited by P. Robinson, 187-199. Burlington, VT: Ashgate, 2003.

Von Clausewitz, C. *On War*. Edited and translated by M. Howard and P. Paret. Princeton, NJ: Princeton University Press, 1976. First published 1832.

Von Zimmermann, J., and D. Richardson. "Synchrony and the Art of Signalling." *The Psychologist* (June 2018): 32-36.

Walter, B. F. *How Civil Wars Start: And How to Stop Them*. New York: Penguin Random House, 2022.

Walzer, M. *Just and Unjust Wars*. New York: Basic Books, 1977.

Walzer, M. "The New Tribalism: Notes on a Difficult Problem." In *Theorizing Nationalism*, edited by R. Beiner, 205-217. Albany: State University of New York Press, 1999.

Watkins, H., and B. Bastion. "Lest We Forget: The Effect of War Commemorations on Regret, Positive Moral Emotions, and Support for War." *Social Psychology and Personality Science* 10 (2019): 1084-1091.

Watson, P. *War on the Mind: The Military Uses and Abuses of Psychology*. Harmondsworth, UK: Penguin, 1980.

Webster, A. "Justifiable War in Eastern Orthodox Christianity." In *Just War in Comparative Perspective*, edited by P. Robinson, 40–61. Burlington, VT: Ashgate, 2003.

White, F. A. "Improving Intergroup Relations between Catholics and Protestants in Northern Ireland via E-Contact." *European Journal of Social Psychology* 49 (2019): 429–438.

White, R. K., ed. *Psychology and the Prevention of Nuclear War*. New York: New York University Press, 1986.

White, R. W. "Social and Role Identities and Political Violence: Identity as a Window on Violence in Northern Ireland." In *Social Identity, Intergroup Conflict, and Conflict Reduction*, edited by R. Ashmore, L. Jussim, and D. Wilder, 133–158. New York: Oxford University Press, 2001.

Wiist, W. H., and S. K. White, eds. *Preventing War and Promoting Peace: A Guide for Health Professionals*. New York: Cambridge University Press, 2017.

Wilkes, G. "Judaism and Justice in War." In *Just War in Comparative Perspective*, edited by P. Robinson, 9–23. Burlington, VT: Ashgate, 2003.

Winter, D. D. N., M. Pilisuk, S. Houck, and M. Lee. "Understanding Militarism: Money, Masculinity, and the Search for the Mystical." In *Peace, Conflict and Violence: Peace Psychology for the 21st Century*, edited by D. J. Christie, R. V. Wagner, and D. D. N. Winter, 139–148. Englewood Cliffs, NJ: Prentice-Hall, 2001.

Winter, D. G. *Roots of War: Wanting Power, Seeing Threat, Justifying Force*. New York: Oxford University Press, 2018.

Wölfer, R., O. Christ, K. Schmid, N. Tausch, F. M. Buchallik, S. Vertovec, et al. "Indirect Contact Predicts Direct Contact: Longitudinal Evidence and the Mediating Role of Intergroup Anxiety." *Journal of Personality and Social Psychology* 116, no. 2 (2019): 277–295.

Wolfers, A. *Discord and Collaboration: Essays on International Politics*. Baltimore: Johns Hopkins University Press, 1962.

Wood, D. *What Have We Done: The Moral Injury of Our Longest Wars*. New York: Little, Brown and Company, 2016.

Zigenlaub, E., and S. Sagy. "Encountering the Narrative of the 'Other': Comparing Two Types of Dialogue Groups of Jews and Arabs in Israel." *Peace and Conflict: Journal of Peace Psychology* 26 (2020): 88–91.

Zwald, Z., and J. Berejikian. "Is There a Public–Military Gap in the United States? Evaluating Foundational Foreign Policy Beliefs." *Armed Forces and Society* 48, no. 4 (2022): 982–1002.

Index

For the benefit of digital users, indexed terms that span two pages (e.g., 52–53) may, on occasion, appear on only one of those pages.
Tables and figures are indicated by *t* and *f* following the page number

Aboriginal Australia, communal fighting through, 48–49
absolutists, 204
Abu Ghraib prison scandal, 159
acceptance of readiness for war
  not supporting war by resisting, 239
  Ukraine war, 231
  war support model (WSM), 218–20, 224f, 225f
actor-observer discrepancy, 105
addiction, 1
adversarial operational psychology (AOP), 215–16
Afghanistan, signature injury in, 29–30
Afghanistan war, 150–51, 175
Africa's First World War, Congo's wars of 1998 to 2004, 27
Agent Orange, Vietnam, 34
Age of Religions, 181
Aitkin, Sir Max, 161
Albright, Madeleine, 26
alienation, 58
Allied Democratic Forces, 208–9
Allison, Graham, 6–8, 236–38, 240–41
All-Party Parliamentary Group for World Governance, 82–83
Allport, Gordon, 114
al-Qaeda, 166
Altemeyer's understanding, authoritarianism, 59
alternatives, 204
altruism, 49–50
American Anthropological Association, 50, 135
American Civil War, 20, 165
American Friends Service Committee, 126
American Holocaust, 35
American Jewish Committee, Department of Scientific Research, 59

American Psychological Association, 37–38, 135, 215–16
American Psychologist (journal), 111–12, 117–18
American Public Health Association, 135
American Revolution, 87
American Revolutionary War, 54–55
America's Army (game), 128–30
analogical reasoning, 104
anarchy rules, international system, 20–23
Anglo-Dutch wars, 141
Angola, children displaced by war in, 32
animalistic dehumanization, 102
anocracies, term, 22–23
anomia, definition of, 58
Ansar Dine, Mali, 166
appeasement of Hitler, 104
Aquinas, Thomas, 186, 191
Arab-Israeli rivalry, 16
Arc de Triomphe, 136–37
Ardrey, Robert, 47–48
Arendt, Hannah, 197–98
armed conflict
  enemy and, 10
  intractable, 112
  Levy-Thompson sense of, 18
Armed Forces, 149–50
Armed Forces and Society (journal), 149–50
armed hostility, outbreak of, 47
Armenian-Azerbaijan war, 53–54, 209–10
Armistice Day, 136–37
arms dealing, shadowy world of, 143–46
arms trade, support for, 219
Arquilla, John, 25–26
Aryan superiority, 79–80
Ascherson, Neal, 234–35
"asymmetric" violent conflict, 25–26
Atomic Bomb Dexterity Puzzle (game), 130
attractiveness of war, 46

INDEX

attractor, 120–21
Augustine, 186, 187–88, 193–94, 206
Austro-Hungarian Empire, 90
authoritarianism, 9, 46–47, 59, 72–73
    Altemeyer's understanding of, 59
    right-wing (RWA), 59–61
Authoritarian Personality, The (American Jewish Committee), 59
authority ranking (AR), 201–2
Authorization for the Use of Military Force, 193–94
availability heuristic, 104, 222–23
Azerbaijan, Armenia and, 53–54, 209–10

Bacevich, Andrew, 6–8, 141–42, 148–49, 151, 182–83, 192–93
Baden-Powell, General, 165
Baghdad Broadcasting Corporation, 164
Balkan conflict, Croatian images of Serbs, 100
Balkan wars, 162, 173
Balloon Site 568 (film), 158
banality, concept of, 197–98
Bandura, Albert, 198–201
Barker, Kathy, 134, 135
Battlefield Vietnam (game), 128–29
Battle of Britain, 19, 139–40
Battle of the Somme, 182
Battleship Potemkin (film), 158–59
Bay of Pigs invasion, Cuba, 159
BBC Promenade Concerts, 77
BBC radio, 210
    Reith Lectures (2018), 37, 247n.111
BBC television, *A Man's World*, 62
Beaverbrook, Lord, 191
Behind Enemy Lines (film), 130–31
Beinart, Peter, 209
Belanger, Jocelyn J., 6–8
belief in a just world theory, 147
Bennett, Beth, 171–72
Better Angels of Our Nature, The (Pinker), 6–8, 39, 213–14
Biden, president, 234–35
Billig, M., 77
bin Laden, Osama, 184
Black Hawk Down (film), 162–63
Black Wave (Ghattas), 94–95
Blair, Tony, 184–85
Blood Rites (Ehrenreich), 6–8, 51–52, 62
Boar War, 165

body bags, 191–92
Boer War (1899–1902), 141
Bok, Sissela, 197–98
Bombshell (game), 130
Bosnia-Herzegovina
    ethnic cleansing, 92–93
    war in, 26–27
Bourke, Joanna, 6–8, 24–25, 62, 69, 128–31, 138–39, 140, 187–88, 191–93, 196, 214
Boxing Day 1915, 89
brain, psychology and, 67–68
British-American Security Information Council, 210–11
British Board of Film Censors, certificate, 158
British militarism, 146–47
British Military Covenant, 149–50, 182–83
British Psychological Society (BPS), 235
Brittain, Vera, 51
Britten, Benjamin, 37
Brockway, Fenner, 204–5
Brooke, Rupert, 53
Brosnan, Con, 203–4
Brother in Arms (game), 128–29
Bryce Report, 157–58
Buchan, John, 100
Buddhism, 181, 185, 205–6
Buddhist ultranationalists, 167–68
Burma campaigns, General Slim, 101–2
Bush, George H. W., 187–88
Bush, George W., 103–4, 142–43, 145, 149, 159–60, 193–94
Bush doctrine, 193–94

Cambridge Review of International Affairs, 170–71, 172–73
Cameroon, 208–9
Campaign for Nuclear Disarmament, 205
Camus, Albert, 82–83
Canadian War Museum, 37
capitalist peace hypothesis, 39–40
Catholic Church, 183
Catholics, 181
causes and values, 178
Causes of War, The (Levy and Thompson), 6–8, 16, 39–40, 94, 117–18, 169
Causes of War and the Spread of Peace, The (Gat), 6–8, 36
Cavell, Edith, 157–58
Cenotaph, 136–37

Centano, Miguel, 6–8, 19, 42, 61–62, 69–70, 75
Central Intelligence Agency, 134–35
Chamayou, Grégoire, 6–8, 142–43, 195–96, 216
chauvinism, 9–10, 81, 90
  cultural exclusivity and, 81–82
  culturalism and, 82
  term, 79–80
chauvinistic, term, 96
Chechnyan war, 71–72
Chief of Chaplains, Washington DC, 183
children
  costs of war for, 32
  as soldiers, 32
China, 103–4
  Chinese-US conflict, 22
  danger of war between US and, 236–38
  propaganda, 101–2
  tension with United States, 6, 22
  United States and, 170–71
Chinese Communist Party, 103–4, 172–73
Chomsky, Noam, 164–65
Christians, 181, 182–83
Churchill, Winston, 139–40, 158, 191
Church of Scotland, 182
Cinderella, 107
circular error probable, 191–92
City of God, The (Augustine), 185
City University of New York, 209
civic nationalism, 80
civic society
  militarism summary, 153*f*
  militarization of, 128–35
civilian(s)
  casualties as costs of war, 30–32
  death by disease during war, 32
  forced displacement of, 31–32
  immunity, principle, 205–6
  injuries during war, 31
Civilisation (game), 130
climate change, 212–13, 240–41
Clinton, president, 234–35
Clooney, Francis, 184–85
close out-groups, 113
Coca-Colonialism, 176
coercion, 47–48
cognitive bias, 105
cognitive complexity, 105–6
cognitive dissonance, Festinger's idea of, 197–98

cognitive simplicity, 105–6
cognitive simplicity versus complexity, 171, 178, 222
cognitive-social, term, 98–99
coherence, conflict, 54
Cold War, 16, 27, 28, 70, 82–83, 92, 100, 107, 134, 143, 160, 170, 210–11, 231
collaborative operational psychology (COP), 215–16
collateral damage, 191–92
collective activity, war as, 55
collective values and beliefs, 58
combatant, definition of, 191–92
commercial pacifism, 39–40
Committee on Public Information, US propaganda and, 173
common in-group identity model, cosmopolitanism, 86–87
commotion (concussion), 30
communal sharing (CS), 201–2
Communist Party, 52
competitive world belief (CWB), 59–60
complexity, concept of, 171
comprehension, conflict, 54
conchies, 204
conflict
  meaning in, 54–55
  relationships with, 54
Conflict: Desert Storm (game), 129–30
conflict-cohesion hypothesis, 109–10
conflict-gives-meaning theory, 56–57
conflict-perpetuating beliefs, 54–55
conflicts, spiral conflict model, 119–22
conflict trap, 212–13
Confucianism, 181
Congo Wars (1996-97 and 1998-2003), 92–93
Congo wars (1998 to 2004), *Africa's First World War*, 27
conscientious objection, war and, 204–5
conscientious objectors (COs), 204–5
conscription, *levée en masse*, 20
consequences, UN criteria, 194
conspiracy theory, 106
conspiratorial narrative, 106
contact hypothesis, 114
contact theory, research, 118
contaminated in-group, 113–14, 228–29
contemplation, war support model, 225–26, 226*f*, 227

cooperation, 214
co-optation, 214
Coriolanus (Shakespeare), 69
Cornford, John, 50–51
Correlates of War Project, 16–17, 27, 41–42
Corruption Perception Index (CPI), 71
cosmopolitanism, 82–87
  term, 84–85
  values and, 9–10
costs of war, 29–34, 44t
  civilian casualties, 30–32
  economic, 33–34
  environmental, 34
  environmental damage, 34
  infrastructure, 33
  societies infrastructure and economies, 33–34
Counter Terrorism Information Strategy Policy Coordinating Committee, White House, 159–60
COVID crisis, 2
Crimean War, 162–63, 165
critical evaluation of their own group, 117–18
Croatia, war in, 26–27
Croatian News Agency, 174
Cromwell's New Model Army, 181
Cross of Sacrifice, 182
Crown Film Unit, Ministry of Information (MOI), 158
Cuba, Bay of Pigs invasion of, 159
Cuban Missile Crisis (1962), 170, 233
cultural diplomacy, term, 176
cultural gap, 10–11, 126, 151, 154
cultural imperialism, 176
culturalism, 81
cultural nationalism, 80–81
cultural openness (CO), 83–84
cultural propaganda, 176
cultural worldview, terror management theory (TMT), 55
culture
  militarism summary, 153f
  militarization of, 128–35
Czechoslovakia, Soviet invasion of (1968), 16

Daily Express (newspaper), 161
Daily Mail (newspaper), 161, 164
Daily News (newspaper), 173
Dam Busters, The (film), 139–40
dangerous world belief (DWB), 59–60

Davies, Frank, 63
D-Day Normandy landings, 19, 90
Dearey, Paul, 183
death
  cost of war, 29
  inevitability of, 56
death instinct, life instinct and, 47–48
decadence, word, 63–64
Defence of the Realm Act (1914), 161–62
defense
  concept of, 184
  military capability, 18
Defense Documentation Center (DDC), 214–15
dehumanization
  animalistic, 102
  mechanistic, 102
  violence-justifying, 101–4
democracy, autocracy and, 22–23
democratic peace, 90
democratic peace theory, 22–23
Democratic Republic of the Congo, 208–9
demon, 102
Denmark, men *vs* women, 67
deprovincialization, 118–19
Der Derian, J., 130–31
Desert Storm, 193
Destined for War (Allison), 6–8
Deutsch, Morton, 119–20
Dismembering the Male (Bourke), 62
distinctiveness threat, 110
Dixon, Norman, 133
dominance, 9–10
Doomsday Clock, 210–11
double effect, doctrine of, 191
double intention, doctrine of, 191
Dower, John, 101–2
Drone Theory (Chamayou), 6–8, 142–43, 195–96
drone welfare, 195–96
Druckman, Daniel, 88
Dublin Easter Rising (1916), 53, 174–75
Duriesmith, David, 6–8, 64
Dutch East India Company, 187

economic interdependence, 39–40
economics, costs of war, 33–34
ecstasy, war mood, 51–52
education, militarization of, 10–11, 132–35
Edwards, Norman, 63
egalitarianism, 36–37

Ehrenreich, Barbara, 6–8, 51–52, 62, 69–70
Ehrhart, William, 130–31
Einstein, Albert, 82–83, 210–11
Einstein, Sergei, 158–59
Eisenhower, Dwight, 145
Elias, Norbert, 39–40
Eliot, T. S., 207
empathic ability, 117
enemy/enemies, 103–4
    dehumanization, 101–4
    identification of, 220–21
    identifying and demonizing, 99–104
    leaders and, 172–75
    negative, demonizing images of 222
    potential, 220–21
    psychological theory, 10
    See also "us" and "them"
enemy image theory, 100
engagement, war support model, 225–26, 226f, 228–29
England, 75–76
English Nationalism (Black), 76
Enriquez, Elaine, 6–8, 19, 42, 61–62, 69–70, 75
entertainment, militarization of culture, 128–35
environmental damage, costs of war, 34
Epistle to Marcellus (Aquinas), 186
equality matching (EM), 201–2
Erikson, Erik, 107
Eros, Thanatos and, 47–48
escalation of conflict, 178
Ethical Theory and Moral Practice (journal), 84, 86–87
ethic of heroic sacrifice, 196
ethics of care, code, 67–68
Ethics of War and Peace, The (Frowe), 6–8, 185–86
ethnic cleansing, Bosnia-Herzegovina, 92–93
ethnic nationalism, 80, 231
ethnic wars, 25–26
Euripides, 107–8
European Federation of Psychologists' Associations, 235
European Union (EU), 75–76, 77–78
evolutionary theory, 84
exclusivism, 92–93
extreme emergency, non-combatant immunity, 191

Facebook, 166, 167–68, 182–83
failed states, 26

fairness, 198
Falklands War (1982), 163–64
Fallen Soldiers (Mosse), 6–8, 50–51, 63–64, 128, 182
far out-groups, 113
Fear and the Freedom, The (Lowe), 6–8, 82–83, 98
Feinstein, Andrew, 6–8, 145
female suffrage, 37
feminism, 68
Ferguson, Niall, 6–8, 50, 51, 89, 161, 182
Festinger, Leon, 197–98
films, militarization of culture, 128–35
Financial Times (journal), 94–95
First Congolese War (1993), 57
First World War, 20, 22, 23–24
    deaths in, 30–31
    Ferguson on, 89
    nationalism, 88–89
    study of letters of Australian soldiers, 50–51
Fiske, Alan, 201–2
Five Hundred Years' War, 35
flash wars, 211
forced displacement, civilians during war, 31–32
ForcesWatch, 132–33, 134
Fore of New Guinea, 48
Francis, Ted, 63
French Revolution, 20, 52, 80, 87
Freud, Sigmund, 47–48
Frowe, Helen, 6–8, 185–86
Full Spectrum Warrior (game), 129–30
fundamental attribution error, 105

Gambia, 208
games, militarization of culture, 128–35
Gat, Azar, 6–8, 21, 27–28, 36, 39–41, 48–50, 66, 149, 200–1, 236–37
Gates, Robert, 134–35
Gaza War (2008–09), 166
Gaza War (2014), 166
gender, attitudes toward war, 66–72
General Treaty for the Renunciation of War (1928), 23
Geneva Convention, 145–46, 189, 190, 193–94, 205–6
Geneva Protocols (1977), 189
George, Lloyd, 161
German militarism, 173

German Youth Movement, 63–64
Gessen, Keith, 235
Ghattas, Kim, 94–95
Gilligan, Carol, 67–68
Global Peace Index (GPI), 71
global prosociality (GP), 83–84
global terrorism, 240–41
globocop
    demise of British, 35
    term, 22
goal of peace, 195
Göring, Hermann, 155
Gray, Glenn, 50–51
Grayling, A. C., 6–8, 17, 42–43, 125, 127, 131, 141, 182–83, 192–93, 194, 196, 197, 240–41
Great Powers, 24
Green Berets, The (film), 130–31
Greenham Common air force base, 68
Gregory XV (Pope), 171–72
Grenfell, Julian, 50
Grotius, Hugo, 187, 190–91
group-based dominance, 79
Guantánamo detainees, 193–94
Guardian (magazine), 208
Guardian Weekly, The (magazine), 208
guerra fiesta, war as a festival, 52
Guinness World Records, 129–30
Gulf War (1991, first), 139–40, 160, 162–63, 164, 173, 187–88, 191–92, 193, 214
Gulf War (second), 193–94
Gunaratna, Rohan, 6–8
Guthrie, General, 149–50

Hague Conventions, 189
Haidt, Jonathan, 198
Haig, General, 182
Hall, John, 6–8, 48
Hamas-Israel conflict, 166
Harris, Elizabeth, 185
Harvard Thucydides's Trap Project, 236
Hathaway, Oona, 6–8, 23–24, 42, 156–57, 194
Hedges, Chris, 46, 53
hegemonic stability theory, 22
hegemony, 22
heroic justification, terrorism, 93
Heym, George, 52
Hezbollah attacks, 58
Hidden Structure of Violence, The (Pilisuk and Rowntree), 6–8, 128, 159–60, 212

Hiller, Patrick, 212–13
Hinduism, 184–85
Hiroshima, 140–41, 191
Hitler, Adolf, propaganda, 158
HMS Sheffield, 164
Hobbes, Thomas, 49–50
Hobsbawm, Eric, 52, 74, 77–78
Holocaust, 108
Holy Communion, 184
Homo sapiens, 238
Houthi rebels, 209–10
How Civil Wars Start (Walter), 6–8, 167–68
Howe, Brendan, 188–89, 192–93
Hughes, James, 94, 160–61
humanitarian intervention, 163–64
human nature
    idea that war is, 46–47
    war and, 47–50
Hungary, Soviet invasion of (1956), 16
Hussein, Saddam, 194
Hutu génocidaires' media, 113
Hutus, Rwanda civil war, 101–2

identity, embedders of, 174
identity wars, 25–26
ideological nationalism, 82
In a Different Voice (Gilligan), 67–68
independence, 170
Independence Day, 77
India, United Kingdom and, 70
individualism, 80
inequality, 212–13
Influence of the Military in Everyday Life in the UK, The (ForcesWatch report), 132
Information at War (Seib), 6–8, 166
information war, 159–60
infrastructure
    costs of war, 33
    war's destructive costs to, 33
in-groups
    defining, 112–14
    identity, 177
    loyalty, 198
    out-groups and, 108–14
    threat to the, 110–12
inherent bad faith, 105
Institute for Creative Technologies (ICT), 129
inter-democratic peace theory, 22–23
intergroup contact theory, 98–99

intergroup threat theory, 111
intergroup violence, 49
inter-male aggression, term, 67
International Brigades, 50–51
International Criminal Court, 24
international hegemon, 22
Internationalists, The (Hathaway and Shapiro), 6–8, 23, 156–57
International Studies Quarterly (journal), 71
international war, 44t
Internet Research Agency, 167
interpersonal contact theory (ICT), 5–6, 114–19
interstate wars, old, 9
intrastate wars, new, 9
Iran-Iraq war, 94
Iraq
    signature injury in, 29–30
    US invasion of, 33–34, 60–61
    US students' attitudes toward war, 66–67
    weapons of mass destruction (WMD), 159
Iraq syndrome, 229
Iraq War, 34–35, 60–61, 150–51, 175
Irish Civil War of 1922–23, 122
Irish nationalism, 94
Irish Republican Army, 130
Irish Volunteers/Irish Republic Army (IRA), 122
Irish War of Independence (1919–21), 122
Iron Curtain, 107
Isherwood, Christopher, 63–64
ISIS brides, 209–10
Islam
    Shia and Sunni, 96
    Shia-Sunni split within, 94–95
Islamic State, 166
Israel-Gaza war (2014), 54–55
Israeli Defense Forces, 21
Israeli-Palestinian conflict, 115–17, 209

James, William, 51–52, 128, 220
Janus (Koestler), 109–10
Jarecke, Ken, 162–63
Jewish Currents (Beinart), 209
Jews, Nazi term for, 101–2
jihadi groups, 163
jingoism, 89
Jinnah, Muhammad, 94–95
journalism, war, 171
journals, 8

Judaism, 184
Jung, Carl, 50, 107
Jungian psychoanalytic theory, 64–65
jus ad bellum criterion, moral rough guide, 188t
Just and Unjust Wars (Walzer), 190–91
just war, criteria, 152
Just War in Comparative Perspective, 183
just war theory, 11–12, 180–81, 205–6
    abandonment of, 192–96
    civilian immunity, 189–92
    justification for war, 185–96
    moral rough guide to making war, 188t
Juvenal, 52

kafir, 102
Kahneman, D., 198
Kalashnikov, Mikhail, 182–83
Kaldor, Mary, 18–19, 20, 26, 28–29, 64, 68, 83, 90, 93, 143, 210, 240–41
Kaldor, Mary, 6–8
Kane, Thomas, 185
Kant, Immanuel, 84–85, 187
Kartapolov, Andrei, 167
Keane, Fergal, 6–8, 53, 122, 174–75, 203–4
Kellog-Brand Pact, 23
Kellogg, Frank, 23–24
Kelsay, John, 184
Kenyan independence, 91
Kindleberger, Charles, 22
Kipling, Rudyard, 182
Kitchener, Lord, 157
knowledge, 117
Koestler, Arthur, 109–10
Korean War, 29–30, 134, 175
Kosovo
    campaign, 193–94
    Croatian children following war in, 32
    war (1999), 175
Kraus, Karl, 164–65
Kruglanski, Arie, 6–8
Kuipers, Benjamin, 135
Kurdistan Workers' Party, Turkey, 58

Lachmann, Richard, 136–37, 151–52
laissez-faire cosmopolitans, 90
Lancet (newspaper), 162–63
Latin American Public Opinion Project, 80–81
League of Iraqi Women, 68

legal arms trade, 125–26
Lemarchand, René, 27
LeShan, Lawrence, 1, 6–8, 38, 52, 53, 69, 98, 107, 162–64, 165
lethal autonomous weapons (LAWs), 211
lethal weapons, development of, 10–11
levée en masse, conscription, 20
levels of analysis, 178
Leviathan (Hobbes), 22
Levy, Jack, 6–8, 16, 22–23, 169
Levy-Thompson sense. armed conflict, 18
Lewis, Wyndham, 50
liberal internationalism, 146–47
liberation, 170
Liberation Tigers, 185
Liberian Women's Initiative, 71
life instinct. death instinct and, 47–48
life's meaning. supporting war and, 53–58
Lindsay-Poland, John, 126, 133
Lippmann, Walter, 164–65
Little Red Riding Hood, 107
Living with Artificial Intelligence (Russell), 211
London School of Economics and Political Science, 26
longevity bias, 147
Lord of the Rings, The, 107
loss of significance, 56–57
Lowe, Keith, 6–8, 31–32, 82–83, 90, 91, 98, 100–2, 240–41
Lusitania (passenger liner), sinking of, 157–58
Lynn, Vera, 19

McGoldrick, Annabel, 169
MacMillan, Margaret, 37–38, 137–38
male institution, war and, 61–72
maleness, definition of, 63–64
Malešević, Siniša, 6–8, 48
Malnutrition, Second World War in Java, 32
Manchester Guardian (newspaper), 161
manhood, definition of, 62
manifesto, term, 156–57
manliness, concept of, 63–64
Mann, Michael, 88–89, 125
Man's World, A (Humphries and Gordon), 62
market pricing (MP), 201–2
masculinity
    aspects of, understanding support for wars, 65t
    fundamental, in military, 70
    war, 69

war-supporting form of, 3, 219
Masculinity and New War (Duriesmith), 64
Mau Mau rebellion, 91
maximizing benefits-minimizing harms, 202
Max Planck Institute, 234–35
Meaney, Thomas, 234–35
meaning in conflict, 54–55
mechanistic dehumanization, 102
media
    propaganda and threat perception, 169–72
    role in engineering public consent to war, 161–72
    role of social networks and social media, 165–69
Melander, Erik, 71
Members of the Legislative Assembly, 71
memorial ceremony, 137
men, women vs., attitudes toward war, 66–72
Menuhin, Yehudi, 82–83
mercenary armies, 18–19
"merchants of death" hypothesis, 143–44
Middle Ages, 18–19, 152
militant nationalism, 64–65
militarism, 3, 78–79
    acceptance of readiness for war, 126–28
    culture and civic society, 153f
    definition, 126
    militarization and, 126, 154, 218–19
    preparedness for war, 155
    shadowy world of arms dealing, 143–46
    support for war and, 10–11, 125–26
    system justification theory (SJT), 147–48
    war support in West, 146–53
    weapons and their fascination, 139–46
    word, 154
militarization
    concept of, 126–27
    of education, 132–35
    militarism and, 10–11, 126, 154, 218–19
    role of games, films and entertainment, 128–35
    term, 127
military
    psychologists working for, 214–16
    sexual specialization of, 70
Military Covenant, 149–50, 151
military ethos, 153
military-industrial-academic complex, 214–15
military-industrial complex, 28, 148–49
military-industrial-entertainment complex, 10–11, 125, 219

military information support operations, term, 160
Mill, John Stuart, 74, 75, 93
Milne, A. A., 204–5
Milošević, Slobodan, 103–4, 173, 174
Milton, John, 156–57
minimal distinctiveness, 108–9
Ministry for Propaganda and Public Enlightenment, Goebbels, 158
modernization peace, 41
monopoly, state's, on violence, 18–19
Montenegrins, 49
moral dilemma, support for war, 11–12
moral disengagement, 5–6, 198–200
  six mechanisms of, 199t
  war support model, 223
moral foundations theory (MFT), 198
moral injury, 30
  suffering, 11–12
  war and, 202–4, 206
morality, 185
morality of war, 179
Moral Maze, The (BBC radio), 90
Moro Islamic Liberation Front (MILF), 102–3
Morris, Ian, 6–8, 20, 22, 34–35, 36, 39–40, 88, 90
mortality-defying theory, 56–57
Mosse, George, 6–8, 50–51, 52, 63–64, 128, 131, 136–37, 182
Mugesera, Léon, 101–2
Munich analogy, 104
Munitions of the Mind (Taylor), 6–8, 135, 157, 159, 160–61, 163–64
Murdoch, Rupert, 194
Muslims, 181
mystery of war support, understanding, 3–4
myths, distortion of reality and, 107–8

Nagasaki, 140–41, 191
Nakba Day, 209
Napoleon, 20, 136–37
national anthems, 77
National Association of Evangelicals, 194
national attachment, 81
national chauvinism, 9–10, 81
National Conference of Catholic Bishops, 187–88
National Health Service, 36–37
national identity, definition of, 76
nationalism, 5–6
  civic, 80

cosmopolitanism and, 84–85
cultural, 80–81
description of, 75–82
distinctions of, 78–82
ethnic, 80
multicultural, 84–85
patriotism and, 74–75, 78–81
people's support for war, 9–10
plural, 84–85
political, 80–81
relevance to "new wars," 91–96
war in defense of, 97f
willingness to go to war, 87–90
Nationalism and War (Hall and Malešević), 48, 88
Nationalism and War (Hughes), 160–61
national pride, term, 86
National Security Strategy, United States, 195
National Survival Game, The (game), 131
National War Aims Committee, 157
Nations, term, 75–76
natural tendency, war and, 4
Nature of Prejudice, The (Allport), 114
Nazi propaganda, 113
Nazis, Germany, 24
Nazism, 108
need for cognitive closure (NFC), 106
negative peace, 212
neoliberalism, 212–13
neuropsychology, 67–68
neuroscience, 67–68
New American Foundation, 142–43
New American Militarism, The (Bacevich), 6–8, 148–49, 182–83
New and Old Wars (Kaldor), 6–8, 83
New Left Review (journal), 125
New Psychology of Leadership, The (Haslam et al), 173–74
New Towns for Old (film), 158
new wars, 9, 17, 25–29
  case of, 113
  intrastate, 9
  nationalism and relevance to, 91–96
  propaganda, 11
New Western Way of War, The (Shaw), 6–8, 152
New York Times (newspaper), 145, 159–60, 162, 170, 175
Nigeria, 208
Nobel Peace Prize, Kellogg, 23–24
No-Conscription Fellowship, 204–5
No More War Movement, 204–5

Northern Ireland, 75–76, 116
  Catholic and Protestant communities, 96
  Catholic and Protestant students, 117
  "Troubles," 163–64, 165
Northern Ireland Campaign, 205
nuclear anarchy, 240–41
Nuremburg trials, 155

Obama, Barack, 142–43
Observer (newspaper), 162–63
obusite (shellitis), 30
October (film), 158–59
Officer and a Gentleman, An (film), 130–31
Official Secrets Act, 164
old wars, interstate, 9
Online Journal of Peace and Conflict Resolution, 127
On the Laws of War and Peace (Grotius), 187
On War (von Clausewitz), 14
operational psychology (OP), 215–16
Operation Restore Hope, 162–63
Opium Wars, 158
Oppenheimer's "baby," 140
optimal distinctiveness, 85
O'Rourke, Sean, 171–72
Orthodox Church, 184
Our Country (film), 158
out-groups
  close, 113
  defining, 112–14
  far, 113
  in-groups and, 108–14
over-simplification
  not supporting war by resisting, 240–41
  Ukraine war, 232
  war support model (WSM), 222–25, 224f, 225f
Overton window, 228–29
Owen, Wilfred, 50
Oxford University, 37

pacifism, 2
Palestine, conflict of Israel and, 115–16
Pan-German League, 182
Paris Peace Pact, 23, 24, 192–93
Partition Voices (Puri), 95
Partridge, G. E., 51–52
passions of war, 51–52
patriarchy, 64–65
patriotism, 9–10, 20, 63–64

  nationalism and, 74–75, 78–81
patriotism good, nationalism bad, 79–80
peace, 170
Peace and Conflict (journal), 102
Peace and Conflict: Journal of Peace Psychology (journal), 215–16
Peace and Conflict Studies (Barash and Webel), 207
Peacemaker, 140
Peace Pact, 42
Peace Pledge Union, 204–5
peace poppy, 137–38
peace psychology, 212
Peace with Honour (Milne), 204–5
Pearse, Patrick, 53, 75, 93, 174–75
Peloponnesian War, 90, 236
Pelosi, Nancy, 237–38
Pemberton, Miriam, 144–45
penicillin, 37
Pentagon, Psychological Operations, 159–60
perception management, 169
  supporting war, 11
Persian Gulf (1990-91) war, 175
personal attraction, of war, 46–47
personal feelings, 58
personal morality, psychological models of war and, 197–202
Piketty, Thomas, 36–37
Pilarczyk (Archbishop), 187–88
Pilger, John, 162–64
Pilisuk, Mark, 6–8, 27–28, 64–65, 108, 139, 144–45, 159–60, 162, 192–94, 212
Pinker, Steven, 6–8, 39, 40–41, 42–43, 49–50, 67, 68–69, 139, 152, 213–14
Pity of War, The (Ferguson), 6–8, 50
Plato, 171–72
political nationalism, 80–81
political organization
  expression, 17
  Levy-Thompson sense of, 17
Political Psychology (journal), 77–78, 81
Political Warfare Executive, United Kingdom, 160
Ponsonby, Lord, 155, 179
Ponting, Clive, 164
posttraumatic stress disorder (PTSD)
  cost of war, 30
  moral injury and, 203
post-war, expression, 15–16
poverty, violent conflict and, 212–13

INDEX   301

Powell, Colin, 193
Powell doctrine, 193
Pravda (newspaper), 158–59
Predator (bird of prey) drone, 142–43
Prejudice, dual-process model of, 60
premature cognitive closure, 104
preparation, war support model, 225–27, 226f
pre-persuasion, 169
presence, conflict, 54
Preventing War and Promoting Peace (McGoldrick), 169
Preventing War and Promoting Peace (Wiist and White), 6–8, 33
Princeton University, 19
propaganda, 37, 105, 152, 240
  Bolshevik, 158–59
  Chinese, 101–2
  contrast between respectful dialogue and, 172t
  as dirty word, 179
  enemies and leaders, 172–75
  history of, 156–61
  importance of threat perception, 169–72
  misgivings about, 175–77
  role of media in engineering public consent to war, 161–72
  role of social networks and social media, 165–69
  supporting war, 11
  term, 157
  Ukraine war, 233–34
  war support, 156, 168–69, 225, 228–29
Protestantism, 157
Protestants, 96, 117, 181, 182
psychic numbing, notion of, 197–98
psychological models of war, personal morality and, 197–202
psychological theory, enemy, 10
psychology, 1
  brain and, 67–68
  neglecting war support, 211–16
  war and, 4–5
  war support and, 9
psychology journals, 8
Psychology of War, The (LeShan), 1, 6–8, 38, 52, 98, 107
Punch (magazine), 101–2
Puri, Kavita, 95
purity or sanctity, 198

purpose, conflict, 54
Putin, Vladimir, 103–4, 231

Qatar News Agency, 167
Q-sorting, 112–13

Radio Mille Collines, Rwanda, 160–61
Radio Swan transmissions, CIA's, 160
Rai, Tage, 201–2
Rambo series (films), 130–31
reactance, 175–76
readiness for war, militarism and, 126–28
Reagan, Ronald, 140
realistic conflict theory (RCT), 111
realist international relations theory, 21–22
reality, myths and distortion of, 107–8
Reaper (angel of death) drone, 142–43
Red Bolshevik Menace, 170
reflective distinctiveness, 110
Reith Lecture
  BBC radio, 37, 137–38
  Living with Artificial Intelligence, 211
relational models, 201–2
relational models theory (RMT), 201–2
Remembrance Day, 137–38
Republican News (newspaper), 160–61
Reserve Officers' Training Corps (ROTC), 134
Resilience Index, 57–58
resilience pillars, 57–58
respect for cultural diversity (RCD), 83–84
respect for legitimate authority, 198
respectful dialogue, propaganda and, 172t
Righteous Mind, The (Haidt), 198
right-wing authoritarianism (RWA), 59–61, 66–67
Risen, James, 145
Rise of the Murch Dynasty, The (BBC TV series), 162
risk-transfer war, 10–11, 152
rivalry, between states, 21
Robber's Cave experiment, 108–9
Rohingya people, 167–68
Roman Empire, 18–19, 35
rooted cosmopolitan, 84–85
Roots of War (Winter), 6–8, 60–61, 65–66
Roots of War and Terror, The (Stevens), 6–8, 38, 46, 64–65, 100–1
Rountree, Jennifer, 108
Rousseau, Jean-Jacques, 49–50, 187

Rowntree, Jennifer, 6–8, 27–28, 64–65, 139, 144–45, 159–60, 162, 192–94, 212
Rumsfeld, Donald, 193–94
Russell, Stuart, 211
Russell, William Howard, 165
Russia
  regime, 103–4
  war between Ukraine and, 6
  See also Ukraine
Rwanda, 101–2, 160–61

Saint Augustine, 190
Saint Basil the Great, 184
Sarkozy, Nicolas, 21–22
Sartre, Jean-Paul, 82–83
Satan, 102
Saudi Wahhabism, 94–95
scholarly journals, 8
Scotland, 18, 75–76
Scott, C. P., 161
Second World War, 2, 15–16, 22, 24–25, 27, 28
  benefits of, 37
  death of "forces sweetheart" Vera Lynn, 19
  deaths in, 29, 30–31
  economic costs of, 33–34
  economic effects on war-affected countries, 33–34
  nationalism, 92
  religion's support for war, 182–83
  theory and research in psychology, 61
  women and gender inequality, 65–66
sectarianism, 94–95
security dilemma, 21
security moms, United States, 71–72
sedative effects, 118–19
Seib, Philip, 6–8, 166, 167, 168
selective attention, 104
self-categorization theory (SCT), 109
self-criticism, 105
Selfish Gene, The (Dawkins), 181
Serbia-Croatia war, 174
Seville Statement on Violence (1986), 48–49
shadow projection, 107
Shadow World, The (Feinstein), 6–8, 145
Shakespeare's *Coriolanus*, 69
Shapiro, Scott, 6–8, 23–24, 42, 156–57, 194
Shaw, Martin, 6–8, 152
Sheppard, Dick, 204–5
"signature injury," traumatic brain injury as, 29–30

Sikhism, 184–85
Singh, Gobind, 180, 184–85
Singh, Gurharpal, 184–85
Sino-Indian War, 16–17
Six Days in Fallujah (game), 130
Sixsmith, Martin, 235
Slovenia, war in, 26–27
Small Arms Survey, 143
social dominance orientation (SDO), 9, 46–47, 59–61, 66–67
social dominance theory (SDT), 66
social identity theory (SIT), 85, 98–99, 108–10
social interdependence theory, 170–71
social media
  propaganda, 165–69
  supporting war, 11
social networks, propaganda, 165–69
societies' infrastructure, costs of war, 33
soft power, 176
soldiers, 18–19
  children as, 32
Soper, Donald, 180
South China Sea, 171
Soviet Cold War Agitprop, 158–59
Soviet Union, 112–13, 170
Spanish-American War (1898), 32
Spanish Civil War, 162, 204–5
Spanish Civil War, The (Thomas), 91–92
Spanish influenza epidemic (1918), 32
Special K, 140
spiral conflict model, 119–22, 225–26
Splatball (game), 131
Stanford University, 34–35, 214–15
starvation, Second World War in Java, 32
state
  anarchy rules in international system, 20–23
  attempt to outlaw war, 23–25
  balance of power between, 22
  rivalry between, 21
  role in war, 18–25
  war and, 20
  development of militarization, 18–19, 244n.18
state terrorism, 27–28
Steinbeck, John, 107–8
Stevens, Anthony, 6–8, 38, 46, 47–48, 64–65, 68–69, 100–1, 103–4, 107–8, 131, 133
Stockholm International Peace Research Institute, 143–44, 210–11

INDEX 303

Storr, Anthony, 52
Strategic Communications Centre of Excellence, 167
Strawser, Bradley, 216
Sudanese Muslims, Black Darfuris, 101–2
suffrage leaders, 69
Summa Theologica (Aquinas), 186
Sumner, William, 84
Sun, The (newspaper), 164
Suppose They Gave a War and Nobody Came? (film), 1, 2
symbolic threat, 111
"symmetric" warfare, 25–26
Symons, Julian, 52
Syria, civil war, 209–10
Syrian conflict, 31
system justification theory (SJT), 147
   defending militarism, 148
   longevity bias, 147
   research, 148

Tajfel, Henri, 108
Taliban, propaganda by, 160–61
Tao te Ching (Tzu), 185
targeted killing, Israel's policy of assassination, 163
Taylor, Philip, 6–8, 105, 157–59, 160–61, 163–64, 175–76
Teilhard de Chardin, Pierre, 51
terrorism, 9, 27–28
   heroic justification for, 93
   3Ns model (need, narrative, network), 56–57, 93–94, 106, 111–12, 165, 217
terrorist, label, 93, 106
terror management theory (TMT), 55–56, 147
Thanatos, Eros and, 47–48
theory of cognitive dissonance, 147
Thirty-Nine Steps (Buchan), 100
Thirty Years War, 30–31, 181, 187
Thomas, Dylan, 158
Thomas, Edward, 89
Thomas, Hugh, 91–92, 94
Thompson, William, 6–8, 16, 22–23, 169
Thomson, Lord, 140
thought wars, 158, 223–24
threat and anxiety, 117
threat perception, 46–47, 178
   not supporting war by resisting, 239–40
   propaganda, 169–72
   Ukraine war, 231–32

war support model (WSM), 220–21, 224f, 225f
3Ns model (need, narrative, network), terrorism, 56–57, 93–94, 106, 111–12, 217
Three Pillars of Radicalization, The (Kruglanski, Bélanger and Gunaratna), 6–8
Thucydides, 236
Thurstan, Violeta, 51
Tilly, Charles, 18
time
   Ukraine war, 233
   war support factor, 225–29
   war support model (WSM), 225–29, 232, 233
Times, The (newspaper), 161, 165, 170
Tomb of the Unknown Soldier, 136–37
Top Gun (film), 130–31
total wars, 19, 44t
Toynbee, Arnold, 51–52
traitors, 113–14
transformed war, term, 69–70
Transformer series (films), 130–31
Transparency International, 71
traumatic brain injury, as "signature injury," 29–30
Treaty of Westphalia, 181
trench warfare, 63
Trojan Women, The (Euripides), 107–8
Tudjman, Croatian leader, 174
Turkish-Kurdish conflict, 112–13
Turner, John, 109
Tutsis, Rwanda civil war, 101–2
Twain, Mark, 80–81
Twitter, 166
Tzu, Lao, 185

Uganda, 208–9
Ukraine
   2022 war in, 152–53
   acceptance of readiness for war, 231
   on British Psychological Society (BPS), 235
   consequence of war in, 210
   over-simplification, 232
   refugees from, 31–32, 230–31
   threat perception, 231–32
   war between Russia and, 6
   war in, 213–14
   war support in, 230–36

304   INDEX

Un-American Activities Committee, 170
UNESCO, 48–49
Unique War, The (film), 130–31
unitary actor framing, 43, 103–4
United Kingdom
   India and, 70
   Ministry of Information (MOI), 158
   nationalism and war support, 75–76
   Political Warfare Executive, 160
   Scotland and, 18
United Nations (UN), 145, 192–93
   Charter of 1945, 24, 194, 205–6
   Commission of Experts, 26–27
   Security Council, 24, 194
United Nations Security Council, Resolution 1325 on Women, Peace and Security, 71
United States
   Air Force, 34
   black propaganda use in, 160
   China and, 170–71
   dangers of war between China and, 236–38
   men *vs.* women, 67
   military spending, 144–45
   9/11 attacks, 27, 79
   security moms in, 71–72
   Soviet images of, 112–13
   tension with China, 6, 12
   women in military, 70
University of Leeds, 157
University of Southern California, 129
University of Washington, 134–35
unmanned aerial vehicles (UAVs), 142, 216
Untermenschen, subhumans, 101–2
"us" and "them," 98–99
   cognitive complexity, 105–6
   defining the in-group and out-group, 112–14
   dividing people as, 104
   enemies and heroes, 123*f*
   in-groups and out-groups, 108–14
   interpersonal contact theory, 114–19
   language importance, 106
   myths and distortion of reality, 107–8
   simplistic thinking, 104, 105–6
   threat to the in-group, 110–12
US Civil War, 32
US Department of Defense, 214–15
US Memorial Day, 138–39
US Naval Postgraduate School, 216

US Special Operations Command, 216
US Strategic Air Command, motto of, 140–41

Vietnam, Agent Orange, 34
Vietnam analogy, 104
Vietnamese Village Reborn (film), 130–31
Vietnam War, 29–31, 141–42, 159, 175, 205
Virden, Jenel, 183
virtual war, 266n.105
von Clausewitz, Carl, 14, 87–88

Wales, 75–76
Walter, Barbara, 6–8, 167–68, 174
Walzer, Michael, 190–91
War (Grayling), 6–8, 17, 125
War (Morris), 6–8, 20, 34–35, 88
war(s)
   acceptance of readiness for, 3
   addiction, 1
   ambivalent attitude of world religions toward, 181–85
   anarchy rules in the international system, 20–23
   attempt to outlaw, 23–25
   benefits of, 34–38
   changing nature of, 25–26
   complexity of causes of, 22–23
   conscientious objection, 204–5
   costs of, 29–34
   declaration of, 121–22
   definition of, 14–18, 44*t*
   ever-readiness for possibility of, 3
   horror of, 2
   moral injury, 202–4
   mystery of support, 3–4
   new, 25–29
   "old" and "new," 14–15
   optimists argument on celebrating decline of support, 39–43
   personal morality and psychological models of, 197–202
   psychological support for, 9
   psychology and, 4–5
   psychology on support for, 9
   readiness for war and, 208–11
   role of media in engineering public consent of, 161–72
   role of the state in, 18–25
   state and, 20

support for, 3
ten points and debates about, 44
Ukraine and Russia, 6
War and Peace (Tolstoy), 37
War and Society (Centano and Enríquez), 6–8, 19, 36, 42, 61–62, 75, 88, 99–100
War Child Annual Report 2009, 32
war fatigue, 229
War in Human Civilization (Gat), 6–8, 36
War Is a Force That Gives Us Meaning (Hedges), 46, 53
war manifestos, 156–57
war memorials, supporting war or peace, 135–39
War of Independence, 160–61
war on drugs, 17–18
War on the Mind (Watson), 215
War Prevention Initiative, 212–13
War Resisters' International, 204–5
Warriors, The (Gray), 50–51
war support
  changing strength of, 47
  competition and danger, 200
  future of, 238–41
  human nature and, 47–50
  individual differences in, 59–61
  in-groups and out-groups, 108–14
  life's meaning and, 53–58
  men versus women in, 66–72
  militarism and, 125–26
  militarism and, in West, 146–53
  nature of men and maleness in 61–72, 65t
  personal attraction of war, 46–47, 50–58, 73f
  propaganda and, 156
  psychology has neglected, 211–16
  resisting readiness for it, 239
  resisting simplified thinking, 240–41
  resisting threat assumptions, 239–40
  spiral conflict model, 119–22
  war in defense of identities, 97f
war support model (WSM), 2–3, 12, 207
  acceptance of readiness for war, 217–20, 224f, 231
  contemplating war between US, UK and Allies, and China, 236–38
  contemplation-of-war, 226f, 227
  engagement, 225–26, 226f, 228–29
  implications for prevention of war, 230–36
  over-simplification, 217–18, 222–25, 224f, 232

preparedness-for-war stage, 226–27, 226f
propaganda, 228–29
recurring themes of, 217–25
summary of factors, 224f
system of interacting and mutually reinforcing parts, 225f
threat perception, 217–18, 220–21, 224f, 226f, 231, 232
time factor, 225–29, 233
war fatigue, 229
war in Ukraine, 230–36
Washington Post (newspaper), 130, 162
Waste Land, The (Eliot), 207
Watson, Peter, 215
weapons
  admiration for, 219
  arms dealing, 143–46
  fascination of, 139–46
  precision, 152
Weapons of Mass Deception (Rampton and Stauber), 159–60
weapons of mass destruction (WMD), Iraq, 159
Webster, Alexander, 184
Weekly Standard (magazine), 194
Weinberger, Caspar, 193
Weinberger doctrine, 193
Weinberger-Powell principles, 193–94
welfare state, 37
Western alliance, Russia and China, 207
What Have We Done (Wood), 6–8, 14, 202–3
White, Shelley, 6–8, 33–34
Why Vietnam? (film), 130–31
Why We Fight (films), 130–31
Wiist, William, 6–8, 33–34
Wilkes, George, 184
Wilson, President, 173
Winter, David, 6–8, 60–61, 65–67, 170
Wizard of Oz, The, 107
women
  femininity, 71–72
  gender inequality and, 65–66
  men vs., attitudes toward war, 66–72
  suffrage, 69
  in US military, 70
women in government (WIG), 71
Wood, David, 6–8, 14, 38, 192–94, 202–3
World Health Organization, 208
World Peace Council, 170
world religions, ambivalent attitude toward war, 181–85

World Rule of Law Centre, 176–77
World Values Survey, 85–86
World War I. *See* First World War
World War II. *See* Second World War
Wounding the World (Bourke), 6–8, 128–29, 214
Wounds (Keane), 6–8, 53, 122, 174–75, 203–4

xenophobia, 89, 99–100

Xi Jinping, 236–37

yellow fever, 32
Yemen, war in, 209–10
Yom Kippur war (1973), 142
YouTube, 166
Yugoslavia, 92–93, 96

Zelensky, President, 231
Zimbardo, Philip, 214–15